WAYFINDING
through the STORM

Speaking Truth to Power at
Kamehameha Schools
1993-1999

WAYFINDING
through the STORM

Speaking Truth to Power at
Kamehameha Schools
1993-1999

GAVAN DAWS
AND
NĀ LEO O KAMEHAMEHA

WATERMARK
PUBLISHING

ISBN 978-0-9821698-3-4

Library of Congress Control Number:
2009924569

Design and production by Marisa Oshiro

Photography and other graphics courtesy of the
Kamehameha Schools Archives, the *Honolulu
Advertiser*, the *Honolulu Star-Bulletin* and
various private collections.

Watermark Publishing
1088 Bishop St., Suite 310
Honolulu, Hawai'i 96813
Telephone 1-808-587-7766
Toll-free 1-866-900-BOOK
sales@bookshawaii.net
www.bookshawaii.net

Printed in China

Contents

◈ ◈ ◈

Foreword
by The Friends of
Nā Kumu o Kamehameha

**The Friends of Nā Kumu
o Kamehameha LLC**

Kēhau Abad

Julian Ako

David Kāwika Eyre

Mark Ewald

Randie Fong

Gail Fujimoto

Kaʻimipono Kaiwi

Keʻala Kwan

Larry McElheney

Robert Ramsey

Jim Slagel

Janet Zisk

Over 150 voices share their experiences of the controversy in the pages that fill this volume. In true Kamehameha style, their melodies and harmonies blend to offer a collective song, a group story. It's an arrangement with many parts, each voice carrying its own timbre, color and texture—its own personal history, motivation and effect.

One might wonder how such a range of voices came together. Gavan Daws listened to each of them, skillfully identifying the prominent melodies and their linked harmonies—the main storylines that unfold in this book. A committee of dedicated individuals also helped to arrange the score—amplifying a moving line here, spotlighting a harmonic line there. However, Daws and the committee did not compose the melodies and harmonies. The lines were already there.

The notes and lyrics are the thoughts and emotions from interviews that David Kāwika Eyre conducted in the years immediately following the controversy—music that flowed naturally from the refrains of the real-time voices of the controversy.

Throughout the pages of this book, many diverse voices speak about the controversy. They include young students, venerable alumni, movers and shakers, average folk, novice and seasoned teachers, Native Hawaiians, kamaʻāina and fresh faces from abroad. Some found inspiration in traditional Hawaiian expectations requiring aliʻi to meet the highest standards or face removal by other more capable and noble leaders who rise to the occasion. Some were stirred by ancient traditions of loyalty to beloved and honored aliʻi—to Kamehameha and Pauahi. Some were moved by universal values of righteousness, the ideals of strong school communities and a duty to serve as role models that youth might emulate. Some were looking at the larger context—corporate excess across America and political corruption in Hawai'i—and the need to remove such noxious seeds, which had grown uncontrollably into the controversy. Some were compelled by the casualties on the front line—students who were missing out on educational opportunities and who would grow up to believe—if no actions were taken—that power and greed prevail, that problems as big as the controversy could not be solved and that their losses were not worth a fight. Most were motivated by all of the above.

While each of these perspectives overlap and combine in ways that harmonized well during the controversy and that complement one another in the chapters that follow, each voice rings clear with a single driving melody, a unifying theme: our shared commitment to Pauahi's will and goal to provide her Hawaiian people with an excellent education in order that they might serve their families, communities and nation.

In *Wayfinding through the Storm*, our chorus joins together in unison affirming that commitment as we speak of our individual experiences, personal reflections and enduring aloha for Pauahi and Kamehameha Schools. We offer this song to remember what occurred, to strengthen the lessons learned and to reinforce the many bonds that unify us as a community as we move forward into perpetuity. ⌒

Introduction
by Gavan Daws

My name is on the title page of *Wayfinding through the Storm*. But the book properly belongs to those who are collectively named there: Nā Leo O Kamehameha—the voices of Kamehameha.

Wayfinding through the Storm exists to tell the human story of a crisis that erupted at Kamehameha Schools in the 1990s and came close to destroying a historic educational community, one of the great institutions of Hawai'i.

The book chronicles what it was like for the people of Kamehameha to labor for years under a regime that ruled by the abuse of power; what triggered the crisis; the devastation it caused and how the Schools ultimately managed to survive and come through.

The tale is told in the voices of Kamehameha. These voices fill the book. They *are* the book. On every page of *Wayfinding through the Storm* are words spoken by people who lived through the crisis years: words of confusion, pain, grief, fear—a descent into the depths of despair. Then, under the most extreme pressure, this despair transformed itself, in individual after individual, into a determination to resist, to organize and to go on resisting, no matter what the cost, in the faith and hope that the good and the right could be restored at Kamehameha.

Fundamentally, *Wayfinding through the Storm* tells the story of ordinary decent people who looked deep inside themselves and found the moral courage to risk everything, to come together and stand up for what they believed in: to speak truth to power. They fought the good fight, and, against all odds, they prevailed.

It was a great struggle. It called upon every ounce of strength in "the better angels of human nature."

The story is an inspiring one—worth recording, worth holding in memory, worth telling and retelling. It carries lessons for life.

Written history often comes out on the page sounding remote, dry, abstract. That was not the way the crisis years were lived at Kamehameha. Those were terrible times.

Things happened at Kamehameha Schools—and to the people of Kamehameha—that were so wrong as to be unbelievable. The Schools had had a long and honorable life as an educational community with an invaluable social mission: to serve Hawaiian children. But now— a mass termination of staff, 170 in a single sweep of the scythe. Parents rousted by campus security. Teachers and staff threatened with interrogation and lie detector tests. Anonymous phone threats at home, rumors of phones being tapped on campus. Spy cameras. Clandestine informants and blacklists. Distrust everywhere, escalating to paranoia, poisoning the atmosphere, so that education could not live and breathe freely. The crisis at Kamehameha threatened the death of good teaching and good learning.

The human cost was heavy, professionally and personally: careers stalled, some of them derailed, relationships ruptured, families split, children damaged.

The severity of the strain showed up medically, body and soul: high blood pressure, heart conditions, raging psychosomatic rashes, a bleeding ulcer, medications for stress, sleepless nights, nightmares, sudden weeping, uncontrollable vomiting fits following forced attendance at ghastly meetings.

The festering crisis erupted as well in language: *malignant cancer, slippery bonefish, Nazi, Gestapo, CIA, a loaded gun on the table, heads are gonna roll, diabolic, satanic, instrument of the devil.* The most extreme words burst out at—of all places—a Hawaiian funeral in Honolulu, where, in the midst of reverent Christian mourning, a Hawaiian teacher from Kamehameha was cursed with death, in Hawaiian, by a top-level Hawaiian administrator.

What did deathly curses and a reign of terror have to do with the proper education of Hawaiian children? The crisis amounted to a corruption and perversion of the historic mission of Kamehameha Schools.

Beyond that, it was a grievous offense against Hawaiian values, against civility, against community, against human decency. Looking back over the entire historical record of Hawai'i in the second half of the 20th century, this crisis is the darkest of stains on the page.

How could it have happened?

The '90s, the most disastrous decade in Kamehameha's history, should have been the best of times.

The Schools, which dated from 1887, were entering their second century of educating Hawaiian children, in accordance with the will of the founding benefactor, Princess Bernice Pauahi Bishop. A Hawaiian high chief, an ali'i nui, she was directly descended from Kamehameha the Great, the warrior chief who founded the unified Hawaiian kingdom early in the 19th century.

Under Pauahi's will, the royal lands that she had inherited—hundreds of thousands of acres—formed the basis of a charitable trust, known as Bishop Estate, administered by a board of trustees, with the income to be dedicated solely to serving the Schools. This was Pauahi's legacy.

By the mid-to-late '80s, all the signs were good for Kamehameha —never better. Bishop Estate had grown spectacularly in wealth, becoming the biggest private charitable trust not only in Hawai'i, not only in the United States, but in the world—worth billions of dollars. The estate was the flagship Hawaiian institution, and it was a supremely powerful financial engine for Kamehameha, the flagship school for Hawaiian children.

Coming into the '90s, both the estate and the Schools were more Hawaiian than they had ever been. For the first time in the history of Bishop Estate, all five members of the board of trustees were Hawaiian. At Kamehameha, for the first time in history, the president was a Hawaiian, and not only a Hawaiian but a proud alumnus who was a living embodiment of the vision of Princess Pauahi.

At the same time, in the broader community, a Hawaiian presence was more prominent than ever. For the first time in history, the elected governor of the state of Hawai'i was a Hawaiian. For the first time, the chief justice of the Supreme Court of the state of Hawai'i was a Hawaiian. And statewide, Hawaiian ethnic identity had never been stronger, both culturally and politically. This was the product of a movement, broad-ranging and deep-running, that went by the name of the Hawaiian Renaissance. It dated from the 1970s, and year by year, decade by decade, it kept gaining strength.

One of the important concepts of the renaissance was "wayfinding." It came from the spectacular voyages of the oceangoing Hawaiian canoe *Hōkūleʻa*, which was navigated across thousands of miles of the Pacific according to traditional principles and techniques—a great and valuable accomplishment, drawing on the past to inspire cultural pride in the present. Wayfinding became a metaphor for the Hawaiian future.

So—important trend lines for Hawaiians were up. Bishop Estate and Kamehameha Schools were flourishing. Great things were predicted, and were expected.

Instead, within a matter of just a few years, the all-Hawaiian board of trustees came close to bringing the estate to ruin with behavior that was worse than bad, that went beyond all bounds. Dubious schemes, hatched behind doors in the boardroom, erupted one after the other in public scandals—ethical, moral, sexual, financial, political, legal, crossing the line into indictable crime.

And the trustees' toxic leadership of Bishop Estate poisoned life at Kamehameha Schools.

Money is the root of all evil. That age-old saying fits what happened at Bishop Estate. The estate had come to be worth billions of dollars. The trustees were each being paid close to a million a year. The boardroom was at the very center of wealth and power in Hawaiʻi. Corruption followed the money.

The list of corrupt practices and reprehensible behavior at Bishop Estate was long. It started with the cheap and nasty—abuse of estate credit cards, padding of travel expenses, commandeering of estate staff and resources for trustees' private purposes and private gain. It spread into business, with trustees profiting personally from investment decisions that they made for the estate—conflict of interest, a legal offense under trust law. It expanded in scale to cronyism—jobs for the boys, non-bid contracts awarded to the "right" people, up to millions of dollars. And it spread into politics—money and influence passed back and forth, under the table, illegal political contributions.

This kind of business and political corruption was common across the United States in the big-money '80s and '90s. Perhaps it was too much to expect that business and politics in Hawai'i would be immune. And in fact they were not. As a matter of public record: during the Kamehameha crisis years, two State senators and two members of the Honolulu City Council were tried and convicted in criminal court and sentenced to jail time, and a mayor of Honolulu who looked to be on his way to the governorship was discovered to be taking wholesale illegal contributions. A former speaker of the State House was convicted of campaign fund abuse and sentenced to jail. A major union leader with insider political connections was convicted on multiple counts of fraud involving huge sums of money and was sentenced to jail. And these were not the only cases giving off the strong smell of corruption.

Watching all this noxiousness work its way through the courts, ending in prison, it could be calculated that, on a percentage basis, Hawai'i politicians and big political players were more criminal than the general population. That was certainly something to reflect upon.

Surely, though, it should not have been too much to hope that better standards would govern conduct in the boardroom of a private charitable trust founded on Christian principles for the education of Hawaiian children. But no. Leadership at Bishop Estate was toxic. And this toxic leadership was at the root of the crisis at Kamehameha Schools.

The trustees of Bishop Estate behaved the way they did simply because they could—because they were allowed to, because nobody stopped them.

On paper, there were legal controls: regular reports to the Probate Court, which governed wills and trusts, by an appointed court master, a lawyer who examined the estate's operations to see that they were in conformity with trust law and with the will of the founder, Princess Pauahi. And under the law, the State attorney general had the power to investigate Bishop Estate.

But the reality was that the trustees could do pretty much whatever they wanted, because nobody moved to rock the boat or blow the whistle—because everyone connected with the estate at a high level was comfortable with the way things were.

The way the system was designed, the way the law was written, Bishop Estate trustees were chosen by the justices of the Hawai'i Supreme Court. The justices were chosen by a judicial selection commission. The judicial selection commission essentially answered to the governor. In other words, everything was political.

In the crisis years, this could not have been more obvious. The chairman of the Bishop Estate board of trustees, Richard Wong, had been the longest-ever-serving leader in the State Senate; he went directly across the street from his Senate office to the estate board-room. The single most powerful trustee, Henry Peters, had been speaker of the State House—in fact, in his early years on the board he continued to be speaker. Gerard Jervis had been a member of the judicial selection committee, an appointment he got because of his close ties with Governor John Waihee. Lokelani Lindsey had worked on Waihee's campaign for governor. That added up to four out of the five trustees, an unbeatable majority—all of them political animals, as the phrase goes. And all Democrats—the party that had been entrenched in power in Hawai'i since the mid-'50s, uninterrupted for four decades.

A few years into the '90s, there was definitely something rotten at Bishop Estate. But nobody in authority was saying so. The Probate Court judge was not saying so. The State Legislature was not saying so. The governor was not saying so. The attorney general was not saying so. The Bar Association, representing the legal profession, was not saying so. The media—the Honolulu dailies and the TV news— were not saying so in any significant way. And the people who worked at Bishop Estate and Kamehameha Schools were not saying so, at least not out loud.

Systems produce situations. Situations lead to individual choices being made. What were the choices for individuals at the estate and the Schools?

Buy into the system—because there were benefits: inside information, preferential treatment, promotion, perks. Or recognize that there were things that were badly wrong, but make a conscious decision to see no evil, hear no evil, speak no evil: just be a good soldier— meaning, at Bishop Estate, be a good secretary or office manager; at Kamehameha, be a good classroom teacher or administrator. Do your job conscientiously. Or just be a time server, do a day's work for a day's pay, and don't take any heed of what is happening higher up. Live your own life—that is enough. Who is to say that anything more should be asked of you?

At the workaday level, the system itself kept people quiet. Bishop Estate and Kamehameha Schools between them had thousands of employees—working people with families, rent to pay or mortgage payments to meet; many of them Hawaiian, with children, and many of them hoping that their children would get to go to Kamehameha. All of them depended on a paycheck from Bishop Estate, and all of them served at the pleasure of the Bishop Estate trustees. If they were moved to want to speak up, what would it cost them? Would it be worth risking their job? Their children's prospects?

Complicating everything was the question of loyalty—a big word in Hawai'i, especially for Hawaiians. Bishop Estate was the great Hawaiian institution. All the trustees were Hawaiian. They had been given the authority to lead. Surely they would lead well. How could they not?—they were understood to be guided by the revered memory of Princess Pauahi, and they constantly invoked her name. Would criticizing them be disloyal to her? The trustees said so, all the time.

There were two people who were in a strategic position to know just how bad things were, and who were in a position to do something publicly decisive about it. One was at Bishop Estate, the other at Kamehameha Schools.

Oswald Stender was an estate trustee. Michael Chun was president of Kamehameha. Stender, who, like the other four trustees, was Hawaiian, was the only Kamehameha alumnus on the board. Chun was the first alumnus to head the Schools.

Both men had very high reputations in the community, especially among Hawaiians. Stender was exceptionally active civically and charitably—an exemplary citizen. Chun was beloved by the students at Kamehameha, for good reason, and this earned him the strong support of parents and alumni.

But neither Stender not Chun had any support in the Bishop Estate boardroom. To the contrary. On the five-member board, Stender was a minority of one—marginalized, excluded, belittled, scorned, abused. Chun, for his part, had to deal with a board majority that constantly and aggressively downgraded the Schools in favor of the business side of the estate—even though the business of the estate was supposed to be conducted solely to the benefit of the Schools. As the crisis began to build, Chun's job was threatened: the board majority was planning to get rid of him.

Stender was so disgusted with what the board was doing to the estate that he considered resigning. That would have made things so public that attention would have to be paid, community-wide: no more see-no-evil, hear-no evil, speak-no-evil. And if Chun had resigned in protest at what was happening at the Schools, it would have created absolute uproar in the Kamehameha community.

Which is to say that Stender and Chun could have led from the front. They chose not to. The advice they were getting—the advice they took and that they gave each other—was to stay on the job and do what they could from inside. But what they could do from inside was limited. For each of them and both of them together, the situation was impossible.

Stender had been trying to get the Probate Court and the attorney general to step up. It had not worked. Could he have done more? Yes, if he had been Superman. He was not, and Bishop Estate was just too massive a boulder for one man to shift on his own.

Nor was Chun a Superman. In the eyes of the students and alumni, he was wonderful; in the eyes of most of the faculty, he was less than that. He was a good, decent human being, none better. But he was a top-down manager, resistant to the idea that teachers had any right to a collective professional voice in decision-making. Over the years, they came to the considered opinion that Chun was not as supportive of them as he could have been—and should have been, in the interests of a genuinely cooperative educational community at Kamehameha.

Chun was what he was, and of course in his position he had all kinds of different interests to balance. And there was one huge destabilizer: he had to do nonstop battle with a super-sized enemy— Lokelani Lindsey, the "education trustee."

One of the amazing things about the way Bishop Estate was run was that in an organization of that size, a multibillion-dollar business, there were no specific written job descriptions for trustees. Chun, the Schools' president, had a job description. Lindsey, the education trustee, did not. She could do what she liked at Kamehameha. And she did.

Lindsey's personality was her philosophy, and she had the personality of a tyrant. She saw herself as all-powerful, the center of the universe. She issued dictatorial commands and demanded instant obedience. She craved attention and surrounded herself with an entourage of sycophants and informants. If anything displeased her, she threw raging temper tantrums. And educationally, she was ignorant and arrogant. She invaded classrooms and terrorized teachers. She abused them and insulted their professional competence. All across campus, she disrupted and derailed programs. She was a disaster.

She was uncontrollable, and the rest of the majority trustees made no effort to control her. They put the care of Kamehameha Schools—the legacy of Princess Pauahi—in the hands of Lokelani Lindsey and left it there.

History by its nature is complex and tangled. But if any one person could be singled out as being decisive in bringing on the crisis at Kamehameha, it was Lokelani Lindsey.

Lindsey was appointed a trustee in 1993. By 1997, the situation she had created at Kamehameha went from difficult to disturbing to appalling to intolerable—beyond intolerable.

It was not going to be changed from the top down. If there was going to be change, it would have to start from the bottom up, meaning with the teachers.

In the spring of 1997, two teachers called a meeting of faculty. If any one event could be singled out as marking the beginning of the open collective struggle of resistance and reform, this was it.

The meeting was just a meeting, not a protest demonstration. The teachers were cautioned by their administrative superior againt organizing it. They went on with the meeting anyway. Only a couple of dozen teachers took the risk of coming—only about 10 percent of the faculty. A second meeting was held, and a third. The initial two teachers became four, and the number of faculty and staff willing to take the risk grew, to some dozens, still an indecisive minority.

This was a start—but a start to what? All they had was a name: Nā Kumu, the teachers—which expressed their belief in their work and a belief in Kamehameha as a worthwhile educational community, dedicated to serving Pauahi's vision for Hawaiian children.

They had no resources. Against the might of the trustees, they looked impotent. In reaction, they developed a working philosophy that was diametrically opposed to the way Lindsey and the majority trustees operated: servant leadership—consensus-driven, humble, prayerful. These were the unlikely weapons of powerlessness.

At the same time that Nā Kumu was forming on campus, a group of alumni, small in number but strong in their sense that things at Kamehameha could not go on as they were, began to meet. They called themselves Nā Pua O Ke Aliʻi Pauahi—the flowers, or the children, of Princess Pauahi.

Nā Pua decided that there should be—must be—a public demonstration. This was historic. Hawaiians had taken to the streets before on Bishop Estate matters—but always in support of the estate. To march against the estate, or, more exactly, against the trustees, was a total reversal, a real head-turner. It would force attention to be paid.

The Nā Pua march of May 15, 1997, was spectacular. It started at Pauahi's tomb in Nuʻuanu valley and ended at the headquarters of Bishop Estate at Kawaiahaʻo Plaza. It drew big crowds, stopped traffic and dominated the news for days.

The crisis at Kamehameha was public now, and from then on it was never out of the headlines.

Over the next months, there was more and more public discussion of the roots of the crisis at the Schools. Everything pointed to the Bishop Estate boardroom.

In August, an essay was published in the *Honolulu Star-Bulletin*, headlined "Broken Trust." It was a bombshell—a fierce indictment of the majority trustees. The march had made this possible, and as with the march, there had never been anything like it.

"Broken Trust" carried great weight because it was signed by four senior Hawaiians, all of impeccable integrity and all with a lifetime of community service. Line those four up against the four majority trustees, compare the two groups for good character, for social conscience, for Hawaiianness, and it was no contest. The fifth name on "Broken Trust" was that of a University of Hawaiʻi law professor whose specialty was trust law: more weight, more authority.

What started with the Nā Kumu meetings and the Nā Pua march developed irresistible impetus with the "Broken Trust" essay. Now it was not just a matter of reform at Kamehameha—it was regime change at Bishop Estate.

The majority trustees resisted, throwing all the huge resources of the estate at the reformers.

One major thing they did was commission a fact finder, a retired judge, to collect testimony and report to them, in the expectation that someone they were paying would report in their favor. Instead, the fact finder, faced with overwhelming evidence of the devastation that Lindsey was causing, told the trustees that Lindsey must resign, get out of the way of Kamehameha Schools. This was another bombshell.

Lindsey's response was to release a report of her own that said essentially that Kamehameha was a mess, incompetently run by Michael Chun, with incompetent teachers who were failing the students—the longer children were at Kamehameha, the worse they did. Lindsey's statistics were cooked. But when they were thrown on the fire along with everything else, they produced thick clouds of nasty black smoke at the end of 1997.

Critical amidst all this furor would be actions taken or not taken by the governor, because the governor directed the State attorney general, who was tasked under the law with responsibility for Bishop Estate. Oswald Stender had been trying for years to get the attorney general to act. But even after the May march; even after the "Broken Trust" essay, which called directly for the attorney general to investigate; even after the fact finder's report, no action was forthcoming. All the governor had said publicly was that he had asked the attorney general to look into things and do a preliminary assessment.

Stender decided to take matters into his own hands. In December 1997, he sued in civil court to have Lokelani Lindsey removed as trustee. He was joined in the suit by Gerard Jervis, who broke away from the majority.

From then on, the main battleground over Bishop Estate shifted to the courts and stayed there for two years. The attorney general finally moved. And—crucially—the Internal Revenue Service also moved. Bishop Estate, as a charitable trust, was basically tax-exempt. If it turned out that the trustees were flouting the law in the way they did business and presented their accounts, the IRS could take away the estate's tax exemption—and that would spell disaster, not just on the business side, but for the Schools, which were the sole beneficiaries of Pauahi's legacy.

While the lawsuits were working their tortuous way through the courts, always with headlines, there was continued disruption at the Schools. Lindsey had stepped down from being the education trustee, but she stayed on the board and kept pushing her campaign against the running of the Schools and her strident criticisms of the teachers.

The uproar got louder and louder when a report of a review of the Schools by an outside accreditation body was leaked to the media. The report praised the faculty and students, and damned the governance of the Schools, meaning the trustees, and especially Lindsey. The trustees' response was to start an investigation, threatening teachers and staff with interrogation and lie detectors. It was hard to imagine a greater insult to an educational community and to the spirit of Pauahi.

While this investigation was lurching along, the trustees released yet another commissioned report of their own, this one costing $400,000. Lindsey's lawyer seized on the report to call Kamehameha "a factory of failure." The phrase made headlines and caused consternation among students and their families. Some of the students—some of them leaders in student government, others ordinary students with their eyes open and their minds active—joined the reform movement, collecting signatures on petitions and demonstrating outside the courthouse where one of the Bishop Estate lawsuits was being heard. Once, when the whole school was assembled at rehearsal for the annual song contest, Lokelani Lindsey's name was announced and booing broke out. There had never been anything like that. Another time, at graduation, Michael Chun got a standing ovation and Lindsey refused to stand, in front of an audience of thousands.

From the beginning, Nā Kumu had been attempting to meet with the full board of trustees, without success—close to 30 attempts, with no meetings, in fact not even any response to written requests. The majority trustees' repeatedly demonstrated contempt for the Kamehameha faculty strengthened the teachers' resolve to empower themselves and led to the formation of a faculty union—something that would never have been predicted at a private school like Kamehameha: more evidence of how bad things were. Organizing the union took upwards of a school year, and it happened, so to speak, over the trustees' dead bodies. But it happened.

All this time, Oswald Stender's lawsuit to remove Lokelani Lindsey was in preparation. It finally went to trial at the end of 1998. Every major event of the crisis years at the Schools was replayed, relived in testimony—high drama on the witness stand, before a packed courtroom, for weeks and months.

In the end, the judge ordered Lindsey's immediate removal. At Kamehameha, there was joyous celebration. Soon after, in other court actions, the remaining trustees were removed.

By the end of 1999—after years of turmoil, uncounted thousands of hours of distraction and millions upon millions of dollars that could have and should have been devoted to the Schools—the estate was under a new and reformed system of governance, and Kamehameha Schools could return to productive education, with a new openness to visions for the future of Hawaiian children in the 21st century.

For everyone at Kamehamaha, faculty, staff and students, there were deep continuing questions to ponder, about duty, about responsibility, about right thinking and right action in the interests of the common good.

That is the story of *Wayfinding through the Storm*.

The estate's side of the crisis years—the legal, political and financial struggle over the control and use of many billions of dollars—is told responsibly and in detail in the book *Broken Trust* by Samuel P. King and Randall W. Roth. The related website, www.brokentrustbook.com, has extensive supporting documentation.

There are other stories from the crisis years that could be told. In particular, it would be good to hear from each of the majority trustees. How would they assess their roles? How would they justify their disastrously damaging decisions and explain their staggering miscalculations? This would make interesting reading, and it would be valuable, as part of the historical record of Hawai'i.

But the years have gone by, and the majority trustees have kept silence (except for Henry Peters, who for a while had a website). Basically, since they were removed from office by the courts, the only time their names have been public has been in connection with more court proceedings.

Two of these cases were Bishop Estate-related. Dickie Wong brought suit in 2002 against the governor and two State attorney generals, claiming that their prosecution of him had been malicious and asking for millions of dollars in damages. He lost. Henry Peters, in 2008–eight years after he was ousted as a trustee—found it in himself to sue the man who had served him for years before then as his senior legal officer at the estate. Peters' claim was that the lawyer had made improper statements before a grand jury investigating Bishop Estate, breaching attorney-client confidentiality.

Gerard Jervis was convicted in 2008 of being drunk at the wheel of his car, pursuing another car at high speed and causing a crash. Lokelani Lindsey was convicted of fraud in a bankruptcy case in 2002 and served six months in a federal prison in Las Vegas.

This was the collective final legacy of the majority trustees who were appointed to serve the legacy of Pauahi.

Oswald Stender, who, for all his troubles in pursuing reform, suffered the indignity of losing his trusteeship along with the others, was elected in 2000 as a trustee of the State Office of Hawaiian Affairs and in 2001 received the highest honor bestowed by Kamehameha Schools, the Order of Ke Alii Pauahi.

Wayfinding through the Storm, for its part, focuses on the crisis as it played out at Kamehameha Schools. That is its constant point of view, its dominant perspective. The whole purpose of the book is to get as close as possible to human experience at the Schools: what it was like to live through those times, when everything was at risk, when there were high-stakes individual moral choices to be made, under the heaviest of pressure, with no certainty that the right would prevail.

That is why *Wayfinding through the Storm* is done as oral history: the story is told by people who lived the story, in their own words.

The heart and soul, the blood and bone of the book, is in the words of more than 200 interviews with Kamehameha faculty, staff, students, alumni, parents and friends.

The interviews were done soon enough after the crisis years for memories to be clear, and long enough afterwards for opinions and judgments to be mature and settled.

For many people, being invited to do the interview was emotional, disturbing. Some could not stop talking; some could not speak at all; some spoke and then were haunted by what they found themselves saying.

Once the interviews were transcribed, people were offered the opportunity to review their words, rephrasing if they wanted to, so that the permanent record would be as close as possible to the truth of their experience. Bottom line: in these interviews, people are saying what they mean, and meaning what they say. In total, their words add up to well over a million.

There were many more millions of spoken words that came from testimony and depositions taken during court cases that were heard during the crisis years. At one point, wrongdoing at Bishop Estate was crowding three courtrooms in Honolulu at the same time, trials running for months, with batteries of lawyers and long, long lists of witnesses. The transcripts of testimony and depositions piled up, rising to tens of thousands of pages, millions of words, all spoken under an oath to tell the truth, the whole truth and nothing but the truth.

There are also a good many words in the book that were spoken for the public record in newspaper and TV interviews. These have been transcribed verbatim.

My part of the work for *Wayfinding through the Storm* was to bring all these millions of words down to not much more than a hundred thousand. How to do it?

First, concentrate on the core story: what happened at the Schools. Things that were going on on other fronts in the crisis—for example, at Bishop Estate headquarters at Kawaiahaʻo Plaza, in the State Legislature, in the State attorney general's office, in the work of private investigators, at the Internal Revenue Service and among alumni—all of these are mentioned in *Wayfinding through the Storm* only if they impacted directly on what was happening at the Schools.

Second, in making use of transcripts, cut to the chase. The way court testimony is taken—question and answer, direct examination and cross examination, lawyers' objections and judges' rulings, all observing proper legal procedure—it might take 20 pages of transcript to establish a single fact. *Wayfinding through the Storm* prunes what was said in the courtroom but takes care not to distort or falsify by omission, at the same time preserving the individual voices of the speakers.

With interviews, follow the same practice—take out ums and ahs, repetitions and digressions, all the wanderings that are part of ordinary conversation. But take pains to preserve the essential voice of the speaker, the way thoughts are framed and expressed, the way the story is told. In *Wayfinding through the Storm*, just as there are all kinds of speakers—faculty, staff, students, administrators, alumni, parents, lawyers, outreach workers, people in all walks of life—there are all kinds of speaking styles, from highly formal to highly informal, from standard English to pidgin, interspersed with Hawaiian. All these different ways of speaking come together to make up the rich collective voice of the book.

There is another kind of richness that is important in *Wayfinding through the Storm*. The text is supplemented and augmented graphically, with historic pictures of the Schools, photographs of people as they were at the time they are speaking of, video grabs, cartoons and reproductions of documents: memos, draft versions of visions of reform, protest petitions with handwritten signatures, official reprimands, an incendiary letter to the editor and more. (One point about reproductions of print material: it will be noticeable that in some originals Hawaiian diacriticals were used, in others not.) The point and purpose of using all these graphics—as with interviews and court testimony—is to bring the book as close as possible to the feel of history as it was being made.

The draft manuscript that I put together, and the graphics, were reviewed, extensively and intensively, by an editorial group at Kamehameha Schools made up of people who lived through the crisis, a number of them people who took a leading part in the movement for resistance and reform. They made decisions on the shape and structure of chapters, and on proportion, placement and emphasis. By protocol and process, the last word on the book was to be theirs.

This is right and proper. Just as the fundamental human truth of the experience of the crisis is theirs—blood, sweat and tears—so the final text of *Wayfinding through the Storm* is theirs.

Now let the voices of Kamehameha, Nā Leo O Kamehameha, speak for themselves.

Kamehameha Campus

Words on a Wall
New Trustees Impose New Culture

Hawaiian values were just words on a wall.
–Mike Chun

PAUL IONA (*'08, Stanford University undergraduate*): I didn't understand what was going on at the time. I only remember this little kid at all these significant events that at the time seemed insignificant. But now, looking back, I can see why my parents were so passionate, so angry.

LEROY AKAMINE (*'52, leader of alumni group Nā Pua*): This passion I have for Kamehameha— I have never forgotten that, and will always come forward to the defense of Kamehameha whenever that is needed.

FORMER BISHOP TRUSTEES

"They were intelligent. And they put the students first, before the pocketbook."
–Nona Beamer

KAIPO HALE (*'68, Schools Hawaiian studies institute*): Kamehameha Schools represents the legacy of one woman's dream and the fact of her direct ties to Kamehameha the Great. And we have the Name. It's our Name.

ERIN MORITA (*'97*): It wasn't until after I graduated that I fully understood what an extraordinary woman she was. I am forever indebted to Princess Pauahi's selflessness.

LAURIE CHEE (*'98*): We honor Pauahi by sharing our minds and hearts, so thoughtfully molded, in balance, with the rest of the world.

TONY RAMOS (*'58, Secondary School principal*): Ke Aliʻi Pauahi provided thousands of keiki o ka ʻāina, native children, the educational opportunities that would not have been available to them otherwise.

LEROY AKAMINE: We need to preserve and protect in perpetuity the trust of our Princess.

KAWIKA MAKANANI (*'66, Secondary School social studies teacher*): Both Papa Lyman and Pinky Thompson were very strong proponents of the Hawaiian Renaissance and what we could do here at Kamehameha to instill in our ʻōpio, our young ones, and our haumāna, our students, the importance of their own Hawaiian heritage.

ELISA YADAO (*Bishop Estate spokesperson*): When I first started, there was a graciousness about the trustees.

ELISA YADAO

NONA BEAMER (*'41, former Secondary School performing arts teacher*): They were gentlemen.

ELISA YADAO: They would not ever disagree among themselves in front of anyone. They never got into it in front of us.

They would never close their office doors. It was unheard of. I mean, you would be in with a trustee, you would be talking about whatever, the door would be wide open. When they spoke with each other, the doors were always open. A small thing, but it was symbolic of the nature of the way they were.

It seems like there was always consensus. It would always resolve, it would always get worked out.

NONA BEAMER

FRED CACHOLA (*'53, Schools director of extension education*): Papa Lyman conducted meetings where he never took a vote. Consensus. It's a style of management mentality that senses when you push and when you don't. You don't go head to head.

MIKE CHUN (*'61, Schools president*): Papa Lyman had control, because everybody deferred to Papa because of the type of person he was. He was a real good person.

LEEANN CRABBE (*Bishop Estate manager of budget and financial planning*): I think ʻohana is such an overused word, but it really, really did feel like an ʻohana. I started very young. You came in respectfully, you tried to understand the culture and work your way into it. Very paternalistic—I keep coming back to that word. But they took care of us.

BOB LINDSEY (*'66, director of Hawaiʻi Island region*): Papa Lyman and Pinky Thompson were always there to help and support. They were good listeners, and I think for them laulima was a guiding principle. They were hands-on, in a good way, a positive way, in a very helping way.

NONA BEAMER: They were intelligent. And they put the students first, before the pocketbook.

NEIL HANNAHS (*'69, Bishop Estate manager, Kakaʻako Improvement*): They had a very powerful bond of allegiance to our founder and to the trust. Papa Lyman and Pinky Thompson, and the others, really saw themselves as indentured servants to the Princess. It wasn't something that you walked away from, a commission you resigned. You served till you died—totally loyal to the institution.

GUSSIE BENTO (*'50, former Heritage Center coordinator*): Basically, Papa Lyman was a kind man.

MIKE CHUN: My experience with him has been one of gentleness and a lot of aloha.

SAM HATA (*Schools director of administration*): Papa Lyman was, I would say, old school, where a personal relation counted for a lot for him. The family meant a very great deal to him. He was one of those, if you trust him and give him your trust, he repaid it in kind. Loyalty went both ways with him—you give him loyalty, he repaid it back to you.

GUSSIE BENTO: You could admire the man, have great respect for him.

PAUL CATHCART (*'69, manager, asset management group region I*): If there's anything, any time that I really treasured, it was the time that we spent with Mr. Lyman, because it was just a whole different perspective.

"Papa Lyman was a kind man."
–Gussie Bento

KAWIKA MAKANANI: He had a very strong link to his Hawaiian background, his Hawaiian heritage—

LAURA THOMPSON (*wife of Pinky Thompson*): —Real, real grounding in Hawaiian language and Hawaiian words—

PAUL CATHCART: —Mr. Lyman constantly reminding us in the boardroom, those of us who were privileged enough to attend trustee meetings, about the importance of Hawaiian, and he would always remind us too about the importance of looking at geographic names, Hawaiian names. They indicate a story, and that's so important.

KAWIKA MAKANANI: He had to live and survive in his world, but even then he did make efforts to push it as best he could, in an environment, an era, in which being Hawaiian was devalued, the Hawaiian culture was devalued.

BRIAN CHANG (*Schools operation specialist*): Papa Lyman was very supportive of education.

SAM HATA: He loved the campus very much.

He was always up here talking to the boys, never hesitate to talk to any of the employees, whether it was a groundskeeper or bus driver. Doing things, getting his hands involved—he was a hands-on kind of guy.

He was very proud of being a Hawaiian. We have a flagpole by Bishop Hall, and we used to fly the American flag and the Hawaiian flag, and he used to tell me, "Why is the Hawaiian flag below the American flag?" I said, "Well, Papa Lyman, that's the law." "Well, I want equal height." So the way I resolved this was, I flew the American flag up at Smith, opposite. So that satisfied Papa Lyman.

OZ STENDER (*'50, Bishop Estate trustee*): That would have been 1948. I was learning to be a draftsman, and Fritz Abplanalp, he was my teacher, he asked if I wanted to do this. I said, sure. He suggested that the top might look like a kāhili. I came out with a

design. We went to the welding shop, did it in copper. It worked out well. I didn't know it was Papa Lyman's idea—I didn't know any of the trustees. We put lights in it, to shine at night. It's still there.

KEIKI KAWAI'AE'A (*director, Hale Kuamo'o*): He kind of tried to keep a certain kind of old Hawaiian standard. When I had to go in about the naming of three buildings, Kekelaokalani, Keku'iapoiwa, and Ke'eaumoku, the first question that he asked me is, "What is the correct pronunciation of Kealakekua ?" He had this big thing about Ke-ala-O-ke-Akua. And that was my quiz as to whether or not I had enough knowledge or not to talk about the naming of these three buildings.

FRED CACHOLA: At the boardroom, I've heard big developers, big guys, practicing how to pronounce some subdivision name before

> "'Why is the Hawaiian flag below the American flag?' I said, 'Well, Papa Lyman, that's the law.'"
> –Sam Hata

they went into the meeting. I've seen people in there shudder when they pronounce a Hawaiian name wrong. He would stop and slam his hand—he had big hands—he would be all over them.

I mean, it could be the make or break of a big development contract. Because these guys couldn't pronounce the name right.

GUSSIE BENTO: He was tough. You didn't do something that will displease him, because he would let you know that, but everything was on the up-and-up, straight up.

PINKY THOMPSON (*Bishop Estate trustee, 1974-1994*): When I first became a trustee of the Bishop Estate, and this was the second month of my trusteeship, they had a presentation for the trustees of the financial plan for the estate. And they went on and on and on and on, and finally I said, "I'm hearing all kind of stuff you're putting on this wall here, but I don't see any connection. What are you connecting it to? And what are you connecting it to that has relevance to Pauahi? What are we in business for?"

MIKE CHUN: Pinky was the guy who had the vision in that area and saw Kamehameha as a different kind of institution, more than anybody else. He saw this institution as not this particular campus on this hill. He saw this institution as being in the community.

PETER KAMA (*'53, member of alumni group Nā Pua*): Oh, I think Pinky Thompson is a wonderful human being. He's great because he committed himself. He went out into the community in areas where he was knowledgeable—very community oriented.

And I think he's a person who demonstrated activities of leadership. He's not the kind of guy to go, "Well, I did this, or I did that." He just got it done. For Hawaiians.

LAURA AND MYRON "PINKY" THOMPSON

KAWEHI YIM (*'79, Bishop Estate communications division*): From the middle '80's, all of a sudden our investments were becoming fruitful for us. We were seeing money that we really never saw before.

ROD FERREIRA (*'52, member of alumni group Nā Pua*): Bishop Estate with all of its opportunities was being exploited by a few of the old boy Democratic network.

FRED CACHOLA: People like Henry Peters and Dickie Wong and Lokelani Lindsey were all politicians.

ROD FERREIRA: A trusteeship was a payoff, and that plum paid them big monies coming from the estate in return for loyalty to the Democratic regime.

MIKE CHUN: The older trustees, all of these guys, had obviously been part of politics, but they never brought the politics to the Bishop Estate. Papa Lyman was a senator, but he was a businessman too, so he had that experience base.

When the Supreme Court appointed Henry Peters, it was the first time they appointed a hundred-percent politician. That's the only thing he ever knew. And he couldn't leave it behind.

LEEANN CRABBE: We still called him Speaker.

Laughter before the coming storm. (Left to right: Gil Tam, director, Administration Group, Trustee William "CJ" Richardson, Trustee Matsuo "Matsy" Takabuki, Trustee Myron "Pinky" Thompson, Trustee Henry Peters, President Michael Chun.)

LEROY AKAMINE: Dickie Wong, he bragged about it, the last day as being president of the Senate, that he was promised he was going to be the next trustee. And the very next day it came out in the papers. It was a done deal; it was set up already.

BRIAN CHANG: Henry Peters recognized that this position at Bishop Estate was even more powerful than the influence he peddled as speaker of the house.

PINKY THOMPSON: When Peters came on, there was a bad shift in the atmosphere. He slid in through Governor Ariyoshi, and he had no real knowledge of the efforts of the school and the direction it should go, other than to drive a power train. He just continuously drove a power train.

MIKE CHUN: I was in Peters' office and he made a comment to me. "Mike," he says, "I'm just biding my time. When Pinky goes—whole new ballgame."

ELISA YADAO: You know, Pinky was a man who existed within a political system but really wasn't a politician. There was that desire to work with these guys. He just wanted to work with them. He wanted to have certain things in place before he left.

I think, on the one hand, they had a great deal of respect for him, because of his age, and the things he had done in the community. But on the other hand, I think they just wrote him off because he was so different from them.

He was a good person, very much dedicated to looking at vision and values and culture. He was dealing with the big picture—things that in Dickie and Loke and Henry's minds were just not that important. And so they kind of marginalized what he was doing. It was starting to slip away.

And frankly, he was feeling his time. He knew he was going to be leaving.

OZ STENDER: When we had to reorganize the board, I suggested that Pinky become the chair, because he had one more year and then he's gone. He's done a lot of good things, and it would be nice for him to end up being the chair—and after he leaves, Henry steps into that position, because he's the oldest in time of trustee, so he can be the chair of the board.

And after that meeting, Henry came to me and said he would prefer to be the finance chair. And I said, "Why?" And he said, "Because I want that job."

NEIL HANNAHS: Because from his days of politics, he understood, why fight over a title? If you had 'em by the purse strings, that's where the power was.

MIKE CHUN: Henry's the type of guy, he wants everything, so he wants the purse strings.

In Henry we trust

"Mr. Peters was the one signing the check."
–Brian Chang

ELISA YADAO: All of a sudden, Henry assumed responsibility for the assets side of the organization.

BRIAN CHANG: Mr. Peters was the one signing the check.

ELISA YADAO: Things were going to be done Henry's way.

BRIAN CHANG: He needs to be personally satisfied. It was not unusual to get a call directly from him asking, "What is the nature of this particular expense?" Sort of being in the army and being a buck private and getting a call from the president of the United States, saying, "When did you clean your rifle last?"

Sort of testing, in my estimation, as to, "What are you doing here? I'm watching you. I'm looking over your shoulder."

◈ ◈ ◈

BRIAN CHANG

NEIL HANNAHS: I was a proponent throughout of communications. Henry never was. In his view, not much good comes from open communications—you know, you build expectations, people scrutinize you, people envied you. So he tried to be very private about what we were.

ELISA YADAO: All of a sudden the doors were closing. Like, you'd go to see a trustee, and the door was closed. I remember the first time that happened. I felt so odd. Because that just didn't happen before.

Things were becoming more difficult on the staff level.

JUDY LAYFIELD (*project coordinator, administration director's office*): It was left up to department managers to determine who got access where, and so it's possible with new locks that an accounting person might not be allowed to walk into Legal—there's intercoms on the doors asking permission to be let in.

ELISA YADAO: We started getting factionalized, depending on who your lead trustee was and who you were reporting to.

And so then you started seeing more of these kind of private dealings—you know, I'm your trustee, you don't need to tell anyone else, just report to me. We couldn't work freely with each other.

KAWEHI YIM: There wasn't that one on one. If anything, the trustees became more secretive. Increased isolation yet still having their hands into everything. And they were very selective as to who they brought in to their inner circles.

ELISA YADAO: They got to the point where the trustees were telling their executive secretaries, "You need to tell me who's going into so and so's office, and who's meeting with so and so." To be their eyes. And I think not any single one of those women was comfortable with it. But, you know, they worked with these guys for a long time, and knew that their allegiance—however they were conflicted about it—was to their bosses. It was hard for them.

JUDY LAYFIELD: It got to where no one wanted to talk about anything, and it's like, well, that's not your business.

KAWEHI YIM: It was like a really lousy feeling.

JUDY LAYFIELD: It was definitely a sense of, well, if I know something you don't, that makes me more important.

BRIAN CHANG: These trustees surrounded themselves with people that were supportive of them. That were subservient to them. They surrounded themselves with yes-men.

FRED CACHOLA: "Mr. Speaker, would you like an umbrella? It's a little wet out there." Ehh—I mean, it's sickening, watching these guys operating in Kawaiahaʻo Plaza like, "I'm taking over this place."

JUDY LAYFIELD: There was a general services division, a department— I thought, my own personal opinion, the staff in there were political appointments, a lot of political plants.

LEEANN CRABBE: The people that were brought in who were certain trustees' people—we knew there were certain things that these people could get away with. Silly kind of petty things, but things that matter down here—

ELISA YADAO: —In a place where so much of your status is determined by these external affirmations. How many square feet you have in your office. How many lines you have on your phone. How big your chair is.

KAWEHI YIM: It's the enclosed offices. It's the prime parking stalls and not having to pay for your parking.

ELISA YADAO: I mean, all of these were indicators of your value to the organization, your importance, your skill.

BRIAN CHANG: So there are certain individuals that had these— spheres of influence. They had power and authority because they had the weight of the trustee's support behind them. Whether or not they really had the smarts to execute was more the question.

"They surrounded themselves with yes-men."
—Brian Chang

JUDY LAYFIELD: I think we lost a lot of good people because of the manipulation. Some just said, "I'm not going to play this game," so they left. And there's others who became puppets.

LEROY AKAMINE: They did not understand that as employees in certain positions, that they were agents of the *trust*. That they worked for the trust and not for their supervisors. They don't work for trustees, they don't work for the president of Kamehameha Schools, et cetera, et cetera—they are agents of the *trust*.

 So that lack of understanding, I think, led them to believe that because my boss said to do this, which you know is wrong, despite the fact that the trustee with all that authority and power had control of only your life, that you just didn't give any parts to the fact that what you're doing is basically wrong, and you should not be complicit in whatever activity that led to a result that was wrong.

NEIL HANNAHS: What it was like in the boardroom changed a lot over time.

I remember our regular trustee meeting dates, you had a published agenda, and anyone could walk in anytime. If you saw something of interest on that agenda, you'd say, I'm going to hear what they're saying about this. You'd go in and be part of the gallery, maybe even chip in from the side of the room and say, "You know, this is what I think," or, "I have a question about this. Thank you." So it was quite open in that way.

Now there would be side caucuses. They would have met privately.

HENRY PETERS
AND NEIL HANNAHS

LEEANN CRABBE: At one point I was making upwards to 24 meeting packets. And then Gil Tam went and revised all of the meeting procedures.

And then the meetings became closed. The doors closed. You were only invited in when you had something to present or the trustees had questions for you.

MIKE CHUN: When I first became president, I would bring in people besides myself—to provide reports on different programs, to have something very substantive. In time, and mainly because of Henry, he said, "No, Mike, leave them, we just want you in the boardroom."

LEEANN CRABBE: A lot of what happened was not recorded in the minutes, simply because they became the executive session items, or they were confidential or attorney-client privilege. They were never recorded.

OZ STENDER: I wanted them to record votes in the minutes. They wouldn't do that.

LEEANN CRABBE: Yet obviously some of these decisions led to actions that were taken. But in trying to go back to the documentation, there was no documentation.

◈ ◈ ◈

KAWEHI YIM: With this board, very rarely did they start on time.

MIKE CHUN: A meeting would be scheduled for 9 o'clock, and I would be there, quarter to 9, 10 to 9. About 9 o'clock, Oz comes in, brings his folder, sits down, says, "Well, where is everyone?" Everybody chuckles, because Loke might be in her office, probably Henry is on his way, Dickie is out there somewhere.

Maybe 9:15, Oz says, "Well, call me when they're ready," grabs his book, goes back into his office. And then a few minutes later, Dickie walks in. He comes in through the ma kai door and he says, "Oh, where's everybody?" and goes out the other door and disappears. Loke comes in the ma kai door, she says, "Oh, where's everybody?" She sits down, she waits a little while, she gets up, she goes back out. Dickie comes back in. "Eh, I can't find my—oh, these trustees." And he'd make fun of it. He says, "Hey, next one comes in here, you lock the door now, okay? Ha, ha, ha." It was embarrassing. It was embarrassing.

KAWEHI YIM: We would schedule guests, some of our business partners, to come in and give presentations, and they were supposedly scheduled to be first on the agenda, and they'd be waiting, and they'd wait and wait, and sometimes they'd wait up to three hours. And the trustees said they have to wait, there are other things to talk about. For them, it wasn't a priority.

BRIAN CHANG: I always came to those meeting with the understanding

"I also give unto my said trustees full power to make all such rules and regulations as they may deem necessary for the government of said schools and to regulate the admission of pupils, and the same to alter, amend and publish upon a vote of a majority of said trustees."

"I direct that a majority of my said trustees may act in all cases and may convey real estate and perform all of the duties and powers hereby conferred; but three of them at least must join in all acts."

–Bernice Pauahi Bishop's will, 1884

that you cannot control these people. You cannot dictate the pace of the meeting, or direct the flow of information. They are in control—it is their meeting. I was taught professionally to release information at key points and to control the environment so that things would hopefully turn out very well.

That could not be done in the boardroom.

MIKE CHUN: I remember Dickie always saying, "Mike, the thing I learned is that five beats four, three beats two, two beats one. You've always got to count your votes."

DICKIE WONG (*Bishop Estate trustee*): The trustees worked like five fingers, one hand.

LOKELANI LINDSEY (*Bishop Estate trustee*): There's a real working-together attitude. It has to do with Hawaiian cultural values. The decisions have to be made as a group, and they're mostly unanimous. We all have a say.

BRIAN CHANG: But you have five different individuals with five different perspectives.

Gerry Jervis had a fiery temper, to put it bluntly. Loke was totally unpredictable. Henry Peters is a confrontational type.

ELISA YADAO: Henry Peters has a remarkable capacity to be a kind person. I can remember my boys, when they were literally babies, running up to him and just opening their arms to him and getting scooped up and having him carry them. And you know he's a big foreboding guy. And they were never afraid of him. He was always good to me. I mean, he yelled at me and screamed at me, and we'd get into it. But I never perceived him to be cruel or underhanded with me. I never did.

ROD MCPHEE (*Punahou School president*): They did not stand up to Henry. I don't think there was anybody who stood up to Henry.

WALLY LAU (*Schools director of alternative education*): I think ultimately Henry was controlling everyone. He was the one.

MIKE CHUN: The way we did business in the boardroom was changed forever.

BOB WHITING (*Secondary School coordinator of learning centers/special events*): The first thing that I saw as an abusive thing was the story about the first meeting Jack Darvill, the president, had when Henry Peters came on the board. He had brought the budget for the following year, and he was completely raked over the coals by Henry in an abusive sort of way, saying he wasn't competent, he didn't know what he was doing, and it was a way of bringing him down or tearing him down. Jack had never been treated that way.

TONY RAMOS: "Me trustee, you staff." That's Henry Peters in the boardroom. His own words—me trustee, you staff.

WALLY LAU: You'd go in the trustees' room—when Henry talk, everybody kind of squeeze their 'ōkole, man.

PAUL CATHCART: I like to ride a bicycle, my road bike, and I was told that to get the most optimum workout, have a heart rate monitor, things you put around your chest and it sends a little beam to your wrist watch and tells you how many beats per minute your heart is beating. I remember going at lunchtime and buying it, and I put it under my aloha shirt, and I said, "Okay, 60 beats per minute." All of a sudden, my phone rings, and us senior managers had a special phone that showed who's calling. It said H. Peters, and I said, "Oh, God, what does he want now?" And I pick up the phone, and he just had some routine question, and I said, "Okay. I'll get back to you, Mr. Peters." I looked at my watch, on my little wrist thing, and it said 180 beats per minute. It was the first tangible indication that even though I thought I was cool, I'm used to all of this abuse, that wow, it's really affecting me. I do have high blood pressure.

MIKE CHUN: My first time, I was asking questions. Then we took a break, and Henry said, "You know, Mike, this is for the trustees. This is not for you." So I got scoldings for asking questions. And I know around the table, and myself included, any question made you the nail.

"... When Henry talk, everybody kind of squeeze their 'ōkole, man."

–Wally Lau

PAUL CATHCART

And these guys were carrying hammers. At some point in time all of us stopped asking questions. I guess that could be taken for not questioning authority.

OZ STENDER

"Oz was really a breath of fresh air."

—LeeAnn Crabbe

OZ STENDER: Nobody wants to tell the trustees anything that's going wrong. Because they get beat up.

When I first started at Bishop Estate, I'd sit in those meetings, and trustees would be screaming and yelling at staff and at guests. I couldn't believe what was going on.

I told them one day, "It's wrong to do that, you embarrass these people in front of everybody. And these people are the ones that are going tell you what's going wrong. But if you scream and yell at them when things are going right, do you think they'd ever tell you what's going wrong? You kill the messenger." That was the attitude in the boardroom. It was so bad. Embarrassing. I couldn't stand it.

JERRY SPRAGUE (*Schools food services, director*): One of my first opportunities to see Henry Peters in action was when I went down to ask for more labor.

Everybody was sitting around the boardroom. Sam Hata was with me. Dr. Chun was there, Neil Hannahs. And Henry Peters started. It wasn't a shout exactly, but it was close to shouting: "All these ungrateful people! Being out sick all the time! What is the matter with them? And why do you need more labor?"

He started banging his fist. Dr. Chun started to say something in response. And I was really upset, so I started to say something. Henry Peters pointed at each one of the trustees, and then he said, "Okay. That's it."

I didn't know what was what. I looked over at Neil Hannahs. He caught my eye. He said, "Get out." So I go out, and he comes out. I said, "What happened in there?" He said, "He was just getting their vote." That's what that was. But he was loud, cursing, banging his fist on the table.

PAUL CATHCART: You have five trustees having to sign a lease document. We're talking about millions, it's going to be affecting a lot of people, and they're just busily signing off these documents. We want their undivided attention. So Henry, a lot of times, just to punctuate a point, he'd grab the documents and just throw them on the table and yell. Or he'd stand up a lot and just pace back and forth. He was very physical, and he moved around, and he'd point his finger, and his voice would increase the volume of it. It was like an opera—he was singing his aria.

A trustee would get up and leave, ostensibly to go to the bathroom or whatever. Trustees are always going in and out, but especially when Henry Peters is going through his aria. They'd come back in five minutes; it's still going on.

My theory is that it was his way, how should I say—I mean, channeling power, enhancing his position as a trustee. He wanted to be the influential trustee, and so his plan was to really send these signals to his fellow trustees that he's somebody to deal with, and therefore, by yelling and screaming the loudest, that he is the man that the other trustees need to cope with and deal with and bargain with in order to get certain issues decided.

MIKE CHUN: If he didn't approve it, it didn't fly.

PAUL CATHCART: Loke would get on our butts, just because, for grammatical things—she didn't know anything else. Henry would start screaming and yelling at us. Loke kind of reveled in it. She fed off all that excitement, and she would throw a few words after Henry would be yelling. None of what she said made sense, because she didn't really know the issues or take time to read the report or what have you, but she just did it to echo or second Henry, kind of tell him indirectly, "Eh, I'm on your side and I believe in whatever crazy things you just said."

ELISA YADAO: Mrs. Lindsey was unhappy. Mr. Peters was unhappy. Mr. Wong was unhappy. They were unhappy to a trustee. And then they made Mr. Stender unhappy.

OZ STENDER: Oh yeah, it's like barking dogs. One trustee had a problem, one dog starts to bark, and they all climb on the bandwagon, start screaming and yelling at everybody.

TONY RAMOS: Just the way they talk, they shouldn't be trustees.

KAWEHI YIM: What words? Unrepeatable.

OZ STENDER: Henry and Gerry, all the time. Gerry, very short-tempered, he'd come unglued a lot. It didn't take much.

NEIL HANNAHS: I am told that trustees now begin all of their meetings with a pule. They should have followed our example a long time ago. Whenever we're called into the trustees' meeting, the first thing a staff member says is, "Oh God, please help me!"

PAUL CATHCART: Henry would start screaming and yelling at us, ridiculing us. Maybe an hour later, he'd call us into the office, and he starts talking to us like nothing happened in the boardroom.

ELISA YADAO: He would say, "You know, my mind is like a toilet, and every day I flush."

KAWIKA MAKANANI: For many people, especially Kamehameha students like myself, we were very happy to have Oz Stender on the board, as the first Kamehameha graduate.

MOMI CAZIMERO

MOMI CAZIMERO (*'51, member of alumni group Nā Pua*): Oz always loved Kamehameha. It just seeped through his pores. He wanted so much, he expressed, to do a good job.

PAUL CATHCART: There was just a lot of excitement on our part when Oz came on board. Oz is somebody who had strong beliefs, and he had this reformist attitude about some of the policies. He would take strong positions.

LEEANN CRABBE: Oz was really a breath of fresh air. He's like a business person. He'd come from Campbell Estate, and he obviously was active in the Hawaiian community. In terms of the way things were supposed to run, he sort of got it. The right things.

BOB LINDSEY

MIKE CHUN: One of the first things he does is this interview and he's quoted as saying, well, he's the first person selected who wasn't part of the good old boys. And that didn't sit well with the other trustees.

BOB LINDSEY: I think Oz is a man of integrity and great strength, always very uplifting, always very caring.

KEIKI KAWAIʻAEʻA: If I were to look at somebody who I thought really represented Hawaiian leadership qualities that you don't see a lot of today, Oswald Stender would really be at the top of my list.

The quiet leadership that he had, it amazes me—what we do to show what we believe in and how we go about doing that in public and in private ways. He's done that in many aspects of our language and culture. 'Cause he really believes it. He never bragged about that.

He can get in the taro patch as well. Where he needs to, he can stand up in those places. If we have students that come out with that kind of integrity, the whole world would be that much more blessed.

BRIAN CHANG: Oz Stender had the real experience. He was chief executive officer of Campbell Estate.

OZ STENDER: I kept harping on doing a strategic plan. We had no strategic plan. They could never find the time to do that. And I think the real reason they didn't want to do that—you do a plan, and you budget to the plan, and then you get benchmarks and goals you have to achieve. And if you don't have a plan, and if you don't achieve anything, or nobody knows—without a road map, you'll never know whether you got there or not. Where is *there?* There was no benchmark for performance.

And that's the way it was at Bishop. I think they were happy not to have a plan. Henry Peters would say, "We are on commission. We earn every dollar. A piece of the action."

HENRY PETERS (*Bishop Estate trustee*): I don't believe in granting favors just to grant favors. You look for talented people who can perform a service we need. We try to give consideration to people in the community who have a service we need. Why not give a job to someone you know than someone you don't? These accusations will always be there because people are jealous.

LOKELANI LINDSEY: A trustee is like a vacuum cleaner salesman—you sell more, you make more. Or a real estate person—if you sell a lot of land, you get a certain percentage of that sale, and you get a higher or lower salary depending on what you do.

GREG BARRETT (Honolulu Advertiser *reporter*): I didn't get the sense that Oz was ever looking out for himself. I felt the sense that Oz was doing this for Kamehameha Schools and was doing this for Dr. Chun; he was doing this for the good of the estate and the native Hawaiian. You can't go wrong saying that.

BRIAN CHANG: Oz was clearly the only one qualified to even be a trustee. But yet, he's the odd man out.

KAWIKA MAKANANI: As more events began to unfold, then I began to see this separation and isolation of Oz Stender from the other four.

MIKE CHUN: Politics steps in. When Dickie came on board and Loke came on board, Dickie and Loke start to line up. She's testing the waters, wind and Henry—okay, that's the power. Being the political animal she is, her decision-making now was based less on substance and more based on politics, and the politics was life with Henry. And Henry and Oz were not—you know, they weren't drinking buddies.

ROD FERREIRA: Oz found himself isolated and shut off in a corner.

OZ STENDER: They wouldn't share anything with me. They had their own meetings. They'd meet down in Henry's office every day, and I'd never know what was going on. They kind of dealt, Dickie, Henry and Loke, all in their little corner, and Gerry for a while. Doing their own thing. And when we got to the boardroom, I mean, they already made up their minds what they were gonna do, and then things just kind of ramrodded.

KAWEHI YIM: Mrs. Lindsey's camp was very disrespectful. Not open disrespect. It was hush-hush, but you'd hear little rumors. Other people, they respected him—but you also didn't want to be seen talking to him.

OZ STENDER: Well, they were all afraid of their jobs. Nobody wants to get fired. And they knew where the power was. They stayed away from me. They'd see me coming, they'd go the other way.

LEEANN CRABBE: There were some things that Mrs. Lindsey would write in the trustees' meeting packet material that didn't have any-thing to do with the business at hand.

OZ STENDER: Her priorities were all wrong. She tells everyone that I hated her from day one. Well, that's not so. I didn't know her to hate her. And I really don't hate people.

LEEANN CRABBE: It was a really uncomfortable situation when we'd go to board meetings. Oz would come into the room—and, I mean, it was like high school the way they treated him. You know, the way they would shun him, their little private jokes. He would talk, and they would talk right over him.

ELLEN PELLISERO (*Bishop Estate communications specialist*): There was a story on Mr. Stender being written for *Imua,* about the Inter-national Relations Group that he was involved with at the university, a real good thing, real popular. Len Tai was working on it with Mr. Stender, and Mrs. Lindsey called her up, and there was a big ring-dang-doo between them. It was almost like the majority didn't want anything positive said about Mr. Stender. It got pulled.

FRED CACHOLA: People like Peters and Wong and Lindsey were all politicians. As soon as Henry Peters knew he had the votes—he had Loke and Dickie—that was it. That was it.

BRIAN CHANG: And my personal belief is that the four of them got together and carved out territory just like they do in the back rooms at the State capitol.

FRED CACHOLA: That's the mentality they wanted. So that they could begin trading, and chum, chum, chum. And that's exactly what happened.

ELISA YADAO: In terms of what Lokelani's areas of responsibility were going to be, they were going to give her Communications and the Schools. And all these things with deals and money, they were going to keep. So—Loke, you go do this.

BRIAN CHANG: What would typically happen was that a spirited discussion would occur, and Oz would be silent on this, and he would subsequently issue a memo to the other trustees. Frequently we got copies of his memos in which he outlined his opinion on the matter. Basically it was a dissenting opinion. I think in most cases his memos were ignored.

LOKELANI LINDSEY: If Mr. Stender objects to something in the boardroom, he writes a memo to us, then that's distributed to these people, and they take his statements out without looking at a total picture and promote them in the news media.

DICKIE WONG: He's written so many memos. Action need not be taken because of a memo to trustees.

BRIAN CHANG: I remember one time Oz mentioning to me that Dickie Wong was berating him to stop writing these memos. Because clearly they were leaving a paper trail.

OZ STENDER: They wanted me to stop writing those memos. I mean, the nerve of them. Mrs, Lindsey, she would say, "You've got no business writing those memos. That's breaching trust." I mean, how is that breaching trust?

NEIL HANNAHS: It just got to the point where Oz couldn't stand it.

BRIAN CHANG: Oz was always very supportive of education. But it came to a point where he was clearly not gonna be supported by a majority of the board.

ROD MCPHEE: When Henry Peters came to power on the board, that's when I started hearing about problems at Kamehameha.

PINKY THOMPSON: I never got a feeling for Henry Peters' efforts in supporting the teachers other than its being a power move on his part. It had nothing to do with the betterment of the Schools. It's completely empty.

BRIAN CHANG: When I came to Kamehameha initially, it was a wonderful place to work. There was tremendous flexibility given to administrators, given to the president, executing the programs in the manner they saw fit. It's certainly changed dramatically since then.

KAWEHI YIM: That us-versus-them attitude.

ROD MCPHEE: The role of the president had changed from running the institution to doing what you are told by the trustees, down to who you hire.

SAM HATA: They start consolidating the power. They want control of who we buy from. Or who you give contracts to. Purchasing and construction. They take all the employees down there.

HAILAMA FARDEN (*'89, Secondary School Hawaiian language teacher*): I was called in to Tony Ramos' office one time and asked, will I go hold signs for Henry Peters—you know, for election.

JAN BECKET (*Secondary School english teacher*): I remember having conversations with Grady Wells, who ran the print shop. He was a very, very decent guy. But Grady was incensed that he was being required to print jobs for politicians, and re-election brochures, and things like that—on the sly, of course. He didn't like it, but he did it, because he was being required to do that.

MIKE CHUN: It used to be, "Mike, you run the school." Henry was the one who said, "No. *We* going run the school."

BRIAN CHANG: From the meetings that I attended, Mike was constantly being beat up by Henry Peters, and particularly by Lokelani.

Mike would basically take it on the chin. He took the higher road. He really did. And I must give him credit for that. Because I certainly couldn't do that.

ELISA YADAO: Henry Peters is through and through a politician, and he was dealing with this realm that was universes away from the campus. And Henry, not coming from the world of academia, had a real problem with people exercising independent thought.

SAM HATA: When you agree to go and testify before Henry and the trustees, you never call anyone Dr. So and So. He doesn't like that

"The school was an adjunct to the goings-on and the concerns and the focus of the Bishop Estate, which was politics and Democratic machine goings-on and support for this politician or that politician."

–Jan Becket

term, Dr. He'll tear that person. Terms like "researcher," "evaluator" —those are all no-no terms. Maybe he's trying to give a message saying, "I don't care if you have a doctorate degree or whatever; I'm just as good as you are."

HENRY PETERS: I've had it up to here with experts.

MIKE CHUN: He views the teachers as elitists, greedy.

ELISA YADAO: He never would want to spend a whole lot of money at the Schools, you know. He was manju—he really would pinch those pennies. And he would say, "I'm checking with Elisa on this. It's a high school, not a college. Why do they need all this kind of stuff?"

MIKE CHUN: Henry liked when he heard stories of me sitting down with bus drivers. "Oh yeah, okay, with the brothers, with the brothers." But he had no value of any stories if I were to sit down with the teachers.

Over the years with that board, it seems to me they would be willing to meet with anybody except the teachers. That the teachers think they're better than anybody else. They think they're special. Who the hell they think they are?

'Five fingers, one glove'

FRED CACHOLA: We're at a retreat to talk about mission, future and stuff like that. The head of land and finance was talking. Everybody in Kawaiahaʻo bowed down to him. I said, "You know, I think maybe the highest and best use of our lands may be in education and culture." And the trustees began to hem and haw, and I thought he was going to growl.

That night at dinner, he sat next to me, deliberately, looking, seeking me out. And he leaned to me and he said, "You know, Fred, I heard what you said about land." I said, "Yeah." And he said, "We make the money, you spend it, we watch how you spend. We don't tell you how to teach. You guys just stay on the hill. Don't come bother us. You let us alone."

And I looked at him, and I said, "Hey, are we working for the same outfit?"

LOIS LONG (*Secondary School speech teacher*): Kathy Kukea was in a meeting with some Kawaiahaʻo Plaza people, and they said, "Teachers are so idealistic." And she said, "How would you have them be?"

BOB WHITING: The letterhead thing that had all the trustee's names on the side, our business is the business of education, all that stuff, that didn't really say a whole lot about the school. It said a lot about trustees.

KAREN WILKINSON (*Bishop Estate policy and procedure specialist*): We were a real estate company. The tail was wagging the dog.

HENRY PETERS: We are big. We are massive. We are wealthy.

KAREN WILKINSON
"The tail was wagging the dog."

OZ STENDER: For those trustees, I think Kamehameha was kind of like a stepchild. They were never interested in being a part of the organization. They were to collect their paycheck, and that's it. I suggested several times that we should cut our compensation.

PETER KAMA: In my opinion, in a sense—so what if they making a million dollars? It's Hawaiians that's making it!

HENRY PETERS: Nobody talked about commissions when this institution had nothing but haoles. I've been sitting back and taking all of this bull for too long, and I'm personally very sick and tired of it.

PETER KAMA: But is it taking away from the students?

HENRY PETERS: We're not apologizing for the success of the institution. I expect a pat on the back on that and not a kick in the ass.

KAWEHI YIM: Having been in both places, I much prefer being on campus. The atmosphere, the environment is really different. You see the kids every day. It's a reminder of why you are here, why you are working.

BRIAN CHANG: Our value was nil in the eyes of trustees.

LOIS LONG: It seemed that the vocabulary that was being used was more business. I remember some of the forms that we dealt with spoke of students and parents as "customers" or "clients." When I first saw that, I just thought, *Oh, there must be a mistake; they must have taken a Bank of Hawai'i form and forgot to change it.* And then I realized, no, no, no, it was how they were using it.

To me, that was just kind of alarming. What's changing here? And I just kind of rebelled. I remember having to fill out some forms, and crossing out those words and putting students or parents.

And when we got a letter—one of the many times when we were

not having contract renewals, ever, until almost school began, or when it did. I got a letter in the mail. And basically it had the first declaration that we were employees at will. And you may be getting a contract, and you probably will. But this attitude is that you are an employee only because we've decided to have you as an employee, even though we've been teaching for many, many years.

And I had never felt that way about my employer, you know—even my unseen employer. It was a change of climate kind of thing.

ROD MCPHEE: It was the trustees' manner of telling the teachers that they were not valued, they were dispensable and could be gotten rid of.

LOIS LONG: I have a garbage thing between the mailbox and my house to throw catalogues away so they don't enter the house. And I was so offended by that letter, I got rid of it immediately. It was a contaminant, you know.

KAWEHI YIM: To me, not having an employment contract would be worrisome. One school year, two days before school started, or one day before school started, they finally got their contracts?

ROD MCPHEE: Because the budget wasn't done? That's one of the dumbest excuses I have ever heard. I heard Mrs. Lindsey say that, and I thought, *I can't believe any rational person would say this.*

KAWEHI YIM: But I think for the majority of people down here, they looked at the faculty as being a bunch of grumblers.

And the fact that for the trustees—it never dawned on them that people's livelihoods depend on this. And yet they were "comme çi, comme ça" about getting these budgets approved and getting these contracts sent out so that we would have teachers for our school. I mean, first and foremost we're a school, but in this culture down here at Kawaiahaʻo Plaza, you know, we're a business.

JAN BECKET: I remember, my first semester, being taken aside by Lee Thomas, who acted as kind of an elderly mentor to people like me, young whippersnappers coming in—taken aside and told, "Around here, the way things work is that the school exists for Bishop Estate, not the other way around." The sooner I realized that, the happier and more content I'd be.

LOIS LONG

"I remember having to fill out some forms, and crossing out those words and putting 'students' or 'parents.'"

FRED CACHOLA: Gil Tam got to be personnel manager. He took the personnel division down to Kawaiaha'o Plaza, and we were the enemy up there. The Schools as a whole. That we were being run wrong. He used words like this in the meetings—"We got to wean those teachers away from this feeling of security, we got to wean them away from this!" And I got so pissed! I said, "Wow!" That you were not to be trusted. That we ought to be looked at more carefully, that everything got to be scrutinized more carefully. That information should be limited, that only certain people should know. This is when—I telling you God's truth—this is when Gestapo mentality started.

KAWEHI YIM: Pauahi was visible as far as a poster that you put in your office. As far as the person she was, and the values she embodied, and as far as what she wanted for Hawaiians in general, it wasn't present.

ELISA YADAO: The trustees instituted a new evaluation procedure whereby we were all going to be graded on how well we adhere to Hawaiian values.

KAIPO HALE: My understanding as to how that all came about is this: Before Pinky Thompson retired, he came to the board and expressed to the Hawaiian Studies Institute at Kamehameha his concern about integrating a series of Hawaiian values institution-wide. It was based on his experiences of *Hawai'i Loa* and *Hōkūle'a*—the training of the crew and so forth—the fact that they had integrated a series of values as part of their program. And he was very adamant and strong in his decision to bring forth that kind of understanding to the table. And that's how it all got started.

OZ STENDER: Lokelani Lindsey supported Pinky on it, saying, "Well, we have to do this, it's a good thing." So she had all these brochures done and all that. And then she never practiced it.

KAWEHI YIM: We went through this whole values classes, the Hawaiian values classes with Kaipo Hale, which I thought was wonderful. But throughout all of the classes you could hear the same questions being raised—"We're not the ones who need this! The people at the top

need it!" It's not the clerks; it's not the secretaries. It's the people at the top, it's the people who serve the people at the top, principal executives—they needed it.

NEIL HANNAHS: The trustees didn't really buy into it.

OZ STENDER: It was lip service.

PAUL CATHCART: All of the staff would always joke that, you know, we got all those Hawaiians in there, and the trustees sometimes publicly would like to make something out of the fact that now you got all Hawaiian trustees. But they were so un-Hawaiian in everything they did.

I don't think Henry was Hawaiian at all. He didn't try to instill any Hawaiian values in us. Once our conscience of Mr. Lyman passed away, and then Pinky felt less and less, he became more impotent. As Henry took over the board's dynamics, our Hawaiianness was gone. It really was. It disappeared.

KAIPO HALE: I offered to in-service them. I said, "Shouldn't we begin with you folks? I want to come into your boardroom and do this."

No—it never happened. Oh, they were too busy; there were many other issues to be addressed. The only person that came was Trustee Stender. He signed up.

"What are we supposed to do with these values? The values have been articulated to help us strengthen the bonds that hold us together. They provide common reference points for how we treat each other ... to care about what happens to other people in this organization.... And when I say all of us, I mean everyone. Not just staff. Not just supervisors. Not just executives. Everyone. And that includes us, the trustees."

–*Pinky Thompson,
August 23, 1994*

OZ STENDER: I stayed the whole day.

KAIPO HALE: No one else came.

NEIL HANNAHS: Attitudes are formed at the intersection of word and deed. And the word was, this institution would embrace certain Hawaiian values. They were emblazoned on our walls, emblazoned in our literature and perpetuated through wonderful classes offered by Kaipo Hale, which all of us were required as staff to attend. Over time it became understood that the trustees, having made this requirement, did not choose to participate in those classes, and that is very troublesome when it comes to something like values, because the leadership really establishes the values. Even beyond that, their actions seemed to be at odds with these values. At the intersection of word and deed was formed a very bad attitude about very wonderful values.

KAIPO HALE: I recall even one time when I saw Dickie Wong's name on the list, that he was going to be in attendance. And he didn't show up. I ran into him in the elevator and it surprised him. I introduced myself. "I'm Kaipo, Kaipo Hale." "Ah, yes." "You were on my list for this morning's class." And he—"Oh, oh, oh"—and he made a mad dash out of that elevator.

NEIL HANNAHS: There was something—I mean, they didn't have good hearts, you know. It's something in the heart that's not there. When you come as rulers of this estate and not as servants, why are you here? Where is your heart? What's the passion to do this work?

KAWIKA MAKANANI: You can be Hawaiian ethnically and biologically, whatever that means, or scientifically, but if you don't have the Hawaiian heart and the Hawaiian values to bring to the task at hand, are you going to translate your task in a very un-Hawaiian way? And this is apparently what was happening with the board. There were things going on that were not following the pattern that had been established by previous boards.

At this particular meeting, Oz Stender volunteered the information that he was very disconcerted that the policy of naming Kamehameha buildings after members of the Kamehameha family was being broken.

And this had to do with the naming of the Hoaliku Drake pre-school in Nānākuli. Hoaliku Drake was Henry Peters' mother.

It seemed to me that this was just a gross example—that people want to push their own agenda to glorify themselves or their families. Hawaiians don't bring this kind of glory upon themselves. Because of Henry Peters' power on the board, and the willingness of three others to go along—I think this was just an inexcusable kind of action and decision-making.

OZ STENDER: Ego.

KAWIKA MAKANANI: The Western values seemed to be much more dominant. The values of acquisition, of individualism and the success of the individual in particular.

ROD FERREIRA: Coupled with the fact—and I'm going to say this—a lot of our own Hawaiians had been co-opted and were part of that structure and they were lining their pockets with Bishop Estate money. We all know that.

ROBIN MAKUA ('78, *Secondary School Hawaiian language teacher*): It happened from the inside, if you consider those trustees the inside, which they were. How the appointments were made, that's where you get the outside influence. What's happening in the outside world just infiltrated and came inside. They brought their outsiders to our inside, and then we got infected.

KAWIKA MAKANANI: And so some of the decisions that were being made that passed as business decisions were obviously linked to supporting their own friends.

NONA BEAMER: The trustees used to be people we trusted.

KAWIKA MAKANANI: Whether or not they got the kickbacks directly from their friends, or indirectly, which would be much more difficult to trace. And it seemed that some members of the board used their position to advance themselves personally.

KAWIKA MAKANANI

"The Western values seemed to be much more dominant. The values of acquisition, of individualism and the success of the individual in particular."

–Kawika Makanani

BRIAN CHANG: All the trustees' credit cards were keyed to a master account. And when this board came into power, they started exceeding the credit limits. So they increase the credit limits.

FRED CACHOLA: Feeding at the trough.

JOE TRAVIS (*'53, member of alumni group Nā Pua*): Dickie Wong said, "Joe, one thing you have to remember in this state—if you've got a position, a good position, and you got money, nobody touches you."

We had a schedule at the Executive Center downstairs in the restaurant there, and he was late. Parked his car right on Bishop Street, right at the corner—No Parking. He went right downstairs.

I asked him the question: "Dickie, you gonna get tagged." That's when he told me about having a good position and you've got money.

At that time, you know, a million dollars a year, the trustees.

JULIAN AKO (*'61, Secondary School dean of student activities*): And getting personally invested in a methane gas investment that the board invested in in Texas. Commingling. That had been aired publicly, and, you know, people like myself were kind of scandalized by the whole thing. There was a time when we began to get these benefits newsletters from Personnel about making your choices and what

Emperors' clothes

have you. And I can remember making some quip among friends about, "Oh gosh, I didn't read about that in the benefits newsletter. How come we didn't know about that information and have that opportunity too?"

FRED CACHOLA: You know, they had the mahiole syndrome, the royal headdress syndrome, and they had the 'ahu'ula syndrome, the royal cape syndrome. Once you put on that 'ahu'ula and the mahiole, and then you put on the palaoa, the royal whale's tooth pendant, you are god. And so in a sense they cloaked themselves with this neo-ali'ism.

WALLY LAU: Do I look at those people as leaders? 'A'ole! 'A'ole! No! No!

FRED CACHOLA: The feeling among Hawaiians as they look at leaders is to search for that sense of aloha, that sense of giving, that sense of service and this sense of being part of them, being with them, you know. Humbleness, humility, as opposed to being arrogant. Giving and serving as opposed to taking and hoarding and controlling.

PETER KAMA: If you're ali'i, you have the authority, you have the power, but you also have kuleana, responsibility—that's one of the Hawaiian values.

WALLY LAU: A leader is one that is honest, that is truthful, that don't play. The Hawaiian leader doing that—'a'ole!

◈ ◈ ◈

ROD MCPHEE: There are so many branches on this tree, but I think the core to me was the original political corruption from the Supreme Court and the governor, which led to the malfeasance by the trustees, and the willingness of the justices to look the other way while all of this was going on. If you can corrupt the Supreme Court, what the hell is left?

I think people have a feeling that some of these institutions are beyond reach. These guys cloak themselves in robes, and how do you get to them?

When the bar association doesn't say anything or do anything? One assumes as a non-lawyer that the bar association holds its mem-

"The feeling among Hawaiians as they look at leaders is to search for that sense of aloha, that sense of giving, that sense of service … Humbleness, humility, as apposed to being arrogant. Giving and serving as opposed to taking and hoarding and controlling."

–Fred Cachola

bers to a certain standard of behavior, and I don't remember seeing the bar association being outraged with this. I don't think the association wanted to get into this jungle, this swamp.

I don't know the dynamics of the judicial selection commission—nor does anybody. We know that they are politically involved, but if they don't see fit to punish anybody for their clear involvement in this, why should the rest of us feel we can do anything?

PETER KAMA: Us, you cannot question them! Their peers can. But what are the peers for those people? There's no peers. The guys that supposed to look over their shoulders—when they reported it, nobody did anything about it. 'Cause who did they report it to? The people that were appointed to the positions by the guys that were trustees.

KEʻALA KWAN (*Secondary School Hawaiian language teacher and department head*): I was saddened that we had Hawaiian trustees in this. I think that was a real feeling probably shared by many Hawaiians. It's like, Oh, man.

We know aliʻi were to take care of their people. It was a reciprocal thing. So if you hana ʻino the people, abuse them, they would get rid of you. There's a moʻolelo about a certain place in the ocean named for the ali'i that always took all the fish, so one day they just kept filling his wa'a, his canoe, until it sank and he died. They named the spot after him. So it goes to say that there were checks and balances against abuse, where it seems this is a situation where the checks and balances weren't working.

BRIAN CHANG: No checks and balances. And they knew it. They knew it.

ROD FERREIRA: The power structure was so huge and so spread out that nobody knew what to do. We were told in no uncertain terms—look, if the political power bloc is in charge and the judiciary is beholden to this political monster, where are you going to go with this?

BRIAN CHANG: I believe we were all stuck. We were dealt—by fate—this particular group of individuals with their own dynamics. And I don't think there was any single individual or group of individuals that could steer this group differently from the course that they had plotted. They wanted to do their thing. They did their thing.

ROD MCPHEE: I think what Lokelani Lindsey did when she came in was just bring everything to a crescendo, so that we all saw that what we had sort of thought—that it was maybe only Henry Peters himself—was now the whole board, except for Oz.

BILL FOLLMER (*Secondary School mathematics teacher*): Lokelani was the key. All the bad things that the top-down management had done in the past with some skill—you couldn't attribute it to anybody. But with Lokelani, the attribution became clear. She was very unsubtle. It was coming from her. And she was proud of it. The offenses became obvious.

   I think the clarity was it. They were doing wrong, and it was out in the open. ✎

"Do I look at those people as leaders? 'A'ole! 'A'ole! No! No!"
—*Wally Lau*

2 Bottles of Coca-Cola
Lokelani Lindsey Enters the Scene

Employees of the Coca-Cola company do not determine how many bottles of Coca-Cola must be produced each year. That's a management decision.
–Lokelani Lindsey

Loke Lindsey at Waihe'e School on Maui

LOKELANI LINDSEY: We were driving to Pā'ia when the most brilliant double rainbow appeared in front of us. When we got back to the office, there was a message to call the chief justice of the Supreme Court. He said, "I just wanted you to know before we release it to the media—I just signed the executive order making you a trustee for Bishop Estate." I must have thanked him 2,000 times. After we hung up, I tried to call my husband, but I couldn't remember my home phone number!

I am awed by the opportunity to help the part-Hawaiian and Hawaiian people statewide. And I'm very humbled by the responsibility.

WALLY LAU: I was one of her best supporters when she became one trustee. I said, "Gee! This will be a good one here, man."

AILEEN SHIROTA (*former secretary to Lokelani Lindsey*): She was a very hard worker. She did everything for the benefit of the children, and she was not afraid to face problems.

KELA MILLER (*childhood friend of Lokelani Lindsey*): She had to really work hard at getting where she's at now. She had to go the extra mile and study extra hard and set her goals really high. She's just one of the women that a lot of us look up to.

ROCKY TOKUHARA (*'76, member of alumni group Nā Pua*): We finally have a woman! As a woman myself, I'm jubilant to finally have a woman on the board!

HERB WILSON (*'61, Secondary School counselor*): I was excited about a Hawaiian woman, an educator, coming on board.

JULIAN AKO: I remember being very excited having someone in the trustees' office who had some background in education, who I thought had come through the trenches, through the ranks, so to speak, as a teacher, and someone who would be able to be an advocate in the board-room for educational programs and for the kids that we serve.

KĒHAU ABAD (*'82, Secondary School social studies teacher*): Looking at her basic background, just on face value it didn't seem like she was well suited. I could think of people out there in the community who would be better. She's not been a mover, a shaker, a doer in the Hawaiian community. Sort of a Johnny Come Lately on the Hawaiian scene—and now she's a trustee? Whereas, other names that people may have considered, somebody like Gladys Brandt—my gosh, think of the stature and the integrity and everything else that comes with somebody like Gladys Brandt.

MIKE CHUN: I can't call her Auntie Gladys, I cannot call her Gladys. She will always be Mrs. Brandt only, because of a depth of respect I have for her, and an awe. She continues to amaze me. She's one of a kind. She has great insights. She is able to communicate like no one else I know. She can operate in any arena. She is one of those who, when displeased, she can say things that are devastating, but with dignity and with class.

GLADYS BRANDT

"She will always be Mrs. Brandt ..."
–Mike Chun

The stories I've heard—when she was principal here, she was a real hard nose, but she was fair. When I talk to kids who had gone to school then, they have a lot of aloha for her.

She's never lost her compassion, understanding of Hawaiians, the problems, the difficulties that Hawaiians are used to having. What I've learned from her stands out in my mind.

GARY OBRECHT (*Secondary School English teacher*): I always saw her as very regal and set apart, and yet she was very down to earth. A beautiful combination of earthiness and kind of being set aside. An ali'i quality in a contemporary setting. Very dignified. Even as a young woman she had class. Not just in how she dressed. She carried herself and treated people well. She was always one individual, and you could trust she would be that individual. Integrity.

NONA BEAMER: Mrs. Brandt, Clorinda Lucas, Flora Hayes, Bina Mossman—wonderful Hawaiian women. The way they carried themselves. They were always a perfect example of a modern Hawaiian woman. But they were quite western Hawaiian, where they dressed to the nines, and the matching hats and the gloves and the bags and shoes. And the way they spoke was always so exciting to me—they spoke such beautiful English. I thought they were wonderful Hawaiian women.

◁▷ ◁▷ ◁▷

MIKE CHUN: The first time I met Loke was when she was deputy superintendent of education for the county of Maui. It was then that I became aware of her political skills and her interests.

OZ STENDER: She was John Waihee's fundraiser on Maui. Very close to Joe Souki, from Maui. He was speaker of the House. She was chosen to run against Linda Lingle for mayor of Maui County.

HENRY MEYER (*Bishop Estate telecommunications manager*): Along with a number of school principals, I had organized a support group for Loke, you know, to kind of support her candidacy, because we felt she was a strong candidate. I took part in the latter part of the campaign by marching house to house on Saturdays with the gang, going to headquarters, that type of thing.

ROCKNE FREITAS (*'63, Schools vice president*): I was introduced to her by a guy named Charlie Duarte in 1982 when I was running for Office of Hawaiian Affairs. We were at the airport, I was flying to Lāna'i, she was coming in. Charlie grabbed me and grabbed her and introduced us and told her that I needed help. And you know how those political things go; you ask everyone for help. So that's how that worked out.

MIKE CHUN: She took great pride in these political skills. She made the comment to me several times, "You know, Mike, Charlie—Charles Toguchi, the State superintendent of education—has been trying to fire me for a number of years, but he can't, because I have the political muscle behind me." She didn't apologize for that.

KEIKI KAWAI'AE'A: She had a lot of power as a district superintendent. People feared her, but they didn't fear her because they respected her—they feared her because of repercussions if they didn't do what and how she wanted to do. That was kind of a common understanding that went through people in the Maui district. People were really afraid of her because of backlash. People said, "You don't cross her, and if you ever cross her, she will get even." She was kind of notorious for that.

CLEMI MCLAREN (*Secondary School English teacher*): I watched her on Maui. There was no consistency, no thread.

KEIKI KAWAI'AE'A: She had a really strange way of administering.

CLEMI MCLAREN: It was more like a monarchy than anything else I can describe. I was never acknowledged or called by name. Ever. We were referred to as "the little elves."

The people who kissed up got the money. And the programs and people, actually the most admirable people who were trying to run a good school and care about kids and education, they mostly got nothing.

And then I got it—it was all about power.

OZ STENDER: The story is, Charlie Toguchi wanted to fire her, because she was demonstrating bad judgment, creating all kinds of havoc with the district people. But John Waihee wouldn't allow it because she was his 'ohana, through her husband. The relationship with the governor— that's the political connection. The connection with the governor is how she got appointed.

"I have the political muscle behind me."
—*Lokelani Lindsey*

CLEMI MCLAREN
"And then I got it—it was all about power."

MIKE CHUN: I had conversations with a number of senior educators from Maui, and they would chuckle and say, "You know, Mike, it was a silent roar of joy when she was named trustee." I said, "Really?" This person said, "Yeah, because we're finally getting her out of the educational system on Maui."

ROBIN MAKUA: People in Maui, and some people here in the DOE, would say, "Too bad for Kamehameha. Good for us, but too bad for you."

SAM HATA: As soon as she got the appointment—lot of people called from Maui, teachers saying, "Oh, thank you very much."

OZ STENDER: The Maui people were so happy to get rid of her. Charlie Toguchi told me that himself. He said he was driving his car one day, and when he heard it on the news he nearly ran into the cars ahead of him.

LOKELANI LINDSEY: I'm sure that I will have the opportunity to visit campus sites, but I think Dr. Chun is doing a fabulous job—therefore, I'll leave the campus operations up to Dr. Chun.

OZ STENDER: But she didn't.

ROCKNE FREITAS: I was sitting in a meeting with Mike in the boardroom and Trustee Jervis said, "You know, we ought to have an office up there; we need to be more visible." And Mike's immediate response was, "I don't want you guys up there—stay out of there."

And so, what are you going to do? I mean, you're kind of in the middle of these damn things. My personal opinion, I want people around; I want people to see what we are doing. And so I kicked him a little bit; I said, "No, let him go." That was the beginning.

BRIAN CHANG: This office was vacant, and it was prime real estate because it was right across from the president's office. She came in one day. She had her entourage behind her. And she came over to my office and said, "Hi! I'm your new neighbor!" in a very friendly kind of way. I went, "Mmmm."

> "I think Dr. Chun is doing a fabulous job—therefore, I'll leave the campus operations up to him."
>
> –Lokelani Lindsey

That was it. One day she was here, she was sitting at the desk, she was talking on the phone. And that was that. Reserved for her. It was kapu.

OZ STENDER: I didn't intend for her to be on the campus. But she gets a parking stall, office, she's up there. And when I talked to her about it one day, she said, "Ozzie, don't you believe in walk-around management?" I said to her, "You're not the manager, you're the policy maker." But that's the way she was.

⬧ ⬧ ⬧

LOKELANI LINDSEY: I wasn't given any written guidelines. There was several different ideas from several different trustees about what I should do. My own interpretation at that time was, I would be in charge of anything that had to do with the school. Reviewing the budget was one of the things; talking to the people there was another.

ROBIN MAKUA: I remember the first time she came and we had an all-faculty meeting, in the band room—

KATHY KUKEA (*Secondary School coordinator of curriculum and instruction*): —Her making some comment along the lines of how the teachers were basically working in a country club.

HERB WILSON: Why would she say that? Why would she say we're spoiled? She was flippant about it, but it hit a lot of people.

KATHY KUKEA: Since I do feel like sometimes teachers do grumble and whine a little excessively, given all that we do have going for us, I remember thinking, *Well, you know, what the heck, she does tell it like it is.*

I thought she was going to be a straight shooter and a tough cookie. And, of course, first time there was a woman on the board. So there were parts of me that thought, *Well, okay.*

Another time, in a meeting in the auditorium, somebody was saying, "Shouldn't Kamehameha be providing education to more kids out in the community?" And she said, "That's not the sole responsibility of Kamehameha Schools; the DOE is responsible for providing education to Hawaiian kids." And again I thought, well, you know what, that's right, and that needs to be said.

ROBIN MAKUA: I remember feeling that she's got a DOE mentality with the Bishop Estate checkbook—we're in trouble.

ELISA YADAO: When she first became a trustee, there were many things she came in unhappy about, based on her experiences as Maui district superintendent. There were people on Dr. Chun's staff that she had talked about having bad encounters with and that she thought very little of. So she walked in the door with that.

LOKELANI LINDSEY: As lead trustee of education, I serve as a liaison between the school and the board of trustees, to support the school's president to the extent he was doing what the trustees asked him to do, to support the school administration with that same caveat and to work with and cultivate the KSBE ʻohana.

KAREN WILKINSON: On her behalf, she had wonderful vision. She was the first trustee that ever talked about education. Thank God she was there to kick ass and worry about education.

CLEMI MCLAREN: She was a PE teacher, a classroom teacher and a vice principal at four schools and a principal. She was Maui superintendent for 10 years. No experience in private schools.

ROD MCPHEE

ROD MCPHEE: There are major differences between public and private schools. The most significant one to me is governance.

In the independent school world, generally, we put great responsibility on the people down where the kids are, and less as you go up the so-called hierarchical line.

In the Department of Education, by virtue of being a bureaucracy—which I don't use in the pejorative sense; it has to be a bureaucracy because it's got 140,000 kids—there's a minimum value placed on discretion at the building level. There's more emphasis placed on following instructions and obeying the rules. And I just am not convinced that the training in a DOE situation in a large bureaucracy is ideal for running an independent school, being a board member of an independent school.

TONY RAMOS: Anybody who was an educator who would listen to her said, "She doesn't know, she doesn't know."

KATHY KUKEA: I got this call from Tony Ramos. He's down at Lokelani's office. He says, "You need to get down here; we're talking about test scores." So I go down there. Never had any interaction with her before except just kind of in passing. Go in her office and she's saying, "I've had some people look at the test scores at the Elementary School, and analyzing, and the kids do worse as the years go by—they start off high and then they drop off earlier." And she said, "I've been analyzing these, and I even know which teachers are good teachers and which teachers are bad teachers. In fact, I can track how kids have done with different teachers. If I were a parent, I could tell you which teachers to ask for in order to make it into seventh grade."

I said, "Ho!" I was trying to be respectful. The funniest thing is that she said, "Look at the scores of this fifth grader. Look what this teacher got out of these kids." And I said, "That's interesting—she's a substitute. There was a teacher on maternity leave, and she was in there for six weeks, a sub."

And then Lokelani would throw out test scores. Mike had this experience with her just throwing aside our test scores, saying these were not significant. And of course we knew that they were profoundly significant. She should have known. There was no way that she could not have known differently if she had any understanding of test scores and education.

So that was a major crack in the old how-great-that-we-have-an-educator-on-board feeling.

OZ STENDER: She would never listen to me. When I would try to give my point of view, she would always say, "Ozzie, I have been an educator for 30 years. You have no experience at all." I always had to say to her, "You're right, Mrs Lindsey."

So what did I do? I got myself on the 'Iolani School board, I got myself on the Saint Andrew's School board, got myself on the Assets School board, Academy of the Pacific board. So now I've got a whole spectrum of education opportunities to learn about education. In fact, 'Iolani, at 'Iolani's expense, sent me to the National Association of Independent Schools conference to learn about governance in private schools, trustees' responsibilities. And it was such an enlightening thing for me.

When I came back, I wrote a memo to all the trustees, that it's

"There are major differences between public and private schools. The most significant one to me is governance. In the independent school world, generally, we put great responsibility on the people down where the kids are, and less as you go up the so-called hierarchical line."
–Rod McPhee

LOKELANI LINDSEY
"I have been an educator for 30 years."

a good idea for you to attend one of these things. The next time they gonna have it, I sent out a notice to everybody, "This is an opportunity." And of course none of them would.

And Mrs. Lindsey, right in the boardroom: "Ozzie, I have 30 years of educational experience, and just nothing they could tell me that I don't already know."

SAM HATA: Seeing that woman around, we thought it was safer to have her office in the administration building, kind of like isolate her. We didn't want her roaming around the campus without us knowing. We wouldn't dare give her anything by the classrooms. Heaven help us if they ever put her in the High School someplace.

CLEMI MCLAREN: But she turned up everywhere, anytime.

LOKELANI LINDSEY: Management by walking around isn't scheduled appearances—just go in and see what's happening at any given time. I wholeheartedly believe in it. A manager's responsibility is to make sure of what is going on in any facet of the organization. Think of how stifling it would be if every visit was scheduled.

TONY RAMOS: She wanted to run this place. She wanted it.

LOKELANI LINDSEY: Basically I'm a team worker. Basically I would like to help people succeed.

English teacher Darrell Schuetz with student Kanoe Mendonca

DARRELL SCHUETZ (*Secondary School English teacher*): I don't know what word to use, exactly. She was dressed in loud colors, and she seemed to sort of strut or maneuver her way into the room in a way that communicated something— "I am important and you're not." Body language, and the stack of Hawaiian bracelets on the wrist and the manner in which she walked around and looked. I don't know how to explain it, except to say that it just made me think this is somebody—"I'm here from above, I'm descending on this room." And going through this in a way that is calculated to achieve her purposes, not ours.

CHARLENE HOE (*Elementary School art teacher*): Lindsey came down and talked to Elementary. She set the meeting at a certain time. Didn't show up for at least 30 minutes, I think almost 45 minutes late. Didn't bother to say anything about, "Well, I'm sorry I'm late." Just came sort of whisking in and, you know, how-come-this-how-come-that, and then gone.

GAIL FUJIMOTO (*Secondary School head librarian*): She wanted to meet with all the librarians. She scheduled the meeting just the day before, and so we had already scheduled classes and were working with kids.

She was over a half an hour late, maybe 45 minutes. When we initially got together and she was late, I said, "We gotta take care of business," and dispersed everyone. And when she did arrive and we weren't waiting for her, she was very indignant. And the fact that she had to sit in the room until everybody came, she was pissed—"How can you make me wait?"

That just irritated the hell out of me. Our first priority is to our kids. So to even call us and tell us we had a meeting the very next day when we had things already scheduled was ludicrous. But on top of that, to expect us to be sitting there in that room, waiting for her—she was totally clueless as to why we weren't there for her beck and call.

LANCE TAMASHIRO (*'98*): She came in to meet with leadership class at the Student Center. We were given slips of paper, to write questions down so she could prepare herself well for each question.

CIARA LACY (*'98*): The questions never resurfaced. She came in— "1,2,3,4—1,2,3,4—break into groups!" We were randomly assigned. One of the teachers came in late. Lindsey spoke very sternly to her and asked her why she was late and told her to get into a group.

ALICE KIMURA (*Elementary School teacher*): We had a meeting, in a second grade room. The kids were doing their Spring multicultural. It was African. They had things hanging, to decorate. Lokelani came in and said, "Why are we meeting in this room? These chairs are too small, and all this laundry is hanging there."

B.J. NAMBA (*Elementary School teacher*): My jaw just dropped.

JOANNE WONG-KAM (*'71, Elementary School teacher*): And we just sat

(Top to bottom): Alice Kimura, B.J. Namba and Joanne Wong-Kam. These three Elementary School teachers eventually left Kamehameha in despair over Lindsey's micromanaging. They were immediately hired by Punahou School.

there, and we didn't say a thing after that—we couldn't, because we were so stunned that she would refer to children's work as laundry.

KATHY KUKEA: We were also hearing about little things like she and Marlene Sai going into Eldon Chun's classrooms, because Eldon had supposedly made some kind of negative remark.

LOKELANI LINDSEY: I don't think I've ever reprimanded a teacher in the classroom.

KATHY KUKEA: Mrs. Lindsey said to this entire group of faculty that the Elementary School teachers had failed to teach the kids to read, which was not true at all, but even if it had been true, to have made such a statement in front of 200 fellow faculty members—

MARYANNE INOUYE (*Bishop Estate human resources*): She had a knack of getting people really mad.

LOKELANI LINDSEY: The trustees asked me to review all of the correspondence and things that went out to the public.

ELISA YADAO: Trustee for communications. The steadfast rule was that she needed to sign off on everything, and everybody knew it.

ELLEN PELLISERO: We had to wait downstairs and have her proof everything and she would put stars on the top. I felt like I was in English class.

ELISA YADAO: For a time in the beginning, I'd have to ask her permission to return telephone calls; I'd have to tell her what I was going to say. It got down to that kind of detail.

She had some strong feelings about my communicating with her and her only, and not with the other trustees—that she would communicate the things from Communications that needed to go to the other trustees.

Basically, my group was hers. And that was it. We were hers.

OZ STENDER: When I did my vision thing, my talk about a future for Kamehameha that I gave at the Social Science Association in town, I sent it out to all the trustees. Anything like that that was going outside the office, I would always send them copies. If they had any reaction to it, I would like to hear about it. Never, never, never a word, until that one.

And when it came in the papers, Mrs. Lindsey went ballistic, said I shouldn't be doing these things without trustee permission. I said, "It's months, Loke, you've had that thing for a couple of months. You could have said something then—how come all of a sudden it's a problem?"

She had a paper there, must have been 10 pages. She said, "I have all the breaches that you committed by writing that." I said, "Well, name me a couple." She started going through it. I said, "Look, Loke, I'm not going to sit here and try to respond to these things. Give me the thing and I'll respond to it in writing."

She wouldn't give it to me—"I'm not going to give it to you! Here-after, don't you ever release those writings to anyone until I edit it." I said, "You can read what I write, but you do not edit what I write."

HENRY BENNETT (*director, Kamehameha Schools Press*): She was quite a presence. Kamehameha Schools Press, under the mandate of Marsha Bolson and Leslie Agard, who reported to Mrs. Lindsey, was forced to submit all materials to her for preview and approval.

HENRY BENNETT

I did protest this specifically to Marsha Bolson, saying that this was a total violation of academic integrity in publishing. And was told that this was an institutional policy, and Mrs. Lindsey's instructions were to be followed. Based largely on Mrs. Lindsey's strength of personality, they would go out of their way to make sure that nothing would be produced that might possibly offend Mrs. Lindsey.

There was a book, *Lei Mele no Pauahi: Music, Past and Present, at Kamehameha Schools,* by Jonathan Osorio and Kanalu Young. Both of them are Kamehameha Schools graduates; both of them are faculty at the University of Hawai'i-Mānoa.

The authors produced a substantial manuscript, what I believed to be a realistic history, which showed a fair number of what might be called warts, especially in regard to the institution's treatment of Hawaiian language, Hawaiian music, Hawaiian hula.

I saw a lot of these elements removed. It was being sanitized.

I have been told that one of the revised type settings was done to remove text reference to the past efforts of Gladys Brandt, ex-principal of the Girls' School, and also a photograph of Mrs. Brandt. The only rationale I can see for such a removal would've been political.

LOKELANI LINDSEY: If a teacher was writing to a parent about a kid, that didn't come to me. If they were sending a notice from the school to the parents that went to all parents, yes.

B.J. NAMBA: This lady is telling me that if I write a note home to my parents, I need to run it by her office. I thought, *That's ridiculous.*

MARIANE HANNAHS (*'69, Elementary School teacher*): I mean, T-shirt design, if it was something like a T-shirt design, it had to be approved by the trustee's office.

OZ STENDER: The T-shirt thing.

I had a niece at Kamehameha. She was a senior. For Hoʻolauleʻa, they had a competition among the students to come up with a T-shirt design.

She was at our house with some of her classmates, and I could hear them talking about waiting for the trustees' decision on the T-shirt—design approval. So I'm a trustee, so one of the girls said, "When are you guys gonna make that decision?" And I said, "We don't make decisions on T-shirts." She said, "Yes, you do." And I said, "We don't." She said, "Yes, you do!" Because that's what the teacher told them. I called the teacher the next day, and she said, "Yeah, Mrs. Lindsey."

Then I found out about all the T-shirts. All these T-shirts that she had to approve.

There was one where one of the classes, an economics class, was going to sell T-shirts for Christmas, and the kids ended up having to give the money back because of the delay. I told Mrs. Lindsey, "Why do you have to approve them?" And she went on and on.

RENEE MARTIN (*Secondary School social studies teacher*): It was a class project, my Business Principles and Management class. One of their requirements was to form a student company within the class and market a particular item. This company wanted to do a T-shirt. A very simple plumeria design. They went ahead and submitted it like they were supposed to. But they never heard. They proceeded with their sale, and they pre-sold something like 3,000 dollars' worth of merchandise, to take advantage of the Christmas market. So everything was going really well, but we were waiting for approval of the design.

TONY RAMOS: These things were supposed to have a 24-hour turnaround time.

HENRY BENNETT: Her approval time generally tended to be substantial —weeks, and in many cases months.

LOKELANI LINDSEY: It takes a long time to read everything.

RENEE MARTIN: As time grew near, my students hadn't heard anything, so I sat down with them and said, "You know, I'm willing to just go ahead and approve it." I was willing to take the risk for them, and I remember one of the students saying, "No, Miss Martin, we don't want you to get into trouble." Because by that time they'd already heard stories about teachers.

JULIAN AKO
AND RENEE MARTIN
"And I just felt, you know, you ass."

So they took it upon themselves, they said no, and they refunded all the money. And then on December 18—I'll never forget this, it was the day before Founder's Day—I got this notice from Trustee Lindsey that said, "Tell the kids to go ahead."

And I just felt, you know, you ass. I mean, you know that school's going to end tomorrow. It was too late already, they'd refunded all the money. I was just livid.

They were concerned about their grades, and I said, "Don't worry about your grades, there were circumstances beyond your control."

I mean, this affected their learning. It totally negated who we were as advisors, guiding these students through the learning process. There was this micromanagement that basically undermined who we were. You know, like—you guys don't know any better, so it's got to come from me. And I'm thinking, *Bull*. I mean, we'd done it before without her and survived.

But for me it was the impact it had on the kids. That just pissed me off more. And just to see the kids say, "No, Miss Martin, we don't want you to get in trouble." To see that the kids had so much more class and concern.

LOKELANI LINDSEY: I approved T-shirt designs. And that came about because a group wanted to use Kamehameha School Lesbians and have it on their shirt. And they wanted to use it on a sign where they were going to have a huge picnic.

OZ STENDER: That's how I found out about the T-shirts. The stupid T-shirts.

◀▷ ◀▷ ◀▷

HENRY MEYER: Well, I think Mrs. Lindsey, being the individual that she was, was sharp in the area of scrutiny.

BRIAN CHANG: Very sharp. I think she's very intelligent. She really did her homework. She was an excellent note-taker. And was able to identify issues. And asked us for responses.

DICKIE WONG: I think as a matter of personal style, and knowing her all this time, that she's a process procedure person. It's what she does. She always questions the board about process and procedures.

HENRY MEYER: I think her weak point was that she got too involved and couldn't distinguish the forest from the trees.

BRIAN CHANG: I don't think she was very creative. I think she was primarily an on-task thinker.

LOKELANI LINDSEY: I felt that as the trustee I could talk to anybody at any time, and management by walking around is a very effective way of managing.

BRIAN CHANG: She's even more a micromanager than Henry Peters. Micromanager, dictatorial.

LOKELANI LINDSEY: Even if it was a custodian who had a mop out on the floor that may have been unsafe, I felt I could talk to that custodian and say, "Remove the mop," rather than go through the president to tell the vice president to tell the head of department to go down and say, "Remove the mop."

JANET ZISK (*Schools archivist*): She was incredible. At the Elementary School, she wanted all the teachers to take an inventory of all their supplies.

LOKELANI LINDSEY: Employees of the Coca-Cola company do not determine how many bottles of Coca-Cola must be produced each year. That's a management decision.

JANET ZISK: Because she had it in her head that teachers were stealing things. Oh, this was not going well.

TONY RAMOS: She had her hand into everything. She called me one night and asked, "Is it true that you expelled a seventh grader for stealing the dorm advisor's underpanties?"

ROD MCPHEE: I mean, Lordy, trustees should not be involved in any of that nonsense.

MARIANE HANNAHS: Questioning a lot of things that we did, or kind of treating us as student teachers rather than as professionals. We also felt put in an adversarial position, where it was either us or them, rather than us working together for the children.

LOKELANI LINDSEY: If I were to say what was the number one thing that caused resistance, I would say accountability. If I had been a teacher and had been in one position a long time and I'd been able to do everything I wanted to do and then all of a sudden I had to be accountable for results or to somebody else who told me to do something different, there would be resistance. Even I would balk at it.

ROD MCPHEE: The only reason school is there is what happens between the teacher and the kids. But there are so many institutions that forget what it's about. It just kind of boggles the mind to think there are a lot of places where the interference level is extreme, and I think Kamehameha has been one of them.

LOKELANI LINDSEY: I don't care if they are a student in my class or they are at the administrative level. If I find things are not being done on a regular basis, I have no problems with evaluating the person as such.

"The only reason school is there is what happens between the teacher and the kids."
–Rod McPhee

ROD MCPHEE: I'd say we had about six or eight very good teachers, predominantly Elementary, leave Kamehameha and come to Punahou, for less money, because of teaching conditions. Because they felt they weren't treated as professionals. So they took a dollar loss. But I would say, we got five superstars—I mean, really super teachers. Five good people in four years is a lot.

KATHY KUKEA: With Mrs. Lindsey, I cannot recall any positive things. ⌣

A Loaded Gun on the Table

Rockne Freitas Takes the Helm

Rockne has this one look where his eyes get real big. And he sits back and said to us, "There's a loaded gun on the table." –Kahele Kukea

MIKE CHUN: The trustees said I needed a vice president.

Lokelani said, "We're not putting it out to search, we already did the homework, we gotta decide."

I had a choice between two. One of them had a lot of baggage, developing a relationship with all those trustees. And no educational background. The other was Rockne Freitas. And I chose Rockne.

ROCKNE FREITAS: Did someone approach me about leaving the University of Hawai'i to go to Kamehameha? All right, that was Mike. Another individual asked me if I would be open to moving. That was Oswald Stender.

TONY RAMOS: Mike and Rockne, you know, went back to little kid days and grew up together.

ROCKNE FREITAS: A long ways. Very long. We don't even speak good English when we're talking with each other.

LOKELANI LINDSEY
AND ROCKNE FREITAS

MIKE CHUN: I was closer to him as a "cousin" than I was to my own blood cousins. His mother was "Auntie," his father was "Uncle." His mother was a beautiful lady, a wonderful person. I loved her very, very deeply. She died too early.

ROCKNE FREITAS
Stand-out football player,
class of 1963

ROCKNE FREITAS: In our culture, when somebody dies, you know, that's a real spiritual time for us, and those who are pallbearers are special people. Mike carried my mother, okay? So no other words need to be said.

MIKE CHUN: The trustees had said, "Loke, you handle this." Her responsibility was education, and so whatever she said on education was on automatic.

All this took place between Loke and me. I did not lobby with the trustees. Rockne and I did not sit down on that. Now, whether he was having conversations with Loke, I don't know. I'm only dealing with Loke.

Job descriptions that would align with the organizational structure—that was determined by Loke. I mean, basically that was her organization. The education side would come to me, the principals report to me, and I'd take care of planning and quality control, and the operational side would report to Rockne.

And that's not how it happened.

SAM HATA: Mike said, "He's coming. And find space for him."

SAM HATA
"Another black hole."

BOB RAMSEY (*campus facilities manager*): Here he is, you know, he's going to be vice president. I remember him coming in to see Sam Hata. He went down to the end of the hall and started talking about how his office would be set up, and it was—knock out these walls, and make this, and we ended up making probably the biggest office in the history of the Schools for him.

SAM HATA: Where did they find the money, I don't know. It's one of those projects I have no idea—another black hole.

BOB RAMSEY: This was going to be, and here he is, start working for him.

ROCKNE FREITAS: I think the mark I make will be in the minds and hearts of our faculty, staff and students. And not something material. And it will not be just me, it will be our team.

BRIAN CHANG: All the directors, everybody, the principals, everybody was assigned to Rockne. Everybody was down at his office. There were three secretaries for Rockne. Three. And one for Mike.

BOB RAMSEY: His sphere of influence grew.

BRIAN CHANG: The meetings used to be called by Mike. All of a sudden, Rockne is conducting the meetings, in Rockne's office.

TONY RAMOS: Rocky was always there. But he was not a micromanager. He's sharp, you know—he knew that he didn't know how to do everything, so he let people do their jobs. He'd say, "Let me know how I can support you." Things got done.

BRIAN CHANG: I think there's a lot of street smarts in there. He's able to take a particular situation, let's say it's a battlefield, and he's able to pick up the points—well, there may be land mines there, and this might be a good attack point here, and there are bushes over there and we don't know what's behind those bushes, so we'd better be careful there. So he's able to analyze a particular situation and figure out the landscape.

JULIAN AKO: We came to believe that Rocky was the connection on education stuff downtown. Rocky was the one who was shaking those things loose with those trustees, cutting through the red tape to get things done.

BOB RAMSEY: That was an additional line in the chain of command that we had to go through now. We couldn't deal directly with Mike without breaking that chain of command.

LOKELANI LINDSEY: I at times gave instructions directly to vice president Rockne Freitas and bypassed the office of president. Freitas was in charge of operations and we were dealing with operational issues.

RANDIE FONG (*'78, Secondary School performing arts teacher and department head*): Tony Ramos, our principal, would make it very clear

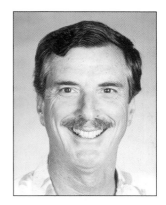

BOB RAMSEY

"… we ended up making probably the biggest office in the history of the Schools for him."

that the routing had changed. Everything would go through Tony to Dr. Freitas to Mrs. Lindsey. That was very, very clear. And that decision-making was hers.

TONY RAMOS: I would get caught between my loyalties to Mike and the role I had been assigned with Loke.

JULIAN AKO: It seemed sort of strange that directives from downtown were coming through Rocky and didn't seem to have Mike's stamp of approval or indication that he was involved with the decision-making. We were starting to realize that Rocky was telling us stuff that Mike never even knew about.

BOB RAMSEY: Right from the get-go, they undermined Mike's authority. Not just by the structure, but also, as we all knew, Rockne's influence was greater and greater.

KAMANI KUALĀ'AU (*'97, student body president*): We saw Rockne Freitas become empowered at the school. There were signs, and so to the people who were looking, it was obvious.

RANDIE FONG: We ended up not speaking with Dr. Chun very frequently at all.

LOIS LONG: He was just kind of out of the picture.

MIKE CHUN: I was no longer empowered. I was placed out of the loop, and yet I was always held accountable. Prior to 1993, I had responsibility and authority. After that I had responsibility.

BRIAN CHANG: Mike was certainly alert enough to recognize what was being done—that he was purposely being removed from being the head of the school, and that those powers and duties were now assigned to Rockne Freitas. So Mike did not know the ongoing operation of the school, what was going on on a day-to-day basis. What student, for example, was being suspended, or even worse, being expelled. And these were things and issues that are close to his heart, because we all know that he has the students' best interests in his mind at all times.

RANDIE FONG: Students would be talking about that all the time. How come Dr. Chun has been put out to pasture?

◈ ◈ ◈

BOB RAMSEY: Rockne Freitas is a survivor, and I attribute to that largely to relationships in politics.

MARIANE HANNAHS: Very astute.

MIKE CHUN: I knew he had a relationship with Dickie Wong, because he ran for office, and I know Dickie had helped him. I later found out he had a relationship with Loke, which he tended to minimize—he was helping her with her mayoral campaign on Maui, like an advisor. And I know Rock's relationship with Larry Mehau and Larry Mehau's relationship with Dickie.

I hadn't really been that closely associated with Rock since we went on to college. Part of that reason was that I knew he had a close relationship with Larry Mehau, and that always made me feel uncomfortable, although I've always had a very cordial relationship with Larry. When his company, Hawaii Protective Agency, was brought in here, he called Rock.

BOB RAMSEY: Rockne was the conduit that brought them in.

MIKE CHUN: Rock came over and said, "Mike, Larry would like to have breakfast. Talk story." And I said, "Sure, fine, what does he want to talk about?" "He wants to talk about the security arrangements."

BRIAN CHANG: It was shortly after Dickie Wong came on the board.

MIKE CHUN: Dickie had said, "We're going to use Larry on this campus." That was the directive.

They were pointing to drug problems on campus, burglaries, loss of equipment.

SAM HATA: Rockne considered himself an expert in drugs.

BRIAN CHANG: We did have our own internal force.

SAM HATA: What they tried to do was degrade our people—they're not competent, etc.

BOB RAMSEY: When Rockne came in, very, very early on, he started expressing concerns about security, talking about incidents that may occur, with, you know, some outside students may come up here and cause some trouble, or some things were stolen or something like that. He would badmouth the guards at the gate, and say they would just wave anyone through, like if you were wearing a ski mask they would let them through.

MIKE CHUN: So I went down with Rock and Larry to the Hungry Lion—I came to learn later that that's where Larry goes for break-fast a lot. Rock doesn't say much; he just stays in the background. Larry says, "Dickie says I gotta be up there, but I want to know if you feel uncomfortable with that." He says, "Mike, I guarantee you this: I'll put nothing but my best people on this campus. And if any

of them stubs your toe, just let me know and they're out of here." He wanted to do a good job on the campus.

He didn't say if I didn't want him there he wouldn't come. I guess he wanted my endorsement.

My response was, "You know, Larry, I don't have any problems with you there. The concern that we have is one of process."

SAM HATA: I got a call. Rockne told me, "Hey, we're going to have HPA on campus." I said, "Wait, I don't want them on my campus." I voiced my concern, and I met with Rockne several times. And of course, the message I got without being told was—get some money to HPA.

BOB RAMSEY: It was inevitable.

MIKE CHUN: We drew up what we wanted in terms of schedule, in terms of performance expectations.

SAM HATA: They dictated how many security guards we should have.

MIKE CHUN: The monies came from our budget.

OZ STENDER: I called Rocky. I started questioning him on it. He said, "Well, talk to your trustees about it." He was kind of snotty about the whole thing. And I said, "Well, how come I don't know about it?" He said, "Well, that's your problem."

I went to see Larry. I told him it was inappropriate for him to do this. Costing the estate a lot of money, and he should step back, and as an alumni, beneficiary, step back on this thing, and save the estate $40,000 a month. He was not happy. He was very upset that I challenged that. And then he got on me to back off. And that he had some information on me. I said, "There's no truth in it. You know it, I know it, so, you know, don't pull that one."

MIKE CHUN: Rock was supposed to handle the contract.

BRIAN CHANG: Sam Hata told me directly that he was instructed by Dickie Wong that this was going to happen. And Rockne Freitas was also there to insure that this was being complied with.

SAM HATA: That's the last I heard of the contract. Never saw a contract.

"I went to see Larry … He was not happy. He was very upset that I challenged that. And then he got on me to back off. And that he had some information on me. I said, 'There is no truth in it. You know it, I know it, so, you know, don't pull that one.'"

–Oz Stender

BOB RAMSEY: It kind of went into a black hole, and nothing ever happened from then on. It showed up as a deficit in our accounts.

BRIAN CHANG: There was no paper trail. It was on trustee instruction.

LARRY MEHAU (*'48, owner of Hawaii Protective Association*): I'm glad it was me. I got a shot at it because I am friends with every one of them. I'm really close with Dickie Wong.

ROCKNE FREITAS: I would like others to view me as a good friend who stuck by his principles. I value honesty.

I'm an optimist. I won't get philosophical now, but this is part of my training and part of what I believe in. I believe that all of us are products of our environment; the nature of man is good.

ROD MCPHEE: Rockne is Rockne. We'll leave it at that.

BOB RAMSEY: You can't just get by with relationships in politics. There's more to it. I mean, the same with Lokelani. They have the ability, if they want to, to be pretty personable and communicate pretty well when they want to get something accomplished and done.

LOKELANI LINDSEY: If everything went through the president's office, we'd never get anything done.

TONY RAMOS: All hires had to go through Loke, even the temps.

BOB WHITING: I had run a curriculum organization already, for President Jack Darvill, so I talked to Rockne and I said I'd be glad to, and he said, "You'll have to report to Mrs. Lindsey." I said, "Well, I'd rather not report to Mrs. Lindsey, I'd rather report to an official at the school. You're the vice president, either you or Mike." And he said, "Are you sure? Because it'd be much better if you report to her, because she understands what she wants in curriculum and everything else." And I said, "I'm a mid-level administrator; I've never reported to a trustee, and no school would allow something like that to happen." He said, "Well, I'll talk to her about it." That's the last I heard of it.

"Never saw
a contract."

—Sam Hata

BOB RAMSEY: When I saw the type of person that Lokelani Lindsey was, and the way she operated, I felt the best course of action for me, personally, would be to avoid her at all costs. Because what I saw was alliances being developed, people forming sides—you're either in her camp or outside her camp. It could've benefited me, of course—maybe even sell my agendas to form an alliance with her like some people. But I didn't want to be in anybody's camp. My loyalty was to the institution, not to any one person. I avoided her like the plague.

LIZ HANSEN (*'67, Schools special events secretary*): Mrs. Lindsey was working through Rockne. I saw him as a mouthpiece for Mrs. Lindsey.

TONY RAMOS: I'd been arguing the fact to Loke that this is an outstanding faculty, an outstanding program. From the day she came on she, she kept criticizing, and Rockne Freitas got right in the mode of criticizing the program too.

WALLY LAU: What bothered me was to see people starting lining up. Different people that surrounded Mike before, everybody starts migrating and shifting.

LIZ HANSEN

KAHELE KUKEA (*'63, Elementary School principal*): Rockne has this one look where his eyes get real big. And he sits back and said to us, "There's a loaded gun on the table." We had to get something done, and we'd better do it right, and if we didn't do it right we were dead. A loaded gun? I mean, are we being threatened here?

WALLY LAU: If you like keep your job or whatever, you'd better start aligning up and listening to me.

JULIAN AKO: I remember being told that Rocky Freitas says, "Heads are gonna roll, and make sure you're on the right side when that happens."

KAHELE KUKEA

OZ STENDER: Gerry Jervis suggested that we organize and Rocky gets to be president, Mike becomes chancellor.

MIKE CHUN: When I look back now, now I'm coming to understand that, yeah, he was brought in to take my job.

◈ ◈ ◈

TONI LEE (*'59, leader of alumni group Nā Pua*): We started hearing the rumbling around—

TONY RAMOS: The whole town did—

TONI LEE: —Through the grapevine and alumni and parents, that Mike's position on campus was becoming a threat, that we were going to stand a chance of losing Mike, that the trustees were getting ready to let him go.

WAYNE CHANG (*'69, Schools director of admissions*): Coming from all different sources, and almost none of the sources had any specifics as to why.

ELISA YADAO: On campus there was a belief that, one, Dr. Chun was going to be fired. Two, there was a strong feeling by the faculty and the staff, and I would believe the students and parents as well, that the campus was being micromanaged, that Dr. Chun had been stripped of his authority, that the place was being run from Kawaihaʻo Plaza, and it was not being run well.

KAMEHAMEHA SCHOOLS

Lead trustee

LOKELANI LINDSEY: I don't think he was viewed as a scapegoat for the problem. I think he was part of the problem. He's not an educator. And I've said that time and time and time again.

ELISA YADAO: Sometimes Mrs. Lindsey would say at meetings, "We don't plan on firing him, but we could fire him tomorrow. We could fire anybody tomorrow."

LOKELANI LINDSEY: Rumors, innuendos and allegations.

RANDIE FONG: I never got the impression in this situation that the grapevine was always carrying untruths. Very often they carry truths as well.

MIKE CHUN: Finally it came down. It came to what it was. That's when I started talking about leaving. Actually, you know, I would start to look around town to see if there were things out there. I was talking to myself, saying, *Well, maybe it's time to leave. I don't know how much I can take.* ✎

"I think he was part of the problem. He's not an educator. And I've said that time and time and time again."

—*Lokelani Lindsey*

4 Four or Five Lei
Lokelani Lindsey Assumes Lead for Education

I go into this meeting, and I got this one lei on, and she's got four or five lei on, and then she says, "You see! I got all of these lei! You only got one!" –Oz Stender

KAʻIMI KAIWI (*Secondary School English teacher*): Right after Lokelani was hired, we were told that she had danced around with her first check, saying, "I will never be poor again! I will never be poor again!"

LOKELANI LINDSEY: It's a Cinderella story, a dream come true.

ELISA YADAO: She grew up very poor. And this is another thing that goes into her whole psyche, you know. She grew up dirt poor, scratched for everything she had.

"She found a place where she could sort of be royalty, you know—hold court. Kawaiahaʻo Plaza."

–Janet Zisk

LOKELANI LINDSEY: I worked in the pineapple cannery. I worked in a travel agency. I worked as a bartender in three different places—Tiki Torch, Crouching Lion, Pat's of Punaluʻu. I washed dishes in a Chinese restaurant, the old Rice Bowl in Kāneʻohe.

MIKE CHUN: One of the comments that she had made to someone— "Christmas came early this year." That really kind of describes her.

MIKE CHUN: She wanted to be liked. She wanted to be appreciated, as we all do. She wanted to please people, especially those who had power.

She was quite preoccupied with things. I'd go into her office and she would say, "Oh, I've gotta show you what I have—Niʻihau shell leis."

That type of recognition was very important to her.

OZ STENDER: I remember going into the boardroom one day. I had a lei. Somebody came in and gave me this lei and I wore it. And I go into this meeting, and I got this one lei on, and she's got four or five lei on, and then she says, "You see! I got all of these lei! You only got one!"

MIKE CHUN: And not only the things but, "So and so gave this to me." It was important for her to have these things, a measure of her status, that people liked her and gave her things. But it was equally important to her for us to know that these were given to her by different people in the community.

JANET ZISK: She found a place where she could sort of be royalty, you know—hold court. Kawaiahaʻo Plaza. There was a major renovation going on, big bucks.

JUDY LAYFIELD: We were tasked with setting up standards. The trustees did not adhere to them. Change this, change that, on a single trustee's direction, primarily Mrs. Lindsey.

MARYANNE INOUYE: Mrs. Lindsey was very angry that we hadn't used solid koa in the trustees' area.

To me, solid koa wasn't even an issue. Koa is almost an extinct wood, so it didn't even occur to me to ask them if they wanted solid koa. I didn't even price it, but it would've been like 10 times more, I'm sure. It took me a while to calm her down on that.

OZ STENDER: One thing she wanted to do was change the board-room table and she wanted to get a koa table in there. In order to do that, you'd have to tear out two walls, take the thing out the window some place. Then build a table and bring it in that way. I mean the cost—But she wanted that table! And I raised all kinds of hell. So

"Mrs. Lindsey was very angry that we hadn't used solid koa in the trustees' area."
—Maryanne Inouye

we ended up keeping the table.

SIGRID SOUTHWORTH (*Secondary School librarian*): Mrs. Lindsey kept telling me that she was a very avid book collector and that she knew a great deal about old books.

I think she had heard about the Van Dyke collection, had heard it was a fabulous collection. She was extremely excited. She thought that buying it was a wonderful thing. So I was to drop everything and work on this, full time. Which I did, on her orders, for seven months.

Every librarian knew about the collection. Robert Van Dyke was a very aggressive collector. I guess I would call him to some extent an indiscriminate collector, in that he had everything.

He and his mother each bought an apartment. He never lived in his—he always lived with her, and no one, but no one, knows where his apartment is. He alluded to keeping some things there, and my suspicion is that that's where the really good stuff is.

These other treasures are things that Mrs. Lindsey did not buy. He certainly didn't make any attempt to let her know that this was not "the Van Dyke Collection" that people have always heard about.

The Van Dyke collection: $421,318.86. No due diligence; not worth having.

OZ STENDER: Van Dyke approached me the year before. I got Sigrid Southworth to look at a sample of the collection. She worked all her life at Kamehameha, and she had been in charge of the Hawaiian collection in Midkiff Learning Center for years and years. Out of her professional knowledge of Hawaiiana, she knew that most of the books were already in the collection in Midkiff, or they weren't worth having. So I didn't take it to the trustees.

Then Lindsey walks it in to a board meeting—it's not even on the agenda. I am not there that day. She and Jervis and Wong decide to buy it, even though it had not been inventoried or appraised. No due diligence.

SIGRID SOUTHWORTH: What she bought was the dregs.

OZ STENDER: $421,318.86. Plus months of staff time—way more than half a million dollars.

BOB WHITING: Sigrid was stuck taking care of this mothy, rattier collection. Every time I saw her, she was just livid.

CRYSTAL ROSE (*'75, attorney for Oz Stender*): Lokelani was had by a crazy old man who had a lot of rubbish. He saw her coming a mile off.

GAIL FUJIMOTO: What I found most distressing about Loke was her unwavering belief that she knew it all. Despite being advised not to purchase the Van Dyke Collection, she did. Despite the fact that technology was being implemented on campus, she made a unilateral decision to purchase and install the Phoenix-based EMG System. She announced it with great fanfare, but it became quite evident early on that this system was not going to meet our student needs. There were lots of bells and whistles in the package, but curriculum software, hardware and support were highly overpriced. It didn't matter that this was not a good fit. Loke knew best and we were told over and over again to make it work. I believe in total this package cost over 30 million dollars. It quickly became a big white elephant. Auē, what a waste.

NONA BEAMER: The Big I syndrome. The power of pride. No humility at all.

There is the Hawaiian saying: I aliʻi no ke aliʻi i ke kanaka. You are who you are because of the people you serve, not because of yourself.

MARYANNE INOUYE: That was, to me, unusual. I didn't see it at all from Mr. Thompson or Mr. Richardson or Mr. Takabuki. Or Mr. Stender, certainly.

KAREN KEAWEHAWAII FARIAS (*leader of alumni group Nā Pua*): Her nature—she needed to put herself in their face and say, "I'm the boss, I decide, I … I … I…."

MIKE CHUN: Her confidant on campus was Wayne Chang.

OZ STENDER: He organized a thing of Lindsey's that turned bad, like the Van Dyke collection—the Shintani Diet. And the pity was, it could have been invaluable for Kamehameha, the school for Hawaiians, the Hawaiian school.

TERRY SHINTANI

TERRY SHINTANI (*author of* Hawai'i Diet): You've got a school with the people in the unhealthiest population.

You know, when I went to Wai'anae—I used to drive from town— I used to say, behind that mountain, the Wai'anae Range, is a forgotten community. And we have the worst health problems out there, from obesity, heart disease, strokes, leukemia—who knows if the radar station is doing that to them. But all of those issues are out there.

And I said, "Well, wouldn't it be great if the best health program could come out of the place that has the worst health." And we pretty much did that, with the Wai'anae diet. To have won a national award for that kind of work—it was like the fulfillment of a dream.

And I thought we were going to do the same thing at Kamehameha. These kids *learn*.

BRIAN CHANG: It was directly implemented by Trustee Lokelani Lindsey.

TERRY SHINTANI: The only person I could get from Kamehameha Schools was Lokelani Lindsey. She said, "This is great. This would really help Hawaiian people if we could get it in Kamehameha." She was the champion of it. True commitment is, you know, you walk the walk. So she coordinated it so that it would happen.

WAYNE CHANG

WAYNE CHANG: The first time I heard about it was through Lokelani. At a volleyball game, actually.

I was kind of given the title of luna, I guess, the person who was going to coordinate things to make them happen with Dr. Shintani. That was from Lokelani. It wasn't a title, it was like, "Wayne, would you coordinate all of this?" I guess I gave myself the title.

JULIAN AKO: Wayne Chang told me Lokelani put in the diet for him.

And he became a person to select who was going to participate and who wouldn't.

WAYNE CHANG: I had input into the first participants. The first 30. And most of that was my knowledge of people on campus throughout the institution who had need of that. People who were either obese, who were diabetic, who were asthmatic or who had hypertension, high blood pressure.

TONY RAMOS: I was just put on this list by Wayne Chang, with an assumption that I was going to be involved in his program. And so was Suzanne, my wife. So we grumbled about this, because we've got to go, right? We did. We participated.

ELISA YADAO: I had some people on my staff who wanted to be part of it, and we couldn't figure out how did you get to be part of this thing. If you weren't in her group, all Loke's friends, then you couldn't be part of the diet.

BRIAN CHANG: The money came out of Dr. Chun's budget for staff development—without him being told. Six figures. We had to over-spend the budget.

TERRY SHINTANI: The programs were great. People were all excited, students excited.

BRIAN CHANG: But here was a program that was not budgeted. It was not approved in our regular operating budget, and yet it was implemented.

TERRY SHINTANI: The plan was—then we do the program for the kids and the dorm. The dorm is great, because the kids eat three meals a day, we can produce data.

It was just a part of a strategy that I'd hoped would take hold. It would be a world model.

We were first and goal and about to score a touchdown—we were all excited—and everything came to a halt. Lokelani got distracted; the whole board was distracted. And it got flushed down the toilet.

◈ ◈ ◈

"The first time I heard about it was through Lokelani. At a volleyball game, actually … It was like, 'Wayne, would you coordinate all of this?'"

—*Wayne Chang*

LIZ HANSEN: I knew Loke and Wayne were friends, and volleyball was a passion.

LOKELANI LINDSEY: A whole group of us went to the volleyball in Las Vegas, 13 of us.

LEEANN CRABBE: The chosen who got to go on the trips with her. Her little entourage. One, I knew him for years, and I would say to him, "Do you know what you're doing? Are you sure you want to do this? It just doesn't look right." He would look at me like I'm naïve—"Wouldn't you go too if you had the opportunity?"

OZ STENDER: She went to Vegas something like a dozen and a half times, starting just a few months after she became a trustee.

She called these trips "business." Now, she is the Bishop Estate trustee for education. But this is Vegas—and I don't think I have ever seen postcards of a campus on the Strip with a Kamehameha Schools neon sign flashing out front.

She met a guy in Vegas and went into a business deal of her own with him on the side, something about secret gold bullion, supposed to be millions of dollars in it for her. Same guy, he had some kind of internet startup going, with a "dating" service called "Love Mate."

The guy never gave back the money. She broke into his office to look for the bullion and he sued her. Then she sued him for fraud. The court asked whether she had evidence of the money and she said, "Of course not! I gave him cash!" That was the most stupid thing I ever heard.

LOKELANI LINDSEY: I visited the estate properties from time to time. I am perhaps the person most familiar with the Las Vegas properties.

OZ STENDER: Here's the trustee for education, taking on all that extra properties work as well. Good for her. But she never put in a written report on the Vegas properties—or about anything she did in Vegas.

Lindsey flew the Love Mate gold bullion guy to the Super Bowl in New Orleans, along with her husband and Rockne Freitas. Then the guy got indicted on federal securities charges. She also went to the Olympic Games in Atlanta, on a chartered jet, along with her husband. These trips were both as a Bishop Estate trustee, and both of them were paid for by companies looking to do business with Bishop Estate.

And she went to the Rose Bowl parade. She loved being in parades.

WAYNE CHANG: At the Rose Bowl, Lokelani was riding in a pāʻū unit. Both sons, they were riders with her. Her grandson was also a rider. I believe she had four outriders, and herself. She also had as a banner and a page, her granddaughter, and myself, Dennis Walsh and Marlene Sai.

For me, it was a very personal trip. It was not a business trip, no. I was Mrs. Lindsey's guest. She paid for me. I went on 12 to 14 trips with her.

NEIL HANNAHS: I was chairing for the Schools in the Kamehameha Day parade one year—1993, the centennial of the founding of the girls' school, the first year Mrs. Lindsey was on the board.

We had the float, and the carcade and the marching band, pāʻū riders and so forth, and we had a host of cars representing graduates by decades of the school for girls, wonderfully decorated.

"She loved being in parades."
–Oz Stender

The five trustees were each riding in a car, and it came time to prepare the signs for the cars. So I asked one of the staff members to ask each trustee what they would like on their sign. The response that we received from Loke was, "Well, what do the other trustees have?" I told her that Mr. Wong would like Trustee Wong, Trustee Peters and so forth. Oz specifically requested something different. He said, "I'd like it to say, 'Oz, Kuʻulei and Uʻilani Stender'"— his wife and his granddaughter. So we went ahead and prepared signs as per these instructions.

We were down at Aloha Tower by the Hawaiian Electric plant, and we're all staged out with the trolleys and the cars and so forth, and Loke comes roaring up to me—"How come my sign is like that?"

She was upset that here in the context of five trustee cars, was this very folksy, friendly aloha sign of Oz, Kuʻulei and Uʻilani Stender. And this led to quite an open—for the public—berating of me by her for not handling this better. It was in view of trolleys full of alumni.

RENEE MARTIN: Another time, we were in a class advisors' meeting, and it came up that apparently Lokelani had asked Julian Ako to find

Christmas parade, Kōnia Field 1996. Seated back row: Julian Ako, Sandy Behenna and Tony Ramos as Santa; seated front: Holly Bohrer, Kathy Kukea, Ninia Richardson

two students to be at the Kamehameha Day parade to pick up her horse's poop. And I just couldn't believe it. So I suggested her two grandchildren, and of course it was like, "We can't do that." And I come back with, "Well, why not?—they're two students, let them go pick it up. Why should any of our other students pick it up?"

I understand that what happened was that Marlene Sai stepped in and I guess basically saved the face of whoever had to make that call. And by my recollection, that's how she became very good friends with Lokelani Lindsey, and became known as the sixth trustee.

BILL FOLLMER: The impact of the majority trustees was huge. I mean the crushing of the leadership. They just decimated the leadership. They selected people who weren't leaders and didn't know how to lead, and didn't develop them in leadership. They controlled information so people didn't know how to challenge rules.

JIM SLAGEL (*Secondary School English teacher*): A lot of it came down on Tony Ramos. He was principal of the Secondary School.

TONY RAMOS : I am responsible for the overall management, direction, of the Secondary School, having to deal with curriculum, the hiring of teachers, the development of curriculum, implementation of that curriculum, the supervision of that curriculum being followed and that instruction occurs at the highest level, hiring of the teachers, the evaluation and supervision of all staff. There are about 300 staff in the Secondary School. Includes a residential program which is the boarding program, where there are 555 residential students from seven through 12, about 200 teachers. Discipline and control of the students, maintain a safe environment where students can learn and grow in a safe place that's a learning community, if you will, and a humane place that is student centered overall. That's what I do or what I am responsible for. I report to Dr. Freitas.

JIM SLAGEL: I've always been fond of Tony. He's a great listener, he's smiling more often than not and he loves the kids. Those are probably my three favorite attributes in an administrator.

TONY RAMOS: Kamehameha is my life. I'm the guy who loses 18 days of vacation a year, and I don't miss it. I lived in the dorms from '62 to '76. I've watched some of those boys grow up to be doctors, lawyers, really make something of themselves. This is a school, but it's a lot more than just that. This is my life.

KATHY KUKEA: He knew his history going back to the first day of the school.

JULIAN AKO: I always believed that Tony is a good person, that he had a really good heart. He was always for the students. He has always prided himself for being a strong advocate for the underdog kid. I think if he had been left to things by himself, he would have come out fine. But I think he got sucked into the politics, the power politics, and where the power resided. He says it was his way of trying to make sure things get done, so it was like having to succumb to that in order to achieve a greater good for the education of kids.

BERNADETTE KAOHI
AND TONY RAMOS
Kamehameha student
body presidents, 1958

HERB WILSON: Big heart, great counselor, a visionary. I think he's constantly on the lookout for new ideas, constantly looking for ways to improve things. But a guy who's so much a part of this whole system that is Kamehameha, that is Hawai'i, that sometimes he has a hard time getting things to gel because he's trying hard to make it fit into the scheme of things. In Hawai'i you do it this way, in Hawai'i you do it that way, but it's the Hawai'i that he knew.

KATHY KUKEA: Tony fit in perfectly with the way things were. He was part of the old boy network; he had all kinds of people skills; I mean his relationship skills were great. All of that served him well. He was going along, behaving the way he was, developing relationships with whoever was in power, because that was the way to get things done. I kind of imagine he didn't notice that the foundation had changed, so that doing that was suddenly siding with bad guys, as far as some of the rest of us were concerned. So I don't see that his behavior ever really changed; he just wasn't paying attention to the principles upon which the place was resting.

RANDIE FONG: Tony has shared this openly, you know, with the department heads—that he sometimes gets burned. He has to be the one to be able to make these policies stick and follow through on them. And that certainly is his job, but sometimes he's not given the full range of the why's and the how's and the who's, and so he has to then, in front of the whole faculty and staff, sort of run in a certain direction, and he doesn't know the background. And if they were displeased, my sense was that he'd have to kind of be on his toes and be ready to defend the trustees' policies even if it changed without him knowing or without him getting information on them.

JIM SLAGEL: He was absolutely in the wrong place at the wrong time. I saw nothing in Tony's personality that equipped him for the storm surrounding the school, which is too bad, because in almost any other situation, his personality would have been perfect. He's non-confrontational. How often do you want a confrontational principal?

JUNKO LOWRY (*Secondary School Japanese language teacher*): He has been an outstanding person, in my opinion. I remember talking to him, and feeling that he too was a player, one who was placed in the middle somewhere, squished, and feeling pretty much empathetic for the role he had to play, even though personally this is not what he preferred to do. When you are a leader, people hang a lot on you, not necessarily your own.

JUNKO LOWRY

LOIS LONG: Tony had a stand with Lokelani Lindsey and his "golden rule"—those who have the gold, rule.

HERB WILSON: People were running into Lokelani and Tony at meetings away from school, on the weekends, breakfast, things like that.

TONY RAMOS: Oftentimes there wasn't time during the school day, so she couldn't meet. So we would say, "Okay, let's have dinner and go over this stuff at dinner." And we did. That was the purpose. These weren't necessarily social dinners. They were to get Secondary School things moving.

HERB WILSON: The assumption is that there was a pretty close relationship developing.

KATHY KUKEA: Mrs. Lindsey liked Tony; she was an educator; she hated Mike Chun. So one can imagine early on feeling pretty seduced into a relationship with Mrs. Lindsey. I can imagine being in Tony's position—I'm so cool, I'm Mrs. Lindsey's buddy, I'm getting nightly phone calls and pastries. I could imagine getting seduced by that.

But as things went on, and Mrs. Lindsey's true colors kept coming out—and there were very few of us who could ever imagine that we could ever remove the trustees—if I had been Tony, and I had this relationship going, and I felt that I was stuck with this lady forever more, if I wanted my school to get anything, I can imagine him trying to work with her, trying to make it work.

HERB WILSON

TONY RAMOS: I don't control that woman.

MARK EWALD (*Secondary School mathematics teacher*): When the situation on the hill started to heat up, there was much talk about what or whose side you were on. Much talk amongst us was about Tony. Is Tony sided against Mike? Is Tony sided with Lindsey and Rockne? Whose side should we be on? What does loyalty for Kamehameha Schools mean? Who should we be loyal to?

KATHY KUKEA: I just don't think he could find it in him, or it didn't go far enough downhill or something for him to cut it off. I mean, there weren't any kids or teachers being shot at dawn.

MARK EWALD: I thought Tony was in a tough position, which may be an understatement. Many of us were worried about losing our jobs. I am sure Tony was no exception.

Although from my point of view, he made some questionable decisions on how he responded to all the orders, requests and situations he was put in by Lindsey, Rockne, Mike, his administration team, faculty and students, I still supported Tony as principal. What would be the alternative if he was fired? Who knows whom Lindsey would have put in that position? I was not willing to take the chance.

I talked with Tony. I always believe that he truly cared for the students and the institution. He was a good man put in the most tenuous position. Every decision he made was scorned by some and

MARK EWALD

cheered by others. Although I think there was more scorning than cheering on the hill.

BRIAN CHANG: There was a breaking apart. In particular, Tony Ramos sided with, or appears to have sided with, Lokelani. Now, in Tony's defense, because I like Tony, he did mention to me that he had been beat up several times. And it only takes a certain number of beatings before you finally cave in. But it became clear to me that his loyalties were not to Mike, and definitely to Loke.

HOLOUA STENDER (*Secondary School performing arts teacher*): I think Tony's similar to Wayne Chang in a sense. They should know better, but they just let themselves get enamored by Lokelani's good side, maybe.

BOB WHITING: We'd go in and talk to him and say, "Tony, you know, you're not doing yourself any favors here, and how can you really support this woman? Look what she's doing to this institution. And to you. This is not helping you at all." He didn't really come out and say, "I support Lokelani Lindsey; I think she's doing the right thing," but that was what the implication was with everything that he did.

JANET ZISK: His unwillingness to support the faculty was very obvious.

JULIAN AKO: I think he didn't want us to rattle the cage with the trustees.

KELLI KEAHIAHI LEE (*'99, organizer of student petition*): I was very disappointed in Mr. Ramos' leadership. During that period he totally forgot about students. He was clearly, like, defending the trustees in all the speeches he gave—you know, they're doing their job, and you shouldn't make it harder for them. I thought, *That's part of politics, right? You pick your side, and then it lies where it falls.*

JULIAN AKO: In different conversations administratively that I've been present at, Tony has articulated to me and to us, that ethically we have a responsibility to support the leadership of the institution and the directions that the leadership takes us. And that ethically or morally, if we don't, if we can't support it, then we should go elsewhere.

⬧ ⬧ ⬧

"When the situation on the hill started to heat up, there was much talk about what or whose side you were on. Whose side should we be on? What does loyalty for Kamehameha Schools mean? Who should we be loyal to?"

—Mark Ewald

DANA TANIGAWA (*'98*)**:** We were always hearing that Mike Chun was going to get fired.

KIM SLAGEL (*Secondary School mathematics teacher*): Even the kids were talking about how Loke was going after Mike.

KAMANI KUALĀʻAU: Mike Chun would never badmouth Lokelani Lindsey. He never said anything.

DUDLEY MAKAHANALOA (*'53, member of alumni group Nā Pua*)**:** We were at a meeting, and Lokelani said, "No, Mike is really not going to get fired"—that everybody at that level serves at the whim of the trustees. Interesting, you know. Bobby Moore jumps up—"Loke, did you say *whim* of the trustees?" She said, "No, I did not, I said *will* of the trustees." If I remember correctly, Dickie Wong goes like this—bomp! "You said *whim*!"

That woman, she was something else.

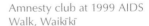

Amnesty club at 1999 AIDS Walk, Waikīkī

KIM SLAGEL: Back in 1991, one of my students, Jen Goodyear-Kaʻōpua, asked Slagel and me if we'd start an Amnesty International club. We did the letter-writing thing for about a year, and then it sort of evolved into a do-gooders club. We'd do beach clean-ups, whatever. Slagel and I attended Church of the Crossroads, and they had an Institute of Human Services feeding ministry, so we had students cook meals for the homeless one Saturday a month.

JIM SLAGEL: We were pretty, I don't know, low-key. We fundraised at school to buy the food. We'd sell popcorn and then have anywhere from 20 to 50 kids show up on Saturday to cook.

KIM SLAGEL: So when things got bad at school, Dr. Chun started to show up regularly to cook with us. He'd bring his own knives and everything. He brought his own cutting board. No controversy, no questions. He'd just stand there next to the kids and chop onions or apples. Us, and the kids, and a couple of parents or alums, and we'd

"He brought his own cutting board. No controversy. No questions. We'd just chop."
–Kim Slagel

just chop. Nobody said anything about the trouble at school. He looked so relaxed, like that was the only time all month he got to be so totally relaxed.

JIM SLAGEL: I think he did it partly to be a good role model and partly to remind himself what it was all about. He got his energy from the kids. They loved him, and he'd talk to them about classes and sports and stuff while they were all chopping, and in the end he'd wipe off his knives and pack up his cutting board, get back in his truck, maybe give a couple of the boarders a ride back to the dorms. I remember thinking I'd rather be going where I was going than where he had to go.

KIM SLAGEL: I felt selfish. Like we got to do the fun stuff all the time, and he had to put up with all the other crap. We all respected him. I was really concerned about his health, but he wasn't being like a martyr.

JIM SLAGEL: He was the guy cutting vegetables because they needed to be cut.

ELISA YADAO: Lokelani could be a lot of fun. And she was a very generous woman. Giving. Small things. She'd always be bringing food.

JERRY SPRAGUE: It was known that she liked lemon bars. Once in a while, when we were making lemon bars for someone else, I would have them make up half a sheet pan of lemon bars, and I would of course take them down personally and take them up to her office. Sometimes she was there, sometimes she wasn't. But she was always ecstatic about it and shared them around and wrote me a nice note thanking me for it.

KAWEHI YIM: There was a delegation from Tonga, and I received a direction to go and set up the boardroom for refreshments. So I contacted Food Services for butterscotch brownies and lemon bars.

But I guess it wasn't set up fancy enough. Lokelani came tearing out—"Who set this up? This is crap in here! I told you I wanted cream puffs! I want cream pastry! They like that stuff. This is crap in here!"

So we went down to Kapiʻolani Bakery and I bought cream puffs, custard pies, everything I could—with my money. Took it back, put it on a nice tray, and I walked into the meeting, which was already going on—and they'd wiped everything out, the brownies and the lemon bars.

EMALIA KEOHOKĀLOLE (*secretary to Lokelani Lindsey*): She asked me to pick up a pair of shoes for her, but I didn't want to do it, because it's not the same style, plus I couldn't find one in her size. We both have big feet.

ELISA YADAO: We'd have to pick up her grandkids all the time.

KAWEHI YIM: Julie Abe, she was our events coordinator, all she got was, "Mrs. Lindsey needs you right now!" Okay, she's grabbing her paper and pen, and she goes down to the Royal Hawaiian, and Mrs. Lindsey wanted her to go and buy her some electric heating curlers. So Julie goes off to Longs, picks up, drops them back off, and she came back, and she was just—"I cannot believe it!"

One day, Elisa called me and said, "You have to go buy some clothes for her granddaughter." Everybody in the trustees' office looked at me and said, "Oh, are you going?" I said, "Do I have a choice?"

ELISA YADAO: I felt it was excessive, but I felt we had no choice. We had to.

KAWEHI YIM: She cared very much about her family.

BOB LINDSEY: Tremendous love for her family.

LOKELANI LINDSEY: My husband and I have seven children between us, and 33 grandchildren.

NEIL HANNAHS: She explained to me that she had bracelets for every child, every grandchild. That's what many women do, and that's how they get so many bracelets. Through their progeny and not through their lavishness. It was not a matter just of accumulated bracelets. It's to create emotional association with their grandchildren.

TONY RAMOS: The first time she came on, she started saying things that were critical of the school. She started in on the middle school. Because her grandchildren were down there. It had trimesters, and she wanted quarters. She thought 12 weeks grading was too long.

So for three or four years I held her off. Finally she said to Rocky that I was insubordinate. So I said, "The hell with it, we'll do it and let it crash." It crashed.

RICK HEYD
"I saw firsthand what the intimidation was doing to our teachers."

RICK HEYD (*Secondary School social studies teacher*): One of the science teachers had called a parent on Maui. During the conversation about grades, she asked the mother if her child had ever been tested for Attention Deficit Hyperactivity Disorder. I didn't hear any of this, but when I walked by, the teacher didn't seem comfortable, and she asked if I wanted to talk to the mom, since I had the student in my class. I spoke to the mom, and things seemed okay.

The student in question was Loke's nephew. I went back to my classroom, and within 15 minutes students were coming into my class and they weren't scheduled to be there. They said they'd been excused from science class by their teacher. I knew what had happened. I ran down to her room. She had been crying and was all upset. Loke had called her and threatened to fire her on the spot for insinuating that her nephew was ADHD. So I saw firsthand what the intimidation was doing to our teachers.

JERRY SPRAGUE: I was sitting at home, watching the World Series, and I got a phone call, and it's from Mrs. Lindsey, and she's wanting to know why she's getting so many complaints from parents, from outer island parents, because their children didn't get any food for dinner.

The next day—and of course after worrying about it all night— I inquired and found out that two young men who were, I think, on the soccer team, got back late to the dining hall from practice, when the kids were done, finished eating. One of them was her grandson. Somehow when either he called his grandmother or she called him, he said they didn't have any food.

I talked with the manager, and he assured me that everything was fine, that the two kids were offered a meal but they didn't want to take it.

So the phone call to me was about all these parents calling up from outer islands. And dinner had only been over by 15 minutes when I got the phone call. So I couldn't see how that activity could have taken place—children calling their parents, all these parents calling up, Mrs.

Lindsey calling me. The children were probably still practically getting back to the dorms from dinner. Didn't make any sense.

So then in the morning, Mrs. Lindsey had a meeting here, and she came into the kitchen, and I happened to be walking by, and she saw me and came over and gave me a hug and a kiss and an apology. She said something about her grandson and a big mixup, and that she was sorry about the whole incident. She didn't apologize for lying about it, but she apologized. It was fine, and we always had a good relationship after that.

OZ STENDER: Lokelani went to another teacher who had given her grandson a failing grade, called her back over Christmas recess and glared at her, threatening her if she didn't change it.

The teacher showed Lokelani some A papers and the boy's paper, and Lokelani put pressure on her to let him do it over for a better grade. And the teacher was afraid for her job, and she changed the grade to a C-. This is even before she has seen the rewrite. So after Christmas the boy comes back with his paper, and it's the same one—all he's done, he's just written a couple of things in in pencil.

JIM SLAGEL: One of the few meetings I remember her speaking—you had to go, and they broke the faculty into two or three groups, and she made the mistake of opening it up for questions, which was always troublesome for her.

And Richard Hamasaki asked, "We're getting more and more kids with special needs. How are we preparing to help with those?" And there was a very long pause as she processed this, and then she said, "Well, I'm not quite sure how they slipped through the cracks, but we're gonna make sure we don't get those kids anymore."

And there was this dead silence. There were 150 educators, and she was saying, "Those kids don't belong here."

NEIL HANNAHS: Just to help me be positive in my life, one thing I'll always choose to remember Loke for is her gracious announcement at the song contest, acknowledgment of my daughter and her class, sopho-

Lindsey presents award at 1997 Song Contest

KAUANOE KAMANĀ

mores. My daughter was a song leader. Someone pitched the altos wrong, and it started on a wrong note. They sang the first couple of lines of the song wrong, and she stopped them in their tracks. They re-pitched, they re-sang the song. Of course, they didn't win. But when Loke gave whatever award she was giving that night, she took the time to acknowledge my daughter. I thought, as a father in particular, and if it had been any child, I would think that was a very, very gracious thing.

KAUANOE KAMANĀ (*'69, associate professor of Hawaiian language, linguistics and Hawaiian studies, UH-Hilo*): We come from a certain understanding of what is good. I think she has goodness; I think she has aloha. But even if within you you have good, if your actions contradict the good things you have—actions speak louder than words.

OZ STENDER: When she's talking to people in a social environment, she is very charming. She can be very sweet. That was part of the disarming part about her. But you get in the next room, she'd come down on whomever she was talking to and being very nice to and, you know, she'd express her true thinking about people.

MELELANI PANG (*'87, Secondary School Hawaiian language teacher*): She used people against other people. Very sad. Very, very sad.

HOLOUA STENDER: She had two sides to her. The good side I really liked. I thought she was warm and huggy-kissy and all that. It's just that when she switched over to being this really condescending, evil, malicious person that you'd see how dangerous she was.

OZ STENDER: You get in a control situation and she freaks out.

LOKELANI LINDSEY: I am a professional administrator and I've taken all the courses necessary to do this. That's how I've been trained as an administrator.

ELISA YADAO: You'd be sitting in her office—I'd go in at 5 o'clock because she'd call me down, we had to talk about something, and then it'd be 20 of 7 before I got out, because she never would deal with me. She'd take all her phone calls and make all her phone calls, then she'd have to go into Henry's office for something. But you could never leave. You just have to sit there and wait.

And she would call me at home. All the time. She would call me up on Sunday morning and make me read the paper to her. I'd be standing, reading her the newspaper on the phone. I don't know why she didn't just have her own subscription. But again, I think it was just that exercise of power.

LOKELANI LINDSEY: In my practice, if you live by policies and you live within the parameters set—but not to implement exactly what is said in the policy, to me, it borders on insubordination if not real insubordination.

OZ STENDER: Mrs. Lindsey has two favorite words: insubordinate and incompetent.

ELISA YADAO: In her mind, people were always stepping over their boundaries. And in my mind they were actually just doing their jobs.

KAREN WILKINSON: She never asked to talk to you. You were always summoned. One time I remember particularly, because of her fury.

KAWEHI YIM: Lashings happened in the boardroom the majority of times, or in her office.

HERB WILSON: I know one administrator—I'm not going to mention the name, let's just say it's a Secondary School administrator—but every time this person went to see Lokelani, this person threw up.

MIKE CHUN: I recall Rockne describing a meeting at which Sandy Wicklein was the subject, and Sandy was there, as well as Rockne, where Loke actually came out of her chair, and Rock said he thought she was just going to come around the table and whack Sandy.

LOKELANI LINDSEY: I can't remember, even, the incident. I know she was in my office with two others, and we had a disagreement.

I think people who know me well know that I'm not volatile, except under rare circumstances.

MARYANNE INOUYE: There were bodies all along the way.

ELISA YADAO: Emalia, her secretary, had her own burdens to bear. We had a conversation one time. She said to me, "I'm going to teach you some Hawaiian. Do you know what the word kauā means? It means, like, slave, right? Loke treats me that way. But that's not what I am, and I won't be treated like that." And the tears are coming down her eyes.

MARYANNE INOUYE

ELLEN PELLISERO: I had a deadline, and it was late at night, and there was nobody else here. I could hear the phones ringing, and it finally got to me. It was Mrs. Lindsey. She just said, "Can you come downstairs and help me look for a tape?"

And I said, "Okay," so I went downstairs, and I was crawling around on the floor looking for this tape for her. I couldn't find it. I was down there for a while, and then she talked to me. Well, now it's 9 o'clock or something, and I'm getting tired, and I still have to get this sucker out, and she said to me, "How are you doing, Ellen?" And I said, "Mrs. Lindsey, I have a rash. You people have given me a rash."

And I pulled my blouse out and I showed her my tummy with my rash all the way across, and I said, "I can't stand it, I just can't stand it." And she started to cry, and I didn't know what to do. I mean, here's a trustee and she's crying.

It just tripped me up, because she's a grown woman, master of the universe down here. She said, "Oh, I'm so sorry," and I said, "Well, I don't know if it can be helped," and then she just cried about how sorry she was about everything, and she's sad all this had to happen. And I didn't know what she wanted from me. Did she want me to excuse the situation? I didn't know what she wanted.

ELLEN PELLISERO

ELISA YADAO: I do think we have an obligation in our portrayal of everybody—warts, bumps and beauty spots. And I'll tell you what—Lokelani could be funny. She could be incredibly generous. And she could be very compassionate. She had those capabilities in her. And she was smart. She was a very smart woman. She had a lot going for her, and she could have been a phenomenal trustee if she had allowed herself to do that.

I mean, I had conversations with her. I told her, "Look, you don't need to be jerking people's chains to convince yourself that you're a trustee. I guarantee, you tell people to jump, and they're going to ask you how high. But if you need to do that every day, then that is going to hurt you." ✎

Lokelani Lindsey and Elisa Yadao. By the end of 1997, Yadao will resign.

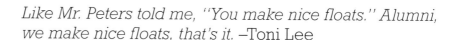

5 Nice Floats
Alumni Association Taken Over

Like Mr. Peters told me, "You make nice floats." Alumni, we make nice floats, that's it. –Toni Lee

APAC (Alumni and Parents Advancement Center) Staff, from left: Sue Botti (administrative assistant), Kimberly Huntzinger (systems specialist/ Webmaster), Marlene Sai (director), Steve Reelitz (parent coordinator), Gerry Johansen (alumni coordinator), Nadine Chang (database assistant), Marsha Meinel (administrative clerk)

MARLENE SAI (*'59, Bishop Estate Alumni and Parent Advancement Center coordinator*): I first met Lokelani almost first days of my singing career, and that was back in the early '60's.

JULIAN AKO: I danced in Marlene's show in the Monarch Room at the Royal Hawaiian Hotel in the '80's, for a year. Wayne Chang was her choreographer.

Loke was named to be the pāʻū queen in the Aloha Week parade. She needed help to pull that whole thing together, and Marlene was the Kamehameha Day honcho—she did that for quite a while.

In 1990, Randie Fong and I were co-chairs for the whole Kamehameha Schools contingent, and Marlene was the overall administrator for the parade, and I had some big run-ins with her. I felt she was getting in the way of my doing my job. I was doing this on top of being dean of student activities, and I needed someone to help and not create obstacles and roadblocks. She had a way of saying, "Nope, absolutely not." I mean, there's no room for discussion or argument. I can remember just shaking my head and wondering, *What is this all about?* Another person who's strong in power and control.

ELLEN PELLISERO: She loved this institution, to a fault, I think. She devoted her life to this institution.

ROY BENHAM (*'41, leader of alumni group Nā Pua*): Mike Chun chose her to run the Alumni Association.

MARLENE SAI: Setting up and organizing and coordinating trustee talk stories, sitting on and being one of the members of this communications committee for KSBE. Handling the trustees' projects. And that one, in particular, is our participation in the Kamehameha Day parade, Christmas parade, and also Trustee Lindsey's participation in the Rose Bowl parade. Things of this nature.

ELLEN PELLISERO: Mrs. Lindsey had always been very kind to her, and she was real loyal. She is a very loyal person. She's always been like that. She came from the old school, just this absolute loyalty.

I was concerned for Marlene. I feel that she was used in many ways. It seems to me that when Mrs. Lindsey came on board, maybe because she was a country girl—I don't mean to speak unkindly— but it seems to me she latched onto Marlene Sai the musical entertainer, not Marlene Sai the human being. I've seen that happen oftentimes, and because I was in the entertainment industry for a long time, I've seen it happen all the time. That's not necessarily a genuine friendship.

ROY BENHAM: When Lokelani came in, Marlene got more power through Lokelani. She knew which side of the apple to polish.

DUDLEY MAKAHANALOA: Gil Tam was president of the Alumni Association. He was Lokelani's boy. And so he sided with everything she did.

It sealed our conviction that the boys are still in the back room, they're still calling the shots. Everything is the same, no changing. Anything that upset the routine or us as alumni, we'd always look the other way, because it's just not the thing to do—to upset our empire.

"When Lokelani came in, Marlene got more power through Lokelani. She knew which side of the apple to polish."

—Roy Benham

"Gil Tam was president of the Alumni Association. He was Lokelani's boy."

—Dudley Makahanaloa

ROD FERREIRA

ROD FERREIRA: The Alumni Association was really just kind of a nebulous thing that was there. It had no purpose apart from whatever they did. I don't know what they did, apart from, you know, whatever they did.

MIKE CHUN: The alumni as an organization has never been trained to question the institution.

DUDLEY MAKAHANALOA: Supposedly we proud to have the Bishop Estate, one of the real strong entities still in the Hawai'i economy, and so forth and so on, still big landholder, and still trying to educate the kids.

ROBIN MAKUA: I think the attitude in the past was that they didn't really have to pay attention to the alumni, because they didn't really need our money, not like other schools, where they're backed financially by their alumni.

Mike Chun and Brook Lee
'89 in alumni float 1999

MIKE CHUN: The culture—other schools look to their alumni a lot differently than Kamehameha has looked to our alumni.

ROBIN MAKUA: It was kind of like, "I'll pat you on the head and we'll feed you, you'll be happy, and that's it. Have these association meetings, come and eat the dry aku and drink the beers. That is what Kamehameha is good for, and mahalo for the pūpū." So we had our chance to give our mana'o, and okay, thank you very much, and everybody goes home and nothing gets done.

TONI LEE: Like Mr. Peters told me, "You make nice floats." Alumni, we make nice floats, that's it.

MIKE CHUN: I served on the Alumni Association, before it was chapterized. I remember the discussions were not necessarily, "We have this issue, what do you guys think about it?" It was, "Okay, this is the issue and this is how we're dealing with it." So you get that culture of not questioning.

And it comes down to, because we are running everything, we are giving you the best deal in town—you don't like it, go someplace else. So there was a reluctance to rock the boat.

ROY BENHAM: And let's face it—for the alumni, the guys who weren't too eager; it was easy then. Just let Marlene do it.

ELLEN PELLISERO: She works very, very hard.

ROY BENHAM: She'd call the meetings, she'd send out the notices, she'd collect the dues and all that kind of stuff.

ELLEN PELLISERO: She had very high standards that she set for herself, and she set those standards for everybody around her, which doesn't always work, because not everybody's going to hit that mark every time in your viewpoint, if you are a perfectionist.

I know Marlene can be tough to deal with. I know it got to people.

FRED CACHOLA: The way she ran things, and the way she looked at information. Same thing as Gil Tam—you know, "We can't let anybody have this, it's ours." This kind of thing, you know, creating a lot of distrust. I refused to represent my class, because she was laying all these stupid rules down.

MARSHA MEINEL (*'67, secretary to Bishop Estate Alumni and Parent Advancement Center coordinator*): She chose the class reps.

NOENOE WONG-WILSON (*'68, member of alumni group Nā Pua*): She just simply ignored those individuals whom the classes had elected to be their liaison.

TONI LEE: I am also my class rep for the class of '59. She tried to fire me from that.

ROD FERREIRA: Marlene tried to pull a fast one on everybody and tried to hold an alumni meeting with representatives of the class that she had self-appointed, and didn't recognize any of the leaders

"The Alumni Association had no purpose apart from whatever they did. I don't know what they did, apart from, you know, whatever they did."
—Rod Ferreira

"And mahalo for the pūpū."
—Robin Makua

who were elected by their classes—including Oz Stender's wife.

NOENOE WONG-WILSON

NOENOE WONG-WILSON: Rod Ferreira got his alumni list yanked out from under his nose by Marlene.

ROD FERREIRA: She just said that that was confidential information and the property of Kamehameha Schools and she was not going to release it.

Marlene would make the presidents of the Alumni Association sign agreements of confidentiality, and you weren't allowed to use it for any other reason except those expressly agreed to by Marlene.

NOENOE WONG-WILSON: Marlene didn't want them to do anything contrary. She pretty much had a stranglehold on the organization.

ROD FERREIRA: The last thing that Marlene wanted was the Kamehameha alumni and people coming on board who were excited about what was going on, to organize. Because she knew that once that element organized, she would lose control. So she threw roadblocks in everything.

NOENOE WONG-WILSON: They didn't move unless they got her blessing.

MIKE CHUN: The Alumni Association and all the chapters, they would correspond with me—"Mike, what's happening?" And I would explain what's happening. They were indignant, the whole thing, but when it came to taking formal action, or writing a letter and saying, we, as the Alumni Association—boom.

MARSHA MEINEL

NOENOE WONG-WILSON: Lokelani and Marlene used to attend the Board of Presidents meetings for the Alumni Association, and they pretty much kept everybody in check.

MARSHA MEINEL: When they had their Board of Presidents meeting, Lokelani would attend those meetings, and sometimes they didn't want her at these meetings. And she goes, "This is mine; I will be at this meeting."

There was a Board of Presidents meeting, on Maui or Moloka'i, and Marlene and Lokelani were both there. I remember Marlene coming back and saying, "The audacity, he asked Loke to leave. How dare!" Marlene was livid. And I told myself, *Why was she there?*

NOENOE WONG-WILSON: I remember one meeting here in Hilo, where our chapter hosted it, and we were at the Hilo Hawaiian Hotel. As much as we were mad at Marlene for the way she was acting and what she was doing with the Board of Presidents and the Alumni Association with her iron fists—as much as we were angry with her, Uncle Roy Benham would attack her in the meetings, unmercifully, I mean, yelling, scream, swearing at her. The moment she would open her mouth, he would start attacking her. And then she would yell back, and it would just deteriorate.

BOB WHITING: She had a temper. She'd get pissed off.

ROY BENHAM: Marlene was taking trips to talk with alumni. And then when she formed this region thing, guaranteed one trip per year to each one of those places.

TOMI CHONG (*'71*): My understanding was to the point where she would—well, she was controlling the votes. She'd take their proxies, go to these meetings, wherever, Mainland or whatever. I mean, it's unheard of. What organization would allow that to take place?

NOENOE WONG-WILSON: Because so much of the membership is represented from the Mainland, the Mainland groups felt unprepared to take positions on any of the controversy that was starting to show its head, because they didn't have enough information. My girlfriend, for example, who is one of my classmates, who was the president of the Washington state organization, was very reluctant to get involved or say anything, or to have the Alumni Association take a controversial position. Even in Hilo, we didn't feel we knew enough. And what little information they did have—I think Marlene played a big part in keeping them quiet.

OZ STENDER: I flew around the country to meet with the alumni regions. And wherever I was going. I would give a memo to the trustees —I'm going to this alumni meeting, and what I'm going to talk about. I remember going all the way to Washington, D.C. The president called me at the hotel when I got there, saying they couldn't meet with me. So I said, "Why?" She said she got a call, first from Marlene Sai and then from Rockne, that they'd better not meet with me. She said, "What do we do?" I said, "You know, I'm here, and I think you

TOMI CHONG

"She was controlling the votes ... What organization would allow that to take place?"

ought to meet with me."

So that was the Washington, D.C., one that I went to. Oregon, I had the same problem—Marlene has been in communication with these folks. And they tried to stop me from meeting with the alumni.

LOKELANI LINDSEY: He traveled the width and breadth of the United States meeting with all these people. They reported it in their alumni newsletters, saying what Trustee Stender said, and a lot of it is very negative against the trustees. ⌒

The Sacrificial Lamb
Extension Education Extinguished

They going take out some other guys too on this one. Extension—you guys was the sacrificial lamb. Watch out, we're coming. –Wally Lau

FRED CACHOLA: Now, the trustees in creating Extension Education Division made it clear to me, "You know, we've gotta do more, we've gotta reach out. Go where the need is—go where Hawaiians hurt."

WALLY LAU: Maybe we didn't literally think about taking it and making a connection to that whole cultural loss kind of thing. What happened? The loss of a culture, and how did it impact?

One of the studies of Pinky Thompson's was the cultural loss stress hypothesis. That one always intrigued me.

At the trustee level, you gotta start off with Pinky. I felt that Pinky, from his social worker experience, one, but also his love for this particular group of kids—I think he was the man at that level. The other trustees, like Papa Lyman, even Matsy Takabuki, the ones I worked with at the time—but it was Pinky who really pushed it.

FRED CACHOLA: The vision he had. I can still see Pinky looking at a chart. There's so many Hawaiians underachieving and way too few high achievers. He said, "I see the skews. These kids are dropouts, and these don't even get on the chart. Well, we'd better move the whole thing."

And there are Hawaiian kids who can't. They don't know how. They come from broken homes.

"There's a great separatism between the elitists and those that need—the maka'āinana. There are Hawaiian kids who come from broken homes. They come from single parents. I'm talking about a house that has seven kids and one parent. And I'm not talking about two or three, I'm talking about 35 percent who are below the poverty line. They come from parents who are in jail. They have parents who have committed suicide."

–Peter Kama

And by the whole thing he meant all Hawaiians, not just the ones on this edge or this edge—but the whole curve gotta move! Move the whole curve! Move the curve!

WALLY LAU: Pinky and Fred were real close.

FRED CACHOLA: I don't know if he would call himself my mentor. But Pinky guided me from the time when he was my social worker at Queen Lili'uokalani Children's Center, when I was just 14. He was mentor, a counselor, a coach—hard to put a name on the kind of role he played in my life. Just by his being there he gave me a lot of confidence. Later on he was my supporter, confidant. He was many things to me.

In the things I did at Kamehameha, I felt confident because he was sitting on that board. I believed in his philosophy, I believed in his mission that we've gotta get out there, we gotta help, we gotta do more. And Pinky was the man who was leading the charge.

PINKY THOMPSON

"Move the curve! Move the curve!"
–Fred Cachola

WALLY LAU: They shared the same vision, so they could really support each other. And I think Fred and I shared the same vision.

FRED CACHOLA: Pinky made it very clear. Your job is to go out there and plant the flag. Do more for more!

My approach was to go right to the heart of the problem, go where they're hurting the most. Where are Hawaiians having the most negative profiles in education? That's what I wanted to hit. Go right to the heart of the problem.

My dream was to make the Hawaiians in Nānākuli and Waiʻanae have just as much of an opportunity as the kids on campus. To bring equity to the legacy and the resources of Kamehameha.

At Waiheʻe, Maui, I went to the parents and I told them, "Kamehameha's been in existence for 85 years, but in all the 85 years, we have never taught a child below five years old. Never!" And they say, "What? You gotta be kidding!" I said, "No, we never had a preschool. And we don't know how to teach them. But do you mind if we come here and learn with you?" And they said, "Oh, come! Yeah, come!"

You know, trust, right? Trust. Honesty. I'm out of the boardroom, and I'm one of them. So I think they begin to trust—to trust me, to trust Kamehameha.

That was the beginning, the fact that Kamehameha was willing to come out into the Hawaiian community. Setting that foundation, setting the trust, setting the cooperation, getting the community to feel that they are being touched by the legacy, you know, Kamehameha is in their community. This was a whole new era for Kamehameha—to be off the campus and in Hawaiian communities.

FRED CACHOLA
"I am one of them!"

WALLY LAU: I think it said to the kids and families that the Princess loved them. They believed it. They really believed that.

The kids, they didn't express it like you and I talking. But they expressed it through their actions, their aloha, by showing what they learned.

When you talk to the parents, they were so grateful for the amount of time and energy and so forth that the Princess would provide. It wasn't my program, it wasn't just my staff. Not me, not Fred, not even Pinky. But for

Bottom left: "Kamehamea was willing to come out."
–Fred Cachola

Bottom right: "For the Princess to say: 'We believe in you.'"
–Wally Lau

the Princess to come out and say, "We believe in you." To me, Princess Pauahi is the aliʻi nui. We have to protect her and her legacy. And for me where that really helped is because the Princess never gave up on us. Her spirit lived in us.

WALLY LAU: More than 25 years, we touch more than 50,000 kids that are in the toughest places in life. Summer programs, traveling vans—paddling, we teach them things, they learn in the loʻi. And all of a sudden, boom, they gonna shut us down.

LOKELANI LINDSEY: The programs were not effective, and students were even regressing in some instances due to the ineffectiveness of the programs.

FRED CACHOLA: Whew! After 25 years of saying, "We got it going! We're moving out there, we're helping Hawaiians, we're developing trust, we're bringing hope." They're people who now believe that the legacy is part of them.

For 25 years we've developed all this trust, aloha, and Kamehameha has maintained such a wonderful cooperative relationship with the DOE and Hawaiian communities. And now to say, "It's all over."

I mean, how we gonna do that? And it was my painful experience to do that over and over—oh, how many times I had to do that.

Man, that hurt!

CHARLES TOGUCHI (*former head of Hawaiʻi Department of Education*): I was shocked, disappointed. There's no question that a lot of Hawaiian kids aren't being served as a result of the elimination of these programs. I think Kamehameha should go beyond serving the best and the brightest. They should serve as many Hawaiian youngsters as they can.

EDMUND LIMA (*parent of student in Molokaʻi program Ka Papa Honua ʻO Keawenui*): I think it was a big-time mistake. Why leave the other kids out?

GEORGE SCHNACKENBERG (*Molokaʻi program Ka Papa Honua ʻO Keawenui teacher/counselor*): Mrs. Lindsey was very adamant in saying that it is not our responsibility to help these children. It is the DOE's responsibility to meet these children's educational needs, and we are not in the business of helping the Hawaiian youth at risk.

ELISA YADAO: We told everyone it was a matter of economics, and a matter of effectiveness. That KSBE had done these studies, and the outreach programs, sort of badly put, were not getting enough bang for the buck.

WALLY LAU: So they gonna build schools on other islands. What they call satellite campuses. And they say no more money for this and outreach both.

ELISA YADAO: It was a horribly difficult decision for them to make, to get rid of these programs, and it was something that was very difficult for some of the people on that board. It wasn't something that I think all of them wanted to do. But they were all committed to opening new schools, which is what happened.

LOKELANI LINDSEY: Never has this happened in Kamehameha Schools history, and it was hard for a lot of people to take.

"We're developing trust."
–Fred Cachola

FRED CACHOLA: The first real threat I saw was when Henry Peters came on the board in 1984.

The first time we meet each other, Henry Peters is running a Model Cities program for Nānākuli. But something happens, I think, to people like Henry. They get in a position of power and politics and they become elitists.

And all of a sudden—Kamehameha is not going to be involved with that kind of riffraff—the low and underachievers. We're going to be involved with the best, the brightest, that's us. Elitist.

I blame some of this on me. I could not get a broader vision of education in Henry Peters' head.

Henry had a model of education for people like himself who could be successful in spite of humble beginnings.

I had one meeting with Henry Peters, and he said, "You know,

Fred, I like the Kamehameha Schools to be like it was when you guys were there."

And I got mad. I know what the school was like when us guys were there—a military institute, very un-Hawaiian, isolated and elitist. That was his conception of good and industrious boys and girls. He wanted that, because that's the part of Kamehameha that he admired. We had been trying to change that for a long time.

He couldn't understand community education, alternative education. His style is, "School is what I understand. If it's something that I don't understand, hey, I can't trust it."

MIKE CHUN: Henry would make these comments. "If it's good enough for Punahou and it's good enough for 'Iolani, then it should be good enough for us to just run this school. I don't know why we're doing all this stuff out there. It's just going to run us dry."

FRED CACHOLA: To my dismay, Peters questioned whether we should be working with kids who couldn't read or whether we should spend any money on dropouts. "Fred, come, I want to talk to you. The dropout kids, the alienated kids—we don't have to fool around with them. If you are a dropout, tough luck. Get plenty more good kids. Aren't we rewarding these kids who are doing bad, by giving them another chance?" I said, "Shit."

WALLY LAU: He would come to me, and he says, "Oh, Wally, you the kind of guy I want teaching my kids, my moʻopuna." The next minute, *boom!*—you're out. Two-sided.

MIKE CHUN: Henry Peters. Comes back to Henry. They're telling me this, Dickie's making these comments, Loke's making these comments—next thing I know, *poom,* they're ready to disband the program, jettison the program. Why? Henry Peters.

I said to Loke, "Why? You supported these programs." And she said, "Yeah, but the Speaker doesn't."

ELISA YADAO: But there was also a feeling that these were programs and people Mrs. Lindsey didn't like, programs that were started under another roster of trustees.

WALLY LAU: To do their studies for them, make their case look good, they bring in a Ph.D, Paul Ahr, from the Mainland, who is Corporate Psychology Center, and this one big accounting firm on the Mainland, Ernst & Young.

FRED CACHOLA: You won't find it in any written contracts, but I bet the marching orders to Ernst & Young were very clear. We have a vision and you guys better help us create this vision. And if it means we gotta chop, well, you figure out how to do that.

KATHY TIBBETTS (*Schools Program Evaluation and Planning*): We had a number of meetings with Paul Ahr. And he said, "Oh, yeah, I'm going to protect this program and no way anything's going to happen." But then things happened just the opposite of what we were promised in meetings. And more and more it seemed he was lying, as events continued to accumulate.

The only thing I can think of is that it was about satisfying the masters, the people who he was being paid by.

KATHY TIBBETTS
"It seemed he was lying."

WALLY LAU: There was a meeting, a retreat that the trustees had at Kuilima. I was asked to attend. Standing there, and they asked me about the data. I told them, "There's the data. And it's public record. This is what I gave Loke. I don't know what Loke's giving you, but it's so different—black and white."

Loke was very furious with me—how dare I show that kine data!

FRED CACHOLA: Wally and I knew that the data from Ernst & Young would be biased. And sure enough, they were using standardized achievement test scores and comparing our alternative education students' scores to the scores of students in conventional schools.

The kind of data that we collected showed that we improved student attendance, we kept them in school, we kept them out of trouble, we brought them through to graduation. How do you measure a mother's tears when she sees the first child in her family receive his high school diploma? How do you measure the value of turning around a whole family's aspirations about education? For the first time families had hope. How do you place a value on that? But people like Pinky, Lyman and Matsy who understood the value were all out of picture, and Henry had his majority.

DUDLEY MAKAHANALOA: We meet regularly. And of course everybody had been listening and with our ears to the door, and you hear about this kind of happening up there.

JOE TRAVIS: The impact was direct, because Fred is a member of our class, and that's why we got totally immersed in it. Of course we could see the wrong; we could see the problem. This is our school and our Bishop Estate. We didn't want to make any waves.

DUDLEY MAKAHANALOA: We knew that anything with Kamehameha should be good.

LOPAKA MANSFIELD
"Something is amiss here."

LOPAKA MANSFIELD (*'62, president of Kauaʻi alumni association*): A vacancy on Kauaʻi's alumni board became available, and I was asked to go and fill that vacancy. I met Fred Cachola there.

That was a good time in my life that I could do, give back to the school. Before that, I didn't know what Kamehameha was doing in the community. I had no idea about the extent of the program. I just thought Kamehameha was Kapālama Heights.

And when they announced that they were going to close, I had a personal connection because of working with Fred on this board. He really talked to us and described what they were doing.

So now I am totally involved, because, wow, this has raised a red flag for me that something is amiss here. Why the drastic measure for a stupid reason? Then I felt something was wrong. Something was amiss. Something was not pono from that point.

WALLY LAU: I smell a rat, when I got a call in the morning from my friends in the DOE—"Loke was here last night; your Hale Hoʻoponopono program, they cutting um." When the DOE find out more than me—

PETER KAMA: Being a proud member of the class of '53, we had a meeting, and we discussed it, and so we called Dickie Wong and we said, "Dickie Wong, we'd like to come and talk to you about this subject."

So we met him at Bank of Hawai'i, some executive dining room. Joe Travis and I went and represented our class. And Dickie Wong invited Gil Tam, who was the president of the Alumni Association.

Joe and I asked the tough questions. And Dickie Wong explained that, well, we hired a consultant, and the consultant said that the continuation of this program will endanger the IRS status of the charitable, non-profit entity.

And I said, "How can it do that? It's been going on for 20-plus years, and all of a sudden now somebody says you are endangered."

PETER KAMA

FRED CACHOLA: That's bullshit. Because I went to the IRS twice. Both occasions with Matsy Takabuki and Pinky. It was my privilege and pleasure to introduce the extension programs to the IRS at Washington, D.C.

At the end of our last meeting, the IRS guy said, "I see what you guys are doing, but you know, this doesn't sound like a school. When you work with pregnant women, that sounds like you're doing health. The kind of research you guys are doing, it's bigger than some universities do. Collaborating with public schools? Private schools don't do that.

"You know, you guys are doing things that we aren't used to. But as long as you have a majority of your resources into things that we do understand, like K-12, then it's fine."

The IRS' general message was, "If you spend at least 80 percent on stuff that is pololei, correct, we can manuahi the rest. The rest is okay."

So that whole IRS threat was cooked up by Loke. It's like, hey, we're gonna play a new game, and the rules you were playing with no count!

PETER KAMA: Dickie Wong said, "Well, I'll call this consulting firm, Ernst & Young, and they'll make a presentation to you."

So we made an appointment. We called the class of '52, and we said, "We gonna go to do this." The class of '53 got together. We hired a lady to take a verbatim record of what happened in that presentation. Each of us were assigned questions that we developed to ask.

Oz Stender was not there. Found out later he wasn't invited. And Henry Peters wasn't there, because he was in Washington, negotiating to get that land for the golf course, getting himself a job on the board of directors that gets paid. That's the reason he wasn't there.

And you know what, what response they gave to us and the people who were present? They're all lies. They're fabrications. Just crap.

FRED CACHOLA: And so I began to look towards Ozzie, yeah. I kept feeding Ozzie that information, the data. Because he would look at it. The others, it was hopeless. No sense taking anything to them because they weren't going to look at it.

OZ STENDER: What really upset me was that they started to cut out the outreach programs—which is all Pinky's things.

I had always been pushing the satellite schools. But my concept was, you build the middle and high school, and you use the elementary schools in the community as a feeder school. My thought was, charter the elementary schools.

No, they want to build the whole thing, own the whole thing, go back to the four-point rule from the IRS—a tax-exempt organization running a school, has to be your building, your students, your teachers, your curriculum.

So they were going to build a school on the Big Island, because that's the biggest concentration of Hawaiians. Problem with that is, Hawaiians are scattered everywhere. If you picked Oʻahu, Waiʻanae, smaller population of Hawaiians than Big Island, but you have the concentration in one area.

But that's what they chose. And because they were building that, Mrs. Lindsey wanted one on Maui. So we had to build one on Maui.

LOKELANI LINDSEY: That decision was very difficult to make. I can tell you there was not a dry eye in the boardroom. But it was necessary in order to meet the needs of the students. We were moving to this other arena.

WALLY LAU: *Go Forward*, yeah.

FRED CACHOLA: Paul Ahr and Ernst & Young were hired gunslingers. When Henry Peters called us in to hear the result of their report, in front of the board, he sat and gloated in glee. He looked at me and he said, "You know what the name of this report should be? *I TOLD YOU SO!*" And he pointed right at me.

TERRY KELLY (*director of Drug-Free Program*): What was the most difficult about all of this was the way it came down—the lies, the misrepresentation, the distortion of the facts. There was no effort to look deeply at these programs and to offer needed resources to shore them up—so for many years, it was like a set up to fail. Fred's favorite saying about working in Extension Ed was "taking a walk on the wild side." In other words, we did push the envelope for KS, so Pauahi's legacy would reach the most in need, those forgotten kids and families that had been left out for generations. KS' Extension Ed. programs were way ahead of their time.

I think the the majority of the trustees at the time, with the exception of Oz Stender—who was like the only one in the sinking canoe, trying to bail out the water—were very self-centered, self-interested and in some cases very bitter and revengeful people. Lokelani Lindsey, Henry Peters and Dickie Wong each had their own hit lists. It was a known fact that both Fred and Wally were on at least one or all of them. It took some time, but eventually, they and everyone under or with them were the first to go.

TERRY KELLY
"… so Pauahi's legacy would reach the most in need."

FRED CACHOLA: Mike Chun was the one who had to tell me officially it was over. He came into my office and just said, "It's all over."

His heart was with us, but Mike was in a rough place. He was too busy just trying to weather his own storms. The threat of getting rid of him was very real.

WALLY LAU: He was powerless. If they had the chance, they would kick Mike out of there anyway.

FRED CACHOLA: I think he was going along with the trustees' *Go Forward* program, trying to administer it as best as possible.

WALLY LAU: Fred and I would go up to Mike's house sometimes and have a little beer and pūpū, just the three of us, and talk.

FRED CACHOLA: But I don't think Mike fully realized how much we were hurting. All of us. We spent a good portion of our professional lives trying to take Kamehameha to places where they never went before, trying to pioneer new ideas in education in its broadest sense, trying to move the entire curve for all Hawaiians.

"Where they never
went before."

–Fred Cachola

CHARLENE HOE: Wong came down and told us, "Oh, we want to give you advance notice because we want to tell internal that we are going to be changing directions, um, that we will be reemphasizing different programs, including this campus." Not to worry, not to worry, because our employees that are currently in certain programs are to be retrained and will be able to go into other programs. And he's giving us advance warning, advance notice, because it's going to be out in the papers soon, like literally in hours. He had to leave us quickly, because he and Mike were going up to the upper campus to tell everybody. I don't know where they went. And they left us. And then within six weeks, hundreds of people got their papers. So to be out-and-out lied to—

WALLY LAU: Then they went to the faculty and told them just the opposite. It's that kind of thing where Dr. Chun would call us in and say, "You guys are gone. And not only gone, but you gone in two weeks." That's the shittiest thing to say to my staff.

Lokelani Lindsey says, "Wally, we're going to have to cut, like, five positions or something." I went, "Ho!" Like what the hell.

So finally at the very end, I said, "Loke, if you gotta cut anybody, cut me. You don't need me. Because I'm way up there." Not knowing that she going kick out everybody anyway. She was so manipulative. Unbelievable.

COLBERT MATSUMOTO (*Master for KSBE*): Your Master is troubled by the turmoil that was engendered by the strategic planning and implementation of the *Go Forward* initiative. What should have been welcomed as the most significant and ambitious educational venture for the Trust Estate in decades turned into an episode clouded by mistrust, misunderstanding, and antagonism that continues till today.

WALLY LAU: So it's all of that. I can live with the decision, but I cannot live with the way they played with people's lives.

KĒHAU ABAD: It was traumatic. It was really numbing.

CAROL KAPU (*KSBE parent educator—Hāna*): It was as if a bomb had been dropped.

KĀWIKA EYRE (*Secondary School Hawaiian language teacher*): And later we come to find out that there was more than enough money to do both—to keep the Outreach programs and to build the two new campuses. It was never that one had to be sacrificed for the other. Never. And it turns out they had $350 million of unspent money at the same time they were taking away these programs from the kids, the kids that needed it most.

OZ STENDER: They were running a surplus. And they were concealing it.

CHARLENE HOE: There was this huge sense of absolute betrayal on our campus. People went into a period of total shock for about a year, and then grief for about a year.

"The way they played with people's lives."
–Wally Lau

KĒHAU ABAD: It was the epitome of what was going on at the time, where very powerful people, for very poor reasons, were able to do whatever they wanted.

Those guys put in so much, starting from scratch, making connections with the community, having the community define what their needs were—creating a very different role for Kamehameha. And what—all for nothing?

WALLY LAU: Why didn't people protest? I think out of fear.

When I talked to people, when we had our alohas privately in small groups, they wanted to. They really did. Campus people, from the janitors to the copy room people, they wanted to. Their empathy and even their sympathy was for us.

But people was so afraid. We did try to collect some money. We was going to put this thing in the paper. We wanted to get the Hawaiian community to say, you know, "We aloha you people." They were afraid of the repercussions that would happen. They were stuck in their fear.

People were worried about—if it happens to them, what will happen to us? Because the word was, they going take out some other guys too on this one. Extension—you guys was the sacrificial lamb. Watch out, we're coming.

MIKE CHUN: When we had that press conference in Midkiff, at that point we said, "Don't worry, we're going to transition people into new positions, and while some programs are going to be cut, we're going to find places for them."

That was the message I delivered, because that was the understanding—that we were going to be able to accommodate everyone. That message came from the trustees.

But I think Personnel, Human Resources, they were kind of stuck, because where they were coming from, I think they knew that wasn't going to be possible. Plus, you can't just shift people around; you have to advertise the position, you have to go through a selection process.

As we started to work out the details, it became evident that all these people had to go.

WALLY LAU: A hundred seventy. Some of these folks working for Kamehameha 20, 30 years. And now—in two weeks, go.

MIKE CHUN: The hard part was trying to keep the organization together, at the same time having to deal with the lives of so many people.

It was a matter of several months. And that's when I had to go back and I had to say, "We're not going to be able to accommodate everyone."

One of the worst days of my life was the final day when I went around to say goodbye.

I just apologized to people, you know—"I'm sorry." I felt shitty. Absolutely terrible. Obviously, I let people down. I could see the bitterness, and it's still there today. The cynicism and bitterness of some who have left. Some were fortunate, they were able to stay within the organization, but they are cynical. And I don't blame them.

LOKELANI LINDSEY: Excellent severance packages were involved.

FRED CACHOLA: They gave us little golden parachutes. There were only certain people who were qualified. They went through a rigorous process. The game towards the end was a numbers game. It was all numbers.

MARYANNE INOUYE: It was a tremendously upsetting time.

The Human Resources folks would go out to work with the separation people. They were doing their duties, the best under the given circumstances—you try to get as much as you can on behalf of people. They were the messengers. They would come back and cry. I think the HR people just had to console each other.

I was going to the doctor, just like a lot of other people—the stress of it.

JANET ZISK: The closing down. That was one of the major traumas I took part in. These people were in horrible shape. They were given two weeks' notice. Two weeks.

And there was absolutely no organized closing down. The only instruction they were given was to make an inventory of everything they hadn't used, all their supplies. Count all the pencils, all the pads and papers, all the leftover computer disks. That was the only instruction.

They had all the files wiped off their hard drives. Somebody came in and cleaned off all the files, so they couldn't print out any final records. Lots of information lost that way.

I'd written a note to Dr. Chun, saying, "How are these programs going to be closed down efficiently? There's a tremendous amount of information here that needs to be archived for our records."

And so he sent Marsha Bolson up all of a sudden to be the person to organize this. She wasn't too thrilled about it—I mean, this is in the middle of the week.

I went with her to the Big Island to close down preschools. I spent about a third of my time just simply holding people in my arms, crying. And these people were crying because these good programs that had helped so many people were being ignominiously closed. They had the whole program set up. Everything was in place. Parents had gotten jobs. And it was closed down. That affected a lot of lives. They couldn't believe how thoughtless and cruel and mean this was. Just incredible.

FRED CACHOLA: I was retiring.

WALLY LAU: This was the last time we were going to be with Fred. We wanted to honor him. So myself and Jean and Kēhau and another person were planning this big thing. And Jean, she was—"Don't make waves, invite him, invite him." Jean was trying to play the politicking. Kēhau was very adamant, who she wanted, who she never like—you know, this is my dad. I mean, *boom*.

FRED CACHOLA: The *I Mua* magazine was doing a beautiful spread on me and my retirement. It was page 11, the full page. And the poor girl had to call me back and say, you know, the trustees pulled it. She said, "Fred, I just want you to know that this is what the page would have looked like, and they pulled it."

WALLY LAU

"I will forgive."

WALLY LAU: I was devastated. Devastated psychologically, emotionally. My spirits was bottomed out. Then it impacted physically—I never knew I had high blood pressure. I was a walking dead guy. Fred was a walking dead guy. Day after his thing, he was in the hospital. A friend of mine had to have his heart transplant. I mean the thing took a tremendous toll. And so I had to leave Oʻahu.

Maybe if I just kept my mouth shut, I would have my job still yet. Wouldn't have lost my house. But it wasn't pono. Pololei for me is in the head, pono is in the heart. And I made the call. Do I regret making that call? Uh-uh.

Why I am saying this is because what happened I will never, never forget. I will forgive. I forgive because the hewa in my heart was so much. I could not live if I kept all this inside me. It would kill me. It would have taken me to my grave. ✑

A Place for Us to Gather
Hawaiian Cultural Center Suppressed

7

*The idea of a place for us to gather ... to heal, perpetu-
ate culture and welcome visitors was very compelling.*
–Randie Fong

PINKY THOMPSON: We need to have a visual statement that articulates Pauahi's Hawaiian background, and it's possible to tie it directly to her great-grandfather, Kamehameha.

We must find a way to develop a program that has its roots in the Hawaiian culture and history of over 2,000 years—it's the missing link that I can see to Kamehameha Schools.

It's our duty and responsibility to make clear that learning is a process that's ongoing, and that our ancient people brought with them a great deal of wisdom that has a place in contemporary society.

I would appreciate if you would struggle with the idea on how we can come up with a program that would, in fact, make Kamehameha the Hawaiian culture educational center of the world and enable our educational material to be shared throughout mankind.

JAMIE FONG (*'78, Hawaiian Cultural Center Project Coordinator*): I was taught the definition of a good aliʻi—a leader who thinks of the people first. The late trustee Myron "Pinky" Thompson was a perfect example of a true Hawaiian leader. He was all about the people and was constantly thinking of how to benefit them.

ELISA YADAO: Randie Fong, during Trustee Thompson's time at the estate, was very much involved in trying to put together a cultural center for KSBE.

JAMIE FONG: In the fall of 1992, Pinky called a group of us together to talk story about the idea of a cultural center. Me, Randie, Bob Worthington and others met at the admin building on campus. Pinky asked Randie to take the lead. Throughout 1993, we met to do research and to gather people's manaʻo. A staff report was submitted to the board of trustees in the fall of 1993 and approved in late January 1994. Two things were authorized in that report: the establishment of Kamehameha Schools as a "Hawaiian culture education center," and the conceptual approval to construct a cultural center facility on the Kapālama campus. A series of workshops began later that year, allowing the Kamehameha community to participate in and guide the process.

KĒHAU ABAD: The concept of a cultural center wasn't new. Those in the Hawaiian community have long articulated a need for a place where Hawaiians could be Hawaiian on our own terms—just for ourselves, for our own sake of keeping our people and culture alive, for our own health and well-being.

JAMIE FONG: I remember the first couple of meetings. Pinky shared his vision of the Center as a storehouse of the mana of Kamehameha I. But he didn't stop there. Pinky said he wanted to introduce a set of core Hawaiian values for the whole institution, virtues that everyone could live by in the classroom and in the boardroom—he emphasized that his trustee colleagues would be expected to live by those values just like everyone else.

"... healing our people by lifting up culture as a primary vehicle."
–Jamie Fong

He had visions to improve the status of Native Hawaiians, and always talked about healing our people by lifting up culture as a primary vehicle. These ideas got us excited. I mean, they really inspired us to make his vision our vision.

RANDIE FONG: The idea of a place for us to gather—to heal, perpetuate culture and welcome visitors—was very compelling.

KĒHAU ABAD: Pinky Thompson was the first to suggest that such a place should be smack dab in the center of the Kapālama campus. The campus programs and the whole institution needed to get re-centered as a Hawaiian place.

JAMIE FONG: A little over 300 people participated in the process over those three years. It was unbelievable how many people came out to help; even alumni and non-KS community members came out. For two years we welcomed them, fed them, engaged them, and then we sat back, listened and recorded what they had to say.

CHARLENE HOE: Randie was able to inspire nearly every staff member to participate in this process.

KĒHAU ABAD: What we experienced in the workshops was truly awesome. People were thrilled that Kamehameha was committed to being Hawaiian.

But what was probably most inspiring was that people were so in sync. Sure, there were diverse ideas at those meetings, but at a na'au level, everyone was coming from the same place. People wanted, as fast as it could be done, a place where Hawaiianness was foundational and not window dressing, where people could connect to precious ancestral wisdom as a source for success in today's world.

RANDIE FONG: Based on the high volume of mana'o and dialogue that came from two years of workshops, specific programs were developed by the committee which at the time included well-respected people who really knew their stuff. They planned a master-apprentice program where students could learn a range of traditional arts from kūpuna and other Hawaiian experts; a staff cultural training program to help

Papa Henry Auwai describes medicinal plants to KS students. Auwai was expelled from Kamehameha in the 1940s for speaking Hawaiian.

teachers and administrators learn and practice Hawaiian culture; a leadership program to promote Hawaiian perspectives of leadership and learn about Hawaiian leaders; a ho'oponopono program to learn and practice conflict resolution skills; as well as a range of other programs that focused on research, hosting, Pacific studies and more. It was just amazing.

JAMIE FONG: Staff and students came up with ideas like traditional food preparation and cooking, cooking in an imu. We need to teach this next generation how to prepare an imu, so that in generations to come we'll be able to practice it and take pride in native cooking, the way our parents and grandparents did.

JAMIE FONG

RANDIE FONG: According to what people shared, they seemed to really feel empowered by the process.

KĒHAU ABAD: All of this positive activity was in such stark contrast with what we were experiencing in our larger Kamehameha existence under the trustee majority. The atmosphere had changed.

RANDIE FONG: It no longer resembled a place that was full of aloha and a place where people were respected.

KĒHAU ABAD: The Cultural Center was an empowering, inclusive, creative, Hawaiian experience.

People saw that. It was so noticeable. So much so that by the second year of our workshops, with the trust that we had built people started saying things aloud in our workshops that were aimed directly at the trustee majority.

Someone would chime in to say that what we were currently experiencing was so un-Hawaiian, not pono, not like what our kūpuna would expect of us.

RANDIE FONG

JAMIE FONG: I was shocked to hear that a staff member who expressed herself in one of the workshops was given a tongue-lashing the next day when she returned to work at Kawaiaha'o Plaza.

We got the impression that there were, I dunno, spies? It was shocking to us since everything we did was honest and out in the open.

Pinky and Oz were the only trustees who attended workshops. I think that's what gave some individuals the confidence to express their mana'o, but to be smacked down by Mrs. Lindsey right afterwards. I felt bad for those people.

That's when it started getting kind of scary.

RANDIE FONG: We sent reports regularly to Mrs. Lindsey and Dr. Chun, and when Dr. Freitas came on board, to Dr. Freitas, and Tony Ramos. As much as we tried to push the Cultural Center proposal to the next stage, it never seemed to go there.

JAMIE FONG: In 1994 we submitted to the trustees a comprehensive report on the Cultural Center. I made copies for the trustees and put them in red folders, each with its own individual videotape showing the large numbers of people who participated, what they said, and how excited people were. Randie delivered the reports directly to Mrs. Lindsey since she was the lead trustee on education. I remember we waited and waited but there was no response.

Randie finally went to meet with Mrs. Lindsey only to find that she had not distributed the reports and videotapes and instead locked them away in a cabinet.

KĒHAU ABAD: We were hearing that our own trustees were a serious obstacle to our becoming a Hawaiian institution. And this was being affirmed in every way by their actions.

RANDIE FONG: I had frequent discussions with Mrs. Lindsey and sent reports to her regularly. She would tell me one thing in our meetings and then right afterwards I'd hear from Tony Ramos or Rockne Freitas that she said the exact opposite. I always got mixed messages. It was like she was purposely trying to cause confusion.

Tony said she feels uncomfortable that people from the institution are coming in and discussing things. Why are all these people involved? Why are you getting everyone involved?

I would get messages from Tony saying Mrs. Lindsey says she is very, very angry with you. He would say things like, you know, Mrs. Lindsey said this is not what Henry Peters had in mind.

It just boggled my mind that she was upset with us for intensely involving our community in the process. You'd think that would be a good thing.

KĒHAU ABAD: I mean, people were talking about what being a

Hawaiian leader means, and it was all too obvious that she didn't come close to measuring up to that.

That's why I believe she shut us down.

RANDIE FONG: But what really threw me for a loop was one particular comment she made. After three years of hard work involving some 300 participants, Mrs. Lindsey had the nerve to say, "All I want is a little hale. That's all Henry and the other trustees want, a little hale. The trustees are very angry about this!"

Not only was she trying to diminish the work of the KS community, she was also sending a message that when it came to our culture, Hawaiians didn't deserve a facility of substance; we should just go outside and do our thing under a tree. That really ticked me off.

She managed to control, micromanage, just about everything else on campus, but she just couldn't get her hands on the Cultural Center project. I believe that's what really upset her the most.

CHARLENE HOE: I worked for two years on the development of a Hawaiian Cultural Center project. That whole process built up a tremendous amount of expectation. Then, ultimately, frustration.

RANDIE FONG: The impression we got from campus leadership was that this was not going to be on the front burner anymore.

KĒHAU ABAD: In the second year of the workshops, Lindsey I think was catching on that the tenor of the discussion and the enthusiasm and power behind the large-group effort could threaten her position.

RANDIE FONG: In the spring of 1996, in the face of mounting pressure from Mrs. Lindsey to disband, the planning committee defiantly held out to June, just long enough to complete a set of program designs. Everyone knew the plans would likely end up on her shelf again, but the committee completed the assignment as planned with faith that their efforts might someday bear fruit.

KĒHAU ABAD: Lindsey shoved the project to the back of her closet, and she wasn't letting it go anywhere.

RANDIE FONG: With all those messages flying, we just decided, okay, probably we should stop.

KĒHAU ABAD: We were totally stuck. If we wanted to help Kamehameha grow to become a truly Hawaiian place, we couldn't do it with her around. It was that simple.

RANDIE FONG: Elisa Yadao was a very good friend during those years. She was in a difficult position of having to appease Mrs. Lindsey's wishes while at the same time trying to serve the greater good by warning people of potentially explosive situations. She was also very loyal to Pinky.

I confided in her all the time, and she always responded with great empathy and concern. Kawaiahaʻo Plaza was a very volatile environment in those days, and I know she must have gotten into a lot of trouble for talking to many of us on the campus, but Elisa was fearless in that way.

JAMIE FONG: To keep the flame burning after Mrs. Lindsey tried to shelve the Cultural Center, Kanaʻiaupuni was created. It was a group of some 150 staff, students and alumni that gathered weekly for Hawaiian choral singing, hula, Hawaiian cultural presentations and community projects.

Kanaʻiaupuni participants practicing their culture. "Keep the flame burning."
–*Jamie Fong*

RANDIE FONG: Soon, Mrs. Lindsey began attacking Kanaʻiaupuni by sending messages through the administration that we were violating rules by charging people a $10 activity fee. Of course there ended up being no violation at all, but the jabs kept coming.

JAMIE FONG: We kept the group alive as long as we could, trying to maintain the spirit of commitment and the growing relationships that were forged during the Cultural Center planning efforts.

RANDIE FONG: To me, our KS community had created its own cultural movement—a cultural revolution, if you will—that in the end did more to galvanize the Kamehameha family than anyone could have imagined.

It is no coincidence that the many who were involved in the Hawaiian Cultural Center Project had also played roles in defending Kamehameha from the trustee majority during the peak of the controversy.

KĒHAU ABAD: The Cultural Center was a collective vision. It's a perfect example of what can happen when a community of good-hearted people come together and dare to dream of what can be.

JAMIE FONG: Lokelani was never able to stop the movement—it was too powerful, way too powerful.

"Dare to dream of what can be."
–Kēhau Abad

8

The Word "Discovery"
Lokelani Lindsey Directs Curriculum Project Fiasco

I remember being told I couldn't use the word "discovery" because it wasn't measurable, so I had to lie about how I taught geometry. —Kim Slagel

JIM SLAGEL: We suddenly had this push to rewrite the curriculum.

JOANNE WONG-KAM: We were told to come in during the summer to work on curriculum. This big curriculum project.

KIM SLAGEL: A huge project that impacted every teacher on the hill.

KĀWIKA EYRE: Loke was of the notion that on any given day, she should be able to walk into any one of the six 4th-grade classrooms and find the same subject on the board and the same pedagogy in play.

"How do we put a single measuring tape on a student's original song or hula about Liliʻuokalani confined to her room?"

—*Clemi McLaren*

CLEMI MCLAREN: How about the very real need to differentiate instruction—that students have different levels of proficiency, different learning styles and interests?

ROCKNE FREITAS: There is a high level of accountability in that format. In the earlier format, there was a heavier reliability on the professionalism of each teacher.

It's more than just grade level to grade level. For me, it's also day to day. That way, we can stay right on top of anybody who is falling in the crack, and get some corrective action immediately to them.

MARYALICE WOODY (*Elementary School teacher*): It was not a question of all of a sudden having to be accountable. It was just having to be all the same. And who makes the decisions? Were Lokelani Lindsey or Rockne Freitas in the classroom? Nope. How do they know?

CLEMI MCLAREN: How do we put a single measuring tape on a student's original song or hula about Liliʻuokalani confined to her room? Where will Trustee Lindsey get the army of observers to check out that everyone is actually doing what they wrote?

KĀWIKA EYRE: Teachers are examining curriculum all the time, daily, at each teaching moment, interacting with students—it's what we do, it's what we breathe in and out.

KAHELE KUKEA: Let's talk about kids and how they learn, and let things develop.

KĀWIKA EYRE: There is never perfect articulation between two levels, two courses or two teachers. It is always a dance of approximations.

Schooling by nature is a messy process. A lot of human messiness. That is just part of being a school.

One must have a certain tolerance for disorder, ambiguities, personalities. At best, we try to play the same background music via a curriculum. But everyone is dancing slightly differently. And that, by my take, is not necessarily bad for kids, as they observe adults and develop a personal take about people and ideas and the general human scene, their place in the world and what they want to make of it.

KIM SLAGEL: But no one took the time to explain the purpose or use of curriculum development.

CHARLENE HOE: There seemed to be sort of an edict from nowhere that we were expected to follow without any clarification.

BRIAN CHANG: There were certain projects where she gave blanket approval. So that was clearly one of her pet projects. And it just sailed through.

> "Schooling by nature is a messy process. A lot of human messiness. That is just part of being a school. One must have a certain tolerance for disorder, ambiguities, personalities."
>
> –*Kāwika Eyre*

> "There seemed to be sort of an edict from nowhere that we were expected to follow without any clarification."
>
> –*Charlene Hoe*

JIM SLAGEL: No philosophical arguments, no paradigm shift, no discussion of import, of merit.

KAHELE KUKEA: I kept pushing on who makes the decision about what is the curriculum? Does the head of the curriculum team make it? Does the principal make it?

TONY RAMOS: It was a collective directive, I guess, probably from Mrs. Lindsey and Dr. Freitas.

KAHELE KUKEA: Finally, we sat with Rockne and we talked it though, and we were saying that the principal should make the decision. I was saying that because I would make a decision based upon the teachers' knowledge of curriculum and instruction and my awareness of what's going on out there and what's best.

Finally, Rockne said okay. Teachers are the developers of curriculum. Principals are the ones who make the decisions.

So in my joy, I wrote a short note to the teachers, saying, "Good news. This has been affirmed in a recent meeting." There was a lot of rejoicing.

Next day, a note comes down to me from Rockne, saying, "I heard what you did. That was premature. As I told you, you should have waited until I was going to talk to the curriculum team. Poor judgment on your part. I want you to rescind that notice." So I rescinded it. I got in real trouble on that.

MARYALICE WOODY

MARYALICE WOODY: When Kahele was slapped down by Rockne and Mrs. Lindsey, all the wind was taken out of our sails. This is just another example of how Kahele tried to support the teachers and the students, while Rockne and Lindsey were just trying to bully everyone.

LOKELANI LINDSEY: If you've had a lot of free rein and all of a sudden you have to become accountable, you are going to have people who are not happy. In my opinion, change comes very hard.

SANDY BEHENNA (*Secondary School assistant principal*): There was a lot of grumbling. The teachers were very upset about it, and the department heads were also.

We needed to have a set curriculum for each individual course that was being taught, and we have over 200 courses.

TONY RAMOS: It was a whole lot to get done.

SANDY BEHENNA: Tony had a discussion with Rockne Freitas about a possible extension. Tony came back and said that there wouldn't be an extension, okay?

JULIAN AKO: We all did what we had to do to get that stupid thing done by the deadline.

ARLIS LEGLER (*Secondary School business department head*): My students knew that I was the department head. And there would be countless announcements over the PA system. And the PA system in my classroom, and probably everywhere, does a little crackle before the message comes on. And it got to the point that when that crackle came on, the students would stop what they were doing and look at me, because nine times out of 10, it was a directive that there was a meeting for department heads, or a faculty meeting.

So we'd listen to the message, they'd look at me, and sometimes my response would be, "Well, you won't get your papers back right away—because I have this meeting, or some such thing." And they knew certain kinds of announcements meant that their teachers would not be able to be there fully for them the next day.

It brought the kids into a fight that shouldn't have been theirs.

ARLIS LEGLER

RANDIE FONG: People were called back and paid to work these curriculum guides. Other people were kind of not called back until the last minutes, and then they didn't receive compensation. It was poorly, poorly managed.

LOKELANI LINDSEY: A lot of people along the line did not do their job and did not get it going, and put barricades in front of getting the project done.

ROCKNE FREITAS: Well, I was trying to manage a position in between these things, and I'm trying to get a result without flame-throwing anybody. And so I tried to pull back a little bit, nudge once in a while, pull back, nudge, pull back, nudge. And I'm accepting some of the blame, because instead of pushing, I nudged.

ROCKNE FREITAS
Trying not to
flame-throw anybody

LARRY MCELHENY (*Secondary School technology teacher*): I remember one meeting in particular that really left an impression on me. It was in the band room. I could see Mrs. Lindsey up there, Tony Ramos, Sandy Behenna, the whole lineup.

It was clear that the school administration didn't know what she wanted. She was saying one thing and they were saying another. I mean, it just became so clear that the right hand didn't know what the left hand was doing. There was blame being shifted from one to the other. It was just really obvious that the thing was dysfunctional.

KATHY KUKEA: She was also out of touch with even her own demands on the curriculum project, and was answering questions in ways that conflicted with what the curriculum leader and I had been telling the teachers.

KĀWIKA EYRE: And she kept looking at Tony for verification.

KATHY KUKEA

"It was just nuts."

KATHY KUKEA: Right. She was pretending that all sorts of things had been under Tony's orders, when of course they had not been. They had been under her orders.

RENEE MARTIN: All the administrators were sitting in the front row, and I felt really bad for them. Whatever question came up from the faculty, she'd point her two fingers at them and say, "Blame your administrators."

KATHY KUKEA: It was just nuts. I thought the whole room was about to blow.

GARY OBRECHT: I must admit, to my shame, that Mrs. Lindsey's personal style offended me deeply.

I remember sitting there with my heart pounding so hard that I knew I needed to speak, but I was scared. Finally, I got up, spoke my mind about the demand, the dedication we had already demonstrated, my horror that the work was not deemed good enough, and so on.

I received thundering applause, and obviously from that day on I was perceived as a troublemaker. I had put myself forward as a potential enemy of our trustee.

RENEE MARTIN: I remember walking back up the stairs and crossing paths with Tony, and my heart went out to him, looking at me and shaking his head, thinking, *Whatcha gonna do?*

KATHY KUKEA: I went back to the Midkiff lounge, locked myself in and cried, just out of a sense of helplessness and sadness over where we were winding up.

CLEMI MCLAREN: It all turned into a huge thing about formatting. And even then, nothing was clear.

CHARLENE HOE: We as the Elementary faculty asked what format should the curriculum appear in. We were never given communication directly. We were never given communication in writing from our direct administration. We tried numerous times to clarify that.

I was eventually given verbal communication on the format the curriculum should take. That curriculum was transmitted to the trustee responsible. And we assumed it was accepted.

In July, I got a call from my principal that I needed to report back. I returned to campus to rewrite that curriculum in the format that was now being recommended for the K to 3rd grade level. And then returned again, on call, to write the 4th through 6th grade curriculum. And in a span of two weeks.

JIM SLAGEL: We got handouts on how to make bullets in the paragraph. Then we'd get a handout saying the bullets were out and numbers were in. Then it was back to bullets.

CHARLENE HOE: So maybe three or four different formats were passed by us to try to meet the requirements.

JIM SLAGEL: Retype this paper into different compartments.

RANDIE FONG: The whole project was so time consuming, and the guidelines to assemble this curriculum guide was communicated so inconsistently, and the guidelines were changed midstream, and it was just incredibly confusing, just tremendous amount of confusion and a lot of disruption.

JULIAN AKO: I can remember being really, really angry, having the curriculum team leader stand up there with a smile on her face, telling us how much we're gonna enjoy what we're about to do, and how wonderful all this was and stuff. And—I hate to say this—I was ready to rip that smile off her face.

KĀWIKA EYRE: This is typical Lokelani Lindsey—making us jump through hoops. We knew she would never be pleased.

JIM SLAGEL: It was easy to picture Lindsey sitting in her office with nothing to do, picking up the phone and calling us and saying something like, "I feel more like indentations and double spacing today."

KIM SLAGEL: Little things, like which words to use in which columns. Putting information in little boxes is weird, even for a math teacher. Teaching geometry, I used a discovery approach to define geometric terms and properties. I remember being told I couldn't use the word "discovery" because it wasn't measurable, so I had to lie about how I taught geometry.

KAHELE KUKEA: Constructivism, the idea you build on prior learning and that people, when they come to new learning, bring their past with them and what they get from it can have a different meaning from student to student. We couldn't use that word. Rockne said, "You can't use that word. Not in your talking, not in your letters, not in your curriculum."

RANDIE FONG: This is about the administrative tone and messages that accompany these directives.

    The messages were offensive—in its totality would be the staff feeling that they thought she thought they were stupid or incompetent.

KATHY KUKEA: To make those teachers work that kind of a schedule for such an arbitrary purpose was, to me, a really unethical thing to do.

    That's when things began looking not just bullyish but absurd.

    And I think a lot of us went from not just feeling angry and pushed around to being frightened of where things were going—not personally frightened, but, oh my goodness, this is really going to go off track now.

LOKELANI LINDSEY: They felt they were overloaded at the time. Had I known that these people had other deadlines along the way that were school-imposed deadlines, I don't think they would have had the deadlines they had from us.

CLEMI MCLAREN: Had she known? How could she not have known? She was a micromanager to the max. She had her informers on campus reporting to her every day. How could she not have known?

KATHY KUKEA: I think when I really knew, or really felt, that we were going to wind up having to take a stance somewhere along the line was when Mrs. Lindsey required the Elementary teachers to come in and completely revise the whole curriculum according to this new format in one week's time, and required them to work around the clock, a 24-hour period, to complete it by an arbitrary deadline of 8 a.m. on a Monday morning—when there's nobody to receive the curriculum. There was nobody there.

JIM SLAGEL: At best, it was a $200,000 waste of time. At worst, it was some moron with no concept of what we were doing imposing her ignorant will on us.

KIM AND JIM SLAGEL
Slagels chaperoning the
Senior Prom 1996

JANET ZISK
"I don't save crap."

KĀWIKA EYRE: And what came of it all? Nothing.

ROCKNE FREITAS: We got caught up with some other issues on campus that kind of raised it out of control, and I took my thumb off of the button on that one.

KIM SLAGEL: I don't think anyone ever looked at the completed work after it was distributed. The binder was so big and heavy my department head used it to hold his office door open.

JIM SLAGEL: It became the stuff of lore—Loke's Doorstops. Teachers still talk about them today.

JANET ZISK: I remember a very thick wad of paper in a very wide-ringed vinyl binder.

I asked Kathy Kukea if I should save it or what, as I was not clear about its history. Kathy firmly suggested that I ditch it, as it was never going to be used. It had been cobbled together by faculty totally worn down by the ill-considered, frustrating, threatening micromanagement of Lokelani Lindsey.

I said to myself, *I know people wonder from time to time why I save the seemingly useless things that I do. However, I don't save crap.* So into the garbage it went. ⌒

Pōwāwae, Football (sic)
Hawaiian Language Stifled

9

She said, "Pōwāwae, football, pōhīnaʻi, basketball, you know, pō means darkness, and darkness is not good."
–Hailama Farden

KĒHAU ABAD: Loke showed up unannounced to my classroom twice. Hawaiian culture once, and Hawaiian history. She came in with a friend of hers, walked to the back of the room, sat down. I acknowledged her presence, you know, welcomed her, explained to her where we were.

We were in the middle of the Territorial period, talking about issues of racism, going over quotes from different people that illustrated this. I said to her, "The students are involved in a discussion, and at any point, please join in if you care to." And out of a clear blue sky she made her announcement, "I'll have you know that I have my master's degree in this."

My students were looking at me like, "What is this?" You know, it was clearly intended to intimidate all of us.

KEIKI KAWAIʻAEʻA: I remember the Hula Pākahi, the hula competition they have on Maui. She was the emcee that year. I was asked to be the language judge for that. And she pulled me to the side and she said, "You know, I have been with some of the best in Hawaiian culture. I was a student of Auntie Edith Kanakaʻole. And I danced hula for many years."

KALEI ʻAʻARONA-LORENZO (*'85, Secondary School Hawaiian language teacher*): She would reference the names. You know, I've learned from this kumu and this kumu. So you're claiming that this is my kumu,

"You know, I have been with some of the best in Hawaiian culture."
–Lokelani Lindsey

and whatever I have, I have that person in me. And that wasn't necessarily what was going on.

DAVID KAUPU (*'51, Schools kahu*): In a letter that I had sent to her, I concluded, as I always do, you know, "Me kealoha," and I lumped "kealoha" together. She is not a Hawaiian speaker, but she grew up in the school of thought that "ke" is an article and should be separated from the root word. In her case, this is the way she wants it done for herself. And so I just remind her, "You know, Mrs. Lindsey, I grew up saying these words and writing these words together, and I'm going to continue to do this. The important thing for me is that the message is communicated."

She never talked to me anymore about that.

DAVID KAUPU
"I lumped
'kealoha' together."

KĀWIKA EYRE: So now here comes Loke making decisions about Hawaiian at Kamehameha. Telling us how she's going to have it taught.

NONA BEAMER: My hānai son, Kaliko Beamer Trapp, teaching at UH Hilo, had received word of a communication from Lokelani: "If it wasn't spoken during Pauahi's time, it would not be spoken at Kamehameha Schools."

KĀWIKA EYRE: We had to freeze the language as of Pauahi's time. At least that was what she seemed to be saying.

EMALIA KEOHOKĀLOLE: There is this controversy in the Hawaiian community for a long time about traditional words versus new words.

KĀWIKA EYRE: Okay, all people in all countries discuss and even strongly disagree at times about what is going on in their languages. Look at the Academie Française, or any of the other national bodies entrusted with caring for their language.

This is no less true of Hawaiian, which has had such a painful recent history and is facing huge challenges. Kamehameha was one of the first schools to ban Hawaiian. Just about right from the start in 1887. Not good! As late as the 1940s, people were being kicked out of Kamehameha for speaking Hawaiian.

So there's a bitter history behind all this, and we feel a lot of passion. These are really matters of life and death for a culture. One of the first proverbs we teach our students is, "I ka ʻōlelo nō ke ola, i ka ʻōlelo nō ka make—in language there is life, in language there is death."

ROCKNE FREITAS: Essentially, Trustee Lindsey felt that we were getting away from the traditional language and going off in a direction that eventually, if we stayed on that path, we would lose our roots and our anchors in that most important part of the culture.

LARRY KIMURA (*'64, assistant professor of Hawaiian language, UH-Hilo*): We have this tremendous gap between the last native speakers.

RANDIE FONG: There seemed to be this category called "traditional Hawaiian" that didn't consider the fact that cultures evolve and change. Traditional Hawaiian—what does that refer to? We're talking about some 2,000 years of evolution of the language. Exactly what centuries are we talking about?

You know, we look at the Hawaiian Bible, we're seeing Hawaiianized Hebrew and Hawaiianized Greek. When we look at the volumes of Hawaiian newspapers that were published in the nineteenth century, we're talking about foreign concepts being indigenized, being Hawaiianized, and that was because Hawaiian people were trying to keep up with the rest of the world. And so this is a reflection of a living culture.

I shared with Mrs. Lindsey that I thought it was problematic that anyone would take language and try to pickle it and prevent it from growing. That negates the entire Bible? That means your name, Lokelani, is invalid?

LARRY KIMURA
"We have this tremendous
gap...."

EKELA KANIAUPIO-CROZIER (*Secondary Hawaiian language teacher*): Language can only live if allowed to live in the century we live in.

MELELANI PANG: You need to have the words that are created so that 'ōlelo Hawai'i, the Hawaiian language, can survive in the now. So that the students can use these words that reflect where they are living. In the now. Language cannot stay stagnant. We know what happens when languages stay stagnant. They die.

It's like Pele! You create new land; you create new words so that there is life! That language is still living. Still molding. Still changing.

Mele Pang and Ekela
Kaniaupio-Crozier at
Christmas festival
mid-1990s

"It's like Pele! You create new land; you create new words so that there is life! That language is still living. Still molding. Still changing."

–Mele Pang

JENNIFER NOELANI GOODYEAR-KA'ŌPUA (left, valedictorian speaker 1992, with classmate Jondi Anderson)

LILINOE KA'AHANUI (*'82, Secondary School Hawaiian language teacher*): The early 1990s were exciting times for Hawaiian at Kamehameha! Lots of life in our 'ōlelo. Enrollments were climbing year after year. We reached almost a thousand students, grades 7-12. All those young Hawaiians learning their language!

JENNIFER NOELANI GOODYEAR-KA'ŌPUA (*'92, Valedictory address*): Aloha mai kākou e nā po'e o ko Kamehameha 'ohana! I kēia ahiahi, ke ho'olaule'a nei kākou i ka puka 'ana o nā haumāna o ka papa 'umikūmāiwa kanaiwakūmālua mai ke kula ki'eki'e 'o Kamehameha.

Before I go any further, I would like to ask all of you, members of the audience, guests and seniors included, a couple of questions. I would appreciate it if you could respond to these questions by simply raising your hand.

First of all, I know this may seem like a strange question, but— how many of you are Hawaiian?

All right, now will you please raise your hand once again if you understood or think you understood what I just said in Hawaiian a few minutes ago? Please keep your hands raised.

Thank you. This, ladies and gentlemen, is one of the most important reasons why I am proud to be a part of the Kamehameha class of 1992. Just a few years ago, the number of students that would have raised their hands in response to that second question would have been considerably less. Today, many more students are able to speak and understand the Hawaiian language, and yet it is more than just their ability that makes me proud.

I see a group of bright young Hawaiian men and women who have begun to realize the importance of keeping our culture and our heritage alive, *and* they have acted on it. I see a group of people who truly have a connection with two very different and distinct cultures—the Hawaiian and the Western. Taught and socialized in the Western system, but at the same time possessing an inborn appreciation and desire for what is Hawaiian, we are able to keep our feet in two different worlds. This is where our advantage lies.

These are exciting times to be Hawaiian. Next year will mark the 100th anniversary of the illegal overthrow of the Hawaiian monarchy. Hawaiian sovereignty is gaining support both inside and outside the Hawaiian community. The Hawaiian people are uniting and organizing in ways like never before. And yet there is still a long road for our people.

However, I know that you have the potential to lead our people to great things. You know what it takes to get ahead in the Western world, and yet you know in your hearts what it means to be Hawaiian. You are the most qualified people, and I have faith that you will become the leaders of a generation of Hawaiians that is ready to reclaim its dignity and self-determination.

E ola mau ka ʻōlelo, ke aloha, a me ka ʻuhane o ka poʻe Hawaiʻi—Let the Hawaiian language, aloha and the spirit of the Hawaiian people live.

Mahalo nō iā ʻoukou. Thanks to all of you

◈ ◈ ◈

MELELANI PANG: We were creating our own curriculum during the summers to keep up with the huge needs. We wanted a really strong, teen-friendly program.

And of course we leaned on whatever resources were out there from the DOE, the immersion program, videos, books—wherever we could pull. That brought in the new vocabulary, *Māmaka Kaiao*, and the new grammar system called pepeke, which had been developed at UH-Hilo.

I would say at the time in at least 50 percent of my teaching, maybe a little bit higher, I used the pepeke. It gave kind of a standard that the students were comfortable with. I think we produce some pretty damn good haumāna, students.

LILINOE KAʻAHANUI: Yeah! Most of the Hawaiian teachers in the state are our graduates.

MELELANI PANG: And then that edict came down from Lokelani, "No, you will not use *Māmaka Kaiao*. And you will not use pepeke system."

KĀWIKA EYRE: So where was this coming from with Lokelani? Out of her own head? We started hearing about a committee she had.

HANA PAU (*Secondary School Hawaiian language teacher*): We went to a meeting and Loke made a remark like, "Oh, I have some people that speak the language who will review the Hawaiian language books, because some of you are still young, you know."

Wow! I was really angry! We have Hawaiian language teachers here that know the language. Why does she have her own group to check my work? Why does she get somebody from outside? I don't

HANA PAU

"If she's going to get somebody to look at my work, why did they hire me?"

"ʻAloha mai kākou e nā poʻe o ko Kamehameha ʻohana! I kēia ahiahi, ke hoʻolauleʻa nei kākou i ka puka ʻana o nā haumāna o ka papa ʻumikūmāiwa kanaiwakūmālua mai ke kula kiʻekiʻe ʻo Kamehameha."

–Jennifer Noelani Goodyear-Kaʻōpua

agree with that. If she's going to get somebody to look at my work, why did they hire me?

KEIKI KAWAI'AE'A: She's not a hūpō nani, not a dumb beauty, if I can put it that way. She knows that she's got to have her pawns in place to keep her status in a certain place. You have questions; you have people to lean on. You make sure you have your committee to kind of help you.

KĀWIKA EYRE: And there were no Kamehameha teachers on her committee.

MIKE CHUN: The sense I got was that the Hawaiian language policy came from Loke because of Kalani Meinecke, who teaches Hawaiian at Windward Community College, and her secretary, Emalia Keohokālole, as part of that group. Loke was taking Hawaiian language in her office once a week. They would come and get together and she was learning the language. It became a friendship.

RANDIE FONG: But they're kind of hidden; they're kind of secret.

KĀWIKA EYRE: What we were asking for from Mrs. Lindsey was a thoughtful, open, intelligent discussion. A normal give and take of ideas. Instead she would go back to her mysterious committee and close the door. We weren't allowed in that room. What we got instead were messengers bringing edicts from on high. Nothing was ever put in writing.

EKELA KANIAUPIO-CROZIER: We were told that this is the way it's going to be, and that the bottom line is there will be no discussion.

RANDIE FONG: We're talking about impacting a generation of people, you know, their native tongue.

EMALIA KEOHOKĀLOLE: I did mention to Loke that if our kids want to go on to the university or to teach at the immersion programs, they would need to pick up this new language. My mana'o to Loke was there's got to be a balance somewhere.

KĀWIKA EYRE: But she wouldn't have anything to do with immersion. It turned out that when she was on Maui, she clashed with the immersion people there, and now she was using the language to get back at them.

And on top of that there were contradictions. The language was supposed to be frozen as of Pauahi's time. But then we were told we had to use only words that were in the Pukui-Elbert dictionary. Well, that dictionary—which is invaluable—was first published in 1957, 70-some years after Pauahi died, and there was a revised edition in 1986, with 3,000 or so new words, including material from the UH-Hilo lexicon committee.

There were so many things that didn't make sense.

KEIKI KAWAI'AE'A: We had several conversations with teachers at Kamehameha. They were really going through stress.

Not being able to teach Hawaiian the way they felt Hawaiian should be taught. To be really micromanaged—those are words that I heard from the teachers—in terms of the curriculum that they were using. The choice of the text, even down to the vocabulary.

RANDIE FONG: It created so much heartache.

KĀWIKA EYRE: Our kids would say they had been approached by Loke at some event—totally out of the blue, say at a track meet—and she would ask them about the word their kumu was using in class for computer. If they said lolo uila, the new word, she would let them know how wrong that was.

KEIKI KAWAI'AE'A
"You make sure you have your committee...."

OZ STENDER: Hailama Farden explained to me what was happening in Hawaiian language. That was the first I heard of it. The issue of traditional Hawaiian never came to the full board. Mrs. Lindsey did that all on her own.

TONY RAMOS: Loke was the nemesis, if you will. I mean the oppressive interference with approving T-shirts, approving communications, Hawaiian language, pepeke and traditional language. The other guys were not interfering.

OZ STENDER: I have no problem with Lindsey having oversight of the school. But do it through the system. In other words, she can't go up there and say, "We've got to change the Hawaiian language, period," without discussing it with all of us.

Then when I brought it up, trustees said, "Well, that's her job." And I said, "That is wrong!"

KĀWIKA EYRE: So there are real differing views here, and this had been going on for a good two years. And during this time, all the orders from Lindsey were conveyed down the chain of command. Still nothing in writing.

Finally we got to meet with her face to face.

KE'ALA KWAN: Here's some background to that meeting. Questions pertaining to Hawaiian language had always been routed either directly through the Kamehameha Hawaiian Studies Institute or to Hawaiian language teachers on campus. Sarah Keahi, who had taught some 30 years in the High School, often got called.

"You are a kanaka. And you need to learn your 'ōlelo kanaka. It's important, especially nowadays."

–Sarah Keahi (with students Liko Hoe '92 and Kekai Olsen '93)

MELELANI PANG: Kumu Keahi. I call her Ma—out of total respect. Definitely my mentor. Definitely someone I look up to, as not only one who really grew the language within me and made me see the importance of it, but one who was really the guiding force in me becoming a kumu.

I still remember her words. "You are a kanaka. And you need to learn your 'ōlelo kanaka. It's important, especially nowadays."

KE'ALA KWAN: In March of 1995, a parent called for help. The parent's daughter, a member of the High School basketball team, was wanting a T-shirt design for the team that would include a Hawaiian word for basketball. Sarah suggested pōhīna'i, the standard term.

SARAH KEAHI (*Secondary School Hawaiian language teacher*): I got a call during one of my classes. It was Loke Lindsey. "Sarah, this is Loki!" Her voice was really hostile. She questioned why my initials were on the request for approval of the girls' T-shirt. She said she disagreed with the use of the Hawaiian word for basketball, and also told me she had a Hawaiian language committee that she consulted with. She was really upset.

I suggested a meeting with her and all Hawaiian language teachers to discuss these things. She agreed to meet.

KĀWIKA EYRE: So the meeting was arranged for April 5, 1995, in Sarah Keahi's classroom, Kōnia 104, the building named after Pauahi's mother.

KEʻALA KWAN: I recall Tony Ramos saying to me, "Mike Chun says"—these are the exact words—"don't fight her, 'cause you're gonna lose." That's one of those things like in the movies. I can still hear it clear: "Don't try to fight her, 'cause you're gonna lose."

HAILAMA FARDEN: An agenda was on the board. Keʻala wrote it—

KĀWIKA EYRE: —In his careful handwriting. He's our boss as head of the languages department. Also a Hawaiian language teacher. So he's the agenda guy.

And then we did the pule, the prayer. Kupuna Elizabeth Kauahipaula gave it, in Hawaiian.

KEʻALA KWAN
"Like in the movies...."

HAILAMA FARDEN: And Loke walked to the board—"Oh, I don't like agendas, I don't believe in agendas." And just erased it.

She sat on the table! And I was offended by it. It's a cultural thing, a breach of our protocol.

ELIZABETH KAUAHIPAULA (*kupuna for Secondary School Hawaiian language classes*): She stood and went on the board. She put all her grandparents' names on the board. She talked about her family, her parents. Her grandparents are Hawaiian.

LOKELANI LINDSEY: I have a great interest in genealogy. That is one of my hobbies since 1960.

HAILAMA FARDEN
"I was offended...."

HAILAMA FARDEN: It is Hawaiian to share your genealogy, when appropriate, because you show your connection.

KALEI ʻAʻARONA-LORENZO: And I remember thinking, *Do you even know who I am? Or do you know what family I come from? What makes your line more special than my line? Or any one else's in the room?*

MELELANI PANG: I got a sense of ho'okano, conceit.

KALEI 'A'ARONA-LORENZO: I just felt ill. I was hāpai, pregnant, but I know it had nothing to do with me being hāpai. You know when you get angry or you are challenged, when you know that something's not right. Someone is just like pushing you. For me, when somebody does that to me, my na'au, my gut, gets really sore. It had everything to do with the things that were being said in the meeting.

I was having a hard time. I didn't smile. I didn't say anything. She picked up on that, and that really upset her.

ELIZABETH KAUAHIPAULA: She just yelled at everybody.

KALEI 'A'ARONA-LORENZO: I literally felt that we were under attack—as Hawaiians, by other Hawaiians. And that whole sense of being put down again.

ELIZABETH KAUAHIPAULA: She yelled at Keahi and all that inside there.

LILINOE KA'AHANUI: We were thinking, *Gosh, what a slap in the face for Kumu Keahi,* who—before we all came on board—checked everything herself. All of the Song Contest things. All of the speeches. All of the graduation stuff. It was disrespectful, especially to Kumu Keahi.

She was disrespectful to Kupuna Kauahipaula, too. She didn't even acknowledge her. And then she put her on the spot.

HAILAMA FARDEN: She started in, "The word pēpē, baby—that's wrong! Kupuna, what's the correct word for baby?"

ELIZABETH KAUAHIPAULA: She came pointing to me—"How do you say baby in Hawaiian?" I got shocked when she came to me and talked to me like that, yeah. I say, "Well, the usual word is kamaiki." And then she started in—"Pēpē is not right!"

KUPUNA ELIZABETH
KAUAHIPAULA

Then afterwards, I told Keahi them, I said, "The dictionary has the word pēpē in there; they don't have kamaiki inside there, or baby right next to pēpē. Why can't she look in there before she talks like that? It's in the dictionary! Why did she do that for?" She was very rude, very rude.

And I felt so bad and when she came point to me like that, like *HOW* do you—? With the tone of voice, just like she was all angry already from outside coming in, you know. The yelling and all that. That's uncalled for, not necessary.

ROBIN MAKUA: It was painful to watch how our kupuna, who we should respect because of her knowledge, because of her wisdom, because of her life experience, had to be subject to this woman who couldn't come close to what Kupuna Kauahipaula had.

HAILAMA FARDEN: And then she kept talking about pō—night, dark. She said, "What's the matter with this in sports? Pōwāwae, football—which is wrong—pōhīna'i, basketball, you know, pō means darkness, and darkness is not good."

LILINOE KA'AHANUI: She said that pōpa'ilima, volleyball, could be translated as "a slap in the night" or "slap the night." It was obvious to me that someone had put all that in her ear. She said there were dark connotations with the word pō, and if the volleyball team had a losing streak, the reason would be that they had that word on their T-shirts.

KALEI 'A'ARONA-LORENZO: And I thought to myself, *Gee, that's only one side of pō. There were a lot of good things that were born in pō!* And Kumulipo.

HAILAMA FARDEN: In my mind I was saying, *Well, from darkness comes everything in our traditions.*

And then I said, "Well, what about pōmaika'i—blessed, blessing?" I did not realize that I may have been impudent or whatever. I was just asking an honest question. She was saying, pō this, pō that—so what about pōmaika'i?

KE'ALA KWAN: There were some other disturbing things.

HAILAMA FARDEN: Lokelani somehow slipped a threat in there that if this thing can't be corrected, then the trustees will make the decision.

KĀWIKA EYRE: This was the first time after two years that we were

ROBIN MAKUA
"Painful to watch...."

really face to face with her. It was pretty shocking. I remember trying to tell her that the strength of our program was the collaboration, the consensus and the closeness to our students that lay at the heart of what we were doing. I told her that we would welcome working with her committee folks—

KE'ALA KWAN: —Trying to have a voice for our teachers on that group that she had. I don't know if she flat-out said, "No, no." I think she said we're too busy as teachers, so we don't want to bother with that.

KĀWIKA EYRE: You could tell by her body language that we weren't welcome.

KALEI 'A'ARONA-LORENZO: The funny thing is that she did it all with a smile. That's why it was so degrading. And I thought, *Do you even know what you did just now? To us?*

EKELA KANIAUPIO-CROZIER: It's this questioning of my ability and my choice as a professional to do what I know is right. That lack of trust really hurt. To be told by someone else what you're going to do in your classroom. That's not right.

It's a lack of trust. No one can work in that kind of environment.

ROCKNE FREITAS: Okay, I called Tony Ramos. I said, "Hey, fill me in on what's happening in the Hawaiian language." I encouraged him to get involved, because he's a hands-on guy.

In the discussion we had, we went back and forth. My understanding was that the problem was how you form new words. Tony's opinion of the situation was that we can't make new words. So I told him, "No, that's not what my understanding is." He said, no, that's exactly what his understanding was.

I said, "Look, we're going to modify what your understanding is to what my understanding is. And if anything happens, you just say Rocky did that. Get hold of Ke'ala Kwan. Just tell Ke'ala, to the best of their abilities, figure out how Kawena Pukui would have made new words. Just go do it the way she would have done it."

I relied on Tony to work it out. It didn't get worked out.

KĀWIKA EYRE: I was in Tony Ramos' office. Tony was making Loke's point that it was the previous board under Pinky Thompson that came up with Hawaiian language policy. So I called Pinky right then and there. I asked him if they had had any discussions as to the use of so-called traditional Hawaiian. Pinky was absolutely firm and clear on the fact that they had never talked about it.

SARAH KEAHI: I said to Tony one time, "You know, you did not stand up for us! You look across the state—most of the people involved in the Hawaiian language are Kamehameha graduates. You should have said to Mrs. Lindsey, 'I stand by my staff. I stand by my staff. I'm sorry, we cannot do this.'"

TONY RAMOS: Remember, I'm pretty much on the receiving end of all this stuff, and not having access to question why. All the administrators were caught in this crossfire with Lokelani.

SANDY BEHENNA: Tony would go in and argue the Hawaiian language policy with Loke. Did he win those arguments? No, he didn't. He was told he had to report back that this is the way it was.

MIKE CHUN: More often than not I was not aware of those meetings. She would call a meeting either directly through her office or through Rock. I didn't know.

In the boardroom, we talked about Loke's involvement in the curriculum, with the Hawaiian language curriculum. I said, "We got unhappy people here." So for Dickie Wong to say that I never communicated that things were not right here and that there was a lot of disenchantment in the morale—in my mind I was being very clear in my communication that, you know, we have some problems up here.

KĀWIKA EYRE: Tony told me later that he had tried to make the case with Lindsey, and that she had yelled at him and threatened him with gross insubordination if he brought up the issue again.

HAILAMA FARDEN: I went to Hilo for the annual native speaker convention to get thoughts from those kūpuna: Are new words such a big deal?

And I remember taking a copy of *Māmaka Kaiao* to Hilo, and we brought up the discussion about the use of new words. I think Larry Kimura brought it up as a panelist. Auntie Mālia Craver grabbed a *Māmaka Kaiao*, stood up, and said—I remember this word she used—hoʻokikina, implore. "Ke hoʻokikina aku nei au iā ʻoukou. I implore you to embrace this book!" This is Auntie Mālia Craver saying that we need to move forward. We need to embrace new words.

I talked to Pila Wilson and we drafted up a petition. To make it very clear—some of these kūpuna are not as strong as others—we wrote it in English and Hawaiian. And we said those who agree with this can sign it.

There was debate on the issue. This is the first time I've witnessed a debate in Hawaiian. Auntie Mālia Craver finally said, "Those of you who agree with me, stand up!" There were about 60 kūpuna. And every person in that room stood up.

ʻAHA MĀNALEO II (*Convention of Native Speakers*): "It is imperative that this precious language of ours continue into the present ... for the benefit of the present time as well as the future, and we therefore support the principle that this beloved language of ours be provided with new words."

"Ke hoʻokikina aku nei au iā ʻoukou!"

–Mālia Craver

KĀWIKA EYRE: Tony Ramos finally made it official on the Lindsey policy. That was just after school started again in late August 1996. He met with the Hawaiian language teachers. I don't even remember if we started with a pule like we usually do. He was sitting there and he began the meeting by shrugging his shoulders, throwing up his hands.

LILINOE KA'AHANUI: Yeah, he threw up his hands and said, "Don't blame me, I'm just the messenger!"

KĀWIKA EYRE: He told us that no material would be allowed from the immersion programs. Nothing from the dictionary of newly coined words, *Māmaka Kaiao*. And, for sure, not the pepeke grammar model that had been in use statewide for some 20 years. That was it. And nothing in writing.

EMALIA KEOHOKĀLOLE: My recollection is that Loke said there was a directive to teach traditional Hawaiian language at the Schools. Not that she sent one, but she said there was a directive.

I could not find anything in our files relative to Hawaiian language, to see if there were any notes or anything I might have put away in there, but there wasn't. There was none.

MELELANI PANG: I think, initially hearing the policy—well, there was the shock, where did all this come from, without even consulting those who are in the trenches day in and day out?

KALEI 'A'ARONA-LORENZO: I remember the meeting being very hostile. Those were ugly days! They were really ugly days. I mean, speaking about broken trust. That's when I think the trust really broke for us. With Tony. And it was really hard to get that trust back. Because of him being "I'm only the messenger."

LILINOE KA'AHANUI: He was supposed to be standing up for us. I think I mentioned in one of Tony's meetings that po'o kumu, principal, means that you are the head teacher. You need to be ahead of us. You need to be in front of us, blocking, taking the hits from the powers that be. Support us in whatever we think is best for our kids. That's who we represent.

KĀWIKA EYRE: Now, after being assaulted by months of absurdities, here comes Lindsey in the *Advertiser* saying that all the Hawaiian language teachers were incompetent. Insult added to injury.

We were now pretty much in open defiance of the Lindsey mandate.

KALEI ʻAʻARONA-LORENZO: I'm a silent kūʻē person. Did I follow the directive? No. So did my kids suffer? No. Because we never followed it. And had we followed it, I think they would have suffered.

MELELANI PANG: I just kept going, 'cause I knew we couldn't put our haumāna at a disadvantage. And so I knew I had to hoʻomau, continue. I knew that all the other kumu felt the same that no way this is going to happen.

KALEI ʻAʻARONA-LORENZO
"Go ahead, fire me! "

KALEI ʻAʻARONA-LORENZO: The whole time I remember thinking, *If you want to fire me, go ahead and fire me! But I'm not going to jump on your bandwagon, because I don't believe in what you are doing. It's not right for our school. It's not right for our haumāna.*

KĀWIKA EYRE: On September 4, 1996, we wrote what was kind of our final memo on all this.

We felt we had to put on record what most concerned us about the situation and how disruptive, even destructive, it was going to be to our program, a program that had experienced tremendous revitalization.

We requested a written explanation of "Traditional Hawaiian." We asked whether input was sought from staff when the policy was developed. And we wanted clarification of the rationale for the policy.

We sent that memo up the chain of command. Never got a written response.

KEʻALA KWAN: Tony Ramos spoke to me, saying that the policy would not be available in written form, and that the trustees had decided there would be no further communication with Hawaiian language teachers regarding the policy. He got that from Rockne Freitas.

KĀWIKA EYRE: So did the mandate from nowhere damage our program? In 1996 when the mandate was announced, more than 900 students were enrolled in Hawaiian classes—a good half of the High School population. A majority of graduates were leaving Kamehameha with at least two years of focused study in the language. Large numbers of our most talented graduates were committing themselves to careers in support of Hawaiian cultural revitalization. By now, the majority of teachers in the statewide immersion and public school programs were Kamehameha graduates.

For a school that had once penalized Hawaiians for using their native tongue and even expelled them for repeat violations, this was a pretty significant turnaround.

But in two years of this language war, the summer immersion classes were cancelled, and enrollments in Hawaiian language at Kamehameha were down 25 percent. That's serious, measurable damage.

HENRY BENNETT: All of the Hawaiian language books which Kamehameha Press was producing at that time were, on Mrs. Lindsey's orders, to be sent to Kalani Meinecke for review and to be published only if it passed with his approval.

I found that he was unreachable by phone or chose to be unreachable by me. He failed to return phone calls, and the materials sent to him would either not be returned or not be returned until repeated requests had been made through Trustee Lindsey.

The Hawaiian language course we wanted to put out ground to a halt because of Mrs. Lindsey's mandate.

LILINOE KAʻAHANUI: The other thing that happened is that our summer curriculum work stopped being funded. This after about six years of paid support.

MELELANI PANG: I don't think a lot of people knew this, but I actually, when a position was made available in the paper for a part-time kumu ʻōlelo Hawaiʻi at Punahou, I went through the whole interview process. And I was seriously thinking about that position.

ROBIN MAKUA: I was ready to walk away. I had called Punahou School for an application for employment, and I did call Dr. Chun.

KĀWIKA EYRE: We lost two teachers, Ekela Kaniaupio-Crozier and Hana Pau. Both felt they had to leave because of what we were going through.

"Summer immersion classes were cancelled."

–Kāwika Eyre

KE'ALA KWAN: I remember Ekela crying at our department meeting at Kōnia. It was a long meeting and we got heart talk coming out.

KĀWIKA EYRE: They were not the only good teachers who left Kamehameha. Three Elementary teachers went to Punahou.

HANA PAU: You know, I read about it, and I felt real bad that I left. You know what I mean? I felt like I kind of deserted you folks. Because at that time, we're family, you know. We're supposed to stick together. We had to. And I felt so guilty when I left because, Oh, look at me! I going home and they're still there. They still have to deal with it. I'm safe at home now.

KĀWIKA EYRE: And things got dirtier. Kupuna Elizabeth Kauahipaula was not rehired that fall semester. Before she came to Kamehameha, she had worked for years in the Waiau Elementary Immersion School and was well known in the community as an advocate for the immersion approach to Hawaiian revitalization. Lindsey retaliation? Who knows!

SANDY BEHENNA: I was told that Mrs. Lindsey did not approve it.

KĀWIKA EYRE: From the teachers' perspective, the administrators, from Assistant Principal Sandy Behenna up the chain through Tony Ramos, Rockne Freitas and Lokelani Lindsey, were now discredited. It was about leadership, and administrators simply pulled rank on us. If schools and their classrooms are not about democracy, they are for nought.

So it got to the point where we just said to our administrators that we would not follow the so-called Lindsey doctrine. We would kū'ē—disobey.

We put it in writing—one sentence—and sent it up the chain of command: "With the interests of our students and the integrity of our discipline at the forefront, we unanimously vote not to honor the verbal mandate."

MIKE CHUN: Yeah. Yeah. I think you were right in doing that. That was the right thing to do.

KĀWIKA EYRE: So I guess we were guilty of gross insubordination. Lindsey's favorite crime. But we called it kū'ē pono—the thought in English would be civil disobedience.

And of course we never got an answer back.

HENRY BENNETT: It was the Hawaiian language teachers who first stepped forward and went public and put their professional careers on the line by saying, "We cannot teach under these restrictions—for the good of the students." They were faced with an actual ethical dilemma. And they simply stood up and said, "No, we won't do it."

LILINOE KA'AHANUI: I think that's when we really came together as kumu. After that hālāwai, that meeting, we knew that that was it. That we needed to stick together. And I remember us saying, "We have to do what we have to do."

KĀWIKA EYRE: This was the moment it turned for me. I said to myself, *This is crazy. There's no working with our administration.* Sure, we had to keep going. Sure, we had to honor our personal commitments to teach our students. But our job now was—we had to get rid of those trustees.

"With the interests of our students at the forefront...."
–Kāwika Eyre

MELELANI PANG: Very much reminds me of one of those mo'olelo, those stories, of the ali'i of Ka'ū who were overthrown and destroyed and killed by their own people because of how ho'okano they were. A eia nō ka hopena! And that's what happened! ✍

10 Shock Waves
Randie Fong Confronts Lokelani Lindsey

It sent shock waves through the campus. —Charlene Hoe

RANDIE FONG: It seemed like there was this degeneration from even 1994 all the way to 1997. Within that three-year period, I cannot even think of the words to describe the condition of the Schools with regard to our institutional esteem. It just plummeted.

ELISA YADAO: We did a study at Kawaiahaʻo Plaza. We had an outside consultant come in and run focus groups. People were very unhappy. Getting close to anarchy because people were so upset. They loved the Schools and hated the trustees. And I think Mrs. Lindsey may have held that for a while. It took a long time before we could get it to the other trustees. We kept trying to get on the calendar, but it kept getting pushed back and pushed back and pushed back.

LOKELANI LINDSEY: I don't recall exactly what it said. I believe I saw it. I just can't remember what was in it.

OZ STENDER: Oh, Lokelani would say, "It's really nothing to it. I mean, a few people unhappy. But don't worry about it." And Dickie Wong told me that one day. I was complaining one day, and he says, "Ozzie, believe me—I deal with these things all the time. It'll go away. They'll get tired of it."

BOB WHITING: It was kind of a "hold your breath" idea of accepting authority. That is, if something comes along that you don't like, if you hold your breath long enough or maintain your course long enough, then those people will leave.

JIM SLAGEL: The only trouble with that was, Lokelani Lindsey was appointed trustee till age 70, which meant she would be around till 2008. A long time to have to hold your breath without screaming.

KĀWIKA EYRE: Ideally, a teacher's first calling is to the students. This is the uplifting stuff—which in a very real sense includes the daily needs of tending to eight periods of very demanding teenagers. School communities are places of relentlessly hard work when you are dealing with 100-120 teenagers, their parents, their crises, their educations, their everything. The daily bombardment is your all-consuming focus.

The point I'm trying to get at is there is not much time and energy for rebellion.

BOB WHITING: If I were Hawaiian in Hawai'i at a time when Kamehameha was really not paying that much attention to Hawaiianness and needed to pay a lot more, what Randie Fong was doing was good, making people more and more aware of what the community was all about.

There were several Song Contests of his that were pretty strongly for Hawaiian causes.

LIZ HANSEN: I think Randie is talented, bright, a musician, teacher, department head. He's very gifted, and he sees the whole picture.

RANDIE FONG

BOB WHITING: Without Randie, without his intellectual and, actually, physical energy, I don't think that Song Contest would have ever gotten to be as good as it was, because he had spectacular, spectacular events.

LIZ HANSEN: He wants it as an educational experience.

ELISA YADAO: Beyond that, my understanding of why he commands so much respect both in the community and in the Kamehameha family is because he is really looked upon as one of the cultural, spiritual leaders of that campus and that organization.

LIZ HANSEN: I know Lokelani wanted to get involved in performing arts, and that was something that Randie just would not have.

I think she wanted him as part of her inner circle, and he just didn't take the bait, because he had more integrity than that, and he didn't believe and support things that she was doing. And Randie's bright.

Randie had a lot of influence—a lot of people love and respect him. In Mrs. Lindsey's eyes, I think she felt threatened. I think if someone else was respected and loved more than her, she felt threatened by that.

ELISA YADAO: Song Contest was, like, a million things. We had to get the students' script, and then it was who's going to sit where, who's going to be an usher, who's going to have what kind of lei—I mean, all these things that needed to go to Loke for approval that many times.

LIZ HANSEN: Kūlana, the proper order of where the trustees should be seated. Mrs. Lindsey did say that they wanted the trustees to sit where they could be seen, maximum exposure, where it was most prominent. Instead of sitting up in the loges during Song Contest, would it be better for them to be on the floor?

BOB WHITING: What the placement of trustees ought to be with relation to other trustees, with relation to the staff, senior staff, minor staff. We'd go through that for hours—

LIZ HANSEN: —How many spaces are they going to have for their guests, that seats should be saved for them all the time, and parking should be saved for them all the time, because we had to assume that they were going to attend and we had to leave those seats open whether they attended or not.

OZ STENDER: And then what to wear.

RANDIE FONG: Mrs. Lindsey would leave messages on my phone, saying, "Run it by Wayne Chang and Marlene Sai." And to me, that's a little curious, because I was involved in the coordination for some 10, 12 years, and I usually go to my own supervisors for approval, Sandy Behenna and/or Tony Ramos. Marlene and Wayne are not even involved in the Secondary School.

TONI LEE: I was fired as a volunteer usher in 1997. I had been a volunteer for 30-some-odd years. I got a letter that said that my services were no longer needed. Signed by Marlene.

LIZ HANSEN: We needed to get the kids learning the songs. For music assistants, we try to hire some past student song directors, because of their experience, their musical knowledge. They're young, they can relate to the students, the students relate to them. They're a tremendous asset.

BOB WHITING: I needed to hire these people right away. I would take requests to Rockne Freitas for Song Contest help that had been pretty much processed by Personnel and everybody else and needed Mrs. Lindsey's signature, since she was the education person. He would put them in his briefcase, and they'd either get lost or misplaced somehow in the shuffle. But from the time he got it until whenever, they'd cause a problem, mostly because they would be delayed, lost, that kind of thing. We couldn't do anything.

LIZ HANSEN: And then they were all "unhired."

One of them, they put him through the wringer, why was he being hired, going on and on. I know for a fact that he was very close to Dr. and Mrs. Chun. And the thinking was that Mrs. Lindsey didn't want him, she didn't want him on campus, and we had to tell him to leave, they couldn't be on campus, they weren't hired.

Dr. Whiting had to justify and justify, write these long memos to Rockne. There had to be justification after justification after justification.

BOB WHITING
AND LIZ HANSEN

BOB WHITING: I wrote all those memos that supported all those guys. We're hiring these people for their skills, not for whatever problems they might have.

Finally, I went down and talked with Rockne. I said, "We have to have these people on board, and we don't have the authorization to hire them. I'm going to hire them. I've got to do it. If we don't do it, we don't have anybody to help us with Song Contest rehearsals. We run a rehearsal for the entire school, and we need to have teachers for all these 1,800 kids." And he said, "Well, do it." So he supported me on that, but nothing on paper.

LIZ HANSEN: They were all re-hired except that one.

BOB WHITING: But God, the mess. It took hours, days, to get that thing done, and people were very, very upset.

LIZ HANSEN: This group that was going to accompany the students was Dennis Kamakahi and his son, David. And Mrs. Lindsey wanted to know why a current student was going to be there on stage, and she didn't think it was a good idea—it singles the boy out for attention.

Randie went to bat, and said this is the perfect example of generations, the continuation of the music through family.

BOB WHITING: Lindsey gave in on that one.

LIZ HANSEN: One program cover had been prepared, and up until three days before Song Contest, that program cover was still a Go. In fact, I think Service Printers was already printing it, and we heard they were asked to stop, that there was going to be a new cover. Mrs. Lindsey didn't like the cover. She wants a different cover.

There was a CD done by Marlene Sai, and the program cover came from the CD insert. Mrs. Lindsey says, "I don't like the CD cover. We need to feature our students." Well, we featured students from the past.

Two photos were changed. One was of a former student who was active in immersion.

All the old covers had to be thrown out. I'm sure it cost us quite a bit of money.

Mrs. Lindsey said, her instructions were, from now on, every program will have Pauahi's picture on it.

BOB WHITING: There were some pretty exotic leis that were done.

But then, Mrs. Lindsey also was concerned about not having a lot—the budget was too high on flowers, let's cut out the flower budget, and only give it to those people who are important in the eyes of the trustees.

Mike used to have this wonderful little party at Neil Blaisdell Center for people he felt were important to the school. Well, it wasn't long after Lokelani came that that party became trustee-sponsored. Mike had nothing to do with it.

LIZ HANSEN: The presentation of awards. From the notes I have, in '97, the New England Mothers' Cup was going to be Trustee Oswald Stender. Then a few days before the program was due, I received a memo that it was going to be Mrs. Lindsey.

LIZ HANSEN: The day before the actual production, we go down to Blaisdell for a rehearsal of all our participants, all our students. We go through the program, to pace the students, to let our speakers know when their turn is, to cue them and so forth.

Kamani Kualāʻau was the student body president. He went up, and his speech was welcoming the audience, the live as well as the home audience, to Song Contest, and also he introduces the administrators, the trustees, as well as any special guests. They're not there for rehearsal, but he names them.

I think he started with Trustee Wong, Trustee Stender, and after he said the name Lokelani Lindsey, there was a very distinctive booing among the students.

JULIAN AKO: I was shocked. I've never witnessed that kind of disrespect to a trustee or the name of a trustee in my previous years of Kamehameha. And I thought, *Something's really not right here.*

LIZ HANSEN: It just seemed like it triggered something in the students, and their response was simultaneous with her name, and it was a shock. I knew the students had heard about the controversy and the problems, and I think some of it was because of the concerns that they had for Dr. Chun, and word gets out of how he was being treated by trustees and Mrs. Lindsey, and that it was now Mrs. Lindsey's turf. I think because there's such high regard for Dr. Chun, and they viewed Mrs. Lindsey as the one taking over. I think this was just a spontaneous reaction. From the classes as a whole.

KELLI KEAHIAHI LEE: I think it was kind of like one of those moments where everybody's thinking on the same page; I don't know where it started. It was probably—most likely it was the seniors. Because they're probably more aware of what was going on.

LIZ HANSEN: How do you handle that? I mean, this was something new. Nobody had—we never even expected this to happen. It was really unexpected behavior, that they as a body really had this strong reaction to Mrs. Lindsey and then also another loving reaction to Dr. Chun's name.

LOKELANI LINDSEY: I worked with students for over 30 years in my career. Usually, something or somebody motivates them to do this. It isn't a natural occurrence. And it never happened before.

KAMANI KUALĀ'AU: I didn't orchestrate that!—even though I was accused of it.

LAUREN LOKEMALIA TONG (*'99, organizer of student petition*): He didn't tell us to boo.

KAMANI KUALĀ'AU: I mean, I was giving a presentation, so even in practice I was in that zone of being nervous, and almost everything is blocked out. So if it was while I was speaking or introducing, then I might not have heard anything.

BOB WHITING: It didn't stand out as important. Tony Ramos, I don't think, saw it as important either. We were both in the auditorium.

TONY RAMOS: That involves children. That involves a student body who had been sitting from 8 o'clock until 1 o'clock in the afternoon in rehearsals. Became kind of a letting-off-steam time.

"I think he started with Trustee Wong, Trustee Stender, and after he said the name Lokelani Lindsey, there was a very distinctive booing among the students."

–Liz Hansen

KAMANI KUALĀ'AU

BOB WHITING: Tony had to get back to campus for something, and he said to me, "Would you mind getting up and just telling, you know, at the end of this whole thing, please, hey, tell them they can't boo, that's terrible, you can't boo anybody." And that's what I did. I'm the one that got up and said to all these kids, "You can do anything you want that evening, but there's some things you shouldn't do, and one of them is to boo anybody. Booing just diminishes all of us, booing was just not a good thing for anybody in a school that prides itself on its politeness and good sportsmanship, so keep that to yourself." I thought that'd be the end of it.

MIKE CHUN: I wasn't there. I heard about it. Dickie Wong didn't say it to me, but my understanding is he told Tony, if they boo Loke that night—he made a threat.

JULIAN AKO: I remember there was a reaction. The trustees became aware of it right away. Dickie Wong was up here beating on Tony's door, Tony Ramos.

TONY RAMOS: Dickie Wong told me, if this ever happens again, you're out of here. He told me we not training attack dogs here.

TONY RAMOS: I talked to the kids on the day of Song Contest— "Look, hey, we're the hosts. Everybody there is our guest. And if you're going to applaud, you applaud everybody equally."

MIKE CHUN: I was nervous that night because what I was on edge about was when we introduced the trustees.

LIZ HANSEN: Every Song Contest, Dr. Chun goes and he encourages the students and also reminds them that they represent their family as well as the school.

MIKE CHUN: I went around, as I do, and spoke to each class. Usually I go and I congratulate them. When I went that night, I said "I'm really excited," *boom, boom, boom*. And then what I threw in there, I said, "You know, I'm so proud of you, we are so proud of you, because we

"I was shocked. I've never witnessed that kind of disrespect to a trustee or the name of a trustee in my previous years of Kamehameha. And I thought, *Something's really not right here.*"

—Julian Ako

know, because there is no other school that would do what we are doing right now. And I know I can count on you folks to do the right thing tonight. In all aspects. You've never let me down." I remember saying this—"You never let me down before, and I know you won't let me down tonight." I never mentioned the incident. I just felt that they knew what I was talking about.

KĀWIKA EYRE: If you look at the video of the trustees, they look absolutely petrified. Not a smile to be seen there. And every time Kamani introduced one of them, they looked terrible. Oz looks like death warmed over.

OZ STENDER: I was worried for Randie. I was worried for Kamani. And I was worried for Michael.

KĀWIKA EYRE: Dr. Chun was looking haggard. When Kamani introduced him, he's looking at his program and he doesn't look up.

LIZ HANSEN: Kamani's delivery was beautiful. There was a tremendous amount of support for Dr. Chun when his name was mentioned.

JULIAN AKO: There was very loud applause and yelling in support of Mike. Not just from the students. It was from the whole arena, including from people in the public. I thought that was kind of interesting.

MIKE CHUN: You know, it's kind of like, wow, I want to be loved like everybody else, but I'm kind of embarrassed when it's public. It's the private conversations I have with kids, when they come up and give me a big hug—that's what I feel more comfortable with. The public part of it, you have mixed emotions. You appreciate it on the one hand, but it's almost like if you show your appreciation publicly, that's not being ha'aha'a, you're not being humble. So I'm torn. That's the kind of emotions that were playing on me.

LIZ HANSEN: It went on and on and on and on. Kamani was so wonderful. He just went on with his speech, and the cheering was so loud that I think the audience missed hearing the next name that was announced, which was Rockne Freitas. I don't think we were able to hear Rockne's name.

MIKE CHUN: It was a big thing. Especially with Loke. And I knew that that wasn't going to help me; it isn't going to help me in the boardroom.

ELISA YADAO: Randie apparently sat down that Sunday and watched the re-run of the Song Contest, and he and Jamie decided at that moment, when they saw and heard Marlene, that was it.

When he told me, I was just devastated.

He wasn't playing games. He really was doing, one, what he felt he had to do, and then, two, if he was going to leave Kamehameha then he was going to try to do as much as he could to help Kamehameha with that departure.

RANDIE FONG: Let's put down my job, because I don't have anything else.

ELISA YADAO: I told him, "Look, you can't just quit. You need to go talk to them, the trustees."

Because of the dynamic of the board, because of the power Henry Peters had, I wanted Randie to go and talk to Speaker first.

Henry was a big champion of Randie. Several years earlier, we had gone to the expo in Japan, and we'd taken the students, and Henry had come along. I think it was one of the first times that Henry saw firsthand how hard the Performing Arts staff worked to get so much out of the kids. Every single one of us worked our asses off on these things, the kids included.

I can remember Henry being backstage with us, and his head was just like a ping pong ball, going back and forth, watching everybody run around—changing kids, and kids going back and on, and just keeping the whole thing together. And he was just blown away. And after that I think he really had deep respect for Randie.

"I will give you my job. Now I want your attention."

—Randie Fong to trustees. Honolulu Advertiser, 5/9/97

"I think it was one of the first times that Henry saw firsthand how hard the Performing Arts staff worked to get so much out of the kids."

—Elisa Yadao

RANDIE FONG: I don't really know Mr. Peters all that well, but over the years he's always shown a lot of aloha for me, and we had a connection where his grandparents and my grandparents were both kahu—they were both ministers at a Hawaiian church, Ka Makua Mau Loa Church in Kalihi.

So I had to go back a couple generations to stand on something to go in and have enough courage to speak so candidly with Mr. Peters.

I felt that if there was anyone who could possibly influence Mrs. Lindsey, perhaps it was Mr. Peters.

I explained to him that the purpose of my meeting was to share this management issue with Mrs. Lindsey and the effect of her behavior on the institution, and the second thing was to let him know that I had decided, along with, again, my family, that, well, I felt I need to put something down on the table in order to be taken seriously, and we had all decided that I would give up my job at Kamehameha so that there wouldn't be any game playing. This is a very serious thing, it's hurting our school, and I didn't have anything else of value to put down.

Mr. Peters was very receptive and very warm. And I think he was also quite surprised at the situation.

When I sensed that it was going well, I had asked Mr. Peters for his protection, and that I feared for retaliation against me, against my family and possibly my son, who is a student there at Kamehameha.

ELISA YADAO: Randie went to see all the other trustees after that. The trustees were all very concerned about him leaving. They didn't want to see him go.

OZ STENDER: When I first heard about the problem, I called him two or three times. First he wouldn't talk to me, didn't want to talk to me, other than that he felt it was a personal thing, and Henry was going to take care of it. Didn't happen. He couldn't get anything out of Henry. Henry avoided trying to solve the problem. And I think that's the only reason he spoke with me. I kept calling him.

After I met and talked with him—I couldn't believe what she did!

RANDIE FONG: It was important for me to speak to Mrs. Lindsey face to face. To do that, I felt I needed to go through Mr. Peters first. I wanted to connect with Ozzie, too, but held off because I needed to look Mr. Peters straight in the eyes and honestly say that Oz wasn't involved. If they thought Ozzie was a part of it, they would never have agreed to meet with me. After I met with Peters, then Ozzie and I had lunch and got caught up. I thought it was the right thing to do to call Mrs. Lindsey out on her behavior, but I didn't want Ozzie to get blamed for it.

ELISA YADAO: He went to see Loke last.

She thought that Randie was insubordinate. She believed that he was running around badmouthing the trustees and her in particular. She didn't think he was that good at his job. Just pretty much everything having to do with Randie, you know, she was unhappy with. She wanted him gone.

RANDIE FONG: I had prepared a memo similar to the one that I had prepared for Mr. Peters to sort of help me keep on track and in case I forgot something. And I placed that in front of Mrs. Lindsey and I had one in front of myself.

And then Mrs. Lindsey said, "Well, I don't want to read, you know, these outlines. Let's talk person to person." And I explained, "Well, you know, it's going to get kind of involved, and I really want you to have a copy of this so that you can refer to it."

And at that point, Mrs. Lindsey stood up from her chair and she started screaming at the top of her lungs, and swearing—which kind of shocked me a little. I wasn't expecting that.

LOKELANI LINDSEY: That is not part of my vocabulary. It's not something I use.

RANDIE FONG: This was about five minutes. Again, that was very shocking.

I said, "If you read the beginning part of the memo, you would see that this has nothing to do with Dr. Chun. This is about your behavior and the manner in which it impacts our schools negatively." And she calmed down, and she sat back down, and then I think at that point was more interested in going through the outline, and we did so at that point.

> My Resignation:
> *For as long as I am here, I believe that you will make life miserable for me, my department and my family. Therefore I feel I must resign.*

I believe it is important that people treat each other with respect and that we should strive to bring out the best in people. I cannot allow myself to compromise my integrity and values.

To demonstrate my sincere intentions, it is important to note that I have no other job to go to, no special deal or employment package waiting for me. I am presently finishing up my resume and plan to start looking for a new job as soon as I can.

After much prayer and lengthy discussions with my family (especially my father whom I respect greatly), I have decided to give everything up with the hopes that some badly needed attention can be brought to this issue. I am willing to give up my current position, medical/dental benefits and my family's security, essentially my whole career—that is how much I love my School and how devoted I am to Kamehameha. I have everything to lose except my integrity.

Randie Fong, Memo to Trustee Lokelani Lindsey, April 11, 1997

ELISA YADAO: I talked to him after that meeting. It was awful. He said that she was practically choking, she was so angry at him. Stuttering and swearing and screaming. And I believe that, you know, because I've seen her be like that with me.

RANDIE FONG: At that point on, I had gotten, you know, anonymous phone calls at my office, nasty calls. I knew it was, in my heart, they were connected with her. Because they were talking about things that no one knew—nothing hit the public yet. And I knew it was, you know, "I think it's time for you to leave, Randie Fong, you have overstayed your welcome," da da da da, all that.

LOIS LONG: I first heard about it from the students. They often introduce us to what is going on on campus. "They're going to fire Randie Fong! That's like firing Mr. Kamehameha!" That's exactly what they said. I'll never forget it. You couldn't have picked a person who was more of the soul of the school from their perspective than Randie Fong.

CHARLENE HOE: It sent shock waves through the campus. ⌒

A Letter to Princeton
Lokelani Lindsey Threatens Kamani Kualāʻau

Mrs. Lindsey said, "I'm not going to do this, but how would you feel if I wrote a letter to Princeton and told them you were a rabble rouser?" –Kamani Kualāʻau

MIKE CHUN: Kamani Kualāʻau. The first time that I recall talking to him, he just impressed me. Came up to me, shook my hand. He was this young kid, seventh grade, very articulate, well groomed. From that point on, we had a nice relationship.

He got involved in Leadership. And that's a group of kids that I have more access to than I do some of the other kids. And so I got to know him through that. And if I had some questions and I wanted to get the kids together, I'd always include him, because he was a good thinker. He was on top of things. He'd take the time to give me his thoughts on a lot of these things.

Kamani Kualāʻau
and Congresswoman
Patsy Mink.

"Kamani's a political guy, and
he liked to be a player."
–*Tony Ramos*

JULIAN AKO: He was an exceptional person as a student. When he came into the leadership program as a freshman, he had already earned the respect of the upperclassmen.

I can remember him as a freshman, speaking at a faculty meeting where Loke and Oz were present. He had asked whether or not he could attend. He was the only student there among the faculty members. He came with this clipboard of questions regarding things such as trustee compensation.

KAMANI KUALĀʻAU: I was always interested in what was next. Being in high school, just thinking about being in the working world and wanting to be a professional. I don't know, I always aspired to be at the top. Or just realizing that you needed to be in a position of power to have something of an effect—you know, to create change and to try to help them move things along. Just kind of aspiring to that. And, you know, being in student government, and that was a natural state from which we could speak on these kinds of issues.

JAMES MONIZ (*'97, senior class president*): He had the trustees' home phone numbers. I remember one time he told me, "Yeah, I can call them at home."

KAMANI KUALĀʻAU: The key is having places to go to have meaningful discussions and meaningful change.

KAMANI KUALĀʻAU: I want things to change and be progressive and innovative and move forward. I was taught that hey, if you want something, you gotta go to those people who can do it. And those were Dr. Chun and then Dr. Freitas and then Lokelani Lindsey.

Mr. Ramos relayed to me through the dean of student activities that I should be following the chain of command and not trying to influence policy at the trustees' level. He came to Leadership one day and taught us some kind of locus of control. He drew a little circle and showed us, you know, you're in this circle, and everything in this circle is what you can control, and outside are bigger circles, and there are things you can't control in those circles. I mean, he was drawing the box and saying you're in the box.

But it's clear that when I went to the people who were in charge, you can get things to happen.

TONY RAMOS: We wanted computers for the dorms. We went through all the forms.

KEOLU BENTO (*'76, Schools boarding department*): In our budget, I was asking for computers, every year. I would never get—

GENE HOTINGER (*Schools boarding department*): —It was like, boarding doesn't count. So Kamani, little adult that he is, he doesn't know that he can't do that, he went directly to Lokelani, because she was the education trustee—

TONY RAMOS: —And the next week—

KEOLU BENTO: —Boom! We getting computers.

TONY RAMOS: Jeez, we ought to send this guy out more often.

KAMANI KUALĀ'AU: My freshman year I traveled to Washington, D.C. My sophomore year, I traveled to the Marquesas and Tahiti. My junior year I went to Washington, D.C., for one semester.

TONY RAMOS: Kamani's a political guy, and he liked to be a player.

KAMANI KUALĀ'AU: Senator Akaka was my sponsor to the Democratic senators, and we ran errands and did whatever else those senators wanted us to do. I was once delivering an urgent message, I think to Newt Gingrich's office, on the House side, or I was picking up, and on the way, running, I almost bowled over Bob Dole. Ran into him. I had Ted Kennedy yell at me for getting him the wrong thing.

Even though Senator Akaka is a senator, and he was my boss, I worked with him for six months and even got to the point where I was calling him Uncle Danny.

KEOLU BENTO: Tony Ramos didn't know that Senator Akaka was coming to dinner. And as a principal and living on campus, he felt he should have known.

TONY RAMOS: Who else knows he's coming to dinner? He's a U.S. senator. Does Mike know?

KEOLU BENTO: After dinner, Senator Akaka goes up to the mike and he talks a little bit about himself and about Kamani. He just praises Kamani too. And then after dinner, he comes down to the dorm, just talks to our dorm. And then we have a photo. I mean that's the only picture I have in the dorm of kids. They're all in long pants and aloha shirts.

KAMANI KUALĀ'AU: The senator came back to my dorm, spent at least an hour with the students. We all sat around in a big circle. Something that has never been done before. He's telling us about the amazing things that he is doing. It was just a great experience.

"Tony Ramos didn't know that Senator Akaka was coming to dinner."

–Keolu Bento (middle row standing far right)

KAMANI KUALĀ'AU: Things were coming down very hard on Lokelani Lindsey. The rumor mill. I didn't attribute every single thing that everyone said was Lokelani's fault or Lokelani's directive. And I called her up and I said, "Hey, I want to talk to you."

I wanted to try and bridge the gap and see for myself and ask questions. When I got to Kawaiaha'o Plaza, she had to go pick up her granddaughter. Her granddaughter wanted food, so we went to McDonalds, and then to her house. She showed it to me, and she was pretty proud of, you know, being able to get this nice house. It was great. There was a pool. And it was huge, and very nice.

Then we were back off to campus, and we did talk about the controversy and the pre-controversy. I was trying to explain to her that people don't think well of you, and I hope that you could try and—you know, I was trying to smooth things over. She appeared to listen and want to understand.

GENE HOTINGER: He had initiated a call to Lokelani, wanted to talk to her, because he was picking up all these vibes about staff feeling insecure about their jobs, about her hands-on administrative style, micromanagement. And so he asked her point blank, "Are any of the staff in danger of losing their jobs?" He shared this with me. I was sitting outside my dorm. Mrs. Lindsey dropped him off in front of his dorm, and they're right, you know, 25 yards apart. He comes over and sits down to talk to me. The reason he was talking to me is because she had used my name as an example. She said, "If you're somebody who is doing their job—anyone who's doing his job doesn't need to worry about it."

KAMANI KUALĀʻAU: I think a majority of the teachers didn't want to touch the issue, didn't want to get involved with the controversy, you know, out of fear for some people. Some confided in me outside of class—I felt I was a sounding board; people would confide in me. If the teachers focused on their subject and taught lessons they had planned to teach and were doing their job, you can't go wrong for doing that.

GENE HOTINGER
"She had used my name
as an example."

MIKE CHUN: In his junior year, Kamani and I started talking about college. So I said, "Where do you plan to go to school?" And he mentioned something like Harvard or some schools, and I said, "What about Princeton?" He said, "I don't know, tell me about it." And I said, "I tell you what, let me have my daughter talk to you." And so Kaʻili talked to him, and she just gave him the sell. She brought out her books and she showed him the pictures. And then he got his heart set on it.

KAMANI KUALĀʻAU: If it were not for Dr. Chun, I would not be going to Princeton.

KAMANI KUALĀʻAU: Coming to the end of our senior year, 1997, I think at this point we felt we were successful in all that we had done related to our roles in student leadership. I was student body president.

I suggested we write a letter to the trustees about our concerns and print it in the newspapers. I felt if we printed it in the newspapers, we were certain to get a response from the trustees.

I intended the letter to speak to our teachers, our faculty, thank them, our teachers through the years. And at some point in the letter, the key would also be to make allusion to the controversy that we believed was going on at Kamehameha.

We were going to put something in the paper and probably put it out after graduation. Maybe the Monday after the Sunday graduation, just to make sure we were graduated before we put our names to it. Caution.

And from that group, it whittled down to James Moniz and me—you know, pick two who wanted to put their names on the line or were willing to put their names on the line. The force of two individuals, not being anonymous, not being "the class of."

Then I got a call from Oz, and he said, "It looks like they're getting ready to fire Dr. Chun."

OZ STENDER: Sometimes the trustees get in this frenzy discussion, and they forget I'm in the room. It was real. On a scale of one to 10? —oh, nine and a half.

KAMANI KUALĀʻAU: I told him about the letter. When I told him we were going to print it in the papers, he said he would help with that, with the costs. I read it to him over the phone.

OZ STENDER: I said that letter wasn't strong enough. You're kind of glossing over things. I mean, if you're gonna do a letter, get to the point of it instead of wishy-washing around it. You're doing it because you want to make a statement that something's going wrong—say something! Because the trustees keep lying about that they never had any thinking about firing Michael.

KAMANI KUALĀʻAU: And he made a suggestion that we address the letter to the justices of the Supreme Court rather than the trustees.

I told James that we should do the letter we had planned right now, and that based on that telephone call, the way we were going to write the letter may need to be changed with respect to Dr. Chun.

JAMES MONIZ: Kamani was very adamant about getting it down; we had to get it done.

KAMANI KUALĀʻAU: James and I put together the beginning of the letter right there and then.

JAMES MONIZ: It felt like we were on a rushed timetable. Sat down, thought about what we wanted to say, wrote down basic dissatisfaction and really sticking up for Dr. Chun. The whole part about being dissatisfied as students and the way that the thing was being run went out the door. The whole thing switched around into being a letter that was going to save his job. It was really a letter in support of Dr. Chun, and that any decision to remove him would be one that would hurt the future of the students, who believe him.

KAMANI KUALĀʻAU: I told James I would take the letter and complete it.

In the morning, I took the letter with me to my classes, beginning with homeroom, and as I went to my first three classes, I asked my teachers if I could read something to the class, and I did read it.

My intention to read the letter to my classmates and schoolmates was because we put on the letter, "From Concerned Students at Kamehameha Schools." And I wanted to gauge the student feeling on the issues, mainly the controversy, to get a gut check from people, to see that we were on the right page, and that I wasn't off base with the way that they were feeling.

Fourth period, I asked my teacher if I could read it, and he said, "No." I did share it with the class in the passing time before class started, but during that period I received a telephone call, which stopped me from reading it to my other classes.

I was to go to Mr. Ramos' office at 1 o'clock, and to be there. I did not have a choice.

ROCKNE FREITAS: I was in a meeting, and usually I hold all the calls. Except if it comes from a trustee, then we interrupt whatever we're

JAMES MONIZ
"The whole part about being dissatisfied as students and the way that the thing was being run went out the door."

doing. Mrs. Lindsey told me, "Hey, I'm trying to find Mike. I can't find Mike. Can you locate Tony for me, and ask him to find Kamani and come on down to the boardroom, as soon as you can?" Which means right away.

That's unusual. Again, I'm an optimistic person, I'm thinking he did something really good, and maybe they want to congratulate him or something.

I had to track down Tony. I told him, "Hey, you know what, see if you can find Kamani and go down to the boardroom." And he said, "What for?"

TONY RAMOS: I said, "What does she want to know? I can ask the questions to him." "No, she wants you to bring him down."

I had driven a student down to a trustee before, for good stuff. You know, Kamani's been down there before. He's had a relationship with various trustees, being taken down. I was aware that he had a relationship with different trustees, that he talked to them and he felt very free of doing that. I mean, here we have a kid who's been to her house or whatever, who has a rapport with her. She wants to talk with him, she wants me to take him down. That's how we responded to trustees.

KAMANI KUALĀ'AU: Mr. Ramos was, I could see, meeting with one of his vice principals. When he finished with that and was passing me to go back to his office, he told me to hold on for a second. He went into his office, grabbed his keys and his folder and came out and told me that Mrs. Lindsey wanted to see me at her office. He told me that while he was at Dr. Freitas' office that morning, Mrs. Lindsey called and asked that he bring me in that afternoon.

TONY RAMOS: In the car, I talked about this whole issue that happened this morning. And I did talk with Kamani about graduation's coming up. Maybe looking to graduation. This whole thing was escalating. Not to get involved with this. Look forward to graduation, look forward to college—a lot of happy things going on for him.

KAMANI KUALĀ'AU: Mrs. Lindsey led us to her office.

TONY RAMOS
"This whole thing was escalating."

A Message to the
Justices of the Supreme Court of Hawai`i
From Concerned Students of
The Kamehameha Schools

May 1, 1997

Dear Justices,

As two students of The Kamehameha Schools, we have received, over the past six years, the finest education that any school in Hawai`i can offer. As a result of this privilege bestowed upon us by Princess Bernice Pauahi Bishop, we have learned what it means to be honest, to have respect for all, and to live each day with integrity.

Sadly, our president, Dr. Michael J. Chun, the man responsible for bringing Kamehameha to this standard of excellence, may soon be asked for his resignation. He has already been empowered to do nothing, and soon insult may be added to injury.

As students who have witnessed the profound aloha that Dr. Chun has extended toward each member of the Kamehameha `ohana and the community of Hawai`i, we find it deplorable that anyone would question his integrity or his leadership.

Though reasons may be cited for Dr. Chun's "resignation," there are other signs that Kamehameha is in a state of turmoil and that this is not an isolated incident. Several of our best teachers will be resigning or retiring at the end of this school year. Many more are dissatisfied with the current Board of Trustees' new leadership and management styles.

All of this is adversely affecting our classmates and our friends. The decline of the quality of the education at Kamehameha will soon show. The best teachers being put in the lowest state of morale will go elsewhere. Something must be done.

Many may believe that the Trustees are ultimately responsible for The Kamehameha Schools; we do not. We hold you, the Justices of Hawai`i's Supreme Court, as the selectors of The Kamehameha Schools'

Trustees, responsible to ensure the integrity of our Schools. We hold you responsible to put politics aside and ask, is this what Princess Pauahi would have wanted? We leave this to your good judgement.

Respectfully yours,

Kamani Kuala`au   James Moniz
President   President
Student Body   Senior Class

LOKELANI LINDSEY: I received information from some students in a telephone call that Kamani Kualā'au wanted them to sign a petition because Oz Stender had called him and had said that the trustees were going to remove Uncle Mike. To come against the trustees because we were going to fire Uncle Mike. And they were explicit that Trustee Stender called Kamani Kualā'au to tell him to do this. They said Kamani had told them.

JANET ZISK: Kamani told me, "Well, first thing Mrs. Lindsey did was take out a file with my name on it, and she took these papers out. I never did get to see what they all were, but she fanned them out in front of her, you know, and started asking me all these questions— why I was opposing her or why I was doing all these bad things."

TONY RAMOS: I didn't know what the questions were. I don't know where she's going to go with that.

KAMANI KUALĀ'AU: She was saying that she doesn't usually call people into her office unless she has three things on them.

She said she had received some telephone messages in which I was mentioned. She read them off of a steno notepad.

One message said that the mother of an intermediate student at Kamehameha had called her and I believe told her that a petition was being done on campus and that intermediate students were being involved and had been pressured into doing this. Mrs. Lindsey said she asked the mother who was doing it, and the lady said she would call back, and she called back and said that it was a student body president.

The next message was from someone who said that I was initiating letter-writing campaigns on campus.

And the final message was from someone who called and said that Mr. Stender had called me the night before, that he told me the trustees were going to fire Dr. Chun, that he told me that I needed to do something about it, and that he told me he would pay to put it in the papers. The message to Mrs. Lindsey, which she read, concluded, "I don't believe such scum would stoop so low as to use a student like this."

I was shocked that, first, people were checking in with her and that I was mentioned, and shocked also as well with the information she had regarding the telephone conversation that I had with Mr. Stender. And the detail she had. Not quite accurate, but very similar to

"I was intimidated when she showed me minutes of teachers' meetings and drafts of letters which she led me to believe she wasn't supposed to have."

—*Kamani Kualā'au*

"He was surprised that I knew as much as I did."

—*Lokelani Lindsey*

discussions that we had had. So I guess I was surprised and baffled that she knew anything about me.

LOKELANI LINDSEY: He was surprised that I knew as much as I did.

TONY RAMOS: Loke had kid informants in the boarding program who would call her up. She had teachers who called, that I didn't know about—she would never divulge.

KAMANI KUALĀ'AU: I was intimidated when she showed me minutes of teachers' meetings and drafts of letters which she led me to believe she wasn't supposed to have.

I denied the first two messages that Mrs. Lindsey mentioned. I told her the first two messages were false.

Much of the conversation during the rest of the meeting centered around Mr. Stender's telephone call to me. And that Mr. Stender had not used me, and that I did not feel used. Because he had not asked me to do something about the information he was giving me. The discussion was friend to friend, so I was telling him what I was planning to do, and not being told by him that I needed to do something. I did it of my own wanting.

Mrs. Lindsey mentioned that Kamehameha is involved with a lot of litigation, that Kamehameha spends over $5 million in litigation. If I published the letter I could add to those problems, cause more problems. And she also said that I could destroy the whole Kamehameha institution.

Well, I certainly took a step back to look at what was happening, because I care so much for Kamehameha. Inside, I was terrified. I wouldn't want to do anything that would hurt the institution, let alone destroy it. And so I was scared, and really contemplating whether that was a possibility, and I really believed that it was a scare tactic to get me not to print the letter, and it worked.

Mrs. Lindsey said, "Do you know you're accused of being behind the applause for Dr. Chun at the Song Contest?"

Up until that point in the meeting, I had been fairly calm. But at this point, I think everything got to me, and I felt that that was an attack on Dr. Chun personally, and so I began crying, and I said that I could not believe that people would disrespect Dr. Chun so much as to believe that the people who applauded him that day weren't doing it because they loved him. And then, I guess, we took a pause for me to

"Do you know you're accused of being behind the applause for Dr. Chun at the Song Contest?"

–Lokelani Lindsey

get myself back together.

Princeton was mentioned. Mrs. Lindsey said, "I'm not going to do this, but how would you feel if I wrote a letter to Princeton and told them you were a rabble rouser?"

LOKELANI LINDSEY: I already knew he was going to Princeton. I said to him, "Kamani, you are going to graduate in a little while. You don't need to be involved in this. Why don't you have fun during the rest of your high school career, and then you are going to move on to college—and make sure that this doesn't influence you in any way."

I said, "You shouldn't listen to things that may not be true. For example, how would you feel about me if I were to call Princeton and say that Kamani Kualā'au was a rabble rouser? I'm not going to do this"—I said it two or three times—"I'm not going to do this, but as an example, how would you feel?"

KAMANI KUALĀ'AU: She was using my name in this third-person story kind of way, to say, you know, "How would you feel if I went around telling people Kamani Kualā'au was a thief or whatever?" She wasn't even pronouncing my name correctly.

Mrs. Lindsey and Mr. Ramos were both saying it was wrong for Mr. Stender to have called me. I began wondering whether or not he could get in trouble for it—maybe he had done something that trustees aren't allowed to do. Mrs. Lindsey said that she would not take any action against him, that basically he would have to deal with his own conscience.

Then she also said that she would not tell anybody about the meeting that day. The only reason we would keep silence was because she hinted that Oz shouldn't have had discussion with me about things that were said in the boardroom. That he could get in serious trouble for that. And there are laws. And she looked at Mr. Ramos and said, "Tony, you're not going to tell anyone, right?" And he said no, he's not going to tell anyone. And so she said that if anyone found out what happened that day, that it would be because I told them. It would be me and on me.

The meeting lasted about two and a half hours. While we were starting to leave Mrs. Lindsey's office, she came out from around her desk toward her door. We hugged. She said she loved me, and I told her that I loved her too. And she said she would never do anything to hurt me, and I said the same thing back to her.

I guess Mrs. Lindsey's office is right next to Mr. Stender's, or adjacent to it on the way out of the trustees' offices. And so as I left her office, I just so happened to see him sitting at his desk there, and I just recall walking very slowly past his office. I hoped that he would see me. I wanted him to look at me and acknowledge my presence. I wanted to run in there. To be safe. And he didn't see me.

OZ STENDER: I didn't know he was there. I didn't even know he was there.

LOKELANI LINDSEY: If I was vindictive, he wouldn't get anything. But I love this kid. I still have a lot of aloha for Kamani. My concern for that young man was that he was getting into something for which he did not have factual information.

Trustee Stender said in the boardroom that I had no business calling a student out of school. And I said he initiated this whole thing by calling the student to tell him to have other students take action against the trustees, which was what was reported to me.

TONY RAMOS: Let me put it this way. I was angered and upset that trustees got students involved in this situation. Trustee Lindsey and Trustee Stender both.

This is highly unprofessional, unethical, for the board, for the politics involved, to get students involved in a controversy like this. Kamani got used. He wanted to play with the big boys, you know. I was concerned about him getting burned with this, because he's still a kid, not realizing what the big picture is. It was a board controversy, and now it's become a student controversy. I was concerned for Kamani. He was a senior, he was almost ready to graduate, he was going to leave Kamehameha School behind and go on to college. And I didn't feel that he should be put in this position. You know, alone and caught in a bind up there between trustee directives.

On the way back to school, Kamani asked the question: "If Uncle Oz says they're going to fire Uncle Mike, and Auntie Loke says they're not going to, we never discussed this issue—who do you believe? Who's telling the truth?" I say, Kamani, "I don't know. I don't know."

LOKELANI LINDSEY
"If I was vindictive...."

KAMANI KUALĀʻAU: Lokelani can do a fantastic job making you believe what she wants you to believe. And I know that from many people who have spoken with her. So it was all very confusing. It was like, well, she was telling you this. But then when you examine the words—I've never had any conversations *in the boardroom* about firing Dr. Chun. Those were her exact words.

Based on my experience of Lokelani Lindsey, comparing information of what she's told people and others showing me—here's the evidence, or here's the reason why that is not true—I just had a cleaner, more honest experience with Oz.

OZ STENDER: He called me in the evening. He sounded very distraught.

KAMANI KUALĀʻAU: I think I was afraid to talk to him. Because the seed was planted that I could possibly be getting him in trouble.

OZ STENDER: I wanted him to be with somebody. And so I called and talked to Bina, Mike Chun's wife, and said, "Kamani's coming up, and kind of mother him a little bit."

After I hung up with Kamani, I called Tony, to find out if what Kamani told me was true. He said, "Ah, yeah." I said, "Well, who else was in the room?" He said, well, just he and Kamani. And I said, "And why didn't you do something?" And he said, "Well, she's a trustee." I said to him, "You know, Tony, even if she's God herself, you don't allow this to happen. *You know you don't allow this to happen.*"

HERB WILSON: It doesn't surprise me that Tony Ramos took Kamani to Lokelani, considering the relationship with Lokelani. I think Mike Chun was being bypassed anyway, and for Tony to have taken things up with Mike might have been treasonous for him to do that in Lokelani's eyes. I think Tony was under a lot of pressure, too.

MIKE CHUN: It wasn't until a couple days later when it started to surface that I found out. I had no idea that he had been called down.

ROCKNE FREITAS: I wouldn't say it's inappropriate. But I would say that it should not be a common practice. Basically, there's such a power differential between the two—when you look at the structural layers between a student and someone at the CEO level, it would have to be something very extraordinary to have me think it's appropriate.

You know, to do a commendation of some sort.

KELLI KEAHIAHI LEE: As a student, you're already in a subordinate position to these people. The idea that they would do that was— really, I lost respect for them.

KAHELE KUKEA: If I had been in the position, I am not sure what I would have done. Who knows what I would have done? But to take a student down to a trustee's office in that kind of—even if he didn't know why—there's no excuse for that. If I did it, I would have said it's time for me to leave this position.

HAILAMA FARDEN: I said, "Mrs. Lindsey, if I wanted to take a student off campus, I would get fired." I said, "How come Tony was allowed to take? Did he ever ask the mother if he could take?" She said, "No, the answer's no."

ROD MCPHEE: If that had been my son, and a trustee had interrogated him in that manner, I'd have gone to court.

LOKELANI LINDSEY: I think it was proper. 〜

12 A Line in the Sand
The Community Responds

People were realizing we just cannot take this anymore.
People were sort of collectively hitting the line in the
sand together. –Kathy Kukea

KĀWIKA EYRE: Nineteen ninety-seven was our year to be re-accredited as a school by the Western Association of Schools and Colleges. The WASC criteria allowed us to revisit national standards of educational excellence. Also, the process was a great chance to look at ourselves in the mirror as an educational community.

Certainly there was much to love about our school, but we all had big bones to pick as well.

KATHY KUKEA: There was this growing feeling in me of how we were sitting on a bomb. Here are all these things going on. The curriculum project. The Hawaiian language thing. Randie Fong was fighting his battles. Kamani got hauled down for his interview. And all kinds of little bullying incidents by Lindsey, little personal one-on-one vignettes, were coming up that were kind of scary.

OZ STENDER: In responding to a rumor that Randie Fong had resigned, I spoke with Randie, and I was appalled at the way he had been treated. The circumstances under which Myron Arakawa, Kenna Ogasawara, Ekela Crozier—and the list goes on—resigned can be attributed to the same problems. And as I understand it there will be others who will follow.

The problem has extended to the students and has come to the attention of people outside the organization. The students' reaction is the booing, the staff's reaction is to resign, the community's reaction is a lot of talk.

We must put a stop to all this now. The more professional response to the problem is to return management of the Schools to the staff.

KATHY KUKEA: So the WASC self-study criteria opened up all kinds of issues about governance that we knew were going to be gruesome.

There wasn't a one of us who could have imagined the trustees would ever be gone. We felt that Mrs. Lindsey would be there long past the retirement of all of us.

KĀWIKA EYRE: Would anyone stand up? Would anyone listen?

KATHY KUKEA: We were trying to figure out a way to have everybody be involved and tell the truth without having to put a guillotine in place on Kōnia field.

BOB WHITING: We went to the trustees and said, "We need to have trustee representation on a group that dealt with governance, and at least one representative from the board of trustees should have been on that group."

Lindsey's the education person. We said it could be anybody. She said if it was going to be anybody, it would be her—but she didn't want anything to do with it, she was too busy to do that, she couldn't be bothered.

KATHY KUKEA: Bob Whiting and I were in charge. I felt like it was quite possible that he and I would be in serious difficulties as a result of what would be coming out of the report. We knew that once it was put in writing and we told the truth and it went to WASC, there would be hell to pay.

But tough. It just was unimaginable to do anything that could have kept the truth from coming out. It was a real invitation. So it was just one of those times where you kind of throw your hands up and say, "What the heck."

KĀWIKA EYRE: There was electricity in the air.

KATHY KUKEA: Tony Ramos was really trying to keep a lid on it, trying to take the edges off a lot of stuff that was coming out. Governance was a biggie. But Tony kept saying things like, "All of these things the teachers are bringing up are focusing on people other than themselves—somebody else has the problem." He was trying to somehow turn it back on teachers. As if they were shucking off responsibility and focusing all on Mrs. Lindsey or the administration or something. He was trying to make it sound like the negativity that was coming was way off base.

But we all knew that there was really no way to truly keep a lid on things in terms of the WASC process. Something was happening where it was coming together, when people were realizing we just cannot take this anymore. People were sort of collectively hitting the line in the sand together.

KĀWIKA EYRE: The WASC self-study allowed us to rekindle our idealism as educators, and to discuss ideas about leadership in an educational community. When the work was done, teachers were left with a common energy of anger and defiance that was inspirational, and it set the stage.

KĀWIKA EYRE: The same day that Kamani Kualāʻau and James Moniz were drafting their letter, April 27, I decided to write something too.

We had worked within the system diligently and sincerely for a long time before realizing that it was pretty hopeless, and that all efforts needed to focus on making change at the top. I remember clearly when I told my department head, Keʻala Kwan, that I was no longer putting any energy into reforming the system from our level or addressing individual school issues, but rather would concentrate on removing the problem itself—which for me was Trustee Lindsey and the culture she had created. That's when I sat down and wrote what I called a Statement of Concern.

The next morning early, I met with my dad, and we talked about the possible consequences. He said that if I was fired and didn't find work again immediately, we could make it for about six months.

It was Monday, it was my birthday, and I wondered what I was doing.

Kāwika Eyre and student Temple Chun on Kōnia Field, May 1997

KAREN KEAWEHAWAII FARIAS: I had two daughters at Kamehameha, my number three, who is Winona Kaweheonā-lani, and number four, Melody, whose Hawaiian name is Kaleolani.

I noticed the two of them coming home and talking among themselves and saying, "Oh, Kumu So-and-so was crying in the back of the class."

WINONA FARIAS (*'98*): My sisters were saying what they heard from the news about various trustees, especially Lokelani Lindsey. And the fact that Dr. Chun was also being kind of, I don't know, condemned for various things, or that he might be at risk in this whole thing.

KAREN KEAWEHAWAII FARIAS: Well, the tension—I felt very bad about it being on campus, affecting the faculty. And because it was affecting the faculty, it was running off into the girls as students and as graduates. There were a lot of overtones. And I said, "This is not good."

I would pick the girls up at school, Melody down by 7th and 8th grade by Keawe Gym, and then I would pick Winona up by Pākī, and then the next year up at Smith. And then I noticed really quickly how the kids were gossiping—I didn't sit in the van, I sat by the tree because it was a lot cooler—and the students were just talking. Everything was coming out, all this negativity, so I knew it wasn't just Melody and Winona.

PETER KAMA: You know, my grandchildren were in school there at the time, and they'd come home and talk about it. It makes you angry. How can they treat our people like that?

KAREN KEAWEHAWAII FARIAS: I always tell my girls, "If you believe there is a wrong, then you should take part in making it right."

WINONA FARIAS: When I know something is going wrong, it's like a physical reaction, rather than a choice.

We were thinking about what we could do. We didn't know what was rumor and what was fact. So all we knew was that we wanted to support Dr. Chun.

So that's when we kind of thought of a petition.

KAREN KEAWEHAWAII
FARIAS

KAREN KEAWEHAWAII FARIAS: Everyone gives me credit for the petition. I did not start the petition. I did not give birth to the petition. My girls did.

WINONA FARIAS
"We just typed it out."

WINONA FARIAS: We could have people sign it. Not do anything derogatory, or make any kind of political stand. It wasn't in any way attacking anyone. Just to say, "We love you, Dr. Chun, and we love the school, and we support people who are trying to make things right."

We just typed it out, and we made all these copies.

When we went to school, my mom made it a point—only before and after school hours, so that you didn't distract from academics and things like that.

So, before school, mostly after school, 'cause we had more time. Mostly it was upper campus. It wasn't even as much us walking around. It was people who had heard about it who were coming to sign. So it was barely even work, because everyone was, "Oh, can I sign it?" So, like, whole groups would take a page and they would sign it and give it back to us. They'd take a page to their friends and give it back to us.

MELODY FARIAS

KAREN KEAWEHAWAII FARIAS: You know, if I were to approach you and say, "I have a petition"—I don't know, but for some reason it has a negative feeling, right at the word petition. So I found that initially when I would say to the student, "Oh, hi, my name is Karen Farias, I'm Melody's mom, and this is our petition," they would kind of walk past me. And then when I just said, "Dr."—and I didn't even say Chun yet—they would hurry back and they would call their friends. They would come in groups.

They came to my van. "Auntie, Auntie, you have the petition? My friend like sign." I'd say, "Hey, school not over yet." "No, but I pau my class." "No, but school's not over; if you can wait, I'll get you soon as school is over."

When they signed, they said, "Hey, is this because of what Lokelani Lindsey is doing?" It was from their lips. I felt good about the fact that we were not poking darts at anybody, but it was already surfacing. I said, "Well, right now we're just supporting what Dr. Chun is doing with the programs and the students." "Oh, yeah, we like Dr. Mike." And there were a lot of little notations from the students—they would write in the margins of the petition, "Uncle Mike, hang in there."

◈ ◈ ◈

KAREN KEAWEHAWAII FARIAS: This particular Monday, at 3:40 p.m., I was approached by Tony Ramos. I was grabbed by Tony Ramos, by the arm. He physically grabbed me.

WINONA FARIAS: Right there in front of everybody.

KAREN KEAWEHAWAII FARIAS: He was angry. And he was very hostile. "Do you know what you're doing? You know what you're doing is wrong."

I don't feel bad, bad for me. But I felt really bad for him, because at that moment with all the students who were standing around there, they saw a different shade of Mr. Ramos, if you will. He was angry.

The next day I called the office and asked for an appointment, if I could meet with Mr. Ramos. And they told me he wasn't available right now. I said, "Let me know when he's available, anytime."

I wanted to tell him that, first of all, I didn't appreciate being grabbed by the arm. Secondly, I didn't appreciate being talked to in that tone. And third, the right way to approach me is to ask me to come and see him in his office. Not take me to Trustee Lindsey's office, but his office. You know, don't just blurt out to the wind and grab me like that.

I called two other times. And to this day I have not had that meeting.

PATRICK AND KAYLIA IONA

KAYLIA IONA (*'74, parent and member of alumni group Nā Pua*): I got a petition that they had put together, and they were circulating on the campus.

We spoke to some teachers at the Elementary campus, and they couldn't even talk, but what they could tell us was that what we heard was true, that they could not do what they felt they wanted to do in their own classrooms.

PATRICK IONA (*'72, parent and member of alumni group Nā Pua*): Loke would come into a class, and if she didn't like how they were being taught, she just abruptly interrupted and started yelling at the teacher in front of the class.

Or the kindergarten teachers were told they had to have the pictures of the trustees, and the kindergartners had to learn who each trustee was. And I'm sitting there thinking, *What are you doing?*

KAYLIA IONA: Pat took the petition and Xeroxed it and went around. We live in ʻEwa Beach, and he started at the bus stop. He went car to car and explained to all the parents that this is what is happening, this is what is going on, will you sign this petition, otherwise Dr. Chun will lose his job.

PATRICK IONA: Some of the parents didn't like it. I think there was fear if you put their name down on anything against the trustees. Many feared that their other children who were not in the Schools would be blackballed and not have the opportunity to attend Kamehameha.

KAYLIA IONA I had just dropped off my son, and one parent grabbed me and said, "What are you guys doing?" I was so mad. I said, "Are you asking if what we are doing is right compared with what the trustees are doing?"

They want their children, their grandchildren, to go to Kamehameha

—but how could they want these children to go to this school under these conditions?

PATRICK IONA: I came up to the Elementary School with the petition. I explained to people, I said, "This is entirely voluntary, and if you would like to support Dr. Chun, sign this petition."

I had probably three-quarters of a page, and then Kahele Kukea, the principal, came out from his office. I guess someone had complained, and he confronted me. And I told him, "Kahele, I'm not forcing anyone, it's all voluntary, we're just supporting Dr. Chun." He says, "Well, I would like you to put it away and not do it on campus." So I said, "Fine, I will." And just as I was about to put away, the security guard showed up.

They brought me up to the security office, and then I had to take out my ID and show them who I was, and did I have children here, yes, and this is the grades that they're in and—

They started to interrogate me about what I was doing. They told me that I was trespassing and they could have charges filed against me.

The captain at that time took me into his office and closed the door. "Because I don't want anyone to hear what I'm saying," and he told me that he supported Mike, but there were others who did not, and he didn't like what he had to do by pulling me into the security, but everybody knew I was there on campus, so he had to do something, and he didn't want to tell me this in front of the other officers, and so he says, "You know, we all have a job to do, and I apologize that I have to do this." So I told him, "Fine."

He proceeded to tell me that right now the campus was very touchy with the situation. He just asked that I don't do it anymore, get any more petitions, signatures on campus, and I said, "Fine." But he said, "I have to take your name and all that, because they'll want to know who you are and stuff like that."

PAUL IONA: I guess some of the parents were afraid of what might happen, so one afternoon we had second recess, and we were playing tetherball, and I wanted to play, and my classmates told me, "No, you can't play, because our parents don't want us to play with you." It was difficult for me. Not understanding what my parents were doing, to me, it was like they're shaming me. Rabble rousers. When that happened, I just got really, really into myself. From then on, I wasn't able to be friends with other people, and I felt that I was being shunned.

One night my parents pulled me and my sister and my brother

PAUL IONA

aside, they sat us down and they told us, "You may not understand what we're doing, you may see us on TV, and you might be afraid, but understand that what we're trying to do is help you, benefit you." My mom's and my dad's biggest problem was that Lokelani Lindsey was going to be a trustee until 2008, and that was the year I would graduate, and they didn't want me to have to be with Lokelani Lindsey for my whole life at Kamehameha.

PATRICK IONA: We got involved for the children at Kamehameha during this controversy and for all future children who would attend Kamehameha.

KAREN KEAWEHAWAII FARIAS: I knew Dr. Chun as a friend. I knew that seeing the kids' little notations in the petitions would make him smile if not cry. So we made copies of all the signed petitions.

Every year, they have the reunion lūʻau, and after I had finished performing, Winona and I went down to the president's house. We knocked. No one was home, but the door is always open. I told her, "You walk this in, and you just put it on where you think they'll find it." And when she came out, she goes, "There's a picture of Pauahi, and I put it under Pauahi's picture."

MOMI CAZIMERO: We had seen things escalate and escalate. The impression that we all had was that the trustees were running this trust as though they owned it. With a kind of abandonment. To fiduciary laws. And to decency in doing what is right and thoughtful and careful.

LEROY AKAMINE: When I look at it, the hierarchy had everything to do with the fear that was instilled upon employees, regardless of what role you play. Because of this threat. It took over your very being, and it was so overwhelming that you did not have a sense of what was happening—all you could understand is that my boss is telling me to do this, so I got to do this.

And there was a big question mark as what they can do—the little old me, what can I do?

For me, the turning point of all of that which resulted in our direct involvement with these wrongdoings is when Mike Chun's firing was imminent, and Randie Fong, who we have a close connection with.

Those two individuals. Mike first, the continuous threats of him being fired, and then with Randie Fong being threatened likewise—we weren't going to stand for that. That was the straw that broke the camel's back.

When it came to a point where we could no longer tolerate, and we had to make a conscious decision—it's now or never—I decided that it's about time that we get directly involved, regardless of the consequences.

We did not even give consideration to how this thing would affect us, directly and indirectly. Not only for our kids who were employees in one way or another, and our moʻopuna was a student, but for our hālau being there on campus.

LEINAʻALA
AND LEROY AKAMINE
"Whenever needed."

LEINAʻALA AKAMINE (*kumu hula, wife of Leroy*): We never gave it a second thought.

LEROY AKAMINE: If the opportunity presents itself, I go direct to the horse's mouth. So I called Oz, who we knew over the years, very close friends.

I told Oz that we have a scheduled class meeting, '52, at my house, to plan for our reunion activities. However, I'm going to take the opportunity, and I'm going to invite class of '53 and others that we know are concerned about our school and what's happening. I said, "Oz, can you attend our meeting?"

And he said sure enough, he'd be more than willing to come to our meeting.

We started calling our classmates, and class of '53—we're sister classes; we do things in tandem.

PETER KAMA: We're a close-knit group.

ROY BENHAM: Leroy and I were already exchanging information. He had a regular list of people that he'd call. I called my classmates.

LEROY AKAMINE: I still am the class president, and having served on the Kamehameha Schools Alumni Association board, I was receiving all these calls from various classes, wondering what was happening. They heard this or that.

TONI LEE: Protocol should be, we should go to the alumni and see what they're thinking. Do they know, do they care? Maybe we could go to them for help. Gil Tam was president, and he was not happy with us, and actually like, brushed us off. We were starting to have meetings, gatherings, and we said, "We have a problem here, are you aware of this problem, do you want to help us on this problem, can we work as a group together?" And he said, "No, we're not interested; you don't know what you guys are talking about."

LEROY AKAMINE: This is why I stepped forward, because I understood that the employees of Kamehameha were threatened, they were fearful about repercussions, real or perceived, and it would take us as the alumni, who are outside of this threat, to do what is necessary.

ROY BENHAM: There were a lot of substantial people at that meeting. There was good representation of classes.

PAULETTE MOORE ('52, *leader of alumni group Nā Pua*): There were members of the class of '41, Roy Benham, Elsie Chu. Generally it was only for '52, but because Oz was coming, we invited other class members to come. And that's why the Kapu sisters were there. Only one belongs to '52. But Dutchie and Carol, they came along too.

DUTCHIE SAFFERY ('57, *leader of alumni group Nā Pua*): It was at that meeting that I heard all of the rumblings. I had been out of touch with everything that was going on, because I'm not a good alumni. I don't attend functions and things. My sisters and my brother are very active. I was merely at the meeting because I was driving my sister, Carol, to the airport, and that was when I heard all these things about Lokelani Lindsey.

What I had walked into was the great concern of several faculty resigning because of what was happening. Randie Fong's name came up. And because I knew him and knew of his fine work, I called him, because I wanted to hear it from him. He did confirm that his job was in jeopardy. I asked him if Kamani's scholarship to Princeton also had been threatened, and he said "Yes."

It was evident that power and money was really controlling.

LEROY AKAMINE: Before the meeting started, Oz and I had talked at length about the threats made on Mike and Randie, and the conduct of the trustees, and how this was unacceptable and that the alumni needed to do something about it.

That's the purpose of that meeting, to gather the alumni and listen to this one trustee that we had, the only trustee that we trusted and had faith, because he was one of us. And he told us that after all this discussion, if the alumni didn't do anything about this, he would be very upset.

I think that was straight from his na'au, and his immediate reaction to what was happening, and the gathering of the graduates at our hale, that it caused him to, I think, identify this as a critical moment, whether we were going to step forward or not.

NONA BEAMER: I had heard about the controversy. My grandson, I guess he might have been a junior, he said that Lokelani had come into his classroom, berated his teacher in front of the class. I was aghast that a trustee would do that. And that was the first direct comment that I had from a family member.

Very shortly after that, my hānai son, Kaliko, came back from UH-Hilo, and he said that they were given a directive, and Lokelani was quoted as saying in this directive that none of the Hawaiian language material from UH-Hilo would be taught at Kamehameha. Unless it was spoken during Pauahi's time, it would not be taught at Kamehameha.

I couldn't believe it was happening. It was so incredible! And I couldn't understand how we allowed it to reach those gigantic proportions.

And then I went to Honolulu to do this interview, and after the interview there was a phone call. I went to take the phone, and there was our dear Sarah Keahi.

SARAH KEAHI: I said, "You know, seems like Lokelani and the trustees don't want to listen to us." I said, "Our people are—it's just really sad. It just hurts my heart that we're having to live in fear and walk on eggshells."

NONA BEAMER: And she said, "Nona, you have to do something about this." Oh, we began to cry together, and I felt at that moment that I had to do something.

SARAH KEAHI
"It hurts my heart."

It took me five minutes to write the letter. I was kind of seething, oh dear, oh dear. I didn't read it over, I didn't edit it. I usually find that a first effort is what you want. Just do it.

I'm sure I was speaking for a lot of people. I just knew that if we spoke up, someone would listen to us. And I thought, *Well, best to start at the top.* It was a short letter, socko, to the point—get rid of the buggers.

OZ STENDER: She called me and sent me a copy of the letter. So I read it, and I called her, and I said, "Auntie Nona! I don't think you should do this. I mean, it's slanderous. She could sue you!" And she said, "I don't care. I'm too old and I don't have any money anyway." And she said, "I'm sending it." I told her she should talk to a lawyer first, but she said no. Good for her!

DUTCHIE SAFFERY: One of the people, Paulette Moore '52, said that there was a letter that she wanted to read. A letter that Auntie Nona Beamer had written and Auntie Nona had asked it be read at this meeting.

ROY BENHAM: Winona called me. I was still a member of the board of the Alumni Association. She called me the morning before the meeting and she read the letter to me on the phone.

I said, "Nona, oddly enough, we're having a meeting on this, so why don't you hold off on the letter, and I'll call you the next day after the meeting, and maybe you might want to change something, or you might not want to send it at all, or whatever."

PAULETTE MOORE: My friend at church, Pauli Jennings, called me up and said that Nona Beamer was writing this seething letter about what was happening at Kamehameha Schools and had asked the *Advertiser* and the *Bulletin* if they would print it. So Pauli called and asked if I could get some of my classmates to sign on to that letter. And I said, "Oh, better yet, I'm going to a meeting. Let me read it at that meeting. And let people at that meeting sign on."

PAULETTE MOORE

Beamer Hawai'iana

P. O. Box 1245   Pāhoa, Hawai'i 96778

May 3, 1997
The Editor
Honolulu Advertiser
Fax: 525-8037

I would appreciate your time in printing the following in the Honolulu
Advertiser. I can be reached in Honolulu at 486-3185 this week-end
only (May 3rd & 4th) and thereafter at: (808) 965-7647 on Hawai'i.

Mahalo nui loa,

AN APPEAL TO THE SUPREME COURT OF THE STATE OF HAWAI'I

Kamehameha Schools trustee, Lokelani Lindsey, has shamed the Hawaiian
people! Her high-handed tactics on campus with students, staff and
faculty have completely demoralized the entire Kamehameha 'Ohana!

The deep concerns have spread through the community, neighbor islands,
and farther.

Mrs. Lindsey's micro-management methodology is an utterly diabolical
plan of a self-serving egoist!

We call for an impeachment and Supreme Court re-dress!

Most sincerely,

NONA BEAMER and countless students, faculty, staff, parents, graduates,
friends and associates of the Kamehameha Schools.

So she faxed me Nona's letter. And I think that was the beginning. When I read Nona's letter and I said, "If this woman is going to take a stand, then I can no longer be hāmau, silent."

ROY BENHAM: At the meeting, we were all comparing stories, and the stories were being validated, in that size group.

Oz spoke. His words were, "There is something wrong up at that school, and we've got to do something about it."

DUDLEY MAKAHANALOA: He was mad—"It's me against them. I would be at the end of the table and they would be at the other end of the table. And they wouldn't care what my decision was because they had the votes."

JOE TRAVIS: In a sense he was orchestrating us to get involved.

PAULETTE MOORE: And then I read Nona Beamer's letter to everybody.

DUTCHIE SAFFERY: It was a very powerful letter.

PAULETTE MOORE: I think what I did was throw gasoline on the fire that was burning in everybody's heart. Because it was a fiery letter, you know. I said, "This is it! We gotta take a stand!"

DUTCHIE SAFFERY: She said that Auntie Nona wanted to know how many would stand with her. And everyone raised their hands.

I wanted to sign in support. I felt that when one took pen to hand and signed your name, it was made a definite move.

Paulette said she was going to pass the letter around the room. And so it was sent around. But as it was being passed, a warning was flagged to everyone to be careful—because if they sign, that they should be aware of how vindictive Lokelani could be.

I didn't watch to see who signed it, or where it even ended up. I didn't ask. I know that I signed it. That was the beginning of my involvement.

PAULETTE MOORE: I remember saying the editor wanted to see signatures. 'Cause in her letter, Nona said, many of them agree with her. Well, who are the many? Give us the names. So everybody over there signed their names.

Except me because my daughter just got her job at Bishop Estate.

I said I would not sign my name. I would do everything else, I would plan, do whatever they wanted, but I couldn't sign my name.

That was very tough.

ROY BENHAM: The next day I called Nona back, and told her it was all good, and here's some of the things we were going to do. And I said, "What did you do with your letter?" And she said, "Uncle, thank you very much, but I mailed it already."

I said, "Oh, Nona."

PAULETTE MOORE: By this time, the news about what was happening at Kamehameha was beginning to filter out. I had people calling me and asking me, "What's all this trouble at Kamehameha?" And people who are non-Kamehamehans calling and asking me.

LEROY AKAMINE: From the meeting at our house, the manaʻo was shared, and the commitment that was made by the graduates there that we're going to come forward and do something.

TOMI CHONG: Nā Pua a ke Aliʻi Pauahi. The flowers, the children, of the chiefess Pauahi. Nā Pua was never organized in a formalized fashion. This was just a group of people. I mean, we were all graduates, who sang the songs, and enough of us who had read her life stories over and over again.

KAREN KEAWEHAWAII FARIAS: How quickly Nā Pua had come into birth. The birthing process was really, really fast. We went straight from conception into the labor room!

ROY BENHAM: And they said, "Roy, you the oldest, you be president." And I said, "Okay, I'll be president."

"Yes, yes, we were friends. He was a gentleman—always a gentleman, polite and kind and of course, he was so good looking and that was a plus factor … We were good friends. We thought, *Well, when we get to our respective colleges, I'll go to Kentucky to visit you and you come to Colorado to visit me.* We went up on the same ship. We held hands."

—Nona Beamer

Top to bottom: Nona Beamer graduates from Kamehameha, 1941; Roy Benham's senior picture, 1941

PAULETTE MOORE: The big question that lingered was, What can we do?

DUDLEY MAKAHANALONA: I think Oz just wanted us to take action.

TOMI CHONG: Oz was asking for support in whatever fashion.

DUDLEY MAKAHANALOA: Oz's daughter got up, and literally tears came down her eyes. She said, "My father, when he became a trustee had black hair." She said, "Look at him today—he's turned white overnight." And she had tears because of that.

TOMI CHONG: The question came—I believe it was from Roy Benham—"Oz, if we pursue the issue and we find that you are part of the problem, meaning you have equal fiduciary responsibility, are you willing to take the brunt of what would happen at the outcome?"

And he said, "Yes." In other words, it's more important to pursue the issue than to protect himself.

KAREN KEAWEHAWAII FARIAS: He said, "Don't worry about me; I have a paper trail." He said he had cc'ed all trustees about any and all grievances.

ROY BENHAM: He said, "If I lose my job, I lose my job. The main thing is that we save the school."

DUTCHIE SAFFERY: And then he left.

LEINA'ALA AKAMINE: That was the last meeting Oz attended. After that, he said, "You're on your own."

TOMI CHONG: We knew there was great potential to touch as many alums, without really having an opportunity to explain to them what the issues were.

DUDLEY MAKAHANALOA: We didn't have the money to go through a lawsuit. So we were talking some sort of a demonstration.

ROCKY TOKUHARA: We got to the end of the concerns, and it was decided that we were definitely going to march to make a statement. That was Auntie Dutchie's idea.

DUTCHIE SAFFERY: When I was invited to come to the Pacific Club and Oz was there, all Oz said was there was nothing he could do. His hands were tied, and whatever transpired had to come from us. Everyone asked, "What can we do?" and out of my mouth I said, "We have to march."

MOMI CAZIMERO: Dutchie Saffery. You know, sometimes it's kind of like an Auntie Nona kind of person—

You know them as sweet people, lovely—all kinds of wonderful adjectives. But the scrapper? The fighter? The person who will put that line in the sand? No, I didn't see that. I only knew Dutchie in this very warm, embracing kind of way. I didn't see the—ringleader! Nor did I see that in Auntie Nona. Until she wrote that letter.

DUTCHIE SAFFERY
"We have to march."

DUTCHIE SAFFERY: After these things transpired from that meeting with the class of '52, I felt that I was on a spiritual journey. That there was something greater than me, who was directing. I would say it's a spiritual guidance from a source that I know is there. On this spiritual journey, I have witnessed this time and time again. I know that it's the Lord's hand that's ahead of us, who has led us through this.

KAREN KEAWEHAWAII FARIAS: Dutchie! Ah, Dutchie—well, I think there are two people in my life who are the two women who are closest to God and hold hands with God that I know of. One of them is my Auntie Flo, and Dutchie would be the other one.

PAULETTE MOORE: I would say Dutchie was our spiritual leader. I would say she would be our wahine kahuna. She never let us forget that who was leading us was God.

DUTCHIE SAFFERY: I was led to write down a march.

That wasn't the first. There were many other things that I was led to sketch—I sketch things that come, and they can come at any hour; they come to reality.

The writing of the march itself was written before it even was mentioned at the Pacific Club. It was already written—on May 5,

"We will walk with pride, because we are the warriors of our Princess. We are going to do it for our future."

—Paulette Moore

1997, at 4:20 a.m. at Milan Chun's house. I woke up knowing that. It was in my head.

So when it came out there and when I was asked, "Where are we gonna go?" I could go right down the line.

PATRICK IONA: She even knew the route, everything.

DUTCHIE SAFFERY: It was to start at the Royal Mausoleum, at Pauahi's tomb, and exactly how the pattern would go, and we had to go past Washington Place, through the Capitol, stop at the Queen's bedroom where she was held prisoner, and sing "Queen's Prayer," past the palace, to Kamehameha's statue, through Kawaiaha'o Church and around Kawaiaha'o Plaza.

PATRICK IONA: May 15 became the march date because the talk-story meeting with the trustees was scheduled for that day and then cancelled.

PAULETTE MOORE: We would not shout and yell. We would be on the best behavior, so our Princess will be proud of us. That means—no yelling.

DUDLEY MAKAHANALOA: Everyone was gearing up already. We had meetings at Kawaiaha'o Church where the final details started getting laid. I remember at one meeting, some of the participants were getting hostile. They wanted to do this shouting match and all this heavy sign stuff, Down with the trustees! and all that business.

So I just stood up, and I said, "Wait a minute, we're not out here to kill these people, we're out to demonstrate," and I reminded them that we agreed at the Pacific Club to do this thing with class.

KAREN KEAWEHAWAII FARIAS: It would be an approach that something needed to be said, but not harshly. And reflecting on our school and our students and all the 'ohana at Kapālama. It should be an approach that Pauahi would be proud of.

PAULETTE MOORE: And we will walk with pride, because we are the warriors of our Princess. We are going to do it for our future. ⌐

The Brink of Something
The Campus Responds

13

Everyone knew that this was something so important—
what's at stake is huge. I remember the feeling of being
on the brink of something. –Kēhau Abad

GARY OBRECHT: I've always had a deep passion for justice. I wanted to be part of something that would pull people together to deal with some of the painful issues. I got involved because of specific issues. First of all, with Randie Fong—he seemed to be in fairly serious trouble. Mike Chun was probably going to be fired or definitely being fired. And that's when I got really emotionally involved. It seemed to be that there were a lot of irrational decisions being made on the part of trustees. People that I truly loved were being threatened. I suggested we could have a meeting.

KĀWIKA EYRE: We put notices, invitations, in the faculty mailboxes for May '97. My name was on there, Gary's name was on there. And within an hour, Sandy Behenna called, and said, "In the office, now."

It was Rockne Freitas and Sandy Behenna and the two of us, Gary and me.

GARY OBRECHT: Rockne was very jolly and was kind of pooh-poohing, that it wasn't that important.

KĀWIKA EYRE: There were veiled warnings.

GARY OBRECHT

SANDY BEHENNA
"In the office, now."

GARY OBRECHT: We were being told, not directly, that we better watch ourselves.

It was left up to us to decide what to do. We said we were going to go ahead and have the meeting, and I think we invited him—"Would you feel better if you came, because then you can see it live, and then you will know what is going on, and if you think we shouldn't be doing anything, tell us what it is." And he didn't come.

KĀWIKA EYRE: We were warned about future involvement but allowed to go ahead.

GARY OBRECHT: We heard through someone that Mrs. Lindsey knew that we were going to have a meeting, and said anybody who showed up at such a meeting would be fired.

I got on the phone with Elisa Yadao, and I remember saying that I don't care if I get fired, but I do not want to put other people in jeopardy. So if this is true, I want to know, so we can cancel the meeting, because I don't want anyone showing up and getting fired because of me, because I invited them. And she went and came back and she said, "Mrs. Lindsey said no, that wasn't true."

KĀWIKA EYRE: The first meeting was in the Choral Room, upstairs.

GARY OBRECHT: I remember calling Kīhei De Silva. I just wanted his opinion—if we had such a meeting, should we have Hawaiian prayers, should we have Hawaiian music?

I was very pleasantly surprised when people actually showed up. It was actually a very respectable number.

JANET ZISK: There must have been 20 or 25 of us. We sat on a length of seats, most of us on one side, all sort of lined up, like birds on a telephone wire, sort of looking to see what would happen. I remember barely having the courage to see who else was there, 'cause it was so frightening—sheer fright.

GARY OBRECHT: It was scary. People who had put their names on the invitation pulled out at the last minute out of fear. I guess I hadn't realized how strong the fear on campus was, when even some of the strongest people were scared. That made me all the more want to do something.

KĀWIKA EYRE: We wanted people to talk, because of the emotional load we were all carrying. We wanted to sing, and we wanted to pule. And don't say anything, but listen—real Quakerly, right? I think we knew that we had to model something which was so unlike what we were getting. We just knew in our hearts that we had to do it that way. Prayer, singing, moments of silence and an expressed understanding that everyone would listen hard, and speak soft, if at all.

HERB WILSON: It felt so good to be there for all of us to speak together. It's easy to be fragmented on that campus, and I think the way we had all been treated, that was encouraged. This was one opportunity for people to be pulled together.

TOM CHUN (*'63, Secondary School science teacher*): That was the first point where I ever saw our teachers get up as one, because they were so incensed. The word pono comes to mind. We talk about pono, but here I saw on people's face genuine concern, like something's wrong.

That's when my jaw started to drop. Because if you don't run around within certain circles, you never hear these kinds of things. And so I thought to myself, *Boy, am I out of the loop.*

I've always tried, like, to be a supporter and go along with the program, and not to rock the boat, but I couldn't stand this anymore.

One of the things I do, if I feel something's right or wrong, and I really believe in it, then I'll jump in and do something. I've already gone through that business with Concerned Parents. So I said, "Now I should be a concerned teacher."

KĀWIKA EYRE: This is what the meeting notes said:

1. *Our faculty <u>must</u> have an organized voice.*

2. *We <u>must</u> speak up. We must assert ourselves as professionals, and we must voice our convictions. The more positive we stay, the more effective we will probably be.*

3. *We <u>must</u> keep in mind—as a focus—the person and the will (i.e.,*

"Throughout this year, we all have been angered, saddened, confused, frustrated, and frightened by the things that have been happening at this school. Recently, we have become aware of colleagues leaving their jobs here in some cases because of these things that have been happening. We all have talked in private about these concerns.... We need to put our heads together and suggest solutions so that we can continue to love this place and work proudly and happily here."

–Gary Obrecht and Kāwika Eyre, from the call to the first informal faculty meeting regarding controversy, 5/7/97

the volition) of our benefactor. We are all here because of her and we must keep this in proper perspective.

4. *We __must__ continue to want to be part of Kamehameha. We cannot be effective if we do not want to be here.*

5. *We __must__ act our conscience.*

GREG BARRETT: Before I even wrote the big story about the unrest at Kamehameha Schools, I knew it was a big story, just from the way people weren't talking and were trying to keep it quiet.

A guy named Charlie called and said he had some information for me about Lokelani Lindsey and that he wouldn't talk to me in public. I said, "Come to my house," and we had coffee out on my deck.

He said he was related to Lokelani Lindsey, so I knew that he wasn't there to snitch on her.

During the course of the conversation, he intimated that he worked for Larry Mehau—and this sounds rather bizarre, but he said he was three rows down in the organization, or something along those lines, and that it was his job to make peace. He said specifically to make nice with people before they got hurt. He didn't say exactly that I was not to report. He lowered his eyeglasses and he looked at me and he said, "You know what I'm talking about, brah?"

And I did, and what he was saying was to stop digging for this story about the unrest at Kamehameha. Of course, I had no idea how deep it was—I just knew there were some problems between Dr. Chun and the faculty and Lokelani Lindsey. When that fella named Charlie came to my house and made a vague threat or left a vague threat, I knew there was a lot to it that I wasn't aware of.

I did think a lot about it at that time, and when I wrote the first

GREG BARRETT
Reporter Greg Barrett with newborn son, May 1997

Honolulu Advertiser headline on Greg Barrett article, 5/8/97

Furor erupts against Kamehameha Schools trustee
Alumni, teachers say she poisons morale, should be impeached?

story, I checked the rearview mirrors a few times on the way home.

Whether this guy was making all this up in fantasy, or had some grandiose image of himself, I really don't know. Very unintimidating fellow—mid-to-late 30s, thin, about 5-10, 145 pounds, Asian, dressed local, spoke local.

I never heard from Charlie again.

KĒHAU ABAD: I was in my homeroom at the start of the day, and I read Greg Barrett's article on the front page, and Auntie Nona's quotes in it. I was elated. Finally, someone is talking about this out loud and breaking through the thick layer of intimidation and coercion that kept so many people silent for way too long. I mean, it had already been years of watching abuse after abuse—from them closing down Extension Ed for no good reason, to Lindsey squelching the efforts that Pinky started and that the Fongs were seeing through to establish a cultural center, all the way to the smaller-scale torment that any given part of the school was enduring at the whim of Trustee Lindsey. Word was getting out about how problematic things were. Finally, she and her buddies on the board were going to have to start answering to people outside Kamehameha, people who weren't beholden to them.

KĒHAU ABAD
"I was elated."

I immediately read the whole article to my homeroom. They were silent; they were listening intently.

They were smart kids—they knew that the trustees had run amok. I remember the kids cheering over it. They were reacting to the article as they might to an action flick when the bad guys get busted.

But I clearly remember them settling down, and one of the quieter girls in class asking me, "So do you think anything's going to change?" When I told her, "They have to," I made my own little promise to myself. I needed to do something, get moving, do something. I remember, too, thinking that if Randie was brave enough to take her on, then we needed to chime in big time to underscore his point. He wasn't speaking on behalf of himself. There were hundreds of us who felt the same way.

"I read Greg Barrett's article on the front page ... and ... I made my own little promise to myself. I needed to do something, get moving, do something."

–Kēhau Abad

And what did it mean for us as a Kamehameha ʻohana to let that abuse go unchecked? We were living with an abusive head of household, silently letting that abuse go on and on, and creating all kinds of strange dysfunctional ways to deal with it. There was a

CHARLENE HOE
"It hit a chord."

whole lot about Kamehameha that needed fixing.

Within a really short time after that day in homeroom, Kāwika gave me a copy of his Statement of Concern. I was so glad that he was starting the forward movement. And I remember thinking that there were other things that I'd want to say in such a statement. But it didn't seem right to fuss with what Kāwika created. So I figured I'd just write a second one. I needed to do something, and for the moment that was it.

I remember also getting a call from Randie. Randie was talking with Oz, who I believe was trying to get a meeting together with a small set of teachers and the other trustees, so that the other trustees could hear directly from us. Because of Randie's and my close connection through our work on the Hawaiian Cultural Center Project, Randie knew very well what my manaʻo was, and that I wouldn't shy away from articulating it if asked. So he suggested that I be included. For the same reason, he suggested another fellow HCCP committee member from the Elementary campus, Charlene Hoe.

CHARLENE HOE: It definitely hit a chord within my own sense, and I know it did within Elementary.

Randie's situation was just a symptom. We had gone from a five-year contract to a one-year contract, with no discussion as to why this should happen. Our employee handbook had become progressively more restrictive, in my opinion more onerous. That became a real threat to us. When Randie decided to leave, that highlighted that fear and frustration.

KĀWIKA EYRE: Right before our second meeting, Tony Ramos called Gary and me into his office. He said he wanted to come to the meeting. Gary said that if the faculty had been listened to earlier, this would not have happened. His comment was not well received.

KĒHAU ABAD: More people showed than I would have expected. It would have been more than 40. I would say it was close to 50. Everyone knew that this was something so important—what's at stake is huge. I remember the feeling of being on the brink of something.

KĀWIKA EYRE: Our statements had a long list of ccs. And Tony held up the statement and said, "Well, you know, it's a really good thing that you guys are trying to do something. But if you're just interested in stirring up kūkae—that's why you're cc-ing it to everyone. If you are really interested in helping, you wouldn't cc it."

KĒHAU ABAD: Yeah, you should just go to Dr. Chun. He wanted it to be just an internal thing.

KĀWIKA EYRE: For the sake of our community, our students, our profession, we had to go public. We had to take our stand and make our statement. It was stand up now on our own feet and be counted, or just shrink away.

TOM CHUN: It was something we all had to make a decision. But the one thing that really bothered me, because I was a Kamehameha student, I was a Kamehameha parent, I was an alumni—I didn't know if by doing this it would take down the school as we know it right now.

But I was thinking to myself, *What is pono? If we are afraid of the truth, we cannot grow, we cannot be strong.* I've seen enough of people who were willing to stand, and that gave me encouragement to stand too. But as an alumni it's real hard to do that, because this is a school that gave me my sustenance, and still does. And there's no way you would want to harm the school. But yet there are people who're in charge that needed to have been, if not admonished, at least brought to some kind of reckoning for the actions that they took.

TOM CHUN
A concerned teacher

CHARLENE HOE: It was the third meeting when we were asked actually to step forward and do the signature, do the compact.

KĀWIKA EYRE: We decided to have T-shirts.

GAIL FUJIMOTO: We originally planned to do the T-shirts for ourselves, but did not know when we would wear them because we were so afraid. We decided to give them to the Nā Pua marchers once we discovered that the march was really going to happen because we felt it would be a very visible symbol of our protest.

I remember going to the silk screen vendor who had a little shop in Kalihi. This guy could do the work "quickly and confidentially." I remember asking him if he ever did work for KSBE and he said no, which was good, because I didn't want him losing business because of us. I remember taking the picture of Pauahi which I got from Janet Zisk with our wording. I described what we wanted and what it was for; he knew immediately that he was working on sensitive material. He gave us a very good price.

GAIL FUJIMOTO
"We were so afraid."

I delivered the shirts to Oz's house the night before the march. I don't remember how many shirts we made, but that was just the first printing. We did four more after that.

KĀWIKA EYRE: I felt very strongly about what I knew as our only opportunity to get the teachers to the right place. And that time was running out, and that we might lose that chance. If we didn't organize at that moment, get the statements signed and to the marchers, then we would be trivialized, trampled on, and it would be awful.

For me, the whole nobility of the profession was on the line, at stake. If we failed to stand up at that time, then all we stood for in front of our kids failed with us.

KĀWIKA EYRE: On campus at this point, the faculty basically is in rebellion. The alumni are in rebellion, with Dr. Chun in mind, supporting him and Oz.

ROCKY TOKUHARA: I'm the kind of people that—pick up the guns, let's go, let's get in the foxhole.

ROCKY TOKUHARA
"Let's get in the foxhole!"

MIKE CHUN: When I first became president, Rocky wasn't too sure about this guy Mike Chun. But there was something about her. What I saw in Rocky was leadership.

And then after I got to know her and talk to her about her time at Kamehameha—just seeing her with her classmates, they kind of gravitate to her. And she has a style about her; she has a spirit about her, a spirit of goodness. Even if sometimes she can be crude to me, and she's tired of me haranguing her about smoking, about swearing. And yet it's brought us closer together.

She has this real loving nature, a spirit of caring. She really has a good heart. Yeah, she was in my foxhole. She's never left my side. She's never left my side.

KĀWIKA EYRE: There were predictions that Mike wasn't going to last the week.

MIKE CHUN: I was a target. I mean, I was in the crosshairs.

KĀWIKA EYRE: The campus was boiling. I remember two of my students being interviewed on TV, one of them talking about the rumors and insisting that students had a right to know, and Keola Dalire talking about the war up there, forcing people to take sides.

MIKE CHUN: My understanding was that a lot had to do with not so much that I was being threatened, but that my role as president was being threatened, and that had to be changed.

Maybe I was the rallying point. But it was just a symbol. People said, "Mike, I going march, you know what—for you." I said, "No, I appreciate your support, I appreciate your aloha, I appreciate your concern. But this thing is bigger than Mike Chun. It's this school. If you marching for me, don't. But if you marching for the school, go down there. Because we got problems."

DUTCHIE SAFFERY: Really what I had hoped would happen was that the students and teachers would all walk off the campus together. I mean, that was to me going to be the biggest impact.

KĀWIKA EYRE: The students were extra jumpy, and the trustees had lost all our trust anyway.

WINONA FARIAS: Those classes, where the teachers were actually doing something, speaking out and trying to change things, they were the ones where we could discuss it. Probably Hawaiian and Social Studies mostly. Other classes, teachers weren't as comfortable talking about it, just "Let's go to our class material" kind of thing.

JIM SLAGEL: This was an exciting time for the kids. The kids were so active.

KĀWIKA EYRE: One of the strategies being thrown around was they were to call in sick and then go to the march instead—and final exams were coming up the next week.

JIM SLAGEL: It wasn't just, you know, "I want to miss a day of class"—kids will do that from time to time if there's a test. These were kids who realized they were on the edge of something really big. They knew the full gravity of this. They wanted to be part of the momentum.

And they knew that the issue was numbers. During our conversations on Kōnia Field, the kids would say, "You know, I'm one kid, but this is one of those times where I'm worth more than, say, a hundred people out in the community." Because if there's a kid out there marching, or students marching, you know, man, that carried a whole lot of weight. The kids are saying, "I can really make a difference here."

KAREN KEAWEHAWAII FARIAS: The first thing that comes to mind is how many students wanted to walk. And my daughters—especially Winona, she wanted to walk. She said, "I really want to do this."

KĀWIKA EYRE: There were rumors of a mass walkout, students threatening to form a procession from campus to the Royal Mausoleum at Mauna‘ala and join up with the Nā Pua march.

DUTCHIE SAFFERY: I thought, *Wow, it would have been dynamite if the teachers had walked with the students—just even walked out of*

the classroom into the middle of the field. It would have just literally stopped them. But it didn't happen.

KAREN KEAWEHAWAII FARIAS: I think in that particular arena, what comes to mind is Dr. Chun coming over the P.A. system and telling the students not to do this.

KĀWIKA EYRE: Mike interrupted classes to make a plea to the students on closed circuit television in every classroom.

He has an uncanny ability to connect with each student individually, even on TV. It's one of the reasons the kids love him so much.

He looked haggard, exhausted. He spoke slowly. He looked straight at the camera. He reminded students of the important reasons for being in school, and their responsibilities with final exams set to begin.

He chose his words carefully, earnest words for young hearts, to touch the deep sense of loyalty that comes with Hawaiian kids—loyalty to family, to Pauahi, to him.

He paused a moment, then leaned forward to the camera. His voice got stronger. He said, "I urge you not to participate in a walkout from class, or in a march planned by alumni and parents this Thursday morning. To do so would disappoint me greatly, and would be a burden which I do not need at this time."

May 13, 1997

To: Kamehameha Schools Faculty and Staff
From: Dr. Michael J. Chun
Re: Events of this Week

A lot has happened in the past week that may cause us to lose focus on our primary purpose—to offer our students the best education possible. The issues brought forth are real ones that require processing, discussion, and opportunities for input from all of us. Teachers and staff have an important role in contributing to the health of this institution. I would not discourage any of you from providing input through appropriate means.

Your concerns are being heard and I am working with our administrators and Trustees to improve the communications process. This morning a meeting was held with two trustees. Trustee Wong and Trustee Lindsey, and your school administrators to discuss the many issues that are of concern to us. The meeting was long and the discussion was honest. I believe much progress was made in identifying the problems and concerns that have led us to your current situation.

Several teachers have spoken with me about the need for a healing process within our 'ohana. I understand that such a process has begun within the faculty as you have developed a statement of concern. I fully support that discussion and dialogue, and would like to facilitate the presentation of your statement of concern to the Board of Trustees. However, I prefer to do this within the 'ohana, as I believe that would lead to a more open dialogue.

SANDY BEHENNA: Mike didn't want the kids to massively leave class. It was very important politically for Mike Chun to be seen as supporting kids staying in classrooms and in being in control of the situation.

KĀWIKA EYRE: It worked.

PAUL IONA: I know my parents wanted me to be there, but at the same time we wanted to respect Dr. Chun's wishes. I did want to go, but I understood Dr. Chun.

KAREN KEAWEHAWAII FARIAS: I think they were told if they left school for any reason than if they were ill or something, they would be given a grade less. I think that was the verbiage. But that still didn't deter their readiness to go. I said, "Well you know, you do what you have to do, and then we'll do what we have to do."

KĀWIKA EYRE: Administration made it real clear that the march day was a work day for us. For the kids, Mike sent out a written note: "Should any student choose not to heed my request and cuts classes or is truant from school this week, his or her absence will be considered unexcused. Consequences for unexcused absences are outlined in your Student Handbook. Keep focused, study hard, and prepare well for your exams. If you do so, we will end the year with dignity and pride, and Pauahi will smile."

MIKE CHUN: No parent ever came to me and said their kid got downgraded because of that. Normally, if a kid was penalized for something along those lines, it would come to me. I mean, it would have reached me. A parent would come see me. It's always because the parents bring it to me. None of that reached me. It did not.

LOKELANI LINDSEY: I went up to talk to President Chun about the march. I told him that I think this is wrong, that he should stop it. President Chun very emphatically told me, "I'm hands off on this. This is Oz Stender's deal." I came back and noted such.

MIKE CHUN: I never said that.

LOKELANI LINDSEY: I didn't say the march was improper. I said Trustee Stender's involvement with the march was improper. I don't feel that Trustee Stender should be out there telling people to march against the trustees.

Protest planned against trustees
Bishop Estate accused of mismanaging school

–Honolulu Advertiser
headline, 5/9/97

DICKIE WONG: You know, I was kind of surprised when it did happen, that there was a plan. First time I kinda looked at it was when there were words coming out that there was to be a march from Mauna'ala, and they were gathering support for that, and other groups in the community were involved. And I'm not sure how they put it together, but they did.

MIKE CHUN: There's no question in my mind that the trustees knew what was going on. I cannot see how Dickie can sit there and say they had no clue of what was going on, number one. Number two, if that is really true, then he should have been off that board. The worst sin is that he didn't know—because that's all the evidence you need that this guy wasn't in this trusteeship for the school, he was in this trusteeship for himself.

The only other trustee I remember talking to about the march was Gerry Jervis. I got a call, and I'm recalling that they felt I had the power to call this whole thing off. And my response was, "I don't have the power, and I wouldn't do it anyway."

I said, "Gerry, don't stop it. The worst thing you could do right now is to stop it. And I'm not going to close down school for this to happen. Our students will have to be at school. If the march is going to be during the school day, they need to come to school. But if it's going to be before or after school, this is their right to do." That's what I told him.

ROY BENHAM: We decided on at the Pacific Club, one, that we were going to walk, and two, that I was going to meet with Lokelani, because there were still some of us who still did not want to take it outside.

No way was I going to meet with her alone. Because I wanted to have somebody else there with me, and I always do that when I meet on this kind of matters. I said, "Tomi Chong will be there." And she was kind of taken aback, and she said, "Okay." So the next day we meet at the Pacific Club parking lot, and we went up to the school in my car.

When we got up to the meeting, Tomi and I are sitting there, and Lokelani comes in and Dickie Wong comes in with her. And she never told me she was bringing Dickie.

TOMI CHONG: After the pleasantries in the beginning and the introductions, it was clear that they had done some research on both of us. Because Loke dropped some names of people—"Oh, you're so and so's friend," and "You work here"—and of course they knew all about Roy and his involvement at Kamehameha—

ROY BENHAM: And sometime during that initial conversation, the fact that she knew we were planning on walking. I was surprised at that, and also she knew about some of the things that were discussed at Leroy's house. So I remember at that time figuring out that there was a mole. Whoever it was.

JOE TRAVIS: People were feeding back information to the trustees. It was obvious that some of the people who were attending the meetings were friends of Dickie Wong's and other trustees. I mean, they were playing both sides, easily—it was wide open.

ROY BENHAM: We got into talking about Lokelani's behavior in the school and the fact that she was usurping Mike Chun's role there. Dickie Wong said, "Well, you know, I'm the chairman and she's in charge of education. And I want her to tell me what's going on."

I said, "Dickie Wong, I remember in the past, if the trustees wanted to know what was going on at the Schools, they would ask the principal, the president. This lady"—and here's Lokelani sitting right here—"you're telling her to find out what she has to do, so she has to go do this, this, this. So basically you're the driving force behind this. If you didn't put those demands on her, she wouldn't be up here poking her nose into everything."

She didn't say two words, really. I had the feeling that because her boss was there, she didn't have much to say. And he just sat and took it.

TOMI CHONG: Before we got there, Roy and I decided that if it was their intent to stop the march, then we would want them to say that. And then we would tell them we wouldn't.

NEIL HANNAHS: My advice had been, go to Mauna'ala, embrace these people, march with them and extend our Hawaiian hand, saying, "If I've done anything to offend you, I apologize. We have tried to do the very best for this institution, the beneficiaries. Clearly you disagree. We commit to sitting down and dialoguing with you to work this out, and to march with you, show some solidarity."

NEIL HANNAHS
"Embrace them."

I don't trust that Loke would have really done that sincerely. Had she done it, I mean, it would have been, lead 'em on, lead 'em on, lead 'em on.

TOMI CHONG: It was a pleasant meeting until Roy said something to the effect that, "If you're here to tell us to stop this march, then we're not gonna."

Dickie pretty much slammed the table with his fist—his hand. And then he started pounding his hand, saying, "You people, you just don't know what you're doing!"

JOE TRAVIS
"Playing both sides."

JOE TRAVIS: The night prior to the march, a dinner was initiated by Dickie Wong. At the Yum Yum Tree.

When he called me, I made it a point to get ahold of Leroy Akamine so I had someone there to support my views.

While we were at the dinner, he asked both Leroy and myself, "Is it okay if Henry Peters joins us?" and we said, "Yeah."

So, Dickie's really angry about this proposed walk and trying to see if he could defuse that by having, you know, the alumni cancel the walk.

He had a chance to halt it. Leroy and I made the comment that if you leave this restaurant and you walk down to Kawaiaha'o where all the alumni were gathered in preparation for the walk the following day—how they was going to conduct themselves, logistics, all about that—all you need to tell the group there is that you will be removing Lokelani from the school. That's all. I think if somebody came up and said, "Hey, Loke's off this campus, we're not gonna march," we would all agree. And the walk will end right there.

And his remark was that Lokelani was the most learned instructor in public education, and she had the credentials for that, and we don't have anybody on the board who has that kind of expertise, and she knows Kamehameha Schools quite well.

LEROY AKAMINE: We had a nice long meeting, but in final analysis, it didn't work, they weren't willing to come to the table and have some serious discussions. What we were offering them was an opportunity to meet with Nā Pua and to discuss all the questions that we had and resolve the Mike Chun issue, but they were unwilling.

JOE TRAVIS: Dickie and Henry walked out to talk about it. They came back and they said they weren't going to.

Finally, Dickie pounded the table and he said, "Okay, let's do it!"—pounding on the table.

LEROY AKAMINE: I said this amongst ourselves, that when this comes to pass, I'm sure that they're kicking themselves in the ʻōkole. You know how you stand up and you bring your leg backwards, try to kick yourself in the ʻōkole—they've done that.

I told Dickie, "Dickie, I'm being instructed that only you can go down and receive the palapala that they're gonna give you."

He said, "Why me?" I said, "Don't send your assistants. And first of all, don't send Lokelani, because, boy, this thing will never end."

KĀWIKA EYRE: We knew we had to have faculty representation at the Nā Pua march. I mean, it was inconceivable that a march about this crisis in our school wouldn't include the teachers. Whatever the risk, our voices had to be heard.

We had written two statements which expressed our concerns. We wanted these statements walked down with the marchers and presented to the trustees with a cover letter. And we felt we as teachers should do it.

CHARLENE HOE: We had two versions of the cover letter. We had the one if we couldn't come, asking someone to please read it. And then otherwise we would have said—

KĒHAU ABAD: We were prepared for either-or.

SANDY BEHENNA: Rockne had told Sandy Wicklein that there was no way the four Nā Kumu leaders would be permitted to attend the march. Period. I assume it was from above.

KĀWIKA EYRE: We telephoned Oz and told him they weren't willing to cover us with substitues.

CHARLENE HOE: Oz was still going to try.

KĀWIKA EYRE: He called Sandy Behenna and told her to arrange for subs for us four Nā Kumu reps in the unlikely event that the majority trustees would support a faculty delegation to the march. She was visibly irritated.

We had to fill out the normal form for being absent and check off the reason. We went down the choices. We weren't sick. Not a funeral. Not really a day off for personal business. I think Kēhau finally laughed and said it must be the professional development box!

KĒHAU ABAD: So this was May 14th, and the next morning, with substitutes covering our classes, we met at an agreed-upon place, Keōua 203, a teacher workroom on the 9th- and 10th-grade campus.

The plan was that Oz would bring Gerry Jervis and Dickie Wong, and we would make our case for representing the faculty on the march.

GARY OBRECHT: Oz finally arrived late and told us that the trustees were mad. They wouldn't meet with us, and we wouldn't be allowed to go down to the march.

CHARLENE HOE: Oz couldn't get them together.

KĒHAU ABAD: The meeting we were waiting for would not occur.

CHARLENE HOE: We didn't find out until super-late.

KĀWIKA EYRE: The march was happening.

KATHY KUKEA: Robin Makua drove downtown to check it out.

ROCKY TOKUHARA: Robin said to me, "Oh, when I knew the march was starting, I didn't have class, so I drove by Mauna'ala and saw all the people." She had other faculty in the car with her. They're all crying.

KATHY KUKEA: My hope was that there would be a lot of people. I was afraid that it would be just this little whimper. And Robin reported back that there were hundreds of people. And we sat there in Midkiff lounge with tears running down our cheeks.

CHARLENE HOE: It was totally clear that, okay, we're not going to be able to join it—but somehow we had to get the faculty's voice down there.

KĀWIKA EYRE: —So we got in Charlene's van—

GARY OBRECHT: —It was a major disobedience.

KĀWIKA EYRE: Me in shotgun, Gary in the middle and Kēhau in the back changing into her disguise. Out of the nice dress she was wearing to meet the trustees and into her jeans, T-shirt, dark glasses and baseball cap. She looked all of 17—just like one of our students. And off we went. ✎

"It was inconceivable that a march about this crisis in our school wouldn't include the teachers. Whatever the risk, our voices had to be heard."

—Kāwika Eyre

14 A Walk of Peace
Alumni March

We felt that this should be a walk of peace, representing our Princess, and that they should be dignified, so we acted accordingly. –Leroy Akamine

Marchers gather at Kamehameha Statue.

LEROY AKAMINE: We'd like to describe it as a walk of peace, but nonetheless, the media picked it up as a march—and this is something that we wanted to emphasize, that this was not a march in the way that marches are held and the strong terms of being forceful and angry. We felt that this should be a walk of peace, representing our Princess, and that they should be dignified, so we acted accordingly.

PAULETTE MOORE: And so what was brought out was that we are children of the Princess. And so we will act like the children of the Princess. With great dignity.

TOMI CHONG: Dutchie did her protocol role.

ROCKY TOKUHARA: Auntie Dutchie was hung up on plumerias. She is a student of Maiki Aiu Lake, who just loved plumerias, and so Auntie Dutchie loves—everything was always plumerias. And that was the thing. All of the Nā Pua people had to bring plumeria leis.

DUTCHIE SAFFERY: Everyone complied and they all wore plumeria leis. Leading the march was Likeke Bell, blowing the pū.

Prior to the march, very early that morning, my sister and I, like at 5:30 in the morning, we went to every place in prayer before the march began. Yvonne Lee drove, and I ran in and out and placed the plumeria lei everywhere, each of the key places. The placing of these lei was important, that there was one hanging by the time the march began. So those lei were all in place and ready to receive everyone.

TOMI CHONG: My role was that I controlled the script. Once we finalized and pasted it up and went down to the copier and had enough to give everybody—the object was to control and manage the people. That became most important to me. That was my role.

We had points of interest where we wanted to stop along the way, and what we wanted to achieve at those points. We organized ourselves so that people would be responsible for those points We had people in charge of certain legs. They took the legs from Mauna'ala to Washington Place.

DUTCHIE SAFFERY: Tomi Chong was responsible for everything that happened up at the Mausoleum. Julie Nurre was the alaka'i, the leader. Pat Iona was assisting her. They were responsible for Kawaiaha'o Plaza when we got down there, and the actual line-up.

ROCKY TOKUHARA: The reason we picked the route was because we wanted to touch the governor. We felt it was important to take our message to the Capitol so the legislators could see. Needless to say why we wanted to be on the Palace grounds. And then we went to the State Supreme Court because they are the ones who appoint the trustees. We wanted to take our concerns to them. And then to the horse's mouth, to the trustees. So from the court building to Kawaiaha'o Plaza.

DUTCHIE SAFFERY: On the map I made, the yellow line was the actual march itself.

ROCKY TOKUHARA: From the inception of Auntie Dutchie's plan to actually getting there and seeing all that actually transpire was totally overwhelming for me. It was so emotional to be there.

MOMI CAZIMERO: I don't think I was the only person crying, by the way. I don't think we hit the high notes in "Keli'i Pauahi."

KĀWIKA EYRE: Many people were wearing white and blue T-shirts that the teachers had made. The shirts had the likeness of Pauahi, with the words "We Care," and "Kū'ē Pono," resist appropriately—those apparently were the words of Lili'uokalani to some of the younger, angrier Hawaiians wanting to take up arms at the time of the overthrow in 1893.

TOMI CHONG: We lined everybody up by decade.

ROCKY TOKUHARA: I mean people, old, old people, classes like the '20s, '30s came. They can barely walk, and they were determined—they were going to walk down the street no matter what.

TOMI CHONG: The '30s, the '40s, the '50s, all the way into the '90s. And it kind of brought order to everybody.

PAULETTE MOORE: The people who turned out were really beyond our expectations. I guess word got around for what was happening at Kamehameha, and people took the day off and came down and joined us.

"By being here I am supporting things that hopefully will make everything right."

–Robert Cazimero '67, KHNL-TV News, 5/15/97

OZ STENDER: Pinky Thompson and Laura came. My wife Ku'ulei—she's an alum, and she's been supportive of me. She wanted to do it, and I said, "That's the right thing for you to do; you have to do it."

ROCKY TOKUHARA: What was so cool is Robert Cazimero and Lee Mann came to Mauna'ala with their pahu.

And as the procession marched out, they beat the pahu. A couple of my friends who are longtime members of Robert's hālau, they brought their hālau kids, and the kids marched with us, too. And they happened to be graduates also. It was surprising to see all those persons there. It was, "Hey Rock, howzit? What's up with you? Kumu told us to come and so we're gonna march with you guys."

GUSSIE BENTO: I was very proud to be there. I cried when we left Mauna'ala.

KAREN KEAWEHAWAII FARIAS: There was that dedication, if you will, the service to begin the walk with. There was a slight drizzle—the blessing, yeah. It was so beautiful.

TOMI CHONG: Once we decided what would be chanted, pretty much everybody picked up on it. Dutch did it from the beginning of the march right through. I think she probably lost her voice. I mean, her energy was just amazing.

Māpuana de Silva and Likeke "Babe" Bell open ceremony at Pauahi's crypt.

DUTCHIE SAFFERY: I had prayed and asked for guidance. I saw Coline Aiu and was telling her about what was happening and the march, and she said, "Māmala Hoa," Kamehameha the Great's Law of the Splintered Paddle.

When I read the words, I knew that was the answer to my prayer. Just the first verse was all that we needed to chant. I would call it out and the others would chant line for line after me—

> *E nā kānaka!*
> *E mālama 'oukou i ke akua!*
> Oh, my people!
> Your allegiance is to our god!

KAREN KEAWEHAWAII FARIAS: Merv Thompson was given the duty of setting up transportation.

Making sure that our elderly, if they wanted to participate in the march, that if they got tired they would be able to be picked at any time. And that was really nice, because those who wanted to come out were driven out, and those who needed to get picked up along the route—they even got a trolley just to do that.

ROY BENHAM: The people were very supportive once they saw the huge—once they saw what we were about. You see, we didn't have any signs, but they had already figured that that's what this was. Usually—"Oh, what the hell you guys doing?—I wanna get through!" Because we were backing traffic up. But nobody's squawking—smiling and waving, just saying, "Way to go!" Marion Joy coordinated the police and got them to donate their time.

We were walking down to Punchbowl and the light turned red so that we could cross the street. Well, when the leading bunch decided to cross at Punchbowl and Beretania, the whole gang decided to cross at the same time. I looked back up the street and here was this whole bunch of people. We had just grown from the time we had started, you know.

KĀWIKA EYRE: From in our Nā Kumu van, I looked way up the street just as the whole march that had been lining the sidewalk seemed to turn on cue, and everyone crossed. The police were holding the traffic and letting everyone cross at once. It was the picture of a beautiful long wave breaking blue and white across the street.

Roy Benham and Dutchie Saffery lead marchers with splintered paddle.

ROY BENHAM: We were in the lead. We went into the governor's house, only just a few of us, and Governor Cayetano was there, and the attorney general, Margery Bronster.

FRED CACHOLA: Toni Lee and Tomi Chong said, "Fred, you do the hoʻokupu, the gifts, to Governor Cayetano." And I did it.

ROY BENHAM: And the governor said, "You guys are right, you're doing something about your concerns, and I think that's terrific for you guys." Nothing specific, just admiring what we were doing.

CRYSTAL ROSE: I was in my office, and I have a very beautiful view that can see this march go through the capitol to the palace. And I was very sad. A day of Hawaiians marching on Hawaiians doesn't sound right to me.

Something had to be done. It was very distressful to me personally that people felt that they had to do it this way, and the trustees being as obstinate as they were to shut it off. And that it required Hawaiians to then march on them.

Not that marches are bad—it's just to think that Hawaiians, that are usually a group that are very open and well-receiving of diverse opinions and diverse people, felt that there was no other choice. And that's what they had to do, you know—and on their own people! These are teachers, these are students.

That is a significant event for me. I think from then on I realized I had to take a more active role.

ROY BENHAM: We walked into the Capitol, and we went outside to the Queen's statue.

DUTCHIE SAFFERY The lei was in the Queen's hand.

ROY BENHAM: And we sang the Queen's song, "Makalapua." Māpuana de Silva, the kumu hula, she led us.

GARY OBRECHT: When we got to ʻIolani Palace, I can remember being almost terrified. Because someone could look right in the van. Kēhau saw someone that she recognized running around snapping pictures.

ROY BENHAM: People were still joining us. They were waiting for us to get there before they joined. So we walked around to the Palace, the Waikīkī end of the Palace. I was showing them where to go, "Go that way." One of the class of '47 gals came and said, "Roy, where are they now?" And just as I was about to tell her, I heard the "Queen's Prayer."

I said, "They're under her window." I was all chicken skin by that time.

DUTCHIE SAFFERY: We had placed a lei at the corner below her bedroom. And we placed another at the Kamehameha statue.

TOMI CHONG: At the King Kamehameha statue, a graduate was stepping forward, and it was a male, and he was very pumped up, like he wanted to rush—to do something negative. And I had to ask him to just calm down.

They had guards in the front of Aliʻiolani Hale. They were all State security. Thank God one of them was a Kamehameha graduate! Cappy Caminos was their head, and I just basically went up to him and said, "Cappy, we're not here to create any problems—why you have all these guys?" And he said, "Oh no, the justice wanted to be real clear about

"These people protesting are … among the frequently silent majority of Hawaiians who are educated, responsible, law-abiding and tax-paying. And they are fed up."

–*Kaui Philpotts, '58 letter to the editor,* Honolulu Advertiser, *5/15/97*

"Tears crept down the cheeks of Kamehameha Schools alumna Lovey Douglas as she stood in shade outside ʻIolani Palace yesterday and softly sang the 'Queen's Prayer' with hundreds of other school supporters. 'It's good to see the Hawaiians get together,' said the 79-year-old Nuʻuanu resident and 1935 graduate."

–*Honolulu Advertiser, 5/16/97*

what was going to take place." And I had faxed out information so that the governor's office would know what would take place at Washington Place and at the State Capitol, and even to the trustees, 'cause you know we were heading down there. So, I mean, it's not like we were hiding anything.

GARY OBRECHT: We went back to the Kamehameha statue and parked right there.

"In love for our benefactress and our schools."

–Carol Kapu and Fred Cachola

"Please know that I have no anger in my heart, only sorrow. I know that this 'Walk' is not being done in anger but in love for our benefactress and our schools."

–Carol Kapu, letter to her supervisor, 5/14/97

KĀWIKA EYRE: We couldn't openly represent the teachers. We decided that Kēhau's dad, Fred Cachola, would be the right person. So Kēhau slips away, in student disguise.

KĒHAU ABAD: I had to get the documents and deliver the documents. I remember them chanting, and I was so proud.

FRED CACHOLA: She gives me the petition. She tells me, "The teachers would like you to present this." And I felt, Wow! I felt very privileged. I said, "Oh, I'd be glad to do that."

KĀWIKA EYRE: They were going to meet with Chief Justice Moon upstairs in Aliʻiolani Hale. Fred Cachola would deliver our teachers' statements. Karen Keawehawaii's daughter Tracie would represent the alumni along with the students. She was carrying the petitions. I had gotten a call earlier saying that Dutchie Saffery's sister, Carol Kapu, would represent Kamehameha Schools employees.

DUTCHIE SAFFERY: She's a graduate, class of '52. She worked for Kamehameha Early Education in Hāna with young mothers and their infants. She had asked for a leave without pay for the day. That was bold.

She received a phone call a day prior to her departure to say that if she was going to participate in the march, she would not have a job. It came from the Kamehameha office.

She called me. She was crying that her job was on the line. I warned her of the dangers of her involvement. She said she wanted to be involved. I said, "You need your job; you have to take care of what your needs are, so don't do this just because I'm doing it. If you choose not to come, I'll understand."

She called me back within the hour and said, "I'm coming. If they fire me, then they fire me. But I'm coming. I must do this."

I said, "Well, you have to know that when you walk down that street, you will have no income at the end of that walk. Is that really what you want to do, Carol?"

And she said, "I need to do it."

PETER KAMA: I think that the conch shell announcement of the arrival and I think the attire of the leadership moving forward and then the masses following—it was so impressive that there could be unity among so many people who would be the beneficiaries.

And then it made us uniform when we got down to the Kamehameha Statue and we see what we described as paid people to photograph who was in the scene. Some people were intimidated and put themselves out of sight from the photographers.

HENRY MEYER: I've been a movie buff since I was a kid, you know, a home-movie type of thing, and I've also been a videographer both on a personal and professional basis. So I've had a lot of involvements with this thing.

I kind of thought this might be a very significant thing, a demonstration against the Bishop Estate and the trustees and such. I felt it would be a good one to just kind of take, for posterity's sake.

ROY BENHAM: When we went upstairs, they ushered us into this meeting room, and the Chief Justice comes in, and the first thing he says to me was, "Mr. Benham, I really admire your folks' deportment, you know, the way you're doing this—it's really terrific. No signs, no rabble rousing."

I said, "Well, we really have some concerns and here's the list. We hope you will be made aware of some of our concerns, and hopefully you can be supporting our efforts to address them." The list of concerns were authentic.

When I handed them to the Chief Justice, he said, "Well, you know, these kinds of things are more for the probate judge"—all this crap. I said, "Sir, you appoint the probate judge. So would you be sure that he sees these?" He nodded and that was it.

As we finished, they started singing "Imua Kamehameha." Then

"'It's a complaint that somebody has, and not a lawsuit,' [Chief Justice] Moon said. 'Until it is an issue before us, we have no authority to act.'"

—Honolulu Advertiser, *5/8/97*

"To the Supreme Court Justices who presently choose to distance themselves from this furor, I say this: You begat five spoiled children; tend to them."

—*Mary Pua'a, '53 letter to the editor,* Honolulu Advertiser, *5/18/97* we shook hands and we left and he thanked us. He said he would certainly look into it.

ROY BENHAM: Then we walked downstairs, going to Kawaiahaʻo Plaza, and somebody came up with the idea, when we go by the church, no singing, so we walked by Kawaiahaʻo Church in silence in deference to the Princess' church.

TOMI CHONG: It was very emotional by that point.

DUTCHIE SAFFERY: Then, as we approached the Kawaiahaʻo Plaza building, our voices got louder and louder, the pace slowed, the words were more direct and a much deeper tone. It was a very bold warning, loud and clear.

PATRICK IONA: At Kawaiahaʻo Plaza—make sure that the crowd didn't get out of control, they didn't damage anything. If we did see people from the outside that were there to antagonize or anything, then we were supposed to work with the police, because we had all volunteer police and they were going to help us make sure they didn't get unruly.

FRED CACHOLA: I'll never forget the shock—as we came down King Street and walked towards Kawaiahaʻo Plaza, there's a bunch of bushes here, and the building, and there's only a narrow gap there. And in that gap is Dickie Wong, and a guy who was Office of Hawaiian Affairs trustee, and some kūpuna, and they're blocking, obviously, physically blocking, shoulder to shoulder—"Okay, you guys not going anywhere, this is it." Very intimidating. I think they wanted everything to end right there.

But the game plan was not to enter there anyway. The game plan was to walk completely around the building and come in from the other side. And we just looked at them and walked right past. And they were looking at us—"Why don't they?" But when we started walking around the building, it was obvious again that they weren't going to stop us from the other side. They didn't have enough people. There were too many of us.

So we came in and started setting up.

HENRY MEYER: I got pictures of them marching into Kawaiahaʻo Plaza.

FRED CACHOLA: And then Pualani Akaka, Reverend Akaka's daughter, who was a preschool teacher and working with Nānāikapono, Nānākuli Elementary Preschool, she came up to me and she said, "Would you please present this petition?" I said, "Wow! We got a petition not just from the school but from Nānākuli! You know, signed by Nānākuli parents—wouldn't Henry Peters love to see this!" And I really felt very honored to be called and to personally present these to Dickie Wong.

KAYLIA IONA: They have kūpuna sitting on benches; Dickie Wong is sitting next to a couple of them. It upset me because the trustees placed them there. They had nothing to do with our concerns, why we were there. They were there for Dickie Wong and Peters and Lindsey and Jervis, telling us, you know, we were wrong in what we were doing.

PATRICK IONA: Telling us, "Shame on you." I'm angry because they were brought in. They were used.

KAYLIA IONA: And these are our elders—of course we're not going to say anything back.

"… they were brought in.
  They were used."

–Patrick Iona

A broken Kamehameha family gathers at Kawaiahaʻo.

ROY BENHAM: We came in the South Street entrance to the courtyard. Now, we didn't know what was going to happen there.

ELISA YADAO: At first we wanted the trustees to talk. But by the end, the day before, and even that morning, it was just, Look, go out there and listen to what they have to say. Or at the very least we wanted to put tables up there, and have food, and something for people to drink, so that when they came down they'd be able to sit and have some refreshment and be made to feel like they were being welcomed and that someone on the trustee level would go down there and listen to them. We had this whole game plan in place. Buy this food, buy these drinks, get the paper plates out, put the tables down, and say, "Here, you know—we want to listen to what you have to say."

Me, I believe that had they done that that day, the thing would have been done.

And Mrs. Lindsey said, "Absolutely not! You absolutely will not! We will not talk to them; they're marching against the trustees!"

You see how we fell into that? People have a constitutional right to do whatever they want. I mean, why couldn't they be out there? Why couldn't the teachers be there? We just handled the whole thing wrong.

HOLOUA STENDER: I thought, *Boy, these guys are really, really stupid.* Because there were so many things that could have happened to make it a positive affair.

ELISA YADAO: We were all filled with incredible sadness, that we had this disagreement in our family that was being played out in such a public way.

I remember seeing Gussie Bento, and that was just one of the things that moved me to tears. 'Cause I was happy to see her, but I was so sad, you know, and she saw me, and we looked at each other, and then I remember thinking, *Here are all these people, so many people that I think the world of, Laura Thompson and all these people.*

Kind of a sickness set in that wasn't just mine alone. That there was just this kind of thud in our stomachs, and I thought, *Oh my God, now we're sinking to yet another low.* It was kind of like being in a tomb. Alternately being in a tomb or being in a bunker.

Dickie Wong said, "I have to go down there. I need to go and at least take what it is that they're giving to us."

Mrs. Lindsey was furious. She was in her office and refused to come out.

OZ STENDER: The trustees agreed that we wouldn't all confront the group. That Dickie was the one, as the chair, to go down and meet with them. And we'd stay away from it. Which is the right thing.

But as they came through the back end of the courtyard—if you notice, those office windows are tinted, so if you keep the lights off you can't see in—well, all the trustees left their lights off and were looking out. And my office—from day one, I took all the blinds down, took all the drapes down. Because there's a pleasant view outside the office. And there's no sun that bothers it, because they get one big kamani tree, and so I never had any blinds on my window. Mrs. Lindsey, who was next to my office, can see that I was waving to people and people waving to me.

LOKELANI LINDSEY: He stood at his window with his curtain wide open, waving to all these people and showing the shaka sign, and they were all waving to him and throwing kisses to him as they marched into Kawaiaha'o Plaza. I viewed the marchers doing this to him. The television cameras captured him doing this to the marchers.

OZ STENDER: And she came over and wanted me to turn my light off. You know, she had the gall—

I said, "We all agreed not to confront the group as a group, but I didn't say anything about my not watching and waving to the people I know." And that was it.

And later they hired some security guy to come and tell me I gotta put the drapes back up, because somebody could get in the tree and take a picture of whatever was on my desk! Would you believe? I mean, the joke! They think I'm a kid or something? Did the drapes go back up? No.

"We were in the parking lot because we didn't want to be caught on camera. And you come back that afternoon and reflect on that, Golly ... am I a coward that I was afraid to be out there marching as well? Like what was wrong with me that I wasn't willing to stand up and be counted. So there was that kind of soul-searching that was going on I think for us down here.

"The way I justified it in my own mind was, Well, I'm the double agent ... I'm undercover ... because I'm getting stuff to Oz. And so ... if the Loke and Dickie people don't know that I'm doing this then maybe in my own little way I'm doing the right thing. And that's how I sort of settled it for myself."

—LeeAnn Crabbe

ROCKY TOKUHARA: Oz was waving from his window. People staring. Staff members would trickle out.

JOE TRAVIS: Lokelani was above with the photographers taking all the picture of all the people walking, coming to Kawaiahaʻo Plaza.

OZ STENDER: I had no idea that they were going to do that. I just saw them out there, which I thought was wrong.

PATRICK IONA: It was like, okay, where's your integrity, guys? I know you guys work with these people, but you know this is wrong, but yet you're still doing it because they're telling you to do it.

PAULETTE MOORE: Gardy Kealoha, he had a job at Kawaiahaʻo Plaza, so his job was to take pictures. Gardy was the one sitting in the patio and snapping pictures of those that marched.

Gardy and I were friends from Saint Andrew's, and when he saw my sister and me, he just put down the camera and laughed and laughed and laughed, and he said, "Oh, no—you two made it down from Maunaʻala?" And so my sister said, "Don't act!" He put his camera down, I don't know, maybe it was out of friendship, right, because that we had heard later that he was snapping pictures of everybody.

ROCKY TOKUHARA: And the joke among the Nā Pua people was, "Smile! You're on Candid Camera!"

ROY BENHAM: I looked up and saw Loke taking our pictures. I said, "Hey, include me in your Christmas card, Loke!"

ROY BENHAM: Dickie Wong comes downstairs. Fred Cachola had the Nā Kumu documents, so I said, "Go ahead, you read them."

FRED CACHOLA: You know, Dickie Wong was trying to maintain face and smile as much as he could. I went up and presented it. I read it from the teachers' Statement of Concerns, where the teachers were saying, "Let our absence here today speak louder than words ever could." So I read that as loud and as clear as I could.

KAYLIA IONA: Fred was very powerful.

FRED CACHOLA: And what a joy there was! Oh, man! The response from the group was just outrageous. I mean they were ecstatic to hear that. They were cheering, shouting, screaming.

And Dickie Wong's jaw just dropped. I mean, his whole face was just—I can't believe what I'm hearing, and pretty soon he was like, I don't care what I'm hearing. I think he's doing his best not to, because he knew that this was coming from a source that he could not bear.

JOE TRAVIS: He always felt he had the protection of the school. And when something coming out from the school that way, that he wasn't aware of—very, very embarrassing. Yeah. He wasn't prepared for that.

FRED CACHOLA: Here it was, the first time that I know of where the faculty and the school staff were saying in public, directly confronting the trustees.

I knew I was just a spokesman at that time, with all the people who are behind this message. I wasn't speaking as an individual; I'm carrying a message from hundreds of people and I'm speaking for them. I mean everybody. When we got down there, it really was a conglomerate of alumni, friends, parents, everybody. A clear showing that there were many, many people. This wasn't just a dissident, a small dissident—there was a widespread feeling that something's wrong.

PETER KAMA: The unity of all the people was wonderful—to show with numbers that you have to recognize that you did something wrong. It was a turning point against the trustees.

MOMI CAZIMERO: At that moment I felt so proud, so proud of us! I felt proud that we were defending Pauahi. Defending our school. Defending our alma mater. I was just awash in emotion, and I felt for the first time we were doing something. You know, there's a difference between talking about wanting to do something and actually doing it. But that day I could not have felt more proud.

FRED CACHOLA: It might have been one of the biggest blows to the trustees, having somebody from inside their house telling them how bad it was, telling them, "You gotta do right."

I don't think Dickie Wong ever in his wildest dreams imagined

FACULTY
STATEMENT
"Faculty members wished to be here with you today to share our statement of concern and our dedication to working towards solutions. We were prohibited from attending. Today's paper reports that "the trustees are very much interested in finding solutions, and committed to starting a healing process for the Kamehameha Schools family." At the same time, we have this morning, once again, been denied our request to send even a small delegation to represent our voice. Let our absence here today speak louder than words ever could."

that that could have happened. That their supremacy and their decision-making would be unquestionable, and that this power to do as they thought was right would never be challenged.

It was a humbling experience for him. Dickie Wong is not the kind of person who is going to feel humbled. But that moment, I think he knew.

PAULETTE MOORE: I was very proud of all these people who had marched. I was proud of the way they acted. And I was proud because I felt that what we were doing that day was the right thing. I just felt overwhelmed that people did this for—for the school. And not for Mike Chun, not for Ozzie, but for the school—and I think the school is personified in the Princess.

FRED CACHOLA: I handed things to Ben Cayetano, I handed things to Chief Justice Moon and to Dickie Wong. And it was only after that I said, "My God, how did I happen to do all that?"

And Dickie Wong said, "We'll take these concerns and we'll get back to you guys."

ROCKY TOKUHARA: Yeah, he said all the right things, "We're gonna talk, and we're gonna this and we're gonna that." Of course, I don't know about anybody else, but I never believed him as far as I could spit in the wind.

KAYLIA IONA: Everybody knew that was just mouth, it was just waha.

ELISA YADAO: Dickie Wong had a huge fight with Loke. 'Cause she was incredibly angry that he had even gone down there. And when he went into her office afterwards, she refused to talk to him. She was so angry because she felt this was a betrayal of her that he went out there.

PATRICK IONA: And I think we sang the school song and pretty much it ended, dispersed.

ELISA YADAO: Then there was the whole thing with the names. The trustees were taking down people's names, writing down people's names. They had people going out there taking their pictures and videotape.

    Mrs. Lindsey had a list. I saw a yellow notepad on her desk that had names on it. They were asking people to identify or tell them. They were asking employees. Other people were asking too.

    All of a sudden the enemies had names—the people who marched. It was all intended to intimidate them.

HENRY MEYER: Well, everybody thinks that Mrs. Lindsey ordered me to videotape, but I videotaped pretty much on my own. She asked if I would be able to do it, and I said, "Well, I'm gonna do it anyway."

    Dennis Walsh and I met up some place out there around the Capitol area, and he was taking still shots.

HENRY MEYER

FRED CACHOLA: I had some words with Dennis Walsh. He took pictures. I took pictures of Dennis Walsh taking pictures. I shot from an angle so that he was clearly taking pictures of the march.

HENRY MEYER: There was a little bit of laughter and lightheartedness in watching it. Oh, there's so and so, you know, kind of taken in a light vein. The tone of the whole thing was rather light in nature and not as bad as it became months after that.

JANET ZISK: Down the road, I was fascinated to see Dickie Wong in the *Advertiser*, talking about the photographing and videotaping of the marchers—for historical purposes. Something about students having to know both the good and the bad of our history.

I decided to encourage him to continue this positive attitude by writing him a letter, requesting the original photographs for inclusion in the archives.

No answer came back. However, some time later, when Oz Stender was visiting me in the archives, he said, "Do you have any idea how close you were to being fired because of that letter you wrote to Dickie Wong?"

Apparently Wong introduced my letter at a trustee meeting, and the uproar it caused was considerable and noisy—it was blue air in there. Finally, probably worn out from shouting unpleasantries, a silence came over the room, and Dickie Wong said, "Why don't we just send them to her?"

And the trustees departed the boardroom to look for the photos and videos. When all returned, the highly paid collective search effort had produced not even one item.

Everything had sort of disappeared. ⌐

The Belly of the Beast
Nā Kumu Forms

Elizabeth Truesdell described one of our early meetings downstairs in Midkiff as taking place "in the belly of the beast." –Larry McElheny

DUTCHIE SAFFERY: I just felt that it was necessary for the teachers to take a daring stand. I recognized the concern of jobs, and that it was even more important that we stand up for them and the students. When Nā Kumu formed and then became involved, that was a very positive step forward for where we had gone ahead and allowed you folks time enough to regroup within your own and step out onto the chopping block.

GARY OBRECHT: I think the trustees thought they could throw aside Nā Pua. No matter how public they were, they could keep blocking them.

TONI LEE: I really thought that we could get into those trustees, talk to them, and it would be done, our job would be over. I thought, *Surely they're going to listen to us.* But they didn't. They dismissed us.

GARY OBRECHT: But when their own teachers are speaking out against them

and disobeying and rebelling and doing things they've been told not to do, I think that was probably harder for them to deal with in some ways. Because they knew that public sympathy would be on our side if they came down really hard. It made it much more powerful with teachers being involved. It made it about education, and not about money and power.

CHARLENE HOE: Nā Kumu is a word that has many meanings. It means foundation. It means guide. It means model. And then, of course, it means, as we mostly know it, teacher.

JAN BECKET: In the early Nā Kumu meetings, speakers often used the word "empowerment." We all came together out of a common vision of what this institution could be, and our place in it.

CHARLENE HOE: Nā Kumu's goal is to have a community of educators in all levels, from trustees through the classroom delivery that work collaboratively, an educational community. Nā Kumu sees a role for all parties in that process. We wanted this organization to truly encompass all of those who were associated with the education of our students.

KĀWIKA EYRE: But the school administration and the trustees didn't see it that way. They didn't want to deal with us—they didn't even want us to exist.

BOB WHITING: Tony Ramos had told the department heads, "You guys are management, so you can't become involved in Nā Kumu."

DARRELL SCHUETZ: Our administrators were saying virtually nothing. Well, nothing, period. It was almost as if there's nothing going on out there, nothing to talk about. They wouldn't talk, and sometimes would almost indicate that they couldn't talk—Well, you know, if you only knew, well, you know—

KAHELE KUKEA: Hard when you're in a position when you have to show one face in one context and another in another context.

DARRELL SCHUETZ
"Our administrators were saying virtually nothing."

BILL FOLLMER: Middle management—they're confused. They operated on a system of personal loyalties. Because their survival depended on that.

ROBIN MAKUA: To me, the administrators folded. Somebody came from behind, kicked them in the knees and they just—they fell.

CHARLENE HOE: I tried to go through, personally, and various representatives on behalf of Nā Kumu tried to go through our chain of command. Individual faculty, myself included, trying to go through informal meetings, to see if we could meet without trustees to discuss these issues. They did not bear fruit in actual discussions.

So Nā Kumu met and decided to communicate in writing, formally, with the trustees.

GARY OBRECHT: Change could have happened much faster if the trustees had been willing to sit down with some people. We've never been able to have those kinds of conversations with trustees. There were opportunities early on, where they could have stopped the whole thing, made peace, and we could have had change without ever dragging it through the courts and so forth.

As a board, they never answered anything from us. Never. Later on, we counted up the number of times we tried to communicate with the board as a whole, for a meeting with all of them, or just for an answer. Scores of times, over months and months, and the number of responses from the board as a whole to Nā Kumu was—zero. With them, we didn't amount to anything.

KĀWIKA EYRE: But a very real strength was that we were such bland, ordinary folk: keepers of children, earners of poor wages, correctors of homework, moonlighters on the side. Nothing much to hide or protect. But with a fierce belief that, in the greater scheme of things, the "we" is so very much more important and powerful than the "I."

Our strengths lay precisely in the fact that we were teachers working with kids. There were no ulterior motives, no hidden agenda. Gandhi, at the moment he let go of everything but his spinning wheel, spoke of the power of being without: the enemy could do nothing when you had nothing. There is great truth to that.

◈ ◈ ◈

KĀWIKA EYRE: The way the Nā Kumu leadership happened—it just happened. Gary Obrecht and I talked, and we sent out the notices for the first faculty meeting. I didn't know Gary very well, just that he had sat in on my first-year Hawaiian language class, he stood up at meetings and he gave a damn good prayer. We talked with other people, including Randie, and the names of Kēhau Abad and Charlene Hoe came up. And that became the four.

GARY OBRECHT: Kēhau was particularly special, because she had been in my English class when she was in the High School. It's so neat to see someone who has graduated and has gone on to become a success and is now a colleague. I just really like that.

KĒHAU ABAD: Charlene and I knew each other from the Hawaiian Cultural Center—this huge effort that was basically squashed.

KĀWIKA EYRE: Charlene has the reputation of being a community activist. And Kēhau does too. I don't know what my reputation is. But I didn't want us to be seen as a bunch of malcontents, a bunch of rabble rousers. Gary was the guy who had been here 30 years. He had style, all the style you could ever want—

CHARLENE HOE: —He had the most style! He made up for three other people!

KĀWIKA EYRE: And he had that old constituency, the conservative Kamehameha teacher group.

FRED CACHOLA: I think from the campus side, clearly the four of you were emerging as leaders. I think the four of you were beginning to speak your hearts and your souls in spite of the threats that might have been real or perceived. And I think from the campus there was this constituency that was beginning to develop only because there were four or five or six of you who were willing to say and help its development. I don't think it would have happened if you folks hadn't come forth.

LOIS LONG: It started with you four—I think real pathfinders in many ways of standing up and not being afraid to stand up. I knew that this fear was around. And seeing people who would put their heads above the masses to be counted was just amazing.

BOB WHITING: I think they were just bigger than themselves.

ELIZABETH TRUESDELL (*Secondary School English teacher*): To have respected and respectable people stand up—it made other people want to stand up as well. Seeing people of unimpeachable integrity, and saying, if they can do it, and be so public in their willingness to speak out, then there has to be people behind them, to buoy up those people who became the faces of that mass.

JAN BECKET: The Nā Kumu leadership did, I think, a perfect job of being vocal and assertive, but only in a way that expressed the feelings of the vast majority of the faculty. There was no attempt to "lead" in the bad sense.

KĀWIKA EYRE: From the first meeting, we defined ourselves as a collective of servant leaders, and simply and purposely did not make available options for individuals to take "lead" roles.

There were never any Nā Kumu elections. We were just called "representatives." And we called ourselves "interim" representatives. It was just that the interim part kept getting stretched. Once, when we tried to get ourselves replaced and didn't succeed, Bill Follmer turned to me and said, "Good. That's why we need you guys—because you are so reluctant. Reluctant leaders are the best kind."

My philosophy—our philosophy—was that authority is not assumed, but is on loan from the group and needs to be constantly re-approved and reaffirmed. Yes, that approval and affirmation have something to do with the qualities and abilities of the leader. But just as important, there has to be a sense in the followers that the relationship is respectful and representative of them and, in a multitude of practical ways, workable. By this view of things, a leader is a facilitator, an enabler, a person who helps people to accomplish their dreams. Leadership is a calling, not a career.

CHARLENE HOE: It was very important to all of us that organizational work was on a consensus basis, that ideas be discussed, sometimes in great length, by all who were interested.

KĀWIKA EYRE: Any time we felt wobbly, didn't know what to do, one of us—usually Charlene—would say, "We've got to go back to the group." The group always knew.

ELIZABETH TRUESDELL

"There has to be people behind them, to buoy up those people who became the faces of that mass."

KĒHAU ABAD: More was going on. None of us had that kind of cha-risma and power that brings people together like occurred with this. If you think about the ensemble of people who were brought together—no way could any of us have done that without that sort of network. It would have been beyond us to try to pull ourselves together like this. We could never have orchestrated it ourselves.

On one very simple level, we really all were praying. And so much of what we did was prayerful. We would go through the process of praying at meetings, and I think that part of our meetings that we didn't just do by rote but we did very meaningful. Even with songs that we would sing, they had that focus that we were looking to Ke Akua for guidance.

We were so desperate. We needed the help so badly. We never knew whether we were going to succeed or fail. It was just so important for us to succeed. So when we did pray about this, we prayed hard. And I know that that made all the difference. And it wasn't superficial. I'm sure Ke Akua understood that. Through our actions, with our prayers, we meant it. He saw that we were there. And my gosh, I think we were standing on the side of right—how could it not in the end come out suc-cessful? Sometimes I wonder, maybe we shouldn't have doubted. But it was just such a hard fight. It really was. It required so many people.

GARY OBRECHT: There were only a few people who were willing to take risks at that time. The number got larger as the months went by. But at first, there were very few people, especially people in the administration, that were willing to have anything to do with us, except behind the scenes. So we used—and I don't mean used in a bad way—the people that were willing to work with us. And they all had their own strengths. The Midkiff Learning Center people were extraordinarily valuable. Gail Fujimoto, Kathy Kukea, Janet Zisk. Sigrid Southworth was very powerful.

LIZ HANSEN: I admired them because they believed in something so strongly that they were willing to put their jobs at risk, their careers at risk, and we, I think most of us in Midkiff, were very supportive of what they were doing, because again, we believed in that.

KĒHAU ABAD: The learning centers were puʻuhonua, places of refuge.

KĀWIKA EYRE: Midkiff was a learning center for the Schools, but also an agitation center for reform.

LARRY MCELHENY: Elizabeth Truesdell described one of our early meetings downstairs in Midkiff as taking place "in the belly of the beast."

HEALANI HUCH (*'66, Secondary School English teacher*): At the first Nā Kumu meeting a week before the march, it was 25 scared birds on a telephone wire. At the second meeting, 40 or 50. A week after the march, coming up to the end of the school year, it was 115. And it kept growing, to more than 200 by the middle of June.

GAIL FUJIMOTO: The morning after the march, I remember seeing the picture on the front pages of the newspaper with marchers wearing our Kūʻē Pono T-shirt. It brought tears to my eyes.

Janet Zisk, wearing Kūʻē Pono T-shirt

The day it hit the paper, I started getting requests from all over the institution, not just the campus but from downtown, at Kawaiahaʻo Plaza. We decided to do another printing.

I identified key people on each campus and asked if they would be willing to help with the orders and distribution. I had no trouble getting help.

Requests kept coming in, not only from inside the organization, but later we were getting requests from the community. We decided to limit it to those within the organization; otherwise, I would have found myself becoming a T-shirt vendor.

Although my husband was leery about my doing this, and I was driving him nuts with all of the checks he had to cash, he supported me by helping me pick up some of the shirt orders. Except for the initial run, we never really had a big stash of shirts because we would only order based on the requests we received. We would do a pickup in the afternoon and I would try to distribute them the next day via our network.

I believe so many people wanted these shirts because they became a symbol of our protests. I felt increasing joy and resolve with each printing, because I knew more and more people were getting behind us. Why else would they want the shirts?

It was also very gratifying to get as many Nā Kumu membership forms as we did.

CHARLENE HOE: Many faculty, both full and part time, assistants, actually paraprofessional assistants, clerical people that dealt directly with students, counselors. Librarians, department heads. Administration, middle level, in particular, as it related to the educational division.

GAIL FUJIMOTO: I was worried because a lot of people on their notes were adamant that it be kept confidential. So I guarded that list at home. I never left anything here at school, nothing on my computers.

JIM SLAGEL: The trustees were going to run out the clock until summer. The kids, like every year, they were already listening to the surf reports and Bob Marley, but the faculty and alumni were hearing drum beats. And the trustees still had the boos from Song Contest ringing in their ears. It was probably going to be a noisy Commencement.

KAMANI KUALĀʻAU: My mother was not sure she could afford to come to graduation. Mrs. Lindsey pulled out two one-way tickets and said, "Here, take this." And of course we said, "No, no." And Mrs. Lindsey said, "No, I feel I need to do this for you." And she gave my mother the tickets. And as is custom when someone offers you something, Hawaiian custom, you do not turn down an offer. And she said, "Don't tell anybody I'm doing this for you."

JAMES MONIZ: He was jumpy, very uncomfortable, because he had to deal with Lokelani on several occasions before we graduated, after the interrogation. When we had our scholarship presentation in the auditorium, she handed him one of the scholarships. He had to go up and kiss her. He was very, you know, not cool with the fact that she could be so nice to him, giving him the scholarship, telling him he's a great student, but she had at one point wailed at him for writing a letter.

OZ STENDER: At graduation, Loke wanted trustees to give diplomas. And I said, "No, Mike Chun, Tony, president, principals, they're the ones who gave the diplomas. Tradition, that's the way it's done."

But they wanted to do all the trustees. One year, we took turns, which was not too smooth. I agreed, just to be a team player. This year I said, "It's not a good idea. With the controversy heating up, I don't think we should put the kids in that position." And one of the kids told me that if Mrs. Lindsey was going to give her, she wasn't gonna take it. And she expressed that as being the sentiment of a lot of the kids. So I told Dickie, "Not a good idea, because you gonna embarrass the kid and might embarrass Loke."

And they printed the program—trustees giving diplomas. And that day, Dickie came up to me in the auditorium, to see if I would do it. I said, "I'm not going to do it, and if I were you, I wouldn't do it." And so when it came time to give the diplomas, all those trustees supposed to do it, they didn't do it. I mean, Mike did it.

Mrs. Lindsey was quite upset about that. She kept looking at Dickie, and Dickie kept looking straight ahead, 'cause he wasn't gonna do it!

That's the only time he took my advice.

LIZ HANSEN: Dr. Chun was on stage, and the students stood up and clapped for him, everybody in that whole arena was clapping for him, and gave him all the support, and then the word started going around that Mrs. Lindsey was sitting.

ELISA YADAO: I can remember looking at her—Oh my gosh, she's not going to stand up! I knew her, and you could see she was angry, so she's not standing up. Loke's not standing up! And that was there for the whole arena to see!

OZ STENDER: I didn't know she didn't stand, because I was looking at Mike. Kuʻulei, my wife, was next to her. She told Kuʻulei that she didn't stand because she had broken her toe or something.

ELISA YADAO: It comes out, "Oh, I broke my toe walking in." Well, that's incredible—because now you can shove your foot back in that shoe and walk on out.

LOKELANI LINDSEY: Because we had a philosophical difference and philosophically I did not agree. And so I was kind of nuha, brooding. I just sat down.

ELISA YADAO: It was Memorial Day, so we come back to work on Tuesday, and everyone said, "How the hell could you have done that?" Dickie more than anybody else. He said, "You shouldn't have done that!" But it was done. Too late. What are you gonna do?

KĀWIKA EYRE: Nā Kumu had made arrangements for the summer, to do two things at once—kind of operate in secrecy, but at the same time get the word out.

CHARLENE HOE: We wrote collectively. Initial documents were drafted by individuals from Nā Kumu. They were brought to a gathering of Nā Kumuʻs membership. They were read paragraph by paragraph and approved by the membership.

KĀWIKA EYRE: We had a friend in Greg Barrett, the *Advertiser* reporter, who had written the first big story on the controversy.

GREG BARRETT: I was never supposed to be an advocate for Nā Kumu. I was an advocate for the truth. It just so happened that the truth appeared to have typically fallen Nā Kumu's way.

GARY OBRECHT: We met down at Kakaʻako park, in a pretty public situation, but there was nobody around who knew us. We were out on a summer afternoon.

GREG BARRETT: I thought it was pretty gutsy. There was a lot of fear, a lot of paranoia, and I remember being surprised that a faculty could fear that. I had covered education in North Carolina. It was public education, and I certainly didn't see that the superintendent wanted that kind of power or influence over the teachers. I was surprised by that, and it also told me something about the whole Bishop Estate-Kamehameha Schools relationship.

GARY OBRECHT: It was just really fun to be with reporters when we had been told from the beginning you are not to speak to the press or to media at all. Fun to sit down with them and talk very openly with them about things we knew they couldn't actually print. We were feeding them information that we chose to feed them, information that they couldn't have gotten in any other way except to have sources at the school. It was a way of getting our side out, and they were willing to take it, whereas we had been told not to do that.

Driving away from there, I was stopped at a stop sign, and Dickie Wong was getting into his Lexus, and he looked right at me and looked right into my car. I wasn't sure he knew who I was, but I had this terrible sense of guilt, because I had been down there, and I had this feeling that he must know I had been down there doing illegal activities. I had the sense that he was watching me, because of the way he looked into the car and sort of stared at me.

There was another day when I was right behind his car for many blocks. And it spooked me a little, as if somehow I was in the wrong place at the wrong time. We had heard rumors that they had pictures of us down at the trustees' office and that they knew who we were and they were watching us. I don't know if any of that was true, so I had this feeling that maybe they cared more about us than we thought they did. I'm not sure—they may not have cared about us at all. But they knew who we were. We heard some remarks.

CHARLENE HOE: Greg did an article about Kamani Kualā'au being interrogated by Lindsey, and we did a letter to the editor, and all four of us signed it, the way we always did, as representatives of Nā Kumu.

"The way Kamani was handled runs counter to sound educational practice. This incident should make it clear that there are fundamental problems within Kamehameha Schools/Bishop Estate: a climate of fear and the threat of personal intimidation, the undermining of the values we represent as educators and the removal of authority from those most directly responsible for the care of students."

KĒHAU ABAD: Each of us knew that being fired was a real possibility. We even joked about it as we composed the letter over the weekend at Kāwika's house. "This could be our last official act as teachers. You sure you guys want to do this?"

I can't remember who said what, but we all agreed, "Yes!" So we did it. We were already in the battle for the long haul. And if we needed to take on the fight from the outside, I believe we were all willing and able to do that.

OZ STENDER: The four horsemen.

KĀWIKA EYRE: The first time Oz talked to the papers was to Greg Barrett, a week or so after we did. In the boardroom, he was still one against four, against the way Lindsey was trampling all over Kamehameha.

OZ STENDER: I told Dickie, "I'm not going to sit back and say it is okay to intimidate students. I'm not going to say it's okay to intimidate teachers. I'm not going to say it's okay to micromanage."

CHARLENE HOE: The interview with Oz was a long one, running over onto three pages. And in the boardroom, Gerry Jervis, Trustee Jervis, hit him with a rolled-up *Advertiser* and told him to get the f--- out.

KĀWIKA EYRE: The next thing we did for publication was for *Ka Wai Ola,* which was put out by the Office of Hawaiian Affairs, meaning that it was aimed at the Hawaiian community. It was about principles of good schooling.

It was scheduled for publication in August.

KĒHAU ABAD: By August Nā Kumu was banned from the campus.

OZ STENDER: That's Lokelani and Henry—why should we give them a place to meet?

KĀWIKA EYRE: We were told verbally by some administrator. We never got anything from the trustees. Eventually, a memo came from Nathan Aipa, the legal officer at Kawaiahaʻo Plaza. The memo said we were banned because we were organizing a labor union, and it was against estate policy to allow this to happen on estate property.

Well, labor law says that if other groups were allowed to use the campus, we should be too. And all kinds of other groups were using the campus. It was Mike Chun's policy to have the school really open to the community, everybody from Girl Scouts to hula hālau to two lua groups, the traditional Hawaiian martial art. We wrote a memo to Dickie Wong listing all these.

The law aside, what we were actually going to do had nothing to do with organizing a union. It was to introduce the faculty to Judge Patrick Yim, who had been appointed by the trustees as a fact finder.

There was real suspicion about Judge Yim. How could we believe that someone appointed by the trustees would report anything critical of them?

We couldn't meet with Yim on campus, so we all went down to the cafeteria at Dole Intermediate School in Kalihi valley. Beadie Dawson was there, which helped people to relax.

ARLIS LEGLER: Judge Yim reassured us that he would not let anything we would say go beyond his ears. And how fearful the majority of us in that room were that he could really do that.

We sat in that cafeteria, and there was a lot of silence between comments. Because we were really uncertain if—if there were spies there that would take it back to the trustees. But also whether he was really trustworthy. And that had less to do with him the individual, as him the situation he was in. It was a very powerful machine we were up against. And as much as people wanted to say things, and to talk to him, there was much fear and much doubt that that would really be true.

And so it took a great deal of courage for the first people who spoke to him. As we learned more, people talked, and then it became not necessarily less fearful, but "I'm not in this alone." It was less likely that an individual would be singled out to lose their job. But that fear was very definitely there. Very definitely.

"We are very pleased. We have succeeded in having what was to be a private, secret report, if you will, now become a report that is going to be out for the public.

"I'm confident that just knowing that the whole fact-finding process is underway is going to be an enormous morale-booster for the students and the faculty."

—*Beadie Dawson, on appointment of Judge Yim, KHON-TV News, 6/27/97*

"Hey fellas, we're probably never going to have another fact-finder for another 100 years. So go. We'll look at his report and worry about that later. But let's help him."

—*Beadie Dawson, Honolulu Star-Bulletin, 8/30/97*

KĒHAU ABAD: Gerry Jervis met with us and told us there would be no retribution. We wanted that on paper, to have a record that that is what he said, so we wrote him a memo.

JOHN TSUKAYAMA (*Hawai'i State investigator*): For talking with Judge Yim, I volunteered to train a group of what we called facilitators, whom we felt could work together and work with various witnesses who could be identified. I gave about eight hours of statement-taking and interview training with them. What the fact-finding process could be like, and how to make sure that it maintained its integrity, keep him honest. And we set up a protocol on how they would operate, by helping these people formulate their recollections and create good, solid, useful statements. Also, we told Judge Yim that we are going to keep a copy

Honolulu Star-Bulletin
headline, 10/29/97

Yim logs 160 interviews in probe of Kamehameha Schools
The fact-finder has received responses to 1,200 questionnaires

of anything that they tell us they gave you, and we will scrutinize your report to insure that their voices are not lost.

So essentially it was to encourage people to go see him, and to put a shot across the bow and tell him we're watching and we have the ability to sharp-shoot your report.

RANDIE FONG: Then, on August 9, came a huge explosion. The *Star-Bulletin* published an essay with the headline "Broken Trust."

BEADIE DAWSON (*attorney for Nā Pua*): "Broken Trust" was explosive. It created an avalanche of dirty water that had been vigorously held back and obscured.

And it caught the governor's attention.

RANDIE FONG: It really was a bombshell. It said, straight out, that the whole political system behind Bishop Estate was corrupt, from the Supreme Court to the boardroom, that the corruption had led to terrible trustee appointments, and the result was chaos and scandal at Kawaiahaʻo Plaza, and crisis at Kamehameha.

All these things had been in the air, waiting to be said, and now they were on the page, in one place, in hard-hitting words.

From then on, nothing was the same.

KAʻIMI KAIWI: "Broken Trust" carried enormous weight. It was Nona Beamer's letter, multiplied a hundred times.

KĀWIKA EYRE: From campus, the way I saw it, "Broken Trust" moved us to a higher, more complex level of engagement with the trustees, because of the stature of the authors and the sophistication and power of the information they presented.

What we on the front lines had been experiencing for years and openly challenging for months was now in print on the front page and on the TV news. Their words affirmed and emboldened our struggles, and—very importantly—provided us protections that hadn't been there before. The writers of "Broken Trust" gave us an imposing shield.

DICKIE WONG: THIS TRUST IS NOT BROKEN. In fact, the exact opposite is true. Kamehameha Schools/Bishop Estate is in a period of unprecedented accomplishments in educational achievement. Our financial position is better and brighter than at any other time in our history—bar none.

It is interesting, and very disturbing, to note how cries of "micromanagement" have now faded from public attacks on the estate as more facts of educational excellence and accomplishments have been brought forth. Now some critics, deprived of

what they thought was a good line of attack, have gone into the gutter making baseless and unprovable charges, sometimes resting on clearly incorrect assertions and second-hand sources with an ax to grind.

These critics have adopted the political tactic: "If you throw enough mud, some of it is bound to stick."

BARB LEE

"The campus was abuzz with all the whisperings."

Honolulu Advertiser headline, 8/13/97

BARB LEE (*Secondary School business teacher*): The campus was abuzz with all the whisperings. We were wondering when they would start investigating some of the goings-on. It took at least three months after the march that passed Washington Place before Governor Cayetano directed Attorney General Margery Bronster to start an investigation into Bishop Estate. "Broken Trust" finally got Cayetano's attention.

◆ ◆ ◆

State to investigate Bishop Estate
Recent charges require action, Cayetano says

GERARD JERVIS (*Bishop Estate trustee*): On a scale of 1 to 10, I'd put the current tension level at about 13.

I don't know of any other time in our history that the very foundation of our existence has been called into question, so publicly, by so many, with such intensity. But I do know one thing: how Kamehameha Schools/Bishop Estate emerges from this situation will depend entirely on how we—as a family and as individuals—conduct ourselves during this very challenging time. If we've made mistakes, we need to find out what they are and correct them. Then we need to move on.

◆ ◆ ◆

HOPEFULLY...FURTHERING THE INVESTIGATION WILL HELP US IDENTIFY THE PROBLEM...

SCRIBBLE
SCRIBBLE
SCRIBBLE

TO THE GUV

A.G.

B.E. BENEFICIARIES

TRUSTEES

KĀWIKA EYRE: We got our contracts four days before school started, so we were all good to be able to pay the rent for another year.

At the same time, there was something darkly somber about the mood of the campus. Not a good way to start the school year.

We had been planning for something in a different spirit, gathering at Mauna'ala, in the presence of Pauahi, to affirm and honor our shared mission, which was her vision.

KA'IMI KAIWI: I was on the planning committee. Others were Janet Zisk, Sandy Tuitele, Gail Fujimoto. Of course, Randie Fong was involved in that as well. That was when things were really tough for him. That's one of the things we were doing during that time period. We were supporting each other as best we possibly could. I guess, prop each other up in the midst of it, 'cause it was really difficult.

GARY OBRECHT: Good people were involved.

KA'IMI KAIWI: We had worked really hard at it. We had support from people. We thought it was going to be really beneficial for the students, for us, for everything.

KĀWIKA EYRE: Word was put out that all were welcome, including trustees. Then, the day before, they canceled it, without explanation.

OZ STENDER: If the trustees weren't so exposed and vulnerable at that point, right after "Broken Trust," all of you would have been fired. They talked about it. They really thought about it, are they gonna punish people like you. I mean, they had mentioned names of people that they knew were involved, and tried to figure out some way they can get to all of you.

KĀWIKA EYRE: I remember Kēhau and I stared at each other when we heard about their decision to cancel. It was another stupid if predictable PR call on their part and would only strengthen support for the faculty in the community. A smart move would have been for them to show up and co-opt the evening—in the same way that Loke should have stood up at the end of the march to offer a mushy-teary apology with appropriate Hawaiian verbiage: "I see that I have erred. I'm so sorry, and I want only to bring the 'ohana together and find ways to ho'oponopono it all to forgiveness." It would have been a crowd melter. Instead of which, they canceled.

We went ahead anyway.

KA'IMI KAIWI
"We were supporting each other as best we possibly could."

SIGRID SOUTHWORTH: People were somewhat scared to go, and for some of us who did, it was again a move that took some risk and some willingness to be vulnerable.

KĀWIKA EYRE: Not a huge crowd. About 60, and again I think fear was a factor, because it was forbidden.

OZ STENDER: I came.

HENRY BENNETT: I decided to attend. It was fairly simple to me. I knew who was involved and I knew who was in opposition, and I have no lack of clarity of which side I chose to be.

I remember being surprised at some of the faces I saw, some people who I had perceived as administrative staff who I had not expected to see.

KAHELE KUKEA: I felt strongly about it. It was just the right thing to be doing. That was a bridge. After that, I felt more connected with the teachers.

KĀWIKA EYRE: People dressed for the evening. There were mu'umu'u and aloha shirts, and many wore shell or kukui lei.

As the dark set around us, we just began.

Māhealani Chang chanted and danced a hula noho in honor of Pauahi. Kaleo Trinidad danced "Hole Waimea" to the chanting of Holoua Stender and Randie Fong—appropriate because "Hole Waimea" invoked the warrior spirit of Kamehameha and his forces, which we needed to emulate.

There are no lights on the Mauna'ala grounds except the one old lamp post near the gate. As the light faded, the candles began to appear, disappear and reappear, snuffed out repeatedly by gusts. A clear memory is the wind blowing out candles and people leaning in to each other. You could see them curved over, leaning to each other to re-light their candles. The dim outline of those leaning bodies for me became part of the lasting symbolic imagery of the evening. And there was singing. Very quiet songs: "Makalapua," "Ua Mau," "Ekolu Mea Nui," "Kanaka Waiwai" and others. Songs in a stronger wind.

The wind also made the bushes above us rustle, and I recall looking up several times at the dim clumps of brush and wondering if trustees' spies were in there.

It was in one of those moments of silence when suddenly a violent burst of light struck us. From above, along the vine-covered chain-link fence that separates neighboring Central Seventh Day Adventist Church from the Mausoleum, flashed what seemed to be the high-beam headlights of a car, lighting up the whole area in a shocking glare of whiteness. Blinding. Stunning us. It was a television crew that had snuck in—despite our prohibition—and started filming through the bushes. Gary Obrecht and I rushed up to tell them they had to leave at once.

The evening ended in prayer as we just joined hands in front of Pauahi.

16 Families and Mortgages
Nā Kumu Leaders Nearly Fired and Teachers Respond

Teachers as a group are pretty timid, and they have families and mortgages and that kind of stuff. —Jan Becket

KĀWIKA EYRE: The school year started, Fall '97, with Pauahi in our hearts. And our defiance of the trustees on our minds.

KĒHAU ABAD: We had heard that Lindsey folks were poised to fire us.

TONY RAMOS: Lokelani shot from the hip—they should be fired.

KĒHAU ABAD: But we were already aware that Oz, Mike and Tony, or some combination of them, had gone to bat for us.

KĀWIKA EYRE: Ever since the start of Nā Kumu, we had spoken not as individuals, but as *representatives*—never in our own voices, but as the voice of all of Nā Kumu. But we were being targeted as individuals.

CHARLENE HOE: There was a consideration of my termination, or more, and that was never clear at that point, what the more might be. I took that as intimidation.

KĀWIKA EYRE: I recall receiving a message that Lokelani had said, "Kāwika Eyre, he'd better watch out."

KA'IMI KAIWI: It was from Oz. I don't think it was in a board meeting, just in one of those meetings that they had by themselves where she made that threat. And Oz had said something to the effect that she'd better not do anything. They were having these kinds of exchanges already, where she was threatening to do things to people, to faculty, and he was saying to her that she'd better not.

TONY RAMOS: I was called down to the legal department, with that lawyer, Gerry Jossem, and the employee handbook, about all what violations occurred by them going public, to the press. At that point, Loke was saying this is grounds for termination, all that stuff. Our attorney, Colleen Wong, said it might be legally right—but I said it might not be morally right.

MIKE CHUN: I don't recall that they ever made a decision to fire, though they wanted to. They wanted to pull the trigger. They had everything set for that, and Gerry Jervis said, "This is crazy—they didn't do anything." I guess what I was saying was, just let it go. I know the best advice I could have given would have been, Look, let's look at what they're saying. And let's talk to them. I didn't even say that. I just said, "Let's let it go." But they weren't about to let it go.

TONY RAMOS: I don't think anybody had the will to fire them. But because I was the principal, like I was the supervisor, I was the person they kept leaning on to do something.

I kept getting calls on my cell phone. Dickie Wong said, "What do you think we should do?" I said, "We have progressive discipline." "What does that mean?" "Well," I said, "first you talk to them. Secondly, you write it out. Third, if this happens again, it could lead to termination."

The legal department wrote this Personnel Form 9. We call it PERS 9. It's for positive strokes, for counseling, for discipline, whatever—you check the right box.

Mike was away while this was going on. He got upset about the fact that we were going to do this.

Meantime, Jervis calls me and says, "Where's the PERS 9?" I said, "I have them." He said, "Well, don't do anything yet. Before you do anything, please talk to me about it." I said, "Fine."

Okay, so we got this phone call to come down to the trustees' office. It's Kahele Kukea, myself, Rockne Freitas and Mike. And Dickie Wong, chairman of the board. And his question is, "Have you done this yet?" And I said, "No." And he said, "Why not?" And I said, "Because Trustee Jervis asked me to wait." He reacted—"Oh, f---, I'm gonna talk to this guy." So my marching orders were to be sure that the PERS 9s were presented.

Now I'm in my office, and I get a call from Loke, and she's on a speakerphone and saying, "Have you done this yet?" I said, "No, I haven't." "Why not?" I said, "Because I gave Trustee Jervis my word that I wouldn't do anything until I spoke with him, and I haven't spoken with him." "Well, ha, ha, ha—do you wanna go with three votes or one vote?" That was said in a joking way, but I think the other two trustees were there.

Was I threatened by that? You damn right, I felt threatened by that. So I call Colleen Wong.

She's on vacation at Waikoloa, playing golf. She calls me back. I say, "Colleen, what do I do with this? I don't want to do anything, because this is all new legal territory."

So I called Mr. Jervis, and I suggested that this be a verbal thing more than a written thing. So Jervis said, "That's good." He said, "Would you give me those PERS 9s?" So I hand-carried those PERS 9s to him, so I didn't even have a copy.

He says, "Run down the points," so that when I'm doing individual meetings, I'm saying the same thing to each person. When it got to the oral conference, he told me, you know, "There are conferences and there are conferences—don't make this a hard conference."

KĒHAU ABAD: We wanted to have all four of us meet together with either or both of the principals at the same time, but they didn't let us. Charlene had to meet separately with Kahele Kukua, and Kāwika, Gary and I had to meet individually with Tony Ramos.

KĀWIKA EYRE: It was cat and mouse in terms of how the meetings finally took place. We were trying to control the process, not hand over the initiative to administration.

We dodged and delayed as long as possible, in part because we needed the time to educate ourselves as to our "concerted effort" rights under the National Labor Relations Board.

GARY OBRECHT: We were given specific appointments with the principal. I just decided I wasn't going up for my appointment. So I didn't. And lo and behold, Tony Ramos and Sandy Behenna came down and actually walked into the department.

As soon as I saw them, I knew it was going to be ugly. That I wasn't in the mood to behave. I told them I would not go up. I don't remember what they said. They were fairly well controlled. They always have been. But they made it clear that I would come up, or else.

I am ashamed of the altercation I had with Tony Ramos. I just felt really rebellious about it. I felt it was no business of theirs to do this—it was a cowardly act on the part of the administration.

I went up with them and pouted and took notes on everything and wrote down everything they said, which was mostly a canned thing— reading from a paper that someone else had prepared for them, reminding us again how we had overstepped and we were not to overstep again.

The funny part of it was when they were done with that part, they wanted me to talk to them. It really hurt them, I think, personally, that our relationships had severed that much that I refused even to speak with them.

Kamehameha teachers silenced
4 faculty leaders get reprimands

Honolulu Advertiser headline, 9/13/97

KĀWIKA EYRE: My turn came later that morning, then Kēhau in the afternoon. Charlene was spared Ramos and Behenna, and had instead a nice, non-confrontational conversation with Kahele Kukea, her principal in Elementary and a Nā Kumu supporter.

KAHELE KUKEA: With Charlene, I made it as informal as possible. Tony had something he'd sent me that was a form letter. I said, "I'm not going to use this." I wrote it out on a yellow pad. So it was meeting the mandate, but probably not in the way they expected. It was an oral, a verbal, and I didn't even make it a reprimand.

KĒHAU ABAD: Tony was clearly not happy with what he had to do. I think on one hand he personally wished we hadn't written the piece, since it didn't place him in a good light. At the same time, he obviously didn't think we should be fired over it.

So he and Sandy Behenna went through sort of the company line about how we weren't supposed to identify ourselves as teachers and speak in that official capacity without sending our message up through the pike to get approval. He did most of the talking, and I think Sandy was there as his witness.

He repeated several times that I was being officially told not to do the same thing again. He also made a point over and over of telling me that he's just keeping a record of the communication in his personal file in his own office, and that it wouldn't be kept in my official file at Human Resources.

I think that was his way of saying that he was trying to comply with what he was being told needed to be done, which I took as "reprimand them in writing," without us really being dinged in a way that would permanently hurt our record. I appreciated that.

JAN BECKET: A petition is a very powerful tool. You know, a little manifesto from two or three people, even if they're elected leaders, just doesn't have the punch, the impact, that a petition can have—it's easily ignored.

It was obvious that people supported the reps. It was a foregone conclusion that people would sign a petition. There just needed to be a mechanism.

JAN BECKET

"It was a foregone conclusion that people would sign the petition."

Why sign such a statement? The steps taken by the administration late Friday afternoon make it imperative that we take a more visible stance, to affirm the existence of our faculty association. The four interim leaders of Nā Kumu have not been acting as individuals these past four months; their actions have been authorized by the rest of us, the faculty of Kamehameha. We need to send that message to the administration and trustees in a clear, strong manner. Only a statement with names on it will send that message at this point, given recent events.

—From Jan Becket's letter accompanying the Nā Kumu petition in support of the four representatives, 9/11/97

Teachers as a group are pretty timid, and they have families and mortgages and that kind of stuff. They need to feel some protection. People wanted to feel that they were part of a large group. They didn't want to be part of 20 or 25 faculty members who could be singled out and labeled as malcontents. They wanted the security of numbers.

So what I came up with was a go/no-go limit, a critical mass point.

A group of us, three or four, went around. We agreed there had to be a hundred signatures. We explained that to everybody. If they trust us with their name, we wouldn't use their names unless there were 99 others at least. That was the agreement.

JANET ZISK: I volunteered to collect signatures. Jan Becket had done such a excellent job of wording the petition, a very courageous thing to do, that although I really dislike asking people to sign petitions—how could I not help out?

I also carried a petition form in my purse, just in case. I got one faculty signature in our local Safeway between the fresh fruit and veggies and the juice and dairy sections, with my cart blocking the aisle. Another signature happened in the Long's parking lot—I passed the petition through the driver's side window as the faculty person was about to take off.

This may sound like a lot of arm twisting on my part, but in truth I didn't encounter much resistance. We either stand together or we sink together. The more people who signed, the less chance of individual retaliation. We act as examples to our students of people who do the right thing, even if it's dangerous. That was my pitch.

LILINOE KA'AHANUI: That's one of the kiddie things. I remember a lot of them talking about the petition. "What? Someone's going to get fired? Kumu Kāwika's going to lose his job?" You know, they're a lot smarter than we think they are.

ARLIS LEGLER: The last thing they needed was for us to lie to them. They needed to know they could depend on us.

LILINOE KA'AHANUI: We were blamed as teachers for a lot of the spreading of information. But we're not the only information givers about this whole situation. Their parents, you know, and these kids can read; they watch the news. As young as they were—freshmen and sophomores—they were fired up and ready to go. Ready to put on their malo and their kīkepa and go wherever they needed to go.

JIM SLAGEL: You signed Jan's petition because four good friends were on the line. It was one of those moments of truth, more so than the meetings in the choral room. You were between classes and you couldn't read the names already on the list. You didn't want to read those names. That would be cowardly. It was almost as if everyone was the first to sign. Everyone had to be a little reckless. I kind of liked that.

JAN BECKET: It's good to have people exercise their voices that way. They need to do that every so often as a faculty. If they don't, then their voices kind of fall silent, and they get into this thing where they maybe expect their leaders to say something, but they're nice and safe and silent somewhere way in the background. It's also good for people to put their names down and actually be part of a larger statement when they feel strongly about something.

KĀWIKA EYRE: So, we were trusted enough, the people had enough confidence in us, that they felt they could trust us with their name on the petition.

On a personal level, I felt tremendous appreciation for the support. I think Jan Becket's leadership on this was as risky as anything we did.

JAN BECKET: It was very effective, that little go/no-go point. It got people to relax, and brought them to be willing to put their names onto something.

KĀWIKA EYRE: We got 160 names, and seven of the signatures were those of department heads, who by employee-employer definitions fall on the side of management—a blow to Tony Ramos, who at this point is fuming about Nā Kumu.

SUSAN ICHINOSE (*attorney*): If it weren't such a hot political issue, I'll bet that the employer could very well have fired you.

KĒHAU ABAD: Of course, they'd have been nuts to fire us. Not just for legal reasons but for the larger picture of what that would mean to all of us—alumni, staff, teachers, students, parents, supporters—all of us who were in the battle together. I was always really comforted by that fact anytime the four of us went walking way out on that familiar limb.

GARY OBRECHT: We didn't get fired, and—

TONY RAMOS: —The PERS 9 never went in your file. Never did. Promise. ⌒

The Tipping Point
Seeds of Teacher Union Form

Based on all that was occurring, we really had no choice. The tipping point for me personally came when I attended the meeting with Bishop Estate's union busters Buddy McGuire and Bob Katz. —Gail Fujimoto

KĀWIKA EYRE: That kind of intimidation, along with everything else that was happening, raised the question of whether the faculty needed organized protection—in other words, a union.

The fact that the question was even raised at a private school like Kamehameha was the strongest possible sign of how bad things had gotten. We weren't talking about floods any more; we were looking to build an ark.

GARY OBRECHT: To be honest, I was very much against the union. I never, ever in my whole life would have seen myself as joining a union as a teacher. I thought unions were not for teachers.

GAIL FUJIMOTO: I'd never been pro-union. I just didn't feel it was professional to be part of a union. And I was very outspoken about that. I was formerly with the DOE, and the teachers decided to strike. I refused to, and I did cross the picket line, and it did hurt, it really hurt to go against my colleagues. But I had to stand up for my beliefs.

SIGRID SOUTHWORTH: I had always said I would not work for a school that was unionized. I just do not think that in education a union should be necessary. Maybe I'm Pollyanna and idealistic, but to me, teaching children and working for an institution that has children at heart is not someplace where I think a union should need to be. Particularly a private school. And I've always said if Kamehameha ever unionized, I would leave.

ROY ALAMEIDA (*'63, Secondary School social studies teacher*): I did not think it would actually happen, because there was the emphasis on Hawaiian values. From the Hawaiian view, when the ali'i takes care of the maka'āinana, they in turn will be cared for. So, I assumed that the trustees and administration would follow that wisdom to stop the teachers from becoming a union. I often thought, *What would Pauahi say to all that was taking place?*

KĀWIKA EYRE: The trustees certainly did not want a union—none of them, including Oz Stender. He was very concerned about our leaning toward unionizing.

Each of us in the Nā Kumu four had contact people that we were responsible for. I was responsible for Oz. So that any time we had issues and needed to communicate or get information, then I would speak to him.

OZ STENDER: I didn't want the union.

KĀWIKA EYRE: He was very critical of it, very fearful of it.

OZ STENDER: Because, you know, you make rules and then all of a sudden you can hang yourself with these rules.

My problem with organizing was not a feeling of animosity, because of the situation—I knew it was self-preservation. I just didn't want to. Be patient and we'll fix things, that was my thing.

The other trustees made those snide remarks—that they felt I was the one putting them up to it. And yet I was the one in the room kept saying, "We don't want this."

BRIAN CHANG: Dickie Wong—here's a guy that started his professional career as a labor organizer. Now chairman of the board, and clearly now management.

MIKE CHUN: Loke accused me of aiding and abetting the teachers in forming a union. To the contrary: for my part, I was very genuine in

"Faculty and students are needed to help reinforce the crumbling brick wall around Kawaiahao Plaza. First fifty volunteers get free parking passes to Royal Hawaiian Shopping Center."

—*Imua Outsider*, faculty-generated parody of *I Mua Insider*, Fall '97 not wanting a union. I had committed myself to do everything I could to persuade the teachers from forming a union.

LARRY MORDAN (*Secondary School science teacher*): Part of the impetus in organizing the union was that there had been a couple of faculty organizations in the past that had been unilaterally dissolved by the powers that be. With a federally recognized union you can't do that.

BILL FOLLMER: Dr. Chun came to the school the same year as I did. It was '88. And the second year I was here, I got sucked into the Kamehameha Schools Association.

The very first year, he attended all the meetings. And the next year, he attended about six.

DIANE TANNER-CAZINHA (*Elementary School teacher*): It became sort of discouraging, because as time went on, obviously he had no interest in it. He would cancel a meeting, you know, have to leave.

BILL FOLLMER: We disbanded KSA on our own, because basically we weren't having the communication. He didn't say you couldn't meet, but it was pointless. Because we were an advisory body to a person who wasn't interested in our advice.

SIGRID SOUTHWORTH: I feel a lot could have been accomplished by Nā Kumu, had it been recognized. I'm sorry our administrators didn't have the courage and the confidence—and I think that's the way I would put it—I think they were afraid of us, and I'm sorry they didn't have the courage and the confidence to come hear what we were saying, understand what we were feeling.

LARRY MCELHENY: I attended the Nā Kumu meetings. I heard Kāwika Eyre speak, and Kēhau Abad speak, and everyone else who was very concerned about what was going on.

So, we'd come back in a little group of teachers that I kind of associate with, the guys that I see on a daily basis. We'd compare notes and say, "Hey, what the heck's going on, and what should we do?"

SIGRID SOUTHWORTH: What was happening to an institution that I loved very much? And to students that I loved. Things were just so wrong. And over my years—my gosh, at that point I'd had

LARRY MORDAN

SIGRID SOUTHWORTH

35 years of working for the Schools, and Mrs. Bishop had become a very close friend. Particularly being the Hawaiian collection librarian—I had read all of her writings. I had read all of the books about her. I felt like I knew her pretty well. And I just felt she was being so betrayed—that what was going on was not what she had in mind for her school. And she would never have participated in political shenanigans such as were going on. And she would have put a very quick stop to that, had she been here. It was just—all so wrong!

HOLOUA STENDER: Someone asked if I would help to lead this process. I guess in the emotions of the moment I just said yes.

I think Diane came on because we wanted to have representation from two campuses.

DIANE TANNER-CAZINHA: I was from the Elementary School. How I stumbled into it was because of Kāwika Eyre and Charlene Hoe and Gary Obrecht and Kēhau Abad. After Nā Kumu was organized and you guys put your signature out there, Charlene asked me could I come to a meeting, could I help.

I said, "Yes, of course, how can I say no; you put your name out in public, a great risk for your job." So I would come and see what was to be done.

HOLOUA STENDER: And so Diane and I started working together and started contributing a lot of time. And we got other people to help us in our efforts.

We had to get people from different parts of our institution to go out and get people to start talking to each other. I think important people were Robin Makua from the eighth grade, and then we had Rita Littlejohn, Joyce Neilson, Becky Tesch, Larry McElheny, Bill Follmer. Those were the people that started talking to others and sort of testing and measuring where everyone else was at. And of course the Nā Kumu meetings.

LARRY MCELHENY: It was just people informally talking, and then an informal structure of people taking responsibility. I think Diane and Holoua were kind of the kingpins.

HOLOUA STENDER

DIANE TANNER-CAZINHA: The task that seemed to need doing and somebody needed to do it was to go out and investigate what it would mean to be a union.

KĀWIKA EYRE: We had a forum where we invited Punahou representatives, and MidPac and ʻIolani. MidPac was the only one with a union.

DIANE TANNER-CAZINHA: Punahou told how they don't feel a need for it, because they have a lot of input and a teacher could make curriculum decisions and so on. ʻIolani said the same thing.

ROD MCPHEE: Now, I understand why the faculty did unionize at Kamehameha, and that's one of the few exceptions that proves the rule. I think that made sense in that setting. I think you needed it for protection.

Some of the most unconstitutional regulations up there. That oath of silence thing, or whatever it was, you couldn't say anything about the school under fear of losing your job.

PETER KAMA: As an individual, you have very little power. But I think as a unit, your complaints will be regarded more respectfully and not treated like—Oh! centipede! Get rid of that son of a gun!

DIANE TANNER-CAZINHA

JAN BECKET: We needed a place to meet, other than Kenny's Burger House in Kalihi, where we met at the very beginning. I called the United Public Workers offices just down the hill and asked if we could meet in their building, the one near School and Houghtailing. They checked with Gary Rodrigues, the president, who said, "No." I later learned that Dickie Wong was in on the early organizing of UPW. I am sure they didn't want to do anything that would go against his interests. Good example of how local politics functions.

BILL FOLLMER: Whereas the machinists—we used their place a couple of times.

DIANE TANNER-CAZINHA: And Tom Chun's church.

JAN BECKET: Kalihi Union, on North King Street. We ended up meeting there for the next year.

MARIANE HANNAHS: At first, when the teachers were trying to unionize, it was only the K through 12 programs. And then Preschool division also expressed an interest.

Our director, Vivian Murray, told us that Suzanne Ramos—she was the Preschool principal—would never allow Preschool to have a union. So, just forget about it.

We had those meetings with Dean Choy at Kapiʻolani Park. The people from Waiʻanae were the ones that were showing up. I was the only one from my site. I think one other teacher came once. We parked away—we were scared to park in the parking lot, ʻcause we were afraid someone would come and take pictures of our license plates. I mean, that's the state of mind we were all in.

Neil came home and told me that Mr. Peters had told him that he needed to talk to me, because Neil was in a delicate position, and that I should not be trying to—it got to his attention that I was trying to unionize the Preschool teachers, which is absolutely false.

I went in to see my supervisor, and I told her, "What shall I do? Where did this come from? How come this is happening? I've never given people cause to believe that. If anything, I've had a hands-off policy. I went to an informational meeting with Nā Kumu in the band room, but so did all the other teachers. So why would I get singled out?"

And she said that she wasn't surprised at all. "Because, you know, the kind of company that you keep, and because of your behavior, because you're very verbal, and outspoken, and everybody knows that you know Mr. Stender and that you sympathize with him and Dr. Chun and that you approve of the union."

Neil and I decided that because of the politics of the situation, that for me to speak up and say something concerning Nā Kumu could be detrimental to him. So we agreed that I would lay low, try and keep a distance from it, not be a ringleader or a person who pushed for union, though I didn't make a secret that I supported that.

And then I got reprimanded.

MARIANE HANNAHS: When Ulu the class rabbit got sick, the children were very concerned. His urethra was blocked by a stone. I think it was a kidney stone. He needed to have an operation—that night or the next day, because we could see that he was failing rapidly. His condition was bad.

I had to leave him at the doctor's. I got home. It was a little before 6. I called my supervisor right away. She wasn't home. I didn't leave a message, but I felt I needed to talk to someone right away. So I called our financial officer for our Preschool site, and I explained to her what had happened. I told her that I knew this was gonna be more than routine visit, but I felt that it was something that needed to be done to save this rabbit, and that I would be willing to be personally responsible for it.

I didn't call Mrs. Murray at all. I figured I had made contact with the school, with the financial officer, and then that was okay.

So the next morning when I went in to see her, I told her that if we didn't have money for it, Neil and I were going to pay for it on our own, 'cause we wanted to save this rabbit, and the children were very, very worried.

At no time did Mrs. Murray tell me that I did anything wrong, or that I needed to talk to anyone else. She even offered to call the principal, Mrs. Ramos, because I had to get back in the classroom, and tell her what was going on.

When I got the bill, I gave it to my supervisor. It was like 600-something. I didn't expect them to pay that much, and we were willing to foot the bill.

The next thing I knew, I was called in and told that I did the wrong thing. That I should have let the rabbit die.

And it just kinda came out of the blue from Mrs. Murray. I didn't expect to have that kind of reprimand, because I followed everything according to the book. I did it with her approval. She didn't tell me not to go ahead and do the surgery, because I had said that I would cover it. And I never committed to any KSBE funds at all. But I was told that I didn't make prudent use of my resources.

I got written up for it in my TRP, my Teacher Review Process. My evaluation was downgraded from proficient in following Kamehameha policies. I got NI, Needs Improvement, 'cause I didn't follow the chain of command.

◄► ◄► ◄►

HANNAHS FAMILY

Left to right: Moanilei Hannahs (KS 2001); Neil Hannahs (KS 1969); Kalikolihau Hannahs (KS 1999); Kahoʻokeleholu Kale Hannahs (KS 1996); and Mariane Holu Hannahs (KS 1969)

MARIANE HANNAHS: We'd keep our children abreast of what was happening, things that were said about Neil, and the kind of situation I was in. And the children knew who we supported and who supported us, let's put it that way.

My children were very depressed about it. They were very conflicted, because they felt a loyalty to their parents and to the school, and they felt their parents' loyalty to the school was being questioned.

They said, "Dad, why don't you quit already?" Or, "Mom, why don't you leave Ulu Pono?"

We had so many dinnertable conversations and even bedtime conversations about what can we do, and I said, "Well, right now all you can do is hold your head up high, and just do what you know in your heart is right." And we'd have to tell them that we have to look at the bigger picture. That we couldn't do knee-jerk reactions. That we had to ride out the storm and become better people, and try to find a way to look at it so that it would strengthen us rather than tear us apart.

◈ ◈ ◈

BEADIE DAWSON

"Beadie Kanahele Dawson was the only Hawaiian attorney to step forward, to listen to our pleas— yes, pleas—and who agreed to help us. I will never forget what she did to help Kamehameha and the beneficiaries. No one should."

–Kaylia Iona, letter to Kāwika Eyre

KĀWIKA EYRE: We got advice that we needed to go talk to the National Labor Relations Board, fast.

We got a lot of information from NLRB, what we needed to do—petition NLRB for certification; take a vote among the faculty, and so on.

And we needed a lawyer. Beadie Dawson made the connections.

DEAN CHOY (*advisor for Nā Kumu and attorney for KSFA*): It was a privilege to participate and to play a role in it. It was from my standpoint a fascinating controversy.

In the practice of law, you don't often get controversy that presents such stark differences of what is right and wrong. The majority trustees were wrong.

They'd done so many bad things that they couldn't hide it all. No matter how many people they got to twist it around and explain it away as something other than what it was—an abuse of power. They were the bad guys. The faculty were the good guys.

JIM SLAGEL: Mike, at the behest of the trustees, sent around a memo saying Bob Katz and Buddy McGuire were coming on campus to "improve communication." As "healers." Sort of like how death heals. Healing like this, we didn't need. These guys were union busters, and they made confrontation out of something that had the potential to be positive for the school. Mike and Oz blew it on that one. They could have called off the dogs.

Bishop Estate signs on reputed union buster

Honolulu Advertiser
headline, 11/15/97

DEAN CHOY: They don't necessarily come as a team. A lot of times, some company will hire Buddy just to be their chief negotiator for a union contract, or just have Bob Katz. Of course, the majority trustees in their infinite wisdom put the two of them together for a double whammy.

TOM CESTARE (*National Labor Relations Board hearing officer*): Buddy is their, well, persuader.

OZ STENDER: McGuire was taking a very tough line. Whether he'd talked to Henry before he came in the room—it sure sounded like Henry kind of dictums.

ARLIS LEGLER: They met with the department heads. It was very unpleasant. They tried to paint a picture of our teacher colleagues as doing this horrible thing by wanting to unionize. They would turn into awful people. They could slash our tires and do all these horrible things. And I was thinking, *I work with these people! They aren't going to anything harmful to us!*

DIANE TANNER-CAZINHA: I never knew any such thing as a union buster.

DEAN CHOY: Unfortunately, in the context of labor-management relations, as far as dealing with unions, the level of what is acceptable behavior for an employer, to discourage a union or to fight a union, it seems to me that what otherwise might be called dirty tricks or bad faith are acceptable tactics.

LOKELANI LINDSEY: I don't think McGuire is known for anti-union tactics. He is a very astute union negotiator and negotiates for union rights. I am not sure the terms of his contract, but I approved his hiring.

GAIL FUJIMOTO: My conversion came slowly, over time. I argued strongly against unionization. But the faculty was backed into a corner. Based on all that was occurring, we really had no choice. The tipping point for me personally came when I attended the meeting with McGuire and Katz. If I had any doubt at that point, they absolutely convinced me that the faculty needed to unionize.

ARLIS LEGLER: We were put in a position where we were somewhat threatened—we were management, and therefore any attempt to unionize was adversely against us. We could not participate because we were department heads. I have this recollection of being told not to be supportive in any way. We could not sign petitions. I knew from my colleagues that money was needed to do the unionizing. And that we were told not to give. I remember putting a hundred bill in an envelope and passing it through a couple of other people so it would get to the union anonymously, because I couldn't do that.

BILL FOLLMER: I came to the Nā Kumu meetings. I was supportive, I joined, I was one of the initial people who signed up. I wasn't a big mover or a player in Nā Kumu itself. I tried to work on the bylaws, so I was a contributor, but that's about it.

I think we were impressed with the Nā Kumu leaders. Four good leaders—just came out of the blue, and they just did a pretty good job.

We were sort of the Nā Kumu supporters and looking for an organization. And I think we realized that we have a lot of talent. You know, if those four could do it—I mean, just looking around, we saw that we had enough of a talent pool to make it work.

Some of the Nā Kumu leaders—minor leaders, not the major four—pulled off and started the union. And they were purposely separate people. We didn't have any of the Nā Kumu four as officials in the union.

KĀWIKA EYRE: We spent a lot of time discussing this, both small Nā Kumu leadership group but also in the big group. Really struggled with it, and came to the point where Nā Kumu was seen as a mix of teachers and some administrators trying to work out as much as possible to reform this institution without having to revert to union leverage of any kind.

LARRY MCELHENY: I kind of have always thought of Nā Kumu as the umbrella, the philosophical high road, and the union as the legal arm of Nā Kumu, to provide some protection. So now they can speak out freely without having to worry about being punished. Speak softly and carry a big stick.

LARRY MCELHENY: We had to set up an organizational structure.

MOANA LEONG (*Elementary School teacher*): A meeting was held at Kalihi Union Church. We went around the room introducing ourselves and sharing what our strengths, and how we thought we could help the union. After everyone shared, we had nominations for president, vice president and treasurer. Diane was the first choice for president, because she had already taken a leadership role on behalf of the teachers, but she declined. Clare Ho nominated me for treasurer, because I had shared that I was very organized. No one else was nominated or volunteered, and the next thing I knew, I was treasurer.

BILL FOLLMER

"We were sort of the Nā Kumu supporters and looking for an organization."

MOANA LEONG

"No one else was nominated or volunteered, and the next thing I knew, I was the treasurer."

MARYALICE WOODY: Everyone thanked Moana for being treasurer, because no one wanted that job.

MOANA LEONG: I took over from Tom Chun and Guy Ontai, who had been receiving checks and cash donations from caring people from both within and outside of KSBE. The outpouring of support was truly amazing, particularly from other private schools and especially from the DOE teachers.

We elected Larry McElheny president and Roy Alameida vice president. Roy had union experience when he worked for the airlines. He had a quiet demeanor. He was happy to stay in the background, but was very qualified to step in. Larry had a calmness about him, and had a lot of experience in community affairs.

LARRY MCELHENY

"I'm willing to take on Bishop Estate."

LARRY MCELHENY: I first came to Hawai'i in 1962 to surf. I fell in love with the place, vowed to come back at some point, returned with my wife and my son in 1970 and have been here ever since.

From some of the experiences I was having in the local community, trying to help the community realize its vision, empowering the local communities, I saw the conflicts between the establishment and this institution. Bishop Estate was basically the establishment, you know.

At the organizational meeting, the nominees were asked to explain a little bit about why they were interested in the job or why they felt qualified. I remember mentioning, tongue in cheek, that I was a plaintiff in two lawsuits. One against McDonald's and one against a giant construction firm from Japan, Obayashi. And I said, "Look, I'm willing to take on McDonald's, I'm willing to take on Obayashi and I'm willing to take on Bishop Estate." And they elected me.

LARRY MORDAN: Larry's quiet, a consensus builder. He's probably kept a lid on a lot of things because he's able to mediate in an even-tempered manner. His ears turn red when he gets mad. But he knows himself well enough to know when to step back.

BILL FOLLMER : He's an amazing leader. But he's got the principles and the organization talent to bring things through, yeah.

DIANE TANNER-CAZINHA: We asked him one time how he got his people skills. He said, when he made surfboards he had to get money out of surfers, so that's how he got his negotiation skills.

BILL FOLLMER: One of the things I like about the union is that we all view ourselves as representatives with no particular personal agenda other than making sure that everyone else's agenda is served and represented. That grew out of Nā Kumu.

DEAN CHOY: Bill first came up to me when I met with the faculty to discuss the forming of the union.

He prefaced his conversation with me by presenting himself as someone who was very conservative, affirming how against unions he was—always been against unions.

BILL FOLLMER: I am a doctrinaire conservative. I like Bill Buckley, Milton Friedman; I like individual liberties, including freedom of choice. At that time I was a member of the National Right to Work Defense Group, which is an anti-union body.

But it turned out that the union was the only kind of organization that could exist, so I was for it.

LARRY MCELHENY: I think a lot of the teachers were not typical union people, so Bill's not unusual in that regard. Maybe a little more than everyone else.

JIM SLAGEL: That such a staunch conservative as Bill Follmer became a leader in the union effort is a testament to how badly the faculty needed protection. I mean, this guy's got the complete first season of Fox News on DVD—and he's rolling up his sleeves with a left-of-left treehugger like Larry, working together as a team and accomplishing the nearly impossible.

This was a "union" in the best sense of the word. The union of ideas. The union of great, divergent thinkers and even greater folks. You were proud to be part of this.

BILL FOLLMER: As a group we want fairness, we want partnership, we want to work with people. You can count on us being honest and straightforward and respectful.

LARRY MCELHENY: We have always, from day one—it's kind of in our bylaws almost—that we don't want to be what was the perception of the typical union: corrupt, abusing power, etc. We want to be the antithesis of that perception, I guess. We want to be democratic and inclusive.

KĀWIKA EYRE: That was an approach that was very attractive to teachers.

DEAN CHOY: From my experience, working with a number of other unions, this union is different. They're a bunch of honorable, reasonable people. The leadership bends over backwards not to put themselves in any kind of self-serving or conflicting position.

TOM CHUN: The thing that makes our union different from any other is that we don't have any paid officials. And I hope it never does. And the union's philosophy, I'm happy to say, is based all on Nā Kumu's philosophy. Almost to the letter, that's what we are, philosophy and mission. ✑

Thirty Students

Judge Yim Reports and Lokelani Lindsey Reports

18

Ninety-seven percent of the graduating class was going on to higher education. And now all of a sudden we have a report coming out that says 30 students can't read. –Patrick Iona

JIM SLAGEL: Somewhere along the way, Lindsey stopped being the lead trustee for education. Or she didn't. If she did, it was in August '97. Or it wasn't. You couldn't tell—there was nothing in writing. Only whisperings making their way up the hill.

Either way, it didn't stop her from acting like she was still the lead trustee. Hers was the loudest voice for firing the four Nā Kumu representatives.

And then she put out an educational report, with the glaring headline that the longer kids were at Kamehameha, the dumber they got. Well, they were smart enough to get that one.

LOKELANI LINDSEY: The purpose of the report was to put everything in focus and present it to the trustees, because the students were not getting the help they needed. There were people who were protecting the president, there were people who were protecting

the teachers, but I was concerned about protecting the learning environment and how our money was being spent.

OZ STENDER: Judge Yim the fact finder came to see us three times.

The first time was to get the trustees to give immunity to anyone who spoke. He was finding that people were reluctant to speak because they were afraid of their jobs and that sort of thing. He's getting phone calls, but people are not telling him anything, and they won't give their names. He wanted the trustees to assure anonymity, and assure him that they wouldn't fire anybody that spoke to him. Of course that was the right thing to do.

Next time, he says he's getting all this stuff, information that was pointing to Mrs. Lindsey as being a big problem, and it's looking very bad, and he's looking for somebody to come in and say the good things, to balance, it was so one way. So each of us trustees went down, and Mrs. Lindsey. He came back and he said, "That's not good enough. I need it from *people* to tell me." I think it was Marlene Sai, or a couple of folks that went down and supported her. And they get Tony Ramos in there, Rockne Freitas, you know, the old team.

The final time he met with the trustees, he said, "The report is very bad."

◈ ◈ ◈

OZ STENDER: The trustees were going to be getting two reports, within days of each other, one from Lindsey saying that things at Kamehameha were dreadful and the other saying that Lindsey was dreadful for Kamehameha.

On November 27, the *Star-Bulletin* published "Broken Trust II."

It had a different group of five putting their names to it. Gladys Brandt, Nona Beamer, Isabella Aiona Abbott, Winona Rubin and Rod McPhee.

Bottom line, she had to go, along with Peters, Wong and Jervis. "Broken Trust" I and II, a one-two punch, and this second punch was aimed right at Lindsey.

LOKELANI LINDSEY: I am an extrovert. You can imagine how difficult it has been for me to remain silent.

The reporters were calling me from all over town, because "Broken

Trust II" came out, and it repeated a whole mess of negative things that I didn't feel were true. They were painting a picture of Kamehameha Schools that I didn't agree with.

Every time I brought something up in the boardroom that needed to be discussed, like my imperative for educational change which was brought up on November 25, a couple days later something would appear in the paper against what I was doing or with lots of allegations and rumors and innuendos of what was going on. I felt this was another one of those things. There was a pattern that was set from way back when, and it just bothered me.

Lindsey, Stender clash on essay

She rebuts the educators' criticism; he says the points they made are right on the mark

Honolulu Star-Bulletin,
11/28/97

I said, "I wish I could take time today to meet personally with reporters to do a point-by-point refutation of the allegations contained in the five authors' letter, but I can't because this is Thanksgiving and I'm cooking a turkey and baking pies."

The defenders of the status quo at Kamehameha Schools obviously believe Thanksgiving Day is just another chance to keep up their relentless attack. But the status quo is not good enough for the children of Kamehameha Schools. I am committed to telling the truth and will do so relentless in my own way in the days to come.

I wish everyone in the Kamehameha Schools 'ohana and community a beautiful Thanksgiving. Mahalo.

OZ STENDER: I kept saying, "It's not Mike who's causing problems; it's Lindsey the one causing the problems, so if you ever make a thing of it, I mean, the thing is going to go right to Mrs. Lindsey."

She is the problem, not Michael. And they knew that, they knew that. They just didn't know how to handle it. And they thought Yim was just going to brush it over. He was their pick.

DICKIE WONG: We asked him to undertake this effort because of his integrity and skill.

OZ STENDER: I don't think they fully expected him to come up with the report he came up with. But they just totally misjudged the impact of all of that. Which is very surprising, you know, being politicians all their lives. Even with compromise and reading the pulse of the community and all that sort of thing. And not paying any attention to it.

But this was so overwhelming, the issues were so overwhelming, everything was so obvious.

KĀWIKA EYRE: Yim's report had 34 ways that Lindsey was bad for Kamehameha.

OZ STENDER: Judge Yim had to get his report out by December. It was so bad he wanted to submit to the court one piece of paper, and one word on it. Pau. P-A-U. Finished. Over.

But in order to do that, the trustees needed to have Mrs. Lindsey step down from the campus. Apologize to the people she offended. And if we would commit to that, commit that we gonna do things differently and better and all that sort of thing, and Mrs. Lindsey would take responsibility for all that she did, he'd send the report, pau, P-A-U.

They wouldn't do it.

Yim calls me, like a couple of days before he has to file this thing, and asks me, "What are we going to do?" I said, "Call Dickie." He said he tried—Dickie won't return his calls. So I said, "Well,

I'll go talk to Dickie." So I got Gerry Jervis. We both go down and see Dickie, and we try to tell him, you gotta convince Loke to do this. To save the situation. And he said, "No, we're not ever gonna do that. That's all a bunch of lies." I mean, he kept repeating what Loke was saying.

All he had to do was make a call to Yim and say, "Loke will step down and we will make her step down." He didn't have to have her agreement to do this. 'Cause she opposed doing it. But he could have said, "We will make her do this." But he didn't.

◈ ◈ ◈

OZ STENDER: Yim's report was under seal, by court order. The trustees got a copy. Nobody else could see it. Nobody outside the boardroom knew what was in it.

Lindsey's report is confidential, for the trustees' eyes only. Nobody outside the boardroom is supposed to know it exists. So after Yim's report scares Lindsey to death—the very next thing she does, she gives her report to the *Advertiser*.

RANDIE FONG: I was sitting in the back of a KS meeting held at a Hawaiian Civic Club Convention in San Diego. Mrs. Lindsey told the audience that when people find out what she knows about the Schools, there would be a dark cloud hanging over the campus. I didn't know what she was talking about. But I remember thinking, *What an odd thing to say in public—and right out of the blue.*

LOKELANI LINDSEY: It's very, very hard for me to go public with this at all. Because, professionally I've never done this before. But I've met with such resistance at the school—and nobody is focusing in on what we're all about. And that's students. And if nothing else happens out of going public but that we start to focus in on the academic progress of students, it'll be the greatest thing I've ever done.

KATHY KUKEA: She was defending herself. That was why she released it. She was trying to say, "This is why I've been an ass. Because the place is a wreck."

MIKE CHUN: There were some very damaging and inaccurate allegations regarding our school—and what was devastating, it was coming

"The longer students stay at Kamehameha, the lower they score on standard tests. More than 30 members of the Class of 1997 could barely read at Grade 12 levels."

—Lokelani Lindsey, Honolulu Advertiser, *12/6/97*

from within and not without. It was coming from our boardroom, and I couldn't believe anything like this would have been allowed to happen.

KĀWIKA EYRE: Yeah. The inside wave. There's a Hawaiian saying about watching out for the inside wave that will swamp your canoe. Lindsey was the inside wave.

ARLIS LEGLER: Dr. Chun called a faculty meeting after school on Friday, and he told us that something would be coming out in the paper on Saturday that would make us so angry, and that it was completely wrong.

In my mind, I couldn't imagine what this could possibly be. So I anxiously waited for the Saturday paper to come—and there's the headlines essentially saying how much dumber our kids were the longer they were here. Speechless. The anger that built in me was just incredible. How could she? How could she?

OZ STENDER: I was appalled and horrified that Mrs. Lindsey knowingly released the report. She knew its release would be harmful to the school. It was unforgivable.

SANDY BEHENNA: As I read it, I could not see any other purpose than to hurt the school and hurt the students.

TONY RAMOS: How could a trustee lambast the school's programs? You don't do that. You don't criticize your own programs in public. That is Administration 101. Secondly, the faculty couldn't understand the criticism. Because we all know what we have, what kind of program we have, and the level of students we're working with and how they're achieving. They're achieving very well. So it's kind of disbelief. Betrayed, if you will, might be a good word that teachers felt.

LOKELANI LINDSEY: I never expected the onslaught of criticism because I released the report.

CHARLENE HOE: Immediately after the release of the report, students came to me and asked, "What does that mean? That I am stupid?" The concern on how the students felt was apparent. They talked to us about their friends who teased them about going to that stupid school.

HERB WILSON: I got phone calls from parents—even parents who were thinking about sending their kids to Kamehameha were suddenly having second thoughts.

PATRICK IONA: Parents are confused. Chairman Wong sent a letter home to all parents, explaining how excited they were about the class that had just graduated. That 97 percent of the graduating class was going on to higher education. And now all of a sudden we have a report coming out that says 30 students can't read.

KATHY KUKEA: How long have we been battling this thing about it's a good school for Hawaiians—we only turn out firefighters and electric line workers. Once something like this goes out in the public, good luck. A week even in the newspaper and that would have been long enough for people to go, yep, I felt they were probably a good school for Hawaiians, and not even a good school at that for Hawaiians.

CORIE CHUN (*'98*): Dr. Chun came on TV during homeroom. He had that I'm-tired-but-this-is-really-important-so-listen look.

MIKE CHUN: Over the weekend, the controversy has escalated to where you are directly affected. Confusion, frustration and a sense of self-doubt have entered your minds and hearts. This hurts me deeply, that you should ever question your self-worth or the worth of your school. I am here this morning to state in no uncertain terms that the school is outstanding, and you are young people with remarkable talents and exemplary abilities. You excel academically, artistically, athletically, and socially; you have done it all.

KIM SLAGEL: He went down the list, excellence across the board. The Christmas concert. Boys' cross-country champions, girls' volleyball champions. Amnesty's meal ministry to the homeless. Increasing enrollment at outstanding colleges and universities—no school sending more graduates to the University of Hawai'i. And SATs were good.

"When asked if her comments in the newspaper might be detrimental to the students, the ever-ebullient Trustee joked, 'Ah, dah little buggahs probably can't read them anyways.'"

–Imua Outsider, *faculty-generated parody of* I Mua Insider, *Winter '97*

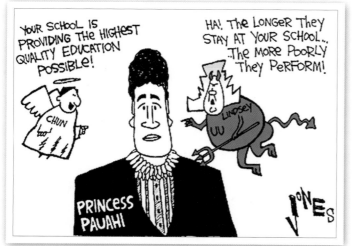

MIKE CHUN: Continue to walk tall, not only because you are sons and daughters of Kamehameha but because you have earned the right to. As you do, I walk with you, as I always have and always will. Next week Friday is Founder's Day. Let us renew our commitment to excel. There is no greater way to honor our beloved princess, or to thank her for this school with which we are blessed. Let us all have a wonderful and blessed day. God bless you all.

JULIAN AKO: When I read the report, I was really incensed. I called Mike Chun up the next morning and I said, "It's not right, what's happening here. It's not right, what's being done to our students, to the name of our program, and I want to be a part of fighting it." I went up to the Heritage Room in the Admin building Saturday morning, and there were a bunch of people there who were concerned, and we all volunteered to pitch in to refute whatever portion of the report we felt we had some knowledge or expertise of to address.

JIM SLAGEL: The trustees gave Mike a week to respond. That was official. Unofficially—

KATHY KUKEA: —It was egregious, and erroneous, blackening reputation. We could have taken the tack that, well, this will all get worked out in the boardroom, and—and, whatever. But I think we had the sense that if we don't immediately say, no, this is wrong, and rebut it, that it would have stood.

ARLIS LEGLER: When she attacked the students, it was like—you don't go there. And we were all a bunch of protective little hens around our students. And probably that was one of the most unifying things. When she put that horrible article in the newspaper, then we just went, no. No. You don't go there. You do not bring the kids in on this. That was off limits.

GARY OBRECHT: We had had a big Nā Kumu meeting. We wanted to publish in the newspaper a letter to the attorney general advocating that all five trustees be removed.

KĀWIKA EYRE: This was major: Nā Kumu is now publicly calling for Attorney General Bronster to remove all five trustees.

KĒHAU ABAD: These were our words: "We implore you to act upon our request and the requests of others in the community to remove immediately the current Board of Trustees. We see this as absolutely necessary if positive changes are to occur at Kamehameha."

CHARLENE HOE: We processed it through the whole group of teachers, sentence by sentence, word by word. Then we added a stack of supportive documents.

GARY OBRECHT: I agreed that I would take it down to the *Advertiser*. At that point, I had never taken anything to them—most of our stuff had been faxed. It was after dark already, and although I talk big about not being scared, I was kind of scared, because I remembered how close the newspaper building is to Kawaiahaʻo Plaza. And I kept thinking about all the stupid things you think about, like, when I get out of my car I'm going to be seen. I think because of the weather, that romantic thing about how nature plays into: it was drizzly, rainy, kind of gloomy, and there were lights on in some parts of the upper floors of Kawaiahaʻo Plaza. I just thought, *I'm real visible.*

You have to go through security. It's that time of night; you have to go through a gate. I had to sign in a book that I was going in—I have to put my name down. And when I got upstairs, the people I was supposed to see weren't there. I think it was Diane Chang, and I can't remember who the man was, but they sat me down, and we had a fairly long conversation and it was pretty reassuring. Anyway they took it, and they agreed they probably were going to put it in the next morning.

We had been told how many times not to communicate with the press, and here I was walking right into their newsroom and signing my name that I was going in there. It was exciting but also kind of scary. But I like that memory.

The next morning it appeared on the front page. Right at the top.

KĒHAU ABAD: Lindsey holds a press conference saying she is no longer lead trustee for education. She said she hadn't been since August.

OZ STENDER: Well, it would be nice if we had known! I told Dickie, "If this is true, we should tell the world about it. Nobody told me about it. I read it in the paper."

CHARLENE HOE: And then what the Yim report said came out publicly, that Lindsey was oppressive and hostile.

LOKELANI LINDSEY: I personally feel that he just listened to rumors, innuendos and allegations. He had already made up his mind. Never did they look at the administration or management of Kamehameha Schools. They only looked at Trustee Lindsey. I don't think I've done anything wrong.

It is obvious that I have become a lightning rod of criticism in the way I have represented the trustees' interest at their request to oversee the performance of Kamehameha Schools. My goal always has been to identify ways to improve the education of our children, and in so doing it is apparent that my forthright style has offended people as I identified areas that I believe required attention.

Trustee Oswald Stender of the Kamehameha Schools Bishop Estate has been the mastermind of an organized campaign to undermine the other trustees and preserve the unacceptable status quo at Kamehameha Schoools. It is my belief that he has definitely targeted me from early on, getting information from people at the school about things that could be used against me, in my opinion.

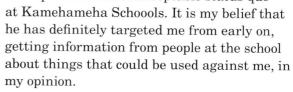

GARY OBRECHT: Next thing—huge surprise—the Supreme Court justices announce that they are not going to appoint trustees anymore.

The justices of the Supreme Court doing a

180 on something like that—no one could ever have imagined it.

KĀWIKA EYRE: While all this was going on, on the campus we were testing the waters to see if there was critical mass supporting the idea of a union. We did this very simply, with a straw vote at a Nā Kumu meeting.

DEAN CHOY: I remember the secrecy in just trying to assemble. There was this fear. People felt that if they spoke out in any way critical of the majority trustees, there were going to be disciplinary repercussions. When Bishop Estate challenged our right to even have a vote to form a union, people felt their jobs were at stake.

KĀWIKA EYRE: A piece of advice Dean gave us was to go out and apply for jobs elsewhere. Gary and I both did. I even interviewed.

DIANE TANNER-CAZINHA: We were either going to win or we were going to be all out of here.

KĀWIKA EYRE: The straw vote favored unionizing. Then there had to be a formal petition to the National Labor Relations Board.

DEAN CHOY: We had these pieces of paper for people to sign individually, that they were interested in forming a union. And you have to take them to the NLRB. And I remember such a concern about keeping those—nobody wanted to see them.

DIANE TANNER-CAZINHA: Not in my office. I didn't want anything in the room. Everything was out of my car. For a year.

JAN BECKET: We needed to get something like 30 percent of the faculty to sign those cards asking for the NLRB to organize an election. Way more than that signed, like 70 or 80 percent.

KĀWIKA EYRE: The signing process was finished by December 19, 1997, which was Pauahi's birthday. Out of respect, we delayed submitting to NLRB until the following Monday.

Honolulu Advertiser,
12/20/97

Cease-fire called for one day
Bernice Pauahi's memory honored

Students at Founder's Day,
Pauahi's birthday

Dean wrote up the submission. It was signed by Holoua Stender and delivered to the NLRB office. The next thing would be in the new year—a hearing, and setting up an election, for the faculty to officially vote Yes or No on having a union.

Mike Chun was asked if he would recognize the union. He said he wouldn't.

CHARLENE HOE: Trustee Jervis was breaking away from the majority. It happened surprisingly quickly. In July, he had been hitting Oz Stender with a rolled-up newspaper and telling him to get the f--- out.

OZ STENDER: He was sitting next to me. He threw it at me. With force. I put my arm up; it hit my arm.

Henry was screaming about my being a traitor, going to the press with all this stuff, bringing down the school, tearing the estate apart, acting contrary to my fiduciary duties, all these stupid statements. I thought Henry was going to punch me that day.

LARRY MCELHENY: After "Broken Trust," Jervis was talking about the need for the trustees to take a good look at themselves and take responsibility for their actions. And by October, he was with Oz Stender, petitioning the court to make the majority—now down to three, Wong, Peters and Lindsey—share board information across the board.

BARB LEE: It appeared to me the rats were starting to jump ship.

It was like Jervis could feel the winds shifting against the trustees and he needed to save his own skin.

By the time of Judge Yim's independent report, Jervis was with Stender that Lindsey had to go.

OZ STENDER: That was the ammunition now—I got this thing, coming from a former probate judge, overwhelming information. He didn't issue it yet. He filed it with the Probate Court, under seal, and then set a hearing date. And I said, the day that report hits the press, "We have to ask Mrs. Lindsey for her resignation. Get her off. We as trustees cannot look the other way."

They wouldn't do it. Dickie Wong wouldn't do it.

So I said, "If you won't do it, I'm going to do it. I'm going to ask for her removal, and then when I'm done with her, I'm coming after you. Because if you do not join me in this, that means you support her.

She did wrong and you support her, you're just as guilty as she is."

That's when Gerry Jervis jumped ship.

We asked the attorney general to do it, and she wouldn't do it; she didn't have the information; the information that Yim had was under seal, not accessible, and therefore they didn't have a case. She wouldn't help, wouldn't even join the petition. And so we said, "Well, we're gonna do this."

Henry says, "What if you lose?" And I said, "I'm in deep shit."

2 trustees petition court

Bishop Estate trustees Gerard Jervis and Oswald Stender put aside previous conflicts to form an alliance against the other three trustees, who they say have left them 'out of the loop' on major decisions

Honolulu Advertiser headline, 11/5/97

OZ STENDER: When I first decided to sue her and asked the lawyers what it was going to cost, they said $2-2.5 million, take a couple of years—and hope you win. I thought, *Gee, if I'm going to spend $2.5 million for some uncertain outcome, it's worth paying $1 million to get a certain outcome.* So I offered her $1 million to resign. I didn't approach her. Told the lawyers to approach her.

She actually considered it. Because we were talking about conditions. We would have a retirement party for her. That's okay. She wanted stupid things, all these stupid ridiculous things. She wanted to have her picture in the trustees' gallery on campus. I didn't know we had such a thing, so I said, "I'll have to think about that." So I called Mike Chun and said, "Do we have a trustees' gallery up on campus?" He said, "No, we don't." I said, "Okay." I don't know where she got that idea. And she wanted, I don't know, a couple of other things.

The last day, Dickie Wong comes in. He knew about this deal we were trying to work out. "Oh, you know, she's a wonderful person—

we keep her on, you can watch her." They needed her. As long as they had her, they had three. I said, "Dickie, I'm not gonna be a housemaid to Mrs. Lindsey, no way. I want her off."

He stands up, he was very upset, and says, "Well, if you don't put an end to this, we're gonna fire Mike Chun, and I've been protecting him all this time." I said, "You wanna fire Mike Chun over this, do it, just do it. It'd be worth it." So after he left, I called Mike—"Mike, you might get fired this afternoon." He said, "Thank you." But anyway, of course they wouldn't. It would have been stupid.

So she turned me down, and I think they convinced her not to take it. I hope they paid her.

BARB LEE: Things were moving in the school's favor. It was a relief to the faculty, especially those who had written letters to Judge Yim. When the Yim report came out, what people had been saying was true—Lindsey was damaging in 30-some ways. This was huge.

LARRY MCELHENY: The Yim report became public in early December, with its 34 ways Lindsey was a huge detriment. The attorney general called her in.

LOKELANI LINDSEY: I feel fine. Nothing to hide. I'll be open and forthright with them. I will stay on as a trustee. I still don't feel I have done anything wrong. I feel like I have upheld my fiduciary responsibility, and I will continue to do this in the best interest of the kids at Kamehameha.

I'm so glad we'll be able to get this over with before Christmas.

ARLIS LEGLER: Well, it was the Christmas parade. I live across the street from Windward Mall, and the parade stages at Windward Mall. So I went over to the parade. And I wore nothing that identified me as a Kamehameha anything. And Lokelani was the parade marshal.

I'm standing around these crowds of people, and the parade begins. And she turns the corner to come down Kamehameha Highway. She's in an open car. And waving and smiling.

There's always excitement at parades, there's noise and all this, and there's children and what not. There was nothing when that woman's car drove by where I was standing. As far as I could hear there was silence before her and after her.

And then people around me are saying very quietly to one another, "How dare she be here! How dare she show her face! What is she doing here?" And my thought exactly: *How dare you show your face in this highly populated Hawaiian community? And smile and think everything is rosy?*

LARRY MCELHENY: On December 29, Stender and Jervis filed suit in Circuit Court to have Lindsey removed as a trustee. ⤶

Union and Disunion
A Governance Disaster

19

How I survived is I pictured Bob Katz and Buddy McGuire coming to school and spending the morning with little kids. Oh, they'd be chewed alive.
–Diane Tanner-Cazinha

DEAN CHOY: Before the union hearings in January '98, there is some discovery you can go through. Even though I request information, Bob Katz doesn't show me anything. He just stonewalls the whole thing. And before we know it, we're at the hearings. So we just blast ahead.

Ultimately we just stuck with three witnesses, because we were able to cover enough ground with those three— Diane Tanner-Cazinha, Holoua Stender and Sigrid Southworth.

SIGRID SOUTHWORTH: Gail Fujimoto volunteered me! She said she would cry in the courtroom. So I had to testify for all the librarians!

DEAN CHOY: I think it was a very real threat that people who did stand out, who took the lead, who stood in the gap, who signed

off on the petitions to organize and form the union, people like Holo Stender and Diane, they would be targeted, they could lose their jobs. So I gave them a lot of credit.

SIGRID SOUTHWORTH: I was close to retiring, so I did not have to worry that way, but Diane and Holo did.

DIANE TANNER-CAZINHA: We got subpoenaed. It was at the Federal Building. You had to get searched. So I'm lining up at the door, and here comes all these reporters and cameramen and photographers with their bags and stuff, and the guards say, "Well, where are you going?" and they say, "Labor Board, seventh floor," and I thought, *Omigod, they're here for us.* So I kept having these flashes, on and off.

DEAN CHOY: In the hearings, one of the main arguments that Bishop Estate used was that the faculty as a group are really *managerial* employees and they are not really qualified to form a union. That was the argument—to take away the ability to form a union, period.

SIGRID SOUTHWORTH: Kamehameha librarians are no way management. We are subject to review all the way up the line for everything we do. And we teach. We are just part of the teaching faculty. That's exactly the situation.

DEAN CHOY: I thought it was just nonsense. I thought it was bad faith. I thought, *We're going to cram it down their throats, and expose it for what it is—bad faith.*

SIGRID SOUTHWORTH: I felt confident about what I had to say. I wasn't scared. I was irritated.

There was a tone of nastiness to Mr. Katz's questions, and Mr. McGuire—they were trying to intimidate us, and I don't think intelligent people need to be intimidated. I don't think it's necessary for professional people to be nasty even in a court situation. And I have to say I think you can handle matters like this civilly.

TOM CESTARE: How could you throw stones at Sigrid? This woman had been there for so long. And she was so knowledgeable, about everything. She's just a treasure of a person. A dream librarian to have at your facility. Her knowledge of Hawaiiana was just stunning.

DIANE TANNER-CAZINHA: I cried listening to Sigrid, because it was just so disgusting. I just thought, *If I were them, I would feel like you want to say to the employer, if you don't want my skills, I'll just say, "Screw you," and I'll take it somewhere else.* But it was sad that we had to come to that point.

DEAN CHOY: They are presenting these arguments and creating a picture that is ultimately a false picture. And they must know it. But why do we have to deal with arguments like this? It's cheating, it's bad stuff.

DIANE TANNER-CAZINHA: Katz is the kind of lawyer that lawyer jokes are written about.

Somebody must have told him we were having these meetings, organizing. He says, "Now is there a room, a teacher workroom?" I say, "Well, you know, there's a Xerox machine." He says, "Isn't there a sup-ply room? Weren't there secret meetings?" And I burst out laughing. I said, "It's a closet."

SIGRID SOUTHWORTH: They were trying to make her management, trying establish whether Diane, as a grade-level chair, lead teacher, was supervising other teachers. I remember a question to her about milk, something to do with milk cartons—whether she had the authority to charge the kids. Management? There was another one about tacky glue. I remember sitting there and sort of snorting and thinking, *Good grief! Do we have to give time to this?*

DEAN CHOY: We went four days. It is ultimately a very unfortunate characterization that you end up making—that the other side is engaging in these kinds of tactics. And that if we could get to a level playing field where we could deal in good faith, there would be so many resources that would not be wasted, that we are wasting now in this process that is taking so much time and so much energy.

DIANE TANNER-CAZINHA: How I survived is I pictured Bob and Buddy coming to school and spending the morning with little kids. Oh, they'd be chewed alive.

TOM CESTARE: One of the things I got from the whole hearing was just how dedicated the teachers and the administration at that school really are. And that to me was really rewarding. Because this was not about money whatsoever. It was about the school more than anything else, and how you folks fit in that school in terms of having good working conditions but also making sure you did right by the kids. I was really impressed by that. I think we all were.

DEAN CHOY: Holo couldn't make the last day. So it was Sigrid and Diane, and we went to Sunset Grill across the street from the Federal Building where the NLRB was, and had lunch, and I told them, "This lunch is a celebration. We won." Because now the record was complete; the truth was intact. And as long as the truth was there, we'd win.

MARK EWALD: In March, the WASC accreditation team had finished their work. It is customary for the WASC committee to give a first reading of their report to the school's core report preparation team. It allows those who put the report together to refute or clarify the committee's findings. I was called to attend this first reading.

We met in the ʻAkahi Student Center. We sat around the large table and listened. I was both stunned and elated at their findings and revelations about our governance situation.

It started out by saying that Kamehameha was a world-class institution that served some of the nicest, friendliest, most energetic, capable and promising youth in the world. It said that the teachers were highly qualified, with a high level of professional commitment. So—so far, so good.

And then it got into how Kamehameha was run. Dysfunctional governance. A perverse application of top-down decision-making "which has openly undervalued, if not scorned, the professional expertise, talent and commitment of the non-administrative staff," producing "an oppressive, intimidating and fearful professional climate."

I thought that no way were these findings going to be presented in the final public report. I thought, *If it is, all hell would break loose, and where would the wrath of the trustees fall?*

ROY ALAMEIDA: The union election had been set for March 13, '98—which turned out to be the day after the WASC report was read to the faculty. It was hard to imagine two days like that, back to back, any time in the history of Kamehameha.

DARRELL SCHUETZ: One of my clearest memories is of Dr. Chun almost pleading with us the day or two before the election to somehow recognize that things were going to be okay and that we didn't need the union.

MIKE CHUN: I was asking for time. Wait a year. I was asking the teachers a question: "Has anybody been fired during this whole period of time?" You know, I haven't let you guys down. The response that came back to me was—"Can you guarantee, Mike, that you're going to be here next year?" And I said, "No, I can't guarantee it." They said, "Well, we want that protection. If we wait till next year it's going to be too late. We need that protection in place now."

ROY ALAMEIDA: Coming up to the day of the election, there was a lot of propaganda. It got pretty intense, and some of it was crazy. An anonymous message came round on a sheet of paper, saying the union would make Kamehameha a hostage and extort all kinds of money from Hawaiian children. "Pauahi's children must not go down in vain. SAVE HAWAIIAN RACE! Vote NO UNION!"

Chun sent out a memo to faculty saying these videotapes, "Election Day" and "Collective Bargaining," would be running on the school closed circuit TV from 8 a.m. to 3 p.m. They had that TV running constantly with some kind of little video on it, and you're "encouraged" to watch.

MOANA LEONG: The videos were totally biased and one-sided. I felt insulted. Did management not think they had intelligent teachers

"Dr. Chun's primary concerns included his beliefs that:

• A union will be divisive, making collaboration in policy formulation more difficult, if not impossible.

• There is no guarantee that some things won't change for the worse.

• The possibility of work interruptions, i.e., a strike, cannot be eliminated."

–I Mua Insider, *KSBE-generated newsletter, 2/13/98*

ROY ALAMEIDA

working for them? Give
me a break. We all saw
through them in an
instant. Instead of warn-
ing us about the dangers
of unionizing, the videos
only served to convince us
more than ever that we
needed to unionize. We
were all disgusted. It was
the last straw.

LARRY MCELHENY: The union election was held in the High School
auditorium from 6:30-7:30 a.m. and then again after school, 2:30-5:30.
NLRB ran it. The ballot was a simple Yes/No choice: Do you want
KSFA to be your bargaining agent or not?

DIANE TANNER-CAZINHA: I was nervous as they counted out loud.
I really didn't know. They were making piles of 10 or something.
I thought surely it would go, because we had a lot of support, but
there were some Nos. When we got to 50, it's like yes, okay. When
he got to 100, then that was the majority. And it went to 186 to 36, a
really resounding majority.

KĀWIKA EYRE: I was deeply moved. Moved to tears. For me it was
like Nā Kumu had landed, had survived, had come into port after a
long and perilous journey through the worst of waters. Unlike many
of my colleagues, I had always been pro-union, and I felt this was the
necessary outcome. I remember Tony Ramos and wife Suzanne were
ashen. They looked like they were waiting for someone to die. I also
remember asking several of my students whom I knew to be involved
in the petition to be there to witness their teachers unionizing. It was
a historic moment.

JAN BECKET: I looked around in those early years and just shook my
head and said, "Forget it, this isn't gonna happen." So, for me personally, it was—it was wonderful to see the faculty vote in that way.

ROY ALAMEIDA Those who said the teachers would not follow through and become a union had to eat their words.

DIANE TANNER-CAZINHA: And then Bill Puette, from the University of Hawai'i labor research center—he had been really helpful, bless his heart—he says, "I didn't want to tell you this, but now you have to get a contract out of them." So I'm like, omigod, aren't we done? And he says, "No, you can't lay your burden down yet." I didn't know. I had no idea.

◀▷ ◀▷ ◀▷

KATHY KUKEA: The WASC report had printed on the front of it, CON-FIDENTIAL INTERNAL DOCUMENT. The trustees hadn't gotten copies yet; they were being printed up on campus at Rapid Copy. But somehow the *Advertiser* got the story, with all the gory details about terrible governance.

It was a huge leak, and very damaging to the trustees. They started an investigation.

JANET ZISK: Well, the leak all started innocuously enough.

I went upstairs to get a cup of coffee. That's where drinking coffee leads you, up the hill of trouble. And I walked past Kathy Kukea's office and she said, "Hi, Janet, the WASC report's been printed." I said, "Wow." And she said, "Yeah, that's the good news. The bad news is that there was a switch of pages, out of order, and so I had to send them all back again to Rapid Copy because I can't send them down to the trustees like that."

She said, "But, you know, if you'd like to look at a copy, I got a copy here." And I said, "Is there any chance I could have it for the archives? I have a box I can put it in. I can close it." That's it. That's the end of it. She says, "Oh, sure, I don't see why not." So I brought it down, put it in its envelope, put it in the box, put the box back there. I didn't look at it or anything. I knew what was in it—I had been at the auditorium when it was read out and everyone stood up and cheered.

The next morning, Kathy comes down, stands just inside the door looking absolutely stricken.

I said, "Kathy, what's the matter?" And she says, "Janet, you know the copy of the last report I gave you yesterday?" I said, "Yeah." She

says, "Can I have it back?" I says, "Sure." So, I went and got it and gave it to her. And I said, "What's the problem?" And she said, "Have you seen the morning newspaper?" I said, "No." And so she shows me the morning newspaper, and the *Advertiser's* got the report in it. I said, "Ho, ho." I mean, that didn't strike me as anything incredibly horrendous. Because my understanding from the previous day was that it would go back to Rapid Copy to have the switched pages rearranged, and then go to the trustees and be redistributed.

And then she said, "This was in the newspaper this morning—and the trustees hadn't even seen the report." And she said, "You know, there's probably gonna be an investigation as to who released this to the press."

BOB WHITING: There were several ways it could've happened—

GREG BARRETT: It was handed off to me. It seems like someone came down and met me in the *Advertiser* parking lot down there by security and gave me an envelope.

BOB WHITING: Maybe I was a prime suspect because I went through this whole thing. They asked me how it happened and all that kind of stuff. I just told them, "Well, it wasn't me."

JANET ZISK: Kathy was one of the two people in charge of the report, and she was in charge of getting it ready for the trustees. And she was on Mrs. Lindsey's black list from before. Obviously, she's the main target.

According to Kathy, when Mrs. Lindsey saw the report published in the paper, and she hadn't even seen the report yet, she said, "I'm going to get that woman's hide"—meaning Kathy—"and nail it to the wall."

LOKELANI LINDSEY: I wanted to make people accountable. I thought it was very presumptuous to release this and I also thought that it was released to serve someone's agenda.

OZ STENDER: First, Mike Chun was supposed to be running the investigation, but then they brought in an outside lawyer, Bill McCorriston.

He came onto campus. People were called in without any notice, and they were not going to be allowed to have their own lawyer. He had a court reporter. And he was going to use a lie detector! A lie detector being used on Kamehameha faculty and staff!

We didn't know that the trustees started this investigation, and it just so happened that Gerry Jervis happened to be on the campus that day when somebody was going to be interviewed. So we quickly got a restraining order to stop it.

GERARD JERVIS: This was new ground that we were breaking because we were interrogating one of our own people using outside counsel. I thought it was like killing a fly with a bazooka.

OZ STENDER: The other trustees made these snide remarks about, you know, we're way off base, we need to be investigated, all that stuff.

MICHAEL GREEN (*attorney for Lokelani Lindsey*): It's outrageous that Stender and Jervis would fight any efforts to find the leak—speaks volumes to their guilty consciences and appears to be a breach of their responsibility to their fellow trustees and to the estate.

TONI LEE: They're lining these people up to fire them and scare everyone else into silence.

KĀWIKA EYRE: Finally they called off their big dog attorney and had the investigation go on using in-house people, administrators. It went on for months.

JANET ZISK: What we didn't know until afterwards, after the first preliminary rounds, is that the first person to be interrogated was Grady Wells, the head of Rapid Copy. And I think one or two of the women who worked there. And this was without anybody's knowledge. Nobody knew. And there is Grady, and he loves the school with all his heart.

KĀWIKA EYRE : Grady was true-blue Kamehameha, always saying that the early days at school had set his course.

JANET ZISK: Grady had always told me with great appreciation and haʻahaʻa spirit how much Pauahi and the Schools did for him, and how glad and honored he was to be able to give back through his work. Then the very institution that he loved and respected, of which he is a loyal graduate, turned on him and treated him like a criminal when he was totally innocent. It did terrible things to him.

KATHY KUKEA
AND PET TIFFANY

OZ STENDER: They had a list of Prime Suspects: Grady; Bob Whiting; Kathy Kukea; Kathy's secretary, Pet Tiffany; Janet Zisk, the archivist and Kāwika Eyre.

JANET ZISK: Kathy was going to be interviewed and was really distressed about it. And then I got this call from Carol Koza, from Personnel, this innocuous call. Instead of saying what she wanted right out, she asked me if she could set up a meeting with me, without telling me what the meeting was going to be about. She wasn't going to volunteer. I had to ask. And she said, "Well, it's about the release of the WASC report."

I found out there was going to be a whole lineup on Monday—Kathy's assistant, Pet Tiffany, who had just retired, and then Kathy and then me. This was all news to me.

I said to Pet, "They've called you for an interview and you aren't even an employee anymore? I don't think that's right." She was very distressed, because she was recuperating from breast cancer, and this is not a good idea, to bring this stress.

KĀWIKA EYRE: It was pretty brutal.

JANET ZISK: That weekend, I called Oz Stender, who hadn't heard about it, didn't know a thing about it. He said, "Let me call around and check." And then I called that really nice lawyer for the faculty, Dean Choy, and he wasn't available, but his associate was. He gave me a lot of information, mainly that it sounded pretty illegal to him, and he told me all the steps to take before I accepted such an interview.

Bishop trustees suspend inquiry

So I had all this information about what I should and should not do. So, first thing in the morning on Monday, I called Nathan Aipa's office—the head lawyer at Kawaiaha'o Plaza—because my rules of the game were: I was going to go with a tape recorder, and I was going to go with my husband, and I wanted a company lawyer to represent me, and I wanted a set of questions given to me, and I would answer those questions only.

JAN BECKET: Watching the absurd little circus that went on with the persecution of the people who were accused of releasing the report— that was another defining moment. I wasn't involved but, you know, I was watching from the sidelines just like the rest of the faculty, and it certainly had an effect, as I think it was meant to. All of those things were meant to be as sort of warnings.

KĀWIKA EYRE: It seemed never to end. It got around to me in October. They were calling me up in class, which I didn't appreciate. My boss, Ke'ala Kwan, told them to leave the classroom off-limits. During the first interrogation, I told Carol Koza I didn't leak the WASC report to the *Advertiser,* and I didn't know who did. She and B.J. Mau wanted to run through it all again. They were dutiful little soldiers. Thankfully, we had our union and Dean Choy sat in on the second round of questioning.

JANET ZISK: In September 1999—September 1999!—I got a letter from Mike Chun. "Dear Janet: The purpose of this letter is to bring closure to the WASC investigation that was initiated over a year ago. I felt it necessary to write you personally since you had numerous discussions with Personnel during this investigation. Please be informed by this letter that the investigation is concluded and no further action is forthcoming. Mahalo for your continued dedication and commitment to Kamehameha Schools. God bless."

KĀWIKA EYRE: It was a form letter. All of the accused got it nearly a year later.

MARK EWALD: Everyone had been waiting to hear from WASC about re-accreditation. On May 11, we heard—only three years. Which really meant that the school was on probation. It was the first negative verdict ever for Kamehameha. It was based on governance, and it had Lindsey all over it. Tony Ramos and the administration were having big discussions whether to appeal. That was for administration to decide.

Out of the loop

MARK EWALD: These were busy times. On May 11, WASC gives the school three years' probation. On May 12, the union elects its officers. And on May 15, there was an anniversary march from Mauna'ala, organized by Nā Pua.

What had the trustees learned from the first march? They continued to be their usual graceful diplomatic selves— they wanted Nā Pua to take out a $2-million insurance policy for coming onto the grounds at Kawaiaha'o Plaza.

TONI LEE: We find it very astonishing and appalling that we who are the beneficiaries have to come up with a $2 million policy to come on grounds that is for us.

KĀWIKA EYRE: By now, Nā Pua and Nā Kumu had zilch respect for what the trustees thought. We would have marched onto the grounds whatever the insurance situation.

TOM CHUN: There was a bunch of us that went on that march. We went, and guys played 'ukulele, and we sang "Ua Mau" and other things, and then we marched all the way down to the courtyard at Kawaiaha'o. *You know*, I thought to myself, *just a year ago or two, this would be unheard of.*

PAUL IONA: I didn't understand what was going on, me and my younger brother and my sister. What we did was, we walked around Kawaiaha'o Plaza. It was slow, because we were being really reverent, and we had a little prayer ceremony, and I just remember thinking, *Oh my God, are the trustees looking at me?* Because we stood right in front of their offices, and my Auntie Dutchy made it very clear that's where we were going to stand. And I was really scared. All I knew is that they were probably watching us through those glass windows that we couldn't see back through. And I was scared. I was really scared. It was quiet but very tense. You could feel it in the air. My mom was holding my hand, because I kind of didn't want to be there, because I knew the trustees were out there. I vocalized that to her, and she said, "No! You be here!" So she had that grip on my hand; I knew I couldn't go anywhere.

KĀWIKA EYRE: The four Nā Kumu reps gave speeches.

KĒHAU ABAD: We are larger, stronger, prouder and more united than ever: students, parents, alumni, faculty and friends of Kamehameha.

TONI LEE: We implore you to open the doors to truth, open the door to begin the healing, stop the stonewalling, stop the legal maneuvering.

KĀWIKA EYRE: Not all the trustees were around. Dickie Wong was hugging the walls of the building, off to one side of the raised platform where Fred Cachola handed him the documents the year before—in the shadows, watching with silent eyes.

He had his say in the papers.

DICKIE WONG: They made an offer that was something different than a year ago: now's the time for healing. They kept repeating the phrase that we ought to be pono, and ought to be haʻahaʻa, humble, and that we ought to get on with the process of healing. I think that's a beginning. One year ago this was never said, and I think that's progress.

I hope as we go forward there will be healing and there will be forgiving. ⌒

Where the Buck Stops
Peterson Reports, Mike Chun Waits

*If the school is a factory of failure, who does it go to?
The principal, the president of the school. That's where
the buck stops.* –Michael Green

KĀWIKA EYRE: If it was possible for things to get more tangled, they
did. In the spring of 1998, while we were trying to teach, the trustees
said they were thinking of moving the estate to the Mainland, they
shut down a useful committee of faculty and administrators and they
paid 400,000 dollars to get another outside consultant, Peterson, to
badmouth the Schools. Joy to the world!

LARRY MCELHENY: So here was Dickie Wong talking about healing—
and the next thing we see in the papers is that the trustees are talking
about moving their operations to the Mainland.

KEKOA PAULSEN (*'77, Bishop Estate spokesperson*): It is one of those
things trustees have discussed from time to time, but it hasn't been
formally presented to the board.

OZ STENDER: Maybe not, but all sorts of things happened without
being formally presented to the board.

KEKOA PAULSEN: There are tax considerations, and certainly an operating climate on the Mainland that is perceived as more welcoming.

LOKELANI LINDSEY: We don't want to work in a place where we're not wanted.

CHARLENE HOE: There was an ad hoc planning committee that was trying to address concerns that had been brought up by the faculty and were coming up with possible solutions or actions. We had met over the summer with administration present.

JULIAN AKO: I think at that point there were administrators who were really receptive to the idea and wanted to see it work.

CHARLENE HOE: It was halted arbitrarily, without input from the participating members. We received a communication from Trustee Wong saying that administration and faculty could no longer meet, and this committee was to discontinue its work. I took that also as intimidation.

HOLOUA STENDER: I would get phone calls against the union, visits from administrators especially, coming to my office and telling me what a terrible thing we were doing—turn back before it's too late!

GARY OBRECHT: A lot of good relationships for Tony were severed during the conflict. Because it's hard to respect people who wouldn't stand up, who had no guts. And who kept saying it was their jobs, and who would publicly say that they had jobs and mortgages, forgetting the fact that everybody else who was standing up had jobs and mortgages. It just galled me that they somehow could think that their families and their mortgages were more important than those of the teachers who stood up or people out in the community who stood up.

SIGRID SOUTHWORTH: I think a lot of administration was just too afraid of losing their jobs or their status or whatever.

GARY OBRECHT: I thought it was contemptible behavior that they would not join us. And it could have made such a difference for them,

"I would get phone calls against the union."

–Holoua Stender

too, if everybody had gotten in and if the whole school had stood up united and had agreed. It would be so better today, too. But no, there was always going to be that dividing line, which definitely occurred then, when the unionization came about, which has always saddened me. The lengths they went to stop the unionizing and to cut off as many teachers as they could from it and to try to use plants to destroy the credibility of the union with faculty members. All the gossip, silliness.

We kept hearing that certain department heads were sources of information. They would take stuff back to Tony and Sandy about what was going on with the teachers. And they were the ones who would agitate against the union. I don't know if any of it was true.

KE'ALA KWAN: Do I wear that T-shirt or not? That's that gray administrative-teacher roles that for me sometimes were conflicting. I don't think I was totally comfortable, because I was in waffle mode. But I can feel okay that I wore the T-shirt. And that's not something we had told Tony them. We were just this ring of commonly T-shirted teachers in front of two administrators.

SIGRID SOUTHWORTH: Two administrators who did have courage and confidence were Julian Ako and Kathy Kukea. They didn't lose their jobs, but they didn't come through unscathed.

JULIAN AKO: The release of the Lindsey report was the turning point for me. It was then that I decided I could no longer be a "loyal soldier" to people who would allow public ridicule and embarrassment, based on inaccurate use of data, to be visited on our students and faculty.

Things got really, really heated as Loke's trial approached. I shouldn't say heated—more and more uncomfortable. I think that Tony and I were lashing out at each other in front of the rest of the administrators. Just having outright disagreements about stuff.

At the beginning of the 1998-99 school year, I was not apprised of the first meeting of the High School A-Team, the administrative team. I was told about the meeting after the fact by one of my A-Team colleagues who wondered why I had not been present. Sandy Behenna is the one that told me, "Tony says he's angry with you and he doesn't want you there." When I asked Tony why I had not been told about the meeting, his response was, "You said you didn't want to play." I corrected him by reminding him that what I had said was that I would not

JULIAN AKO

"I could no longer be a 'loyal soldier' to people who would allow public ridicule and embarrassment ... to be visited on our students and faculty."

participate in any teacher-bashing. My statement had been prompted by administrative discussions about playing hardball with the teachers after they had voted to establish their union.

KATHY KUKEA: With me, really it started most with WASC. Bob Whiting and I were co-chairs. Bob and I had come in trying to get the group to go somewhere, and Tony would derail things in one way or another. It's not that he had any notion of doing deliberate whitewash, but every single meeting he was trying to stonewall what was coming out, either by blaming the teachers for not being able to look after themselves, defending the trustees, or defending Mrs. Lindsey or something. So every steering committee meeting was just this difficult situation. So there was a real struggle between Bob and I and Tony—not overt, but there was this constant head butting. I suppose that's when things really started to go downhill between Tony and I. I was undoubtedly pissing Tony off on multiple occasions.

JULIAN AKO: All of the other High School administrators except for Kathy Kukea and me got their merit pay raises at the beginning of the 1998-1999 school year. Everyone else's had been done in the summer of 1998. The reason we didn't get ours was that Sandy Behenna and Tony Ramos had not completed our performance appraisals, which was a prerequisite to receiving the raises. Repeated requests to have the appraisals completed went unheeded. And I think I even wrote a note to Sandy Wicklein expressing concern that it had not been completed.

We had to resort to requesting the intervention of the Personnel Division. The appraisals were finally completed at the end of December 1998. In fact it was the night before Christmas. Kathy's, I think, went longer than mine. My appraisal had many negative comments in it, among them the charge that my colleagues on the A-Team were complaining that I was contributing to divisiveness on the team. When I asked each one of the team privately about the comment, they were surprised and indicated that they didn't know what I was talking about.

◈ ◈ ◈

KĀWIKA EYRE: Six months after the Lindsey Report and the Yim Report, the trustees came out with yet another bought and paid for report by an outside consultant. The Peterson report cost 400-plus thousand dollars of Pauahi's precious money.

MICHAEL GREEN: The Peterson report is going to vindicate Mrs. Lindsey. The school is a factory of failure.

JUNKO LOWRY: The students were crushed. They were so crushed— Well, after all, we're stupid. We're stupid Hawaiians.

CIARA LACY: I felt hurt. I felt embarrassed. Kamehameha means a lot to me, and I would hope that if there were problems, they would be addressed in the school and not displayed across the state.

RICK HEYD: Some of my students had taken to bringing an extra shirt to school, so when they left school they wouldn't be seen with the KS logo on their shirts, because they were embarrassed with the school and had to deal with ridicule from other kids and adults if they were identified as KS students.

GLADYS BRANDT: My concern is the faculty and parents have been disturbed by something that has been allowed to linger as long as it has, and now the students are involved. That's a no-no as far as I'm concerned.

JAN DILL (*'61, leader of alumni group Nā Pua*): The children of Kamehameha are being exploited for the personal gain of your trustees. The resources that were spent on the Peterson report are a fraud—a fraud perpetrated by the majority trustees, because it was an attempt to defend their own self-interest rather than to reach forward for the betterment of Kamehameha schools.

TONI LEE: The saddest part is that the kids have to face it for another year.

◈ ◈ ◈

MICHAEL GREEN: If the school is a factory of failure, who does it go to? The principal, the

LAURIE CHEE

"I graduated from Kamehameha with an honors diploma and was accepted to Santa Clara University. Kamaile, our salutatorian, placed in the 98th percentile nationwide for SAT scores and will be attending the University of California at Berkeley. Ciara, Jasmine and Lance have been accepted to Yale, Harvard, and MIT, respectively. I can't speak for my entire class, but 98 percent are going on to higher education.

"So, please excuse my ignorance, Mr. Green and Trustee Lindsey, but where did I fail you? Where did we fail you?"

–Laurie Chee, '98, letter to the editor, Honolulu Advertiser, 7/28/98

president of the school. That's where the buck stops.

OZ STENDER: The Peterson report said Chun wasn't up to the job. He "lacks the educational background and leadership skills the Schools need to take them successfully into the next century. This is not to say the board is blameless; but the incumbent has lost the confidence of the board and staff."

ROD MCPHEE: I don't care who the person is, the conditions at Kamehameha over the past five years would have made it impossible for anyone to lead that school. The board has created an impossible situation and criticized him for not rising above this.

KĒHAU ABAD: The board majority will not be persuaded by moral or legal arguments nor by the force of public opinion to serve the best interests of Kamehameha or its students. Such advocacy on Dr. Chun's part would have resulted in his termination, which would not have been in the best interests of Kamehameha.

JULIAN AKO: Mike is very, very visible to the kids and they love him for it. I think that they believe that Mike listens to them. The fact that he takes the time to go to two-three different activities in one night so that he can show his support for the kids means a whole lot. I can remember when I was in the classroom full time, how much it meant to kids for the teacher just to say, hey, that was a good football game Friday night. And I think the kids feel like Mike takes that kind of interest in them, even though we're a large school, in a way that they don't see frankly from the other administrators here at Kapālama. And it means a lot.

MARIANE HANNAHS: I know he had his hands tied in many ways, and I really felt sorry for him, because I could see he was a man in conflict. You could see it was just taking its toll on him, you know, the internal conflict. I mean, physically he was just horrible.

MIKE CHUN: It was horrible during that whole period in terms of the ups and downs, ups and downs, ups and downs.

TONY RAMOS: He had countless opportunities to step forward and show some leadership, and he blew it over and over.

NEIL HANNAHS: Ultimately, my sense of it is that Mike never signed up for all this. Who would have? I think his view was being an alumni, the number one blue and white guy, the keeper of the old traditions, and I think the number one warrior in the sense of kind of a popular leader.

LEROY AKAMINE: Tradition is very important. He continues that to this day.

"Our confidence in Dr. Chun has perhaps wavered over the past years largely because of his inability to defend Kamehameha and the students and staff from the harms the educational trustee Lokelani Lindsey and the board majority have inflicted upon us through their perverse and top-down management style."

–Larry McElheny,
KITV News, 7/31/98

NEIL HANNAHS: I don't think he ever signed up to be a warrior in the sense of first in the battle.

ROD MCPHEE: Mike's stance was to say nothing, and I don't know whether he hoped it would go away, but I think, by saying nothing, he was avoiding getting sucked into it, and so he wouldn't say anything. I know when Loke was shooting her cannon off and so on, he never said anything that I know of publicly.

BOB WHITING: I thought, ethically, he rose above a lot of the name calling and that kind of stuff; he just rose above it.

PATRICK IONA: I was disappointed—well, not disappointed, I was more sad because he didn't take a stand. Like Rocky Tokuhara said, "Mike needs more balls. He needs to stand up and show his colors and just tell them." Face the fire. With all the support that he had behind him, I really felt that if they tried anything at that point, it would have been a serious mistake on their part. I felt that if he stood up and said what he had to say, they wouldn't touch him.

MIKE CHUN: I should have publicly gone to the paper and disagreed with the board and taken them to task. When the television people came and said, "Will you have a statement?" instead of saying, "No, I don't have a statement," saying, "Yeah, I think they're a bunch of yo-yos and we gotta get rid of them."

JULIAN AKO: He said to me that he contemplated resigning. He told me that he thought maybe the thing he should do is just resign and go outside and fight it from the outside, and not have to deal with what he was having to put up with and stomach.

OZ STENDER: And I told him, "You can't! You know, you can't do that." I said, "If you do that, she wins, they win. And what have you gained? Nothing! You need to be there. We need to fight this thing together."

KATHY KUKEA: It was clear that Rockne Freitas would have been put in Mike's place.

LEROY AKAMINE: There was two people there on campus, Loke and Rockne, that were committed to oust him, and Rockne to replace him.

KATHY KUKEA: And we always have to remember that it was not inevitable that the trustees would be removed.

OZ STENDER: When it was all over, the important thing was that Mike still be there to be able to help piece things back together again and provide leadership for the institution. And if he did anything in a public way that would give the trustees the pretext to fire him, then all that opportunity for him to continue to serve the institution would have been lost.

KAHELE KUKEA: I think he would have been dumped. He probably feels some guilt about taking that role and not stepping forward. I can understand that. I feel some of that too. But you kind of feel like you can make your big statement and then you're gone. You'd be remembered as a martyr and you wouldn't be there to maybe protect your people.

LEROY AKAMINE: His responsibility was to bear all pain and to suffer indignation, embarrassment.

MIKE CHUN: Just stay focused on the kids, and do what you believe is right. Turn it over to God. ⬎

The End of Their Gauntlet
Surveillance and Threats

21

The jeers and taunting only increased until I reached the end of their gauntlet and set out for home. Watching my back. –Kāwika Eyre

LOKELANI LINDSEY: You know, Kamehameha Schools is a very small institution, and everything I do or don't do is transmitted up there, and everything they do or don't do finds its way down some way.

TONI LEE: She had every pulse of what was going on this campus.

TONY RAMOS: She had a standing thing about people letting her know what's going on.

BRIAN CHANG: We knew that there were people in the organization that were very, very interested in finding out what was going on.

ELISA YADAO: If you burped at an inappropriate time, somebody was on their cell phone calling Loke on her cell phone.

PATRICK IONA: There was those that would tell us we got to watch who we're talking with, because we don't know, this teacher or this PTA or whatever is going to report us.

RANDIE FONG: Mrs. Lindsey had a way of knowing all kinds of things. You would walk into her office, or you would give her a call, and she said, "I received six phone calls this morning saying la, la, la, la—why is that happening?" I would say, "Well, I don't know what you're talking about. Who are these people?" "No, I can't reveal their names." And that would be a pattern of interaction with her—I got a phone call this morning, or I heard this, someone came into my office and told me this.

PATRICK IONA: We were at a meeting, and Dickie was at the microphone with Henry, and they asked if you had any questions. So I raised my hand, and they had all their secretaries or whoever, they asked who you were, what class you were, and there were people writing your names down as you spoke.

GARY OBRECHT: Some of the things that were going on were really bad. The strongest fear I had was, what if there really was that secret network of spies, and they watch what we do, and they really are listening to our phone conversations? We really believed those things. A lot of people believed them constantly. I had flashes of thinking maybe they were true.

KĀWIKA EYRE: Part of what Nā Kumu was about was flaunting the chain of command, the insider boy network of our administrators and the whole way schooling was being conducted. Our response was complete openness and inclusiveness. So we used the phones, email and fax machines with impunity. However, as a precaution, we tried to keep everything short, and use names sparingly.

BOB RAMSEY: I can't say that I have hard evidence, and I may have been just paranoid. but I would hear ominous clicks on my phone at times, and it's funny, because I don't hear those now, and I don't recall hearing it prior to all this stuff going on. But when I heard them I would immediately change tone. Everybody was really uptight. It was real scary.

OZ STENDER: I thought that our offices were bugged. I became more conscious of talking on the phone. I would turn up the radio. But then one day I was sitting in Dickie's office and talking to him, and Stella, my secretary, was in my office, and she could hear the conversation.

You see, the walls don't go all the way up to the ceiling, so there's really no soundproofing.

There were other things that would surface where somebody somehow knew about a conversation I've had on the telephone.

KAWEHI YIM: I had to come into the office one Saturday, and Elisa had talked to me and said, "Just so you know, there's going to be someone in here who's going to be checking the lines to see if there are any bugs." I said, "What kind of bugs?" In my very innocent—I'm thinking cockroaches, right. "They want to see if somebody is tapping our phone lines."

JUDY LAYFIELD: As part of the office renovations, as we were doing work, or as the contractors were doing work, they were asked to look out for things that might be planted and to take them out.

KAREN WILKINSON: I was part of that group that worked with the outside consultant who worked to check for bugs, and I remember one time at 2 o'clock in the morning, we went through Mrs. Lindsey's office because she thought her office was bugged. But there was nothing. We didn't find anything.

OZ STENDER: They ordered a sweep. But they announced to everybody they're gonna do the sweep. Why would you announce it? You gonna do a sweep, you do it in the middle of the night when nobody knows.

LEEANN CRABBE: We would go to the gym after work. I have an enclosed office—we wouldn't even change our clothes in here! The only place, if we had to change clothes, we would do it within a bathroom stall, because we knew it was illegal for them to have cameras

"This is a matter under investigation and we're not going to comment on it right now."

–Kekoa Paulsen, KSBE spokesperson, KHNL-TV News, 4/30/98

in the bathroom. There's stuff like—people wouldn't even pick their nose in their cubicles because they don't know if there are cameras on them. That's how it felt.

I would go home and tell this to my husband. He thought I was crazy. But it really did feel that way here. But it was like we could only talk to each other in the workplace, because no one else really understood. I think if you had talked to anyone else on the street, you know, they would have thought you were crazy.

OZ STENDER: I used to get nasty calls at my house. People wouldn't identify themselves. Scream and yell at me and hang up. People told me, you know, take your name out of the book.

I'd get letters. A lot of anonymous stuff. Now whether Mrs. Lindsey wrote it and had somebody send it?

LEI-ANN STENDER DURANT (*'73, daughter of Oz Stender*): People drive by. Some people weren't nice. You know, they'd yell things.

OZ STENDER: My son said, "Dad, you gotta watch your back."

Freeman Guards, they're friends of ours, they wanted to help me, put a security guard on the house. I just felt, if someone was going to do something to me, let them do it.

Mrs. Lindsey had a private eye, Matt Levi, watching me. And that kind of worried me. Then a couple of days later, my tire was flattened, purposely punctured, somebody used a knife to puncture it. That kind of worried me a little bit.

I never felt Mrs. Lindsey would ever be a part of somebody doing something vicious. One time she said she had a letter in her hand that I had written to the Supreme Court justices. I hadn't. I said, "Show it to me." She said, "No. It's confidential."

It was all the paranoia.

GARY OBRECHT: There was a story in the papers about threats. Rockne Freitas got a piece of paper with writing in block letters saying that Peters, Wong, Jervis and Lindsey better resign, or else. Freitas put out a notice about increased security, and to watch out for unattended packages. Lindsey's attorney got threats. The lawyer for Nā Pua got threats. The attorney general got threats.

MARGERY BRONSTER (*attorney general, State of Hawai'i*): Usually by supposedly well-meaning friends who said they had heard it from enemies. I didn't know how to read it. There were so many calls. I had no idea what their connection was to anyone. I got very paranoid after 10 calls in one day. I think Oz told me to be paranoid, to watch out. Friends and others suggested caution. There were consultants and attorneys for the Bishop Estate who indicated that it was a good thing that I was from the Mainland, because I could always go back there to work.

◈ ◈ ◈

LAURIE CHILDERS (*Bishop Estate computer division*): I was in the Computer Division in Information Services Division. I basically was in charge of the Kawaiaha'o Plaza system, the computer network and the servers.

I absolutely loved working for the estate. I thought it was a great thing that they did. I loved being on campus. I did all the early networks and all the computer classrooms in the High School.

Then one morning, a person in my office came in that said Mrs. Lindsey was in here over the weekend with some of her people and they deleted a lot of files and he'd like to make sure those files cannot ever be restored. They wanted me to get rid of it. That's what they were asking me to do—make sure whatever was deleted

could never be restored.

This was when the attorney general was investigating Bishop Estate, investigating the trustees. I didn't want to go to the files, get rid of all the files. I remember at the end of the conversation saying, "I don't think I can do that," so I walked out of the room.

My boss talked to the director of ISD, and he said, "Let it be." I told my husband about it, and he said, "You're in big trouble, because that's withholding evidence, and you could go to jail for that."

He called the attorney general's office, and two investigators came up to our house and did a deposition. Then I was supposed to go into court and present all this information. I had a subpoena delivered to my house, at night.

Richard happened to come home from work early, and someone called our house threatening—

RICHARD CHILDERS (*husband of Laurie Childers*): Local voice, no hello, nothing. I remember the exact words, which is, "Tell that f------ haole bitch that if she testifies, she won't live to see another day."

I called the AG's office to tell them what happened, and they freaked out, and 15 minutes later we had two armed sheriffs over at the house.

LAURIE CHILDERS: That night we had armed guards outside the house.

RICHARD CHILDERS: I found out later that somebody had called and threatened the attorney general as well, which is part of why they took it so seriously—same description of the same voice, happened at almost exactly the same time. They were probably sequential calls. Who? Isn't clear, but it was somebody that thought that intimidation was the appropriate thing to do. Not that that would be a great surprise over what was going on at the time.

LAURIE CHILDERS: A lot of locals called me that I worked with, and they all told me to watch my back. They just said, because they knew

I wasn't from here, you know, this is really serious, take care of your family, take care of yourself, don't let your daughter out of your sight. I was very scared; I was very scared for my daughter.

RICHARD CHILDERS: For a while, we had an armed guard going to pre-kindergarten with my daughter to the Montessori school, and the guard would sit there in the classroom. What a horrendous thing for a four-year-old kid.

Prior to the time that the threat occurred, when Laurie had first come forward and told Kamehameha about what had happened and made an official statement, and we had told Oz Stender, Oz Stender in writing had told her that if there were any threats, to please let him know. I mean, clearly, he anticipated it in advance, and Oz was the only one out of the entire bunch I would give you a plugged nickel for. He was always personally appalled at what had occurred.

LAURIE CHILDERS: I left the estate because of this.

RICHARD CHILDERS: Our entire lives were uprooted.

LAURIE CHILDERS: Richard just said, "We're out of here."

RICHARD CHILDERS: I'd been 17 years in Hawai'i and I would've been there till the day I die. We've adjusted, you go on in life, but it certainly was a horrendous event. There was a period of time where I really felt like we were living inside a John Grisham novel, and it was very strange.

We put all that behind us and our lives are very different now. We find things that we still talk about. It'll probably still be my choice when I retire to come back to Hawai'i. I love the place; I love the people.

◈ ◈ ◈

CYD GASPAR ('99, *organizer of student petition*): I saw my teachers who were close to me really struggling with this thing, and it was taking a toll on their health. It didn't take a toll on the classroom experience at all. But you could see the frustration and the worried-ness and on announcements, their readings every day, all kinds of different stuff.

"Although KSBE and the AG have certainly had their differences in recent weeks, both can and do agree that even so much as a hint of a threat against any KSBE employee is not acceptable and will not be tolerated by either KSBE or the AG."

–I Mua Insider, *KSBE-generated newsletter, 10/31/97*

CYD GASPAR

"I saw my teachers who were close to me really struggling with this thing, and it was taking a toll on their health."

I think it was Keahiahi Lee that had come to me first and talked to me, and said something to the effect that we should do something, that Kumu Kāwika was talking about something, and it's big, it's really big.

Kumu Kāwika and I talked about the benefits, the goods and bads, what a student's voice could do in the community, what impact that would have.

That same day after school, I was sitting in Kumu Chun's room, Tom Chun, and he and I had gotten to be pretty close. He was my homeroom teacher for junior year. Kumu Chun and I—he had helped me make my first ʻukulele. We went to Keawewai on the Big Island, to go and plant koa trees. And I was sitting up there, and I told him about what I was going to do, a petition. He turned on his computer, and I don't remember if it was him or me that said half of it should be in Hawaiian:

> *We, the undersigned students of the Kamehameha Schools, wish to show our support of the Attorney General and her petition for the immediate removal of the current KSBE trustees for the benefit of all ke aliʻi Pauahi's beneficiaries.*

> *ʻO mākou nā haumāna o ke kula ʻo Kamehameha nona nā inoa ma lalo iho. Makemake mākou e hōʻike i ko mākou kākoʻo i ka Loio Nui o ka Mokuʻāina ʻo Hawaiʻi nei a me kona makemake e hoʻokuʻu ʻia nā Kahu Waiwai o ke KSBE.*

Right after Kumu gave me the petitions, I was kind of at a standstill. I was just, what are we supposed to do with this? Just say, here, sign it here? Just sign your life away, if you get in trouble, it's whatever.

KELLI KEAHIAHI LEE: Definitely. That was part of the fear factor. A hundred percent. The idea that a teacher, or you, could be yanked out of whatever—you know, that's like, Whoa!

CYD GASPAR: I went down to Kōnia Circle, to go stand with my friends after school, and my friend Brandy said, "What are you gonna do with that?" I said, "What does it look like? Why don't you look at it, why don't you read it?" So then she read it, then she said, "Cyd, you're gonna get in trouble"—No, you shouldn't do that, you might get suspended, or it might go on your record. What if you get kicked out? What if this, what if that?

KELLI KEAHIAHI LEE

"That was part of the fear factor."

It was only a small group of people at Kōnia that day. I think we had two sheets filled up. The next day, I think we met with Keahiahi Lee and Lokemalia Tong, and we kind of talked about it. I said, "Oh, here," and I gave it to them, and they said, "Oh, good," and they left with it. It wasn't a planning group; it was just really spontaneous, just do it because it has to be done kind of thing.

KELLI KEAHIAHI LEE: Our group of friends, there's like 10 of us, we all had some.

LAUREN LOKEMALIA TONG: We had people in band, in student leadership, I was in gymnastics—mostly girls.

KELLI KEAHIAHI LEE: We made a whole bunch of copies, and we split them up, and we figured out who has a free period when—someone was down at the lunch at 'Akahi; someone was in the library.

Student petition seeks trustees' ouster
Kamehameha seniors collected the signatures over a four-day period

Honolulu Star-Bulletin, 10/24/98

LAUREN LOKEMALIA TONG: It's the grapevine they talk about. The Kamehameha grapevine. I mean one person, and by second period it's all over campus.

KELLI KEAHIAHI LEE: The attitude of the class was, I think, they were willing to follow. They just needed someone to put it in motion. I mean, not everyone can juggle school and all of sports and all of that and be worrying about what the administration is doing at the same time. And with senior year, you're applying for college, and you have a lot of things that are going on.

I would say the majority of the class had some sort of feeling about it. But I think there was a lot of fear. And then there was a level of apathy. And when you have those two things together—

LAUREN LOKEMALIA TONG: And you don't want to screw up. Just in

"We don't know exactly what is going on. All we know is that we are hurting, and we're trying to do what we can to get back to our education and to keep focused."

–Shelby Decosta-Galdeira, '99, student body president, KGMB-TV News, 10/24/98

"In my estimation the student petition is a statement that the students want immediate closure to this. They want the healing to begin. Their lives cannot be put on hold. They want to be students. They want to concentrate on school."

–Beadie Dawson, KGMB-TV News, 10/24/98

case you get kicked out by doing something. And so it's very scary.

KELLI KEAHIAHI LEE: Our really good friend was senior class president, so she's, you know, on our shoulder, saying, "Don't get caught. Watch out." She was good, because she was always, like, be careful, do this, do that, stay away from this. She was kind of good to have.

When I think about it, what also helped us was that the teachers allowed us to do it in class. I mean, it didn't disrupt from class. Some of them were, like, "Oh, good, you need to do this." And others were like, "Okay. I don't see this."

KELLI KEAHIAHI LEE: If you look at the majority of the leadership in the teachers, it all came out of the Hawaiian language and Hawaiian studies kind of areas.

That's where you have teachers who are invested in being Hawaiian, in the Hawaiian people. The advocacy lesson is something that's like an underlying theme in a lot of the Hawaiian language classes. Like, over time you learned you can do something about—

LAUREN LOKEMALIA TONG: —The issues of the school. And it was just being a Hawaiian in general, being there for your people. This does affect you. Whether you think it does or not, it does affect you. And it's going to affect your children and your grandchildren. And if you don't do something now, or just get involved somehow, then it may not end up being the way you could possibly make it be.

KELLI KEAHIAHI LEE: To the credit of our class, we got so many juniors and seniors to sign over the course of about two days.

CYD GASPAR: I remember on the last day, gathering everything together. About 800 signatures.

KELLI KEAHIAHI LEE: Then we hid them. We were, like, hmmm, we should probably put this somewhere where they can't really look. Just, you know, paranoia. We ended up putting it in our friend's locker in the Ka'ahumanu workout place, 'cause anyone can have a locker in there; you just have to get a lock on it. So she was kind of further detached from us—that locker was kind of nameless. In case they decided to go through ours, it wouldn't be there.

Trustees order student probe

Henry Peters denies the estate is going after students supporting removal of trustees

KĀWIKA EYRE: The demonstration—though nobody called it that— was going to be outside Circuit Court, downtown. It was agreed that we would all wear blue and white, preferably the Kūʻē Pono T-shirts from the '97 march—Gail Fujimoto got us a new printing of the shirt. And we would wear ti-leaf leis, symbolizing our need for protection from abuses by the trustees and our effort to protect Pauahi's trust.

We did a briefing sheet to hand out. Mike Chun had sent a memo forbidding Nā Kumu to use faculty mailboxes, but we decided to anyway. And of course the kids doing the petition knew about it. It was going to be late afternoon, after school hours, so anyone was free to go.

KELLI KEAHIAHI LEE: We made fliers ahead of time that said, "Come to this day and fight for your school."

LOKELANI LINDSEY: I had phone calls from various people at the Schools saying several teachers were indeed telling the students to do these things.

TONY RAMOS: Mike calls me, saying Loke's on the phone saying that she has someone on the other line telling her that Kēhau Abad's putting up this sign for the kids to go down. "Tony, send somebody down." I called Kēhau—somebody's putting up signs for the kids to go down and march on the courts. We're trying to keep the kids out of this.

SARAH KEAHI: I was walking over to the court, and I saw all these people with signs, red and yellow signs, something like SUPPORT THE TRUSTEES, SUPPORT THE TRUSTEES.

The trustees' supporters were shouting, "You're not Hawaiian."

As we were walking in, these people were saying, "Shame, shame!" you know, at us and the staff. And they made some ethnic comments about the staff. And I turned around and I said to this person something in Hawaiian—"Ah, hilahila, hilahila."

KELLI KEAHIAHI LEE: A few people said, you know, the whole shame on you kind of thing. "You're a student! They take care of you!" But I was just beyond that. I was like, "Well, that's an interesting opinion to have. But I have a stack of petitions in my hand, 800 students long." So it didn't affect me at that point.

LEI-ANN STENDER DURANT: I wanted to see what would happen. It was really bad. And I just broke down in tears because the way they treated me, people who knew who I was, and them taunting. And I saw Aunty Momi Cazimero and Uncle Roy Benham holding SAVE STENDER or some sign like that. And I just broke down, because in this sea of people, there were two people who wanted to keep Stender.

HAILAMA FARDEN: Henry Peters' guys were around. They bussed them in, under whose money I don't know, bussed them in from Wai'anae. And that was sad, because I grew up with a lot of these people.
I'm looking at my people, and I say, "I love all these people. I grew up with all these people." I look at some of them, some of these

"kūpuna—well, you're like all my aunties. You know, I just have to say, okay, I disagree. I won't disrespect them. Because I love them, I grew up with them. And it was so hard that day; we had to walk past them to the court.

The hardest thing for me was Henry Peters' wife making eye contact with me and saying, "How could you bite the hand that feeds you?" And I said, "I'm doing this no nā keiki, for the children."

DUTCHIE SAFFERY: I think one of the most fulfilling times for me was when the students and teachers came and spoke outside the court. That for me was probably the greatest time beside the march itself. These young people, the students, got up and they spoke. It was almost like everything was worth all of it, and truly we had made a difference. And that these young people were able to be their own person. That was probably the happiest time for me.

KĀWIKA EYRE: When people talked about the Nā Kumu speeches, Kēhau's stood out.

KĒHAU ABAD: I remember feeling all day long that I really needed to find some space, because, you know, here we were coming from a full

"You can't have *ho'oponopono* if the values aren't shared. If aloha doesn't mean aloha, it's really difficult to come to common ground. Looking at all the *pilikia* (trouble) that has swirled around the estate in the year and a half, none of us would have taken that first step. But we need to stand up, be accountable. This is a battle to protect the values of Pauahi and the legacy of Pauahi. And the children sit at the heart of it."

—*Jan Dill, '61, Honolulu Advertiser, 9/11/98*

day at school, you know. Throughout this whole time we had our whole real jobs to take care of, and so I remember that whole day being really busy, not having found time to, um, clear my thoughts and really center myself. I had some, just some real cursory thoughts jotted down—what are some of the manaʻo that I wanted to share, but of course that's only about one, you know, one-tenth of what you gotta do to deliver it. And I just didn't really have—I knew it wasn't gonna come from me that day, 'cause I just didn't have it, and I said, "Where am I gonna go with this?"

So I needed to get on the side and just really pule very hard, very, very, very hard, 'cause I needed help desperately. I just needed to, um, ask Ke Akua to take care of it.

I sat off somewhere by the plants somewhere, until I saw it was time, and then I, I walked forward.

KĀWIKA EYRE: Leaving, there was a walkway from the courthouse in the direction of Punchbowl. The sign holders lined up on both sides of it.

KELLI KEAHIAHI LEE: I didn't have to walk through it. But I was, like, wow. I felt more sympathy for the teachers and the alumni. Because, you know, as a student there's that level of protection, where they can't be as fierce with us—I mean, we were still kids.

Nā Kumu reps Kēhau Abad, Charlene Hoe and Kāwika Eyre

DUTCHIE SAFFERY: The trustees' supporters were shouting, "You're not Hawaiian!" to those of us dressed in white and blue.

KĒHAU ABAD: Yelling things at us. Calling me and my dad blank blank haoles.

HAILAMA FARDEN: You know what it reminded me of? When you go to the racist museum. There's a racist museum, and you walk through, and they have recordings of yelling and hissing, "You f------." It was like that, walking through this thing as these people were yelling at you.

KĀWIKA EYRE: We'd heard it before. Oz told us that the Nā Kumu leaders were sometimes mocked by the trustee majority as the three haoles and the one Filipina.

SIGRID SOUTHWORTH: I didn't let them bother me. But the feeling that I came away with was that I felt sorry for them. We were there because we had real convictions and we went on our own. We got ourselves there. To be bussed in at somebody's behest—I felt sorry for them for being used, being used. And to form a gauntlet—what a crude thing to do. But I didn't let it bother me. I didn't mind walking between them, and I held my head high.

KĀWIKA EYRE: I walked straight ahead, thinking I would keep my eyes fixed, my head up and my mouth shut. The taunts started immediately: "Who you, haole, talking out about Pauahi's trust?" "Eh! Go back where you come from, haole!" "Who you tink you was, haole?" Then, against my promise to myself, I did the worst thing I could possibly have done. I responded. I told them off in Hawaiian. That, of course, infuriated them all the more, and the jeers and taunting only increased until I reached the end of their gauntlet and set out for home. Watching my back.

KELLI KEAHIAHI LEE: One thing that I'm still sort of nervous about and slightly afraid about is that some day this may come back and bite me in the foot—like, hurt my children's chances of getting into Kamehameha. And I hope it doesn't. I hope that we all, like, just progress and not dwell on something that was significant, but the important part is that we got past it. I just hope that can happen. ⌣

"Cayetano is using country club Hawaiians like Gladys Brandt and Walter Heen as human shields to hide behind. The high muckety-muck of the Hawaiian community is a very arrogant group that are letting themselves be used because they want to control who becomes trustee next. It is all desperation politics."

–Henry Peters,
Honolulu Advertiser,
10/27/98

22 Thanksgiving Day
And Bad Times with Buddy McGuire

Although we were disgusted with Buddy McGuire for making all of us, including the management team, negotiate on Thanksgiving Day, we did our best not to show it. When we took a break for lunch, our KSFA team shared everything we had to eat with Buddy and the management team. –Moana Leong

DEAN CHOY
"Marching orders are to give you guys a hard time."

DEAN CHOY: It was pretty predictable that Bishop Estate was going to give the union a real hard time in negotiating a contract. In fact there was feedback from a number of sources—leaks, if you will, from the management side—that you guys better watch out because they're going to give you a hard time. It usually would be somebody who would know somebody or was related to somebody, or is related to somebody they know who works over at Kawaiahaʻo Plaza. Somebody would tell a faculty member. That faculty member would let me know. They hear the scuttlebutt around the office that they are really upset with the union, and marching orders are to give you guys a hard time.

OZ STENDER: Dickie saying, "Good!" They looked at the union as providing them a weapon. McGuire was laying out the program of how they are going to negotiate the contract and the issues. They came up with a lot of things that they felt, we could get the teachers. That was the whole attitude—how we gonna use this opportunity to beat up on the teachers? They had dos and don'ts. And all the don'ts were stupid don'ts. And benefits, they could cut out benefits.

BILL FOLLMER: We formed the union just prior to the summer of '98.

So we were going to negotiate over the summer, yeah? Buddy used the entire summer about ground rules.

DEAN CHOY: We didn't get our first meeting till September.

BILL FOLLMER: He purposely waited till school was started.

DIANE TANNER-CAZINHA: I made a very sincere effort to do things after school and before school, on the weekends. For myself, I vowed that it would not affect my class. Teaching is so draining, and with the little kids that I have, second grade, it's body and soul, heart and soul, and so you can't—your mind can't be elsewhere.

MOANA LEONG: The first negotiation team was our KSFA executive board, which included the three officers and one representative from each division: Larry McElheny—president, Roy Alameida—vice president, myself—treasurer, Bob Hamilton—unit 11/12 rep, Bill Follmer—unit 9/10 rep, Rick Heyd—Middle School, and Diane Tanner-Cazinha—Elementary.

DIANE TANNER-CAZINHA: Every Thursday we had to go, from Labor Day to May. Right after school, we would jump in the car. To the Federal Building. An enclosed federal building, so the guy would frisk you coming in. This is the pits.

We're dragging every box and bag, papers and things, and try to have coffee for Bill, and I'd have a Coke, and there was a soda machine and a candy machine, so we'd have that and whatever we could get. So I said, "Buddy, can I get pizza?" And he says, "You can't, because the building's locked. You can't bring in any food."

LARRY MCELHENY: We didn't have any real dinner Thursday nights for a year.

RICK HEYD: I remember my son hating Thursdays because I never came home for dinner.

MOANA LEONG: A week before Thanksgiving, our team speculated as to whether Buddy McGuire would make us negotiate on Thanksgiving Day. We all decided that if he asked for it, we'd try to persuade him not to, because we all wanted to be with our families. If that failed, however,

"Not surprisingly, the majority trustees continue to use delay, diversion, and adversarial tactics in their negotiations with KSFA. These attempts to disenfranchise the teachers who are charged with educating Hawaii's children strengthen KSFA's support of the attorney general's petition for the immediate interim removal of all the trustees. As long as these trustees remain in power, Kamehameha Schools cannot be expected to reach its full potential."

–Larry McElheny, letter to the editor, Honolulu Advertiser, 10/1/98 we all agreed we'd be prepared to negotiate on Thanksgiving Day. And that's exactly what happened.

Maddie Oshiro, our KES librarian, was so appalled to hear this news that she met us downtown with a large bag of goodies she and others at KES collected for us to eat. I had picked up my kālua turkey earlier that morning from school and taken it to my parents' house in Waipahu. My mom helped me pack containers of food, kālua turkey, stuffing and candied yams, plates, napkins and utensils to take for lunch, since we had no idea how long we were negotiating that day. While there were less than a handful of members from the management team that came, our entire KSFA negotiation team showed up in a united effort to show them they were not going to break us. I was so proud of us that day!

Although we were disgusted with Buddy for making all of us, including the management team, negotiate on Thanksgiving Day, we did our best not to show it. When we took a break for lunch, our KSFA team shared everything we had to eat with Buddy and the management team. It was tempting not to. But with Larry McElheny as our president, he was always steering us to take the high road. We were able to hold our heads high after that meeting.

BILL FOLLMER: The regular after-school meetings were four to six hours, and the air conditioner went off at 5 o'clock. He just put us through the wringer.

LARRY MCELHENY: The first round of negotiations was total head-butting. They were trying to squelch the union; they were trying to kill the union.

BILL FOLLMER: We came in with a straight plain vanilla contract. It was less than a page. Maintenance of benefits, with just cause—that's all we wanted.

The first nine meetings, the only thing they and we agreed to was the one-sentence preamble to the contract.

DIANE TANNER-CAZHINA: They would say something gobbledygook— that was Buddy's thing—then we would have to go to Dean the next day, and he would say, "No, that's not correct," and then we would go back, and Larry would have to call Katz and say such and such.

DEAN CHOY: It became obvious that they couldn't stop the nonsense. So I got plugged in to the meetings, from about the 10th meeting. But I can't stop the nonsense either. They rejected everything we ever presented to them.

BILL FOLLMER: Rejected out of hand as "unacceptable"—that was Buddy's favorite word. And then they presented their own set of proposals and absolutely insisted that we couldn't go anywhere unless we worked with their proposals.

 With Buddy and Bob Katz, it was strictly a power battle. They were into all sorts of restrictions that would make it almost intolerable.

 In place of our one-page proposal, they came back with a 37-section counterproposal with all sorts of stuff that was absolutely pointless and meaningless. And stupid, like we can't use faculty mailboxes on campus. And lots of things were clearly unacceptable—you know, the pay cut. And some stuff that was sort of sinister.

MOANA LEONG: Bill relished picking apart management's unreasonable proposals, and particularly Buddy McGuire's ludicrous arguments. He came to every team meeting with a complete analysis of our previous negotiation session and with a plan of action for our next one. Who knows how many countless hours he spent on KSFA work, but he seemed to thrive on it.

JIM SLAGEL: His tenacity earned Bill the nickname Bulldog. I'm guessing management had some other names for him.

BILL FOLLMER: The first series of notes were done by hand, but then I brought my laptop in. I was trying to copy word for word. I would get about 80 percent. Other people taking notes with time indexing allowed me to fill in the gaps. I'd type them up and pass them around and everybody would fill in, and then the next day or that weekend I'd go over it and fill in the blanks.

 There are certain people who count on wearing you down. Negotiations, for instance, it's a wearing-down process. And if you don't go in there to wear them down versus them wearing you down, and give them that sense of that, then you're going to hear a lot of stuff that you don't want to hear.

DEAN CHOY: Buddy's had a lot of experience negotiating contracts,

"Rejected out of hand as 'unacceptable.'"

–Bill Folmer

30 years. When I saw their initial draft, my perception is that he took the most onerous provisions, the most onerous to a union, and the ones most heavily slanted to a manager, put them all together and then added even more onerous stuff he just dreamed up on his own—Let's really screw these people.

BILL FOLLMER: Buddy's job was to drag it out. His real gift is being able to say things that have no meaning. And that's a tremendously effective tool when you're at a negotiating table. You ask a question and he comes back with something that has no meaning and then you've got to sift through that.

He had various ways of saying things that were sort of different. You'd never catch on to what he was saying. It's really hard taking notes on that. You're trying to take notes on something that makes no sense at all.

DIANE TANNER-CAZINHA: We all had to write everything down, every word, because—you had to look back when Buddy said, "I never said this." We all had to flip back and say, "No, on October 8th, you said such and such." We would spend time going over word by word.

And then Buddy and Bob would leave the room to "caucus."

BILL FOLLMER: For hours. And we would be sitting in there with the air-conditioning off.

DIANE TANNER-CAZINHA: Yeah, it did drive me crazy.

DEAN CHOY: I wasn't particularly surprised that we got a lot of grief. I was surprised ultimately at the magnitude of the grief, magnitude of the junk that just got dumped the union way. But I wasn't surprised that there was bad faith on their part and that they would use specious arguments and reason.

That took the negotiating team by surprise. I think to the faculty, members of an educational institution, it was a real revelation that people would lie. That people would say things that they didn't mean. That they would waste your time and act in bad faith. So there was a certain amount of outrage that that was the kind of behavior that they were being subjected to.

MOANA LEONG: I purposely sat next to Diane every negotiation session and told her that when she felt herself losing her cool, because of the insanity of the arguments we were presented with, to grab my hand. Or I would grab her hand to signal her to take a deep breath and calm down.

DEAN CHOY: To me, the best example of negotiations that were just a waste of time were over the bulletin board.

DIANE TANNER-CAZINHA: Every union shop has a bulletin board. I said, "I know, I can go to Kāneʻohe Marine Base or Barber's Point, and they have a bulletin board. It's not so burdensome." But the next day, we spent hours on it.

BILL FOLLMER: Initially there was only going to be one bulletin board for the whole school. And that was because Buddy didn't really know the structure of the school. He knew nothing about how the school was organized. We're four campuses. One bulletin board would mean that three-fourths of the teachers would never see it.

LARRY MCELHENY: They conceded that it was acceptable to have bulletin boards in each of the unit offices. But then we just spent hours and hours talking about who's going to pay for them? And who's going to pay for the installation?

It was just bizarre.

DEAN CHOY: Buddy and Bob were making such easy money. I don't know what they were charging Bishop Estate for their services, but I'm sure they weren't cheap. And all they would do is come in there and waste time. A tremendous waste. It was a travesty. To spend hours and hours to talk about the configuration of a bulletin board.

Other things too. If you were on campus and you wanted to talk about union business, you've got to get in your car, go off campus, go to the guard shack and make a request through the guard that you want to talk about a KSFA subject. The guard then has to call some human resources director, and say, "This person wants to do that," and they say yea or nay. And if they say yea, then you can go back up campus, drive back up, and then start your conversation.

That was their proposal. And the thing is they insist on it. They defend stuff like that.

"IT'S CONTEST TIME AGAIN

If you added up the cost of the ads we place in the newspaper to bash the AG, the $400,000 we're paying the Peterson firm, and the salaries of Katz, McGuire, and McCorriston, how many new students could we educate with that money? Round your answer to the nearest Hawaiian."

–Imua Outsider, *faculty-generated parody of* I Mua Insider, *Spring '98*

BILL FOLLMER: Their overall strategy was: We're going to make these guys negotiate a year and see if they still have the support of their people. If you don't get a contract in a year, your union can be de-certified.

So they dragged it out, and for any reason at all. That's what's called bargaining in bad faith or surface bargaining.

From the start, we made an attempt to document completely everything that went on in negotiations, so that when we made our case to the NLRB—unfair labor practice, surface bargaining—we would have the evidence.

DEAN CHOY: Their strategy went from unfair labor practice to unfair labor practice. We got up to five unfair bargaining practices.

Honolulu Advertiser
headline, 12/8/98

Estate accused of unfairness to teachers
National board supports union

LARRY MCELHENY: The way it goes—they engage in unfair labor practices. They do things that are illegal. The NLRB sides with KSFA. They say, "You're right, they're breaking the law. So charges can be filed."

BILL FOLLMER: Eventually they could see that they weren't getting anywhere—five unfair labor practices had gone by.

The trustees—the IRS was after them; everybody was after them. It was a very good historic consequence. We had everything going for us. And the unfair labor practices put them in even more trouble.

LARRY MCELHENY: Bishop Estate didn't like that.

BILL FOLLMER: So they were anxious to get the unfair labor practices out of the way so they could deal with the legal matters.

LARRY MCELHENY: In the end, we didn't file on the unfair labor practices. They see that we're right, and they say, "Okay, you drop these charges, and we'll give you language you want in the contract."

I think with the impending trial on the unfair practices, we were one more nuisance the trustees didn't want to deal with. They were taking in too much water over the sides.

BILL FOLLMER: The trustees had been subpoenaed. I think it was one or two days prior to a judge stepping on an airplane from San Francisco and coming out here for a trial.

And that's how we got our contract.

DIANE TANNER-CAZINHA: It took a whole school year. We finally actually started in September '98, and we finished in May '99. Nine months. Term labor.

RICK HEYD: When we had finally prevailed and got them to agree to a contract, Buddy invited all of us to dinner to celebrate and show us there were no hard feelings. Roy Alameida, who never raises his voice and was pretty quiet at the negotiation table, said the best line of the entire negotiation: "No, thank you, I'd like to spend my dinner with people whose company I enjoy."

Kamehameha contract ratified
Faculty, Bishop Estate satisfied with vote

Honolulu Advertiser
headline, 4/29/99

At the signing of the initial contract: (clockwise, from top left) Diane Tanner-Cazinha, Rick Heyd, Sandy Wicklein, Bill Follmer, Roy Alameida, Moana Leong, Mike Chun, Adm. Robert Kihune (ret.), Larry McElheny

LARRY MCELHENY: During my tenure as president, we worked hard to stay on the "moral high ground." It wasn't easy, given some of management's tactics, but we held ourselves to a high standard in this regard. I think the current union leadership adheres to these same values.

I often think of KSFA as an insurance policy against the abuses of the past. People buy fire insurance for their homes but they rarely, if ever, file a claim. Our minimal dues buy us peace of mind.

There have been many positive changes at Kamehameha, but these changes are not necessarily permanent. The fact that a union exists has improved the atmosphere for teachers, in my opinion. It's sustainable as long as the members are supportive. ⌐

Lokelani Lindsey Removed 23
A Rainbow around the Sun

Maybe, you know, this is the Princess.
–Kelli Keahiahi Lee

JANET ZISK: I said this continuously for years: I would like to put in one day without hearing of something horrible happening to somebody or some horrible situation happening. Just one day. And some days I would get through the whole day and I'd get home and say, "Huh, nobody told me anything horrible today that had happened to them." And during the evening the phone would ring and somebody would say, "Janet, you really need to know this."

ADV. SAT. May 2, 1998 A-6

LARRY MCELHENY: I mean, money, conflicts of interest, KSBE lobbyists taking politicians to Korean strip bars on the estate credit card, and just total arrogance and abuse of power and finally you just go—aaargh.

BARB LEE: It's like an ongoing soap opera. It never stops. You couldn't make up stories like this. It's getting embarrassing to even tell people

Casino, bar charges made on estate cards

Former state Sen. Milton Holt ran up about $21,000 on Bishop Estate credit cards at local strip clubs, restaurants and Las Vegas casinos between 1993 and 1997, according to documents subpoened by the state attorney general.

"Most of the transactions with the KSBE credit card were legitimate school purchases. To avoid future misunderstandings, clear such purchases with your department heads. Drinks under $25 may be paid with petty cash funds, Black Jack tables require work orders from maintenance, and lap dancers must be cleared through Personnel."

–Imua Outsider, *faculty-generated parody of* I Mua Insider, *Spring '98*

where you teach. The Milton Holt escapades are too much. We heard he had an office on campus but there was no furniture in the room. It was apparent the estate had bought a State senator. He had exclusive use of an estate credit card. The charges were excessive—Korean hostess bars, all kinds of drinks and food for he and his pals.

Then there was Terrance Tom's monthly retainer for his loyalty to the estate. It just went on and on.

It was only a matter of time before it hit the fan. When the Feds— the Internal Revenue Service—start looking at your dealings, you better know it means trouble. There was talk the school could lose its tax-exempt status. This would kill everything Princess Pauahi had set up for the children over a hundred years ago.

IRS tells trustees to resign or risk tax-exempt status

Bishop Estate could face bill for millions in taxes annually

KUʻULEI KALILIKĀNE *('03)*: I am a student at Kamehameha Schools and would like the trustees to know they are embarrassing our school. Children who go to school each day feel humiliated when they get dropped off from the bus in uniform and a person comes up to them and harasses them about the trustees and how the school sucks.

JANET ZISK: I had a picture of Pauahi in my office, and I used to stand and look at that picture every day, and I would say to her, every day, several times a day, "Please help us. I know this is distressing you terribly. But the one thing you could do to help us is just somehow or other get the door open a crack."

◈ ◈ ◈

JANET ZISK: I think of Pauahi when she chastised in public members of her household who fell away from doing the right thing. She was responsible for them, and they were responsible to her, and when they fell away from their duties, they heard about it. Not only was she a truly good person, but she had backbone, and never hesitated to do the right thing, no matter who was involved.

LARRY MCELHENY: Finally, people can only take so much, and they're willing to stand up and say enough is enough. It just becomes outrageous, and the contradictions are so obvious that you just have to throw your hands up in the air and say, "That's it."

5 trustees get raise, maybe to $1 million
"We're not apologizing for the success of the institution."

Henry Peters, *Honolulu Star-Bulletin*, 4/29/99

OZ STENDER: I wasn't getting help from the attorney general's office, not from the masters, not from the Probate Court, nobody. Before the public pressure thing, before the Yim report, you think anyone will step up? No way.

I was gonna quit. That's the easy way, quit. I told Herb Cornuelle, "I'm walking out of here." And he said, "If you do, you're leaving things to the wolves. You believe in your heart that this thing is wrong, fix it. You can't fix it from the outside; you can only fix it from the inside."

Why take the hard road? It's a deep emotion, you know. One, family. Two, people you don't know, but think you are a jerk because you're doing this. And then you got the people that you have to deal with, the employees that you have to deal with. There are so many things out there that just bare all your emotions. And so there's always doubt. I mean, you know, one, is it worth it? Two, would we ever achieve it? Three, am I off base? Am I barking up a tree? Why not quit, call it a day, we can all go home, I can sleep at night. So there's all those things. There's no clear answer. There's no clear answer. And if you lose, you lose bigger than just losing; you lose everything.

So … I filed the petition to remove Lindsey.

It was unfortunate that we had to go through all that. Because it was very traumatic for a lot of people. Just to get the witnesses. I went to talk to the teacher groups, and to the staff. I told them, I'm sorry to remove Mrs. Lindsey, but I need your help. Can't do it without witnesses to what she did, and she's entitled to face her accusers.

KAMEHAMEHA SCHOOLS

In the overall context, all is not well on the hill

Throughout the turmoil of recent months, spokes-people for the Kamehameha Schools have attempted to create the impression that all is well on the hill, that the students are learning in a relatively normal environment. For fear that our silence might be misconstrued as tacit agreement, we are compelled to respond.

Our students are doing remarkably well, given the stormy atmosphere above them. In all day-to-day activities, they are — as has been said — "focused." Yet many of them are questioning how such a climate can persist. Gathering facts is only an early step in the learning process. Students must place these facts in context and — based on a moral system established by family, fostered by cultural and spiritual influences, and nurtured by teachers, peers and community leaders — search for truth.

Such critical thinking does not exist in a sterile lab. For our students, it exists in the midst of the now 2-year-old "controversy." We implore them to think, but what have the trustees and their minions left the students to ponder?

Is all well on the hill? Let's put the question in context:

■ The same week that some of their classmates were expelled from school for violating the Kamehameha Schools zero-tolerance drug policy, the students saw the trustees support and continue to employ embattled estate "Special Projects officer" Milton Holt following positive tests for crystal methamphetamine use.

■ Earlier students heard trustee Lokelani Lindsey cite distorted data to minimize their academic accomplishments and forward her own self-serving agenda.

■ They read of allegations of trustees stealing money left by their benevolent princess for their education, resulting in trustee Henry Peters' indictment and the investigation of Trustee Richard Wong.

■ Continuing revelations of inappropriate — even unspeakable — behavior have resulted in a total loss of respect for some of the most visible representatives of their school.

■ Students have been mocked by friends and questioned by relatives, reducing the healthy skepticism of their youth to a numbing cynicism. Humiliation has supplanted pride.

Students and staff at Kamehameha are held to high standards. The student and staff handbooks, outline behavior for which there is zero tolerance. Students realize that their failure to follow the rules will result in severe consequences.

However, in the current context, students have begun to question an apparent double standard; are not those in positions of power — special projects officers and trustees — held accountable to the same degree as those with less power?

Unfortunately, we live in a world infected by hypocrisy and corrupting ambition. We live in a world infected by vice, greed, sexual indiscretion and drug abuse.

However, that diseased world should not be forced upon the beneficiaries of Bernice Pauahi Bishop's vision, not by the stewards of her legacy, not by those empowered to protect her legacy. We are appalled that these corrupting influences have not yet been removed from our school. All is not well on the hill.

Na Kumu o Kamehameha
Organization of Kamehameha Schools staff members

You gotta look her in the eye in the courtroom and tell the bad things she did. If we lose this—and there's no guarantees—there's no confidentiality, of course, and if we lose this, she's going to end up screwing us, fire everybody involved.

But even with that, I had more than 200 people sign up. Only used like 20. But it shows how bad things were.

DAVID GIERLACH (*attorney for Lokelani Lindsey*): This state has never seen anything like this case. This is a huge case, and it involves hundreds of thousands of documents and hundreds of witnesses.

BEADIE DAWSON: Litigation is rarely pleasant, but this case before First Circuit Judge Weil was long and painful to everyone except most of the trustees, who seemed oblivious and convinced they were going to be exonerated.

Their self-serving management of the trust assets and the school told a forbidden story: Lokelani and most of the trustees considered themselves the beneficiaries; the students' and faculty concerns fell on deaf ears, a footnote to trustee actions and decisions. Only Oz stood firm in his understanding of fiduciary duty.

MOMI CAZIMERO: The courtroom always struck me as a place I didn't want to be. But I was determined to go.

By then we were having these ongoing meetings, the alumni and so forth. Because many of them work and couldn't go, had other reasons why they couldn't go and knew that I was committed to going, they asked me if I would take notes. I took notes, with the idea that I would share.

Lokelani's lawyer, Michael Green, and his team always sat on the right side. And then Crystal Rose and Doug Ing and Oz were just to the left. That became the Oz side—the his and the hers sides. So we ended up on the left, and once we sat on that side, we always stayed there. So as soon as there would be a break, because that witness would be over and then they would be bringing a new one in, we'd look

"That fist of power, that continued climate of fear and intimidation at the Kamehameha Schools, must stop now."
–*Crystal Rose*, Honolulu Star-Bulletin, *10/31/98*

and we'd wave them to come over and sit on our side.

OZ STENDER: I was surprised at the number that volunteered to give testimony. Because if we lost the case, you'd all be fired. And life would be misery. And she could sue everybody for defamation of character and all that sort of thing. And it's amazing how people came out of the woodwork with stories I didn't know about.

MYRNA CUNDY (*former Secondary School English teacher*): On the whole, they were nervous, but that's logical.

JOEL TRUESDELL (*Secondary School science teacher*): I knew that when I went down and testified against Mrs. Lindsey, that if she doesn't get thrown out, I was gonna be looking for another place to work.

JOEL TRUESDELL

"If she didn't get thrown out, I was gonna be looking for another place of work."

BOB WHITING: My wife was so concerned that I could lose my job. I told her I had to tell the truth. These are my friends that I am associated with at the school, and they know what I know, and if I were to get down there and make a-- of it, what would that say about me as a person?

MYRNA CUNDY: Sigrid Southworth may have shown the most exhilaration in being given the chance to tell her story. Charlene Hoe had such a graceful presence that she made a very confident, articulate witness. Kathy Kukea was one of the best witnesses. She and Julian Ako were superb. They know their business, and it came across.

JOEL TRUESDELL: In my mind, I had full respect for those administrators and people who went down and testified, told the truth and took her on.

"I was concerned that they might not consider my education there as good enough to attend Yale."

–Ciara Lacy, '98, KHON-TV News, 11/27/98

OZ STENDER: I had students who volunteered.

KĀWIKA EYRE: Ciara Lacy, Lance Tamashiro. They had had experience of Lindsey at school.

LOKELANI LINDSEY: I asked Mr. Green not to cross-examine them. As a lifelong educator, I don't believe students should ever be used in this manner.

OZ STENDER: To me, that was a ploy. She couldn't have found any students to stand up for her.

MOMI CAZIMERO: Kamani Kualā'au was a very studied kind of witness. He was always thinking and thoughtful. And I knew that made Green very anxious. And impatient.

KEOLU BENTO: Kamani handled it real well. I thought Kamani won.

MOMI CAZIMERO: Green asked Sarah Keahi a question—and that's what I mean about the lawyer playing the role: he would ask the question and he would walk away. Not really facing. He'd be walking sideways. That's why I said he was kind of dramatic. He would ask, and he would kind of do a slow turn and start walking away. And she said, "Look at me when I answer you!" The way a teacher would. He was not even being respectful enough to look at her when she was answering the question he asked.

MYRNA CUNDY: One amusing memory I have of the attorneys in the courtroom happened before the judge entered. Green had a question for Crystal. I don't remember the question, but Crystal responded, "How would I know? I'm a graduate of the factory of failure."

MOMI CAZIMERO: These people who are coming to be witnesses are doing it knowing that they can possibly lose their jobs. These are people who are really courageous. But they love Kamehameha. For everyone who takes that stand, I'd like to be able to thank them. To hug them. That's the Hawaiian way.

So I made sure other people knew I had a "job." And my job was to go out there and go hug these people, you know. And so even if I came a little bit late, and somebody was sitting in that corner, they moved in and I sat on the end. And I always immediately followed the witness out, and my question was, "Do you want the mommy hug?" It wasn't "Momi." It was "Mommy." Because how do you walk up as a woman and just ask somebody if they want a hug? I offered mommy hugs to the Kamehameha campus witnesses because I admired their courage. I saw them as true warriors, because each of them put themselves at risk of losing

"I felt that in a way Mrs. Lindsey was attempting to use the students to prove her point that Dr. Chun was doing a bad job. And that she didn't really care about the personal reaction of the students."

–Lance Tamishiro, '98, KHON-TV News, 11/27/98

their jobs for testifying against Lokelani Lindsey. I admired their courage and their conviction.

And nobody turned me down, nobody turned me down. They took the hugs. And in every witness I felt an emotion. I could feel the tremor in their body. And some of them would even tear.

MIKE CHUN: During the trial, I would still be meeting with her. And we would be praying together. I would initiate it. I would just offer, you know, "Loke, you're under a great deal of stress. I'm under a great deal of stress. Nobody is enjoying what is going on right now. So—can we pray?" And she would say, "Yes." She'd never turn me down. She said, "Yeah." And so I'd just hold her hands. We'd stand there and I'd pray. I would pray for her. I would pray for the school. I would pray for all those who were trying to do what was right for the school. And I would pray that she would be comforted. And she would be in tears, you know, imploring me, "Why is everybody after me? Why do they think I am an evil person? I am not an evil person."

KIM SLAGEL: That night the news showed Randie Fong testifying about Lindsey when he was going to resign, and she went into a frothing rage and used the f-word: "Who the f--- does Mike Chun think he is?" And she mouthed "liar" at him.

RICHARD CUNDY (*former Schools director of personnel*): Mouthed. We saw her. She was over to our right, and we were maybe in the second row, but we could see her profile, and we saw her mouth the words.

MYRNA CUNDY: We could hardly believe it!

MOMI CAZIMERO: You know, Lokelani made nothing but bad stink eyes at the witnesses. The glare!

BOB WHITING: On the stand, in looking at her attorney, he positioned himself slightly to the right of Mrs. Lindsey's eye, so that when you

MYRNA CUNDY

looked at him, you also had to look at her. And that's the only time I ever saw her glare at me. I'm sure she was there to intimidate whoever was there.

KATHY TIBBETTS: When I left the witness stand, she had just—the malevolence in her, in her expression, in her eyes. I remember leaving the courtroom, and for a few days after that, checking intersections real carefully. I didn't want to step off the intersection, you know, in front of her car, because I was sure she'd run over me.

MYRNA CUNDY: Often after one of the "good guys" would testify, particularly the younger members of the staff, or even someone more experienced like Randie Fong, I'd leave the courtroom and go to talk to the person or pat him on the back, simply because I thought that what they had done was a gutsy thing to do. I wanted them to know that I was supporting them, and there were lots of others who were, also.

One comes to mind—an Intermediate teacher who Lindsey was pressuring to change a grade or something like that. I don't remember her name, but I think she was very frightened to be on the witness stand. I don't think she wanted to talk with me. She was so relieved that she was finished, she just wanted to leave.

OZ STENDER: I was very pleased about the fact that she volunteered, because we didn't even know that story. And then told the story the way she did. And Mrs. Lindsey had no defense. Well, she didn't try to challenge her on any of it, which I thought was kind of interesting. I don't think she remembered. You know, we're supposed to provide the witness list to the other side a week before they come on. And the day the teacher came on, she walks between Green and me to the stand. And Green turns to Lindsey and asks, "Who's this person?" And Mrs. Lindsey couldn't remember. I mean, you would think if you made someone change a grade, you would remember an incident like that. But she said, "Oh, I have no idea."

OZ STENDER: We had Mrs. Lindsey on the stand for three or four days.

MOMI CAZIMERO: She just went on day to day as though she never

even saw herself of being in any situation of concern. I thought, *Either
she doesn't get it, or she's a real duck. It just rolls off her back.*

MYRNA CUNDY: We happened to meet at the same restaurant at
lunch a couple of times, and she'd smile and talk.

While she was in the courtroom, she would take notes. Her cell
phone would ring—it seems like frequently—and she would get a "look"
from Judge Weil.

RICHARD CUNDY: I think we did not believe what she said and wondered how she could believe it herself.

MYRNA CUNDY: Kathy and Julian both spoke to the standardized
test scores and how Lindsey had grossly misinterpreted them. They
wanted to make it perfectly clear that she didn't know what she was
talking about.

She was absolutely convinced that she was right and had no sense
of what kind of trouble she was in.

OZ STENDER: So halfway through the trial her lawyer comes in and
wants to settle. So I said, "The offer is off the table."

BEADIE DAWSON: As expected, attorney Green's closing arguments merely served as an attempt to bolster his client Lindsey—but it was not enough to counter the overwheming evidence and courageous testimony against her. Trustees and directors of boards are supposed to follow a basic rule—trustees make policy in the best interest of the trust. Administrators, executives and staff carry out those policies. Period. Lokelani never understood this basic principle.

MICHAEL GREEN: Oz Stender's credibility is at the heart of this case. I truly believe the evidence in this case shows this campus was whipped into a frenzy. The trial has been an ordeal beyond words.

MYRNA CUNDY: Doug Ing's closing was very dramatic—well paced, well written and excellently delivered. Impassioned, it was. His love for Kamehameha Schools came through loudly and clearly.

MOMI CAZIMERO: As part of his closing, he read the students' statement of appreciation and it brought tears to all of us, including Judge Weil.

OZ STENDER: They said, yeah, very powerful. Would you believe I missed it, because we had a trustee meeting that morning.

KĀWIKA EYRE: Judge Weil made her ruling on May 9, 1999.

BAMBI WEIL (*Circuit Court judge*): It is hereby ordered that the Petition for Removal of Trustee Marion May Lokelani Lindsey, filed on December 29, 1997, is hereby granted, effective immediately.

KĀWIKA EYRE: I think it was Greg Barrett from the *Advertiser* who called me in my Hawaiian 5 class. We had a kupuna speaking and so I didn't interrupt. These were many of the same kids I had two years earlier in Hawaiian 3 when Rockne Freitas ordered Gary and me to get up to the office.

 It had been a long two years. I looked at my kids and I just felt that finally help had come.

"It wasn't Lokelani Lindsey who orchestrated a very well organized campaign against the Bishop Estate and against a trustee. I think the person that actually should go down in history as bringing down this estate is Oz Stender."

—*Lokelani Lindsey,
KHON-TV News,
5/7/99*

"We, the students of Kamehameha Schools, In appreciation of our founder, Bernice Pauahi Bishop, Pledge to develop our potential in all we do, To strive to meet our responsibilities, To progress to the best of our ability, To carry ourselves with dignity and pride.

"So we, the people of Hawai'i, For whom she cared so much, Give thanks on this day of remembrance, And remain forever indebted to her."

—*Kamehameha Schools'
Student Statement
of Appreciation*

GAIL FUJIMOTO: When news came that she was out, we rejoiced. Absolutely rejoiced. I remember in the staff lounge in Midkiff, there was hugging, crying. I think I even screamed in here.

SIGRID SOUTHWORTH: It came via a phone call. My phone rang, and I remember letting out a war hoot. There were kids in the Hawaiian room, and I remember them looking at me.

People just began to pour in the minute they were out of class, and there were 15 and then there were 25 and then there were 35. It was definitely something that was seen as part of a major celebration.

And Bob Hamilton walked in with his violin, walked through the library and into the lounge, playing the "Hallelujah Chorus" on his violin! Which brought the house down. And as soon as he finished that, he started in on "The Wicked Witch Is Dead" from *The Wizard of Oz*.

KIM SLAGEL: Within an hour, I had 30 computer messages from all across the country from kids—once one kid got it, he shot it everywhere. Everybody was just jubilant.

JOEL TRUESDELL: We couldn't teach the next day. That's all the kids wanted to talk about.

KIM SLAGEL: You look at these 17- and 18-year-old kids and wonder how they would sort this out later. The junior and senior classes were pretty much robbed of the typical high school experience.

KAMAILE NICHOLS (*'98*): I see myself at 12 years old, standing, arms full of books, in the cool pre-dawn fall morning, waiting for the school bus. I'm thinking about how my day will go, when the bus pulls up to the curb. I step up into the bus, and, like always, I am greeted with a warm smile that combats the cold morning, and the

sound of my bus driver's voice, "Good morning, darling." A small gesture of aloha that began another day at Kamehameha.

And as I stepped off the bus at school, I thanked my bus driver, Ray, by name—as did each of my classmates on that bus—completing the cycle of aloha that came to be expected of each of us. This routine of shared respect and courtesy was something that saturated the air at Kamehameha, but I have rarely found in other settings since. When I stepped through those bus doors, I entered a world that saw the best *in* me and expected the best *from* me. I feel blessed to have grown up in such a place.

LANCE TAMASHIRO AND
KAMAILE NICHOLS

CIARA LACY: Kamehameha gave me the strength of, well, me. As globalization, communication, commercialization, and every other "tion" swiftly contribute to worldwide homogenization, I have never questioned who I was or where I came from or any other existentialist mumbo-jumbo. I am a Hawaiian.

AURORA KAGAWA (*'99*): For instilling in me community values that were an extension of lessons learned at home—for providing a community which supported me and reminded me of the reason why it did so—Aloha au iā Kamehameha.

I realize that "giving back to the Princess" is about "passing forward" in some way. Kamehameha has always provided me with an awareness that there is a place for my efforts in the larger Hawaiian community. Time has taught me that finding my role is part of life's journey.

AURORA KAGAWA

CIARA LACY

LAUREN LOKEMALIA TONG

Remember those core Hawaiian values? They stuck with me. It worked.

CIARA LACY: Kamehameha solidified who I am. It took me one step further from just having the koko, the nature, to giving me the nurture, too. Because of Kamehameha, I know my language, know my dances, and know more of my own people. Through Kamehameha, I know me. Sure, I'm an ethnic mutt like many of us Hawaiians, but I've been immunized against the darker elements of life, because I have a culture and an identity.

This planet of ours, its shaky and shifting mess and masses, its easy ability to leave us feeling small and unimportant, intrigues me, rather than intimidates me. For every ocean I travel and every city I see, I have a culture and value system to filter this information, and a paradise to return to.

Mahalo e Pauahi, mahalo e Kamehameha, a mahalo i nā ʻaumākua.

KELLI KEAHIAHI LEE: There was a rainbow around the sun!

LAUREN LOKEMALIA TONG: Above Kōnia.

KELLI KEAHIAHI LEE: And everyone was looking at it. And we were blinding ourselves because this is the sun, and there's a rainbow all the way around. And I thought, *Could that perhaps have been a pono thing? Maybe, you know, maybe this is the Princess.*

Epilogue
by Neil Hannahs

Never doubt that a small group of thoughtful, committed citizens can change the world. Indeed, it is the only thing that ever has. –Margaret Mead, cultural anthropologist

By the end of December 1999, trustees Gerard Jervis, Lokelani Lindsey, Henry Peters and Richard Wong had resigned under threat of removal, and trustee Oswald Stender had voluntarily surrendered his position on the board. The chain of events that included Winona Beamer's letter of outrage, "Broken Trust" articles, marches, removal trials and seemingly endless tribulation had come to a dramatic climax. But the story was far from over.

Interim trustees David Coon, Francis Keala, Robert Kihune, Constance Lau and Ronald Libkuman assumed full control of the helm of Kamehameha Schools. Their mission was to right the listing canoe and move it into compliance with the expectations for governance the Internal Revenue Service, Probate Court and attorney general had of Pauahi's charitable trust.

This entailed stabilizing operations, formulating a Strategic Plan, appointing a Chief Executive Officer and initiating measured delegation of authority held at the trustees' level of leadership. Macro-management of fiduciary concerns, policies, strategies and plans was to replace the micro-management of curriculum, leasing, T-shirts, investments and anything else that might capture a trustee's fascination or align with a personal agenda.

The interim trustees had charge of an organization battered and

The Values, Vision, Mission, Guiding Principles and Goals of the Strategic Plan were informed and inspired by the input received from:

- Over 1,200 participants in 24 community meetings during the initial scoping phase;

- 386 individuals who submitted a completed survey of Hawaiian educational needs;

- 29 community leaders who agreed to be interviewed;

- 2,010 respondents to a telephone poll of the opinions of a representative sample of the Hawaiian community conducted in the analysis and Plan development phase;

- 427 volunteers who served on 16 issue-focused work groups;

- 92 individuals who shared thoughts by letter, Internet, phone or fax;

- Over 1,000 attendees of 43 community meetings in Hawai'i and the continental United States during the Plan review phase; and

- 944 respondents to a survey circulated to elicit comments on a draft of the Plan.

reeling from several years of emotional pummeling. Its survival was not a foregone conclusion. Yet alumni, students, staff and other stakeholders were energized with hope and determination that a phoenix would rise from the ashes.

A Strategic Plan, meaningfully informed by stakeholders, was to provide the keystone around which the fractured organization would be re-assembled. The Plan, as well as the process for its development, would heal wounds incurred during the controversy and also affirm values, outline goals and chart an ambitious course into the future.

The court and trustees anticipated that this work would be performed by consultants and indeed, KPMG, the big five accounting firm with a global network, was retained based on its assemblage of a team from across the nation with expertise in the areas of education, governance, real estate and asset management.

But members of Nā Kumu and others who had played key roles during the controversy advocated strenuously and successfully for a larger, facilitative leadership role by staff who understood Kamehameha Schools' mission, culture and issues. Nathan Aipa, Julian Ako, LeeAnn Crabbe, Neil Hannahs, Charlene Hoe and Kathy Tibbetts came to assume coordinating kuleana for this vital endeavor.

The Plan set a new standard for inclusiveness. The Schools reached out to staff, students, the Hawaiian community, general public and best practice leaders through core planning teams, community meetings, interviews, opinion surveys, issue work groups and thought leader presentations.

The range of representation is telling of the underlying philosophy that guided this work. Kamehameha's Strategic Plan amounted to much more than a statement of heady aspirations. Process mattered and contributed to re-building relationships as the threads of individual efforts were woven into a broader, stronger, cohesive fabric. The endeavor was referred to as "Wayfinding." (See sidebar on page 348.)

SEEING THE ISLAND

The "Kamehameha Schools Strategic Plan 2000-2015" (see sidebar on page 354) begins by promising an institution grounded in the Christian faith and Hawaiian worldview embraced by Ke Ali'i Pauahi. The three-sentence Values Statement expressed first in Hawaiian and then restated in English recognized that the Schools' leadership maelstrom precipitated from a callous and arrogant drift from the example and intentions of our Founder.

Rather than set forth a prescriptive list of values … so many *words on a wall* … the Statement exhorts servant leadership. The controversy demonstrated that individuals must rely on their own moral compass in making difficult choices about what is pono and what is not.

Therefore, the Statement offers the brilliant points of light reflected in our Founder's life and legacy as navigational stars to help us maintain course through even the most turbulent seas. We must determine our own path, but Pauahi can serve as a beacon to light our way in all that we undertake on her behalf.

> *'O kēia ka manaʻo pono no ka ʻohana Kamehameha e hoʻomau i ko Pauahi kuleana me ka haʻahaʻa a me ka hana pono.*

> *Therefore, it is fitting for the Kamehameha Schools ʻohana, called upon to carry her legacy forward, to humbly do so through good thoughts and deeds that reflect the values of stewardship in her Will.*

The Values Statement is followed by affirmations of Vision, Mission and Guiding Principles, as well as seven Strategic Goals and Priorities. Robert O'Neill, the managing director of the KPMG consulting team, expressed his opinion about the Strategic Plan.

> *KS has not only met, but exceeded the Court stipulation and IRS requirements for a comprehensive and integrated financial and strategic planning process that ensured the active involvement of key stakeholder groups in performing strategic planning to further the educational mission of KS.*

O'Neill's professional judgment provided welcomed and appreciated affirmation. But it was manaʻo about the importance of vision expressed by soon-to-be-trustee Nainoa Thompson at a Strategic Plan thought leader presentation that resonated in the hearts of stakeholders with ancestral traditions of voyaging and discovery.

Nainoa shared insights learned from his mentor, master navigator Mau Piailug. One story recalled Nainoa's preparation for his first performance test as a non-instrument navigator for a long distance voyage on the double-hulled canoe, *Hōkūleʻa*.

On several successive nights, Mau asked Nainoa to drive them to the lookout point on the southern coast of Oʻahu near the Hālona Blowhole. Each evening, while peering southward at the dark horizon, Mau would ask Nainoa, "Can you see the island?" Though eager to please his teacher, each time he was asked, an incredulous Nainoa admitted

(Continued on page 350)

Goals of the Strategic Plan

The Plan then sets forth seven Strategic Goals and Priorities.

Goal 1: Kamehameha Schools will provide and facilitate a wide range of integrated, quality educational programs and services to serve more people of Hawaiian ancestry.

Goal 2: Kamehameha Schools will work with families and communities in their efforts to meet the educational needs of people of Hawaiian ancestry.

Goal 3: Kamehameha Schools will cultivate, nurture, perpetuate and practice ʻIke Hawaiʻi (which includes Hawaiian culture, values, history, language, oral traditions, literature and wahi pana—significant cultural or historical places—etc.)

Goal 4: Kamehameha Schools will foster the development of leaders who focus on service to others.

Goal 5: Kamehameha Schools will optimize the value and use of current financial and non-financial resources and actively seek and develop new resources.

Goal 6: Kamehameha Schools will mālama i ka ʻāina: practice ethical, prudent and culturally appropriate stewardship of lands and resources.

Goal 7: Kamehameha Schools will continue to develop as a dynamic, nurturing, learning community.

[The concept of Wayfinding
was introduced at a meeting
launching the analysis and
development phase of the
Strategic Plan process.]

Wayfinding

A quarter-century ago, the Polynesian Voyaging Society was founded to replicate heroic feats of our ancestors. It was an ambitious test to validate bold assertions which have been told and retold with pride and conviction by our kūpuna:

- that these islands were deliberately settled through a series of migratory voyages in double-hulled canoes;
- that the vessels were directed by skilled navigators who found their way without instruments across a vast expanse of uncharted ocean by relying upon their ability to interpret Nature's clues;
- that the incredible achievements revealed in our chants and oral histories about journeys to a mythical homeland called Hawaiki were more than fanciful lore.

The Polynesian Voyaging Society has produced many shining moments, and its accomplishments have surpassed our wildest expectations. Credit for these results can and should be spread widely through our community. It took a village.

Among the most deserving of praise are the individuals who dedicated themselves to acquiring traditional navigational skills. Led first by Nainoa Thompson and later joined by Chad Baybayan and others, they began as apprentices seeking knowledge from the Micronesian navigator Mau Piailug. Now, they are masters in their own right and teachers of a new generation.

Along the way, these navigators redefined their role and became wayfinders. The new title better captured the broad responsibilities they shouldered and leadership demanded of them. Chad discussed this evolution in the journal he kept on *Hōkūleʻa*'s voyage to Rapa Nui.

"Wayfinding is more than guiding the canoe. It is about nurturing a crew of friends by building positive relationships on the deck and among the communities we visit. It is also about the tradition of honoring our ancestors, and the culture and heritage they represent.

"Lastly, it is about cherishing the spirit of the many friends and supporters who fill *Hōkūleʻa*'s sails through their effort and work.

"As navigators and as a crew we would 'raise' the islands we were seeking if we all did our jobs. But how we felt as a crew about the totality of the experience is as important a goal as making landfall."

The words of Baybayan and the achievements of the Polynesian Voyaging Society offer inspiration for the undertaking at hand … the development of a Strategic Plan for Kamehameha Schools. If the ordeal through which we have suffered has taught us anything, it is that the credibility of the product will be a function of the process. Our Plan's proposed landfall will mean little if we do not nurture positive relationships, honor our culture and feel good about the voyage.

For this reason, we have:
- reached out for the input and participation of stakeholders, as well as the

larger community;
- designed core planning teams and work groups to be broadly representative of our organizational hierarchy;
- included a feedback phase allowing us to explain our decisions and rationale to the stakeholders, as well as invite further comment; and
- imbued the entire process with our Christian beliefs and Hawaiian cultural values.

We have also transformed the original planning construct into an ongoing cycle of assessment, accountability and adjustment. Strategic planning is not something we do merely to satisfy a court requirement; it will be something we do because the process enriches "the totality of the experience."

There is further relevance of the voyaging metaphor. Travel by canoe over the open ocean can evoke sensations of thrill and exhilaration that can only be achieved in the presence of real peril and uncertain outcome. In these situations, hard work and competent preparation offer the best remedies for quelling our angst and averting catastrophe.

This applies to our planning efforts, as well. The results we seek will not just happen. We must give generously of our time and energy. And we must bring our best thinking and talents to the task.

No doubt, there will be days when we are perched on the bow of our vessel feeling like "kings of the world." Then, too, there will be other times when the rough going and our fear of the unknown will have us bent in misery over the side. We are not strangers to these tests of our endurance, resilience and faith. And our past has left us wiser. We must anticipate the low points, support one another through them and, as we have recently demonstrated, survive.

In our noble quest, do not underestimate your capacity to make a profound contribution. Consider the life of God's humble servant leader Mother Theresa, who once said,

"There is a light in this world, a healing spirit more powerful than any darkness we may encounter. We sometimes lose sight of this force when there is suffering, and too much pain. Then suddenly, the spirit will emerge through the lives of ordinary people who hear a call and answer in extraordinary ways."

We must never forget that we have not ventured forth for our own enjoyment and self-gratification. We carry precious cargo, the value of which exceeds our ability to measure. With us ride Nā Pua A Ke Ali'i Pauahi, the beneficiaries of our founder and the hopes and aspirations of a people … in a word, our future.

And so it is that we invite you to come aboard and assist us as we endeavor to take every reasonable step to assure safe passage to a landfall where the children of Hawai'i will rise to achieve their greatest potential, where they reach their Hawaiki.

Should we be successful, and we must, perhaps then we will have earned the right to be called the wayfinders of Kamehameha Schools. I mua e nā poki'i!

that he could not see Tahiti and questioned how it could even be possible. Hearing that, Mau would return to the car and Nainoa would drive him home in silence.

It took many nights before it dawned upon Nainoa that the island Mau sought was not to be found on the horizon but in Nainoa's mind. Mau understood that navigators who lack vision of their goal are incapable of charting a course to a destination. Their canoes are doomed to aimless wandering.

The "Kamehameha Schools Strategic Plan 2000-2015" enabled the 'ohana who man Pauahi's great vessel to "see the island" and regroup for the voyage to a place where kānaka maoli can achieve their highest potential.

ARE WE THERE YET?

The Kamehameha 'ohana celebrated completion of the Strategic Plan with fanfare and cultural pageantry. Respects were paid to Pauahi at Mauna 'Ala, followed by a signing ceremony and pā'ina to mahalo those who contributed over the 18-month process. A press conference showcased the Plan for the wider community and announced Kamehameha's new beginning.

Hopes ran high and expectations soared even higher. Stakeholders were anxious for long-discussed changes and benefits to materialize. The question at hand shifted abruptly from "What should be the Schools' new direction?" to "Are we there yet?" The stakeholders had done their part; now it was a leadership issue.

Successor trustees were named near the end of the Strategic Planning process. The interim trustees were acknowledged for yeoman's efforts under very difficult circumstances, and the new trustees stepped into the leadership role. Two of the interim trustees, Robert Kihune and Constance Lau, joined new appointees Douglas Ing, Diane Plotts and Nainoa Thompson, as successor trustees. While their terms of office were staggered, it was clear that this board would shepherd the organization for the next decade.

Leadership below the trustee level was much less settled. The new position of chief executive officer, as well as a host of other high-level posts, was created and advertised. Reaction to these opportunities to control Pauahi's assets and programs might be likened to the breaking of a vacuum seal. Resumes from all corners of society rushed into the vortex.

Candidates included a mix of those who had long served the mission;

alumni expatriates who were seeking a ticket home; social saviors; Hawaiian activists; business opportunists; political insiders and staff who sought advancement after years of laboring under an oppressive regime. It was an eclectic range from soldiers in the Hawaiian movement to carpetbaggers.

The trustees' appointments reflected their collective backgrounds, beliefs and comfort zones. It became clear that they pinned their hopes on those with strong western credentials. Palapala was paramount. For instance, when introducing Hamilton McCubbin as the inaugural CEO, Chair Kihune made a point to note how impressed they were by the thickness of Dr. McCubbin's curriculum vitae.

They also leaned toward those with experience outside of the organization over those who had served Kamehameha and our stakeholder population. This signaled limited confidence in appointing internal candidates to senior leadership positions.

It was as if all who were present through the controversy were deemed dysfunctional ... goods damaged by their association with inept trustees and by time spent operating in systems that fell short of best practice. Outsiders, who professed overnight conversion and commitment to the Schools' mission, were considered more qualified and less of a risk than insiders who were tarred by their service during contentious times.

The most prominent exception was Rockne Freitas' selection to be Executive Director of the newly-formed Ke Aliʻi Pauahi Foundation. This promotion sparked questions and concern. Many in the Kamehameha ʻohana advocated that he and others be held accountable for their role and activities during the controversy. While some could understand the trustees' desire to put the past behind us and commit to the healing process, few could fathom how Rockne came to be singled out for reward and elevation to a position that he held, albeit briefly.

Initially, the gap between lofty expectations for new and improved Kamehameha leadership and the reality of performance by the team put into place was so wide that some stakeholders would mutter cynically, "new dogs, same fleas." But by the mid-point of the 15-year Strategic Plan horizon, a majority of the key executive positions had turned over at least once and the situation was much improved, a function of both better performance and a tempering of expectations.

The selection of relative strangers to the mission and the fits and starts caused by attrition resulted in some stumbling out of the blocks as the Schools raced toward its Strategic Goals. To their credit, stakeholders, who were anxious for the new vision and programs to unfold, displayed laudable patience.

Notwithstanding, a less than perfect start, after the first half of the Strategic Plan's term, much about the Schools had indeed changed. While these are not the Kamehameha Schools of the 1990s, it is unlikely that many within or outside of the organization would declare victory and suggest the vision has been achieved. The progress is undeniable; however, we are not there yet.

E TU I TA HOE ULI

But is it fair or reasonable to expect a people or an institution to ever achieve a state where conditions leave little else for which to hope or aspire? If life is a journey, do we ever truly get there?

An alternative view would recognize that in the decade following Kamehameha Schools' darkest and bleakest moments, this 'ohana came together to recommit to values of servant leadership and to rededicate themselves to Pauahi's mission.

With this renewed sense of purpose, we have accomplished significant and unprecedented milestones that have only emboldened us to raise our sights, envision new worlds and set higher goals.

Visions of Well-Being

At the forefront of our agenda might be the continuing quest to achieve a state of holistic well-being. The Schools has always possessed the desire and competencies to address educational needs and account for the number of stakeholders participating in programs, their academic achievements, SAT scores, National Merit awards, graduation rates or degrees accumulated. But what of the other dimensions of their well-being: material and economic, emotional, social and cultural, and physical? Some would turn a blind eye to these needs out of fear of "mission creep."

But would Pauahi be satisfied if education targets are achieved, yet beneficiaries die young, are displaced from their homeland, fail to practice and perpetuate their language and cultural traditions, have broken families or lack meaningful employment opportunities? For years to come, the Schools' leadership will likely grapple with striking the appropriate balance between maintaining a focus on education and influencing non-cognitive domains of well-being through direct or nuanced efforts.

Visions of Fulfilling Ali'i Kuleana

For years, Kamehameha toiled to be a school for Hawaiians, but not necessarily a Hawaiian school. Many generations of kānaka maoli were carefully and thoroughly groomed to be what the dominant society wanted them to be. There were few opportunities and little encouragement for students to acquire more than the barest rudiments of our culture. We spoke of ourselves in the third person … a people that used to be. We learned songs without meaning and concepts that were not meant to be practiced.

But that is not the case today. The seeds of cultural revival sown during the Hawaiian renaissance of the 1970s took root in the 1980s, overcame the controversy of the 1990s and now flourish in the 21st century. Kamehameha is currently evolving from a school for Hawaiians into a Hawaiian school and is emerging as a leader in probing the depths of our indigenous worldview in the arts, literature, curriculum development, well-being assessment, publishing, cultural assets research and restoration, as well as land, water and resource management.

It has been a stunning turn of events, but even these wonderful accomplishments fall short of stakeholders' hopes that we someday assume the mantle and kuleana of our ali'i legacy … an organization not merely attentive to the needs of our students and lands, but rising to the pleas for leadership in addressing the wide spectrum of issues that confound our lāhui.

Visions of Self-Determination
And is it beyond our imagination and reach that individuals vested with deep knowledge of Hawaiian culture, as well as an education in western disciplines and broad worldly experience, would someday populate each and every leadership position of these Schools, thus ensuring a measure of self-determination and governance of the legacy of Ke Ali'i Pauahi that has eluded the grasp of our people for more than a century?

E 'imi kākou i nā alaka'i … e hō'ihi i Ke Akua … e aloha kekahi i kekahi … e mālama i ka 'āina … e 'ōlelo i ka 'ōlelo makuahine … e nānā i ke kumu … e kūlia i ka nu'u i ka 'oihana a kākou … e 'auamo kuleana … e kūkauka'i me nā 'ohana a me ke kaiāulu.

No doubt, these paradigm shifts will challenge current beneficiaries and stakeholders, as well as those yet unborn. The powers that uphold and prolong the status quo will not yield without a demand.

(Continued on page 356)

Kamehameha Schools
at the Mid-Point of the Strategic Plan

The Strategic Plan mandated a myriad of changes in institutional governance, educational services, endowment management, community engagement and cultural commitment.

Institutional Governance

- **Strategic & Tactical Planning:** The Education, Endowment and other groups conducted extensive reviews of their operations and results to set targets for near- and long-term transformational outcomes, as well as priorities to discipline the allocation of resources.

- **Delegation:** Investment, spending and a host of other policies have been adopted to link the amount of educational funding to the size of the endowment and allow authority to be delegated under a new CEO governance model. These reforms have propelled Kamehameha to the forefront of best practice.

- **Regulatory Compliance:** All of the concerns have been resolved that were identified by the Internal Revenue Service in the closing agreement that led to the draconian step of removing trustees.

Educational Services

- **Three Campuses:** The removed trustees' decision to build campuses on Maui and Hawai'i was affirmed, student bodies were expanded to serve grades kindergarten to 12, sites were selected and new flagship campuses were constructed at Pukalani and Kea'au.

- **Outreach:** On the other hand, the mid-1990s scuttling of community-based outreach and enrichment programs was reversed, leading to the reinstatement of many programs and the addition of new initiatives.

- **Early Education:** Expanding the reach, delivery models and coordination of early education services has been a high priority.

- **Charter Schools:** Corporations were established to allow Kamehameha to pool monies with the public school system in support of Hawaiian-focus charter schools.

- **Financial Aid:** More resources have been directed toward financial aid to support the enrollment of Hawaiians in preschools, other private elementary and secondary schools and post-high school programs.

Endowment Management

- **Business Model:** Portfolio planning, due diligence discipline, asset allocation targets and proactive business strategies were integrated into management of the endowment, and its value grew at a pace exceeding benchmarks.

- **Balanced Scorecard:** Return expectations have been redefined, and many visible land use commitments have been implemented to optimize a balanced scorecard of not just economic returns, but also educational, cultural, environmental and community benefits.

- **Place-Based Learning:** Agriculture and conservation lands across the state have emerged as exciting "4th campuses" serving over 20,000 learners annually through place-based eco-cultural stewardship curriculum and activities.

Community Engagement

- **Partnership Approach:** Numerous partnerships with other educational institutions and community groups have been formed to leverage investment and engage others in Kamehameha's mission.

- **Ke Aliʻi Pauahi Foundation:** A foundation was created to stimulate and receive funds and other contributions to support mission-related activities.

- **Service Learning:** Activities that foster lifelong commitments to service learning have been woven into programs at all levels to build community capacity, as well as to perpetuate in students the Christian and Hawaiian values of aloha aku, aloha mai exemplified by Pauahi.

Cultural Commitment

- **Hawaiian School:** Commitments have been made to help restore the vibrancy of Hawaiian language and culture, construct the Kaʻiwakīloumoku Hawaiian Cultural Center on the Kapālama Campus, and emphasize the importance of acquiring cultural knowledge (ʻike) *and* incorporating culture into our way of life (nohona).

- **Curriculum & Training:** Curriculum development, teacher training and other efforts designed to have a force multiplier affect have been launched to broadly enrich general and cultural instruction throughout the community.

- **Sense of Place:** Numerous programs have been implemented to enable students to strengthen knowledge of their sense of place and genealogical connections to lands and communities.

As it has always been, survival will entail a struggle and will be the reward of those with the courage and capability to meaningfully influence the course of their lives.

Shortly before the arrival of Captain Cook at Waimea, Kaua'i, a priest foretold of impending and dramatic change. This prophecy, memorialized in "Ūlei Pahu I Ka Moku," warns that "our sacred councils will be no more ... the images will be useless ... and Hawaiians will be as nothing...."

To avoid this fate, the priest admonished his people to hold fast and control their own destiny: "E tu i ta hoe uli, i tohi i ta pale tai!" Seize the steering paddle and press it to the canoe's side. The chant continued: Resist the onslaught of tide and current; steer free, steer clear.

Before his retirement, having witnessed the attitudes and behavior that would ferment and devolve into the controversy, trustee Myron Pinky Thompson also issued a warning inspired by ancestral wisdom.

'A'ole make ka wa'a i ka 'ale o waho, aia no i ka 'ale o loko.
A canoe is not swamped by the billows of the ocean, but by
the billows near the land. Trouble often comes from one's
own people rather than from outsiders.

Demonstrating tremendous fortitude, the intrepid 'ohana of Kamehameha Schools ultimately rose en masse to seize the steering paddle to navigate free and clear from ka 'ale o loko ... from the waves near the shore ... the waves from the inside that threatened to swamp Pauahi's canoe.

There are valuable and enduring lessons to be garnered from the many tests of integrity and individual acts of bravery and protest that were required to cast off the chafing yoke of control applied through force and intimidation by leaders who proved to be unfit for service and undeserving of their trust responsibilities.

The noble traits of character exhibited and cultured in this test of survival will serve our people well as we launch new journeys in the years ahead to islands we have seen only in our minds.

From the harbor of my heart,
The task completed but in part.
The cruise of life just now begun,
Sail far and wide with star and sun.
Sail on O my soul.

Lessons Learned

KĀWIKA EYRE: On so many, many levels, it was indeed a wayfinding through the storm. The lessons learned? For one, it was about finding our way as a school, and about showing our students the right way. It was about the living of our values. About pono and Pauahi and the essential humility of servant leadership. It was about the centrality of the student-teacher relationship, and the grace of solidarity among teacher colleagues. It was about courage and persistence and the speaking of truth to power. And ultimately, it was about how goodness triumphed on Pauahi's campus.

RANDIE FONG: In the face of unspeakable adversity, the Kamehameha Schools family united—and against all odds—managed to overcome the forces of power, lust and greed. Our community's courage and perseverance a decade ago have paved the way for Pauahi's legacy to impact unprecedented numbers of Hawaiians today.

JULIAN AKO: "I aliʻi no ke aliʻi i ke kanaka." A chief is a chief because of the people he serves. Four of our trustees had lost sight of this basic wisdom offered to us by our kūpuna and placed our people in positions of having to make difficult choices guided by their personal moral compasses.

OZ STENDER: All stakeholders of the Kamehameha Schools must always be vigilant that the trustees who are chosen to manage the trust are truly qualified to carry out the mission of Ke Ali'i Pauahi's legacy. These qualifications shall include intelligence, experience, commitment and a passion to serve the children of Pauahi.

GAIL FUJIMOTO: I learned what true servant leadership looks like, and Oswald Stender is the embodiment of that concept. All of us who are, have been, and will be a part of Pauahi's legacy owe him our debt of gratitude and would do well to follow his example. Like Pauahi, he has a servant's heart.

PATRICK IONA: Never be ashamed for standing up for what you believe in. There are many who will shun you and never fight the battles but will be the first to step forward to claim the rewards.

KE'ALA KWAN: Courage in the face of conflict and fear is not easy, but we are each capable, with the help of Ke Akua and each other, to stand up and speak out for what is right.

DUTCHIE SAFFERY: The power of prayer and unwaivering faith was proof that what is impossible to man is possible in the Lord. Pauahi's legacy is protected for her children.

GARY OBRECHT: We need to speak up. The controversy taught me that all of us have a place in this institution, and although things often will not go as we would like them to go, we should still speak up to point out problems, inconsistencies, wrongs, possible wrongs. Sitting back and accepting wrong is wrong on our part.

SIGRID SOUTHWORTH: The solidarity among the faculty was inspirational. The great percentage that stood together to speak out against what almost all of us perceived to be morally wrong was impressive. We didn't intend what we were doing to be a lesson, but students saw and learned. It was a good lesson.

JAN BECKET: Conceived as a result of the controversy, KSFA has been a strong, independent faculty voice. KSFA plays a vital role in our internal system of checks and balances by helping to move us all towards a collaborative governance model and away from the old plantation model. Ultimately, it serves the very best interests of Pauahi's legacy and of her pua.

BILL FOLLMER: We formed a union because it was the only type of organization that had legal standing and could not be abolished or ignored by our leaders. We thought that once we guaranteed our existence and established our intent to be a different kind of union, one that would not interfere with operations or try to run the school, that management would consult with us and use our collective classroom expertise. It was a sad lesson learned that management had little interest in that expertise.

ELISA YADAO: It is true that time heals. But equally important is the need for us to remember what we felt, what we did and how we struggled in those dark days at Kamehameha Schools. I am extraordinarily grateful to the authors of this book for their thoroughness, their thoughtfulness and the telling of this story through the voices of the people who lived it.

JANET ZISK: Early in the controversy, an administrator admonished several of us to keep students uninvolved as they were "just kids, unaware and not interested." To the contrary, what we learned was that students watch adults around them and our behavior spoke louder than words.

LAUREN LOKEMALIA (TONG) HASTINGS: You need to speak up in order to be heard. No one will know your feelings, thoughts, or ideas if you keep quiet. Speak up and out for what you believe to be pono.

KAYLIA IONA: My children at the time were very young. Both were in the Elementary School. They were afraid, as I was at times, but looking back now, becoming involved was the RIGHT THING TO DO. We love Kamehameha and what it gave us and what it continues to give us today: family, pride of one's heritage and school, and aloha.

PAUL IONA: I have a deeper appreciation for the school because of what I was exposed to. Because of my family and what they did for the school. And I wouldn't have it any other way. ∽

Acknowledgments

The Friends of Nā Kumu offer our deepest mahalo to Gavan Daws for his dedication to having our story told. Mahalo to Neil Hannahs for graciously agreeing to provide the Epilogue for the book. Our gratitude also goes to a committee of volunteers—Alohi Aeʻa, Healani Huch, Kuʻualoha Hoʻomanawanui, Kaʻimipono Kaiwi, Brandi Nālani McDougal and Michael Puleloa—whose assistance was crucial in reviewing and editing the text. Mahalo to Tiana Companion, who endlessly gave of her own time to help with technical aspects of production. Our appreciation goes to Michael Young, Luryier "Pop" Diamond and Kamehameha Schools for their generous agreement to provide photographs for the book. We would like to thank the *Honolulu Advertiser*, the *Honolulu Star-Bulletin*, KGMB-TV News, KHON-TV News and KITV News for allowing the use of material from their publications and broadcasts. Finally, we are very grateful to Dick Adair and Clay Jones for making their newspaper cartoons available for this book.